SUPER
FREAK
ONOMICS*

*THE SUPE
SUPER ILL
EDITION

R DELUXE,
USTRATED
THEREOF.

DESIGN BY NUMBER 17, NYC

ILLUSTRATED EDITION

SUPERFREAKONOMICS

GLOBAL COOLING, PATRIOTIC PROSTITUTES AND WHY SUICIDE BOMBERS SHOULD BUY LIFE INSURANCE

STEVEN D. LEVITT & STEPHEN J. DUBNER

ALLEN LANE
an imprint of
PENGUIN BOOKS

ALLEN LANE

Published by the Penguin Group
Penguin Books Ltd, 80 Strand, London WC2R ORL, England
Penguin Group (USA) Inc., 375 Hudson Street, New York, New York 10014, USA
Penguin Group (Canada), 90 Eglinton Avenue East, Suite 700, Toronto, Ontario, Canada M4P 2Y3 (a division of Pearson Canada Inc.)
Penguin Ireland, 25 St Stephen's Green, Dublin 2, Ireland (a division of Penguin Books Ltd)
Penguin Group (Australia), 250 Camberwell Road, Camberwell, Victoria 3124, Australia (a division of Pearson Australia Group Pty Ltd)
Penguin Books India Pvt Ltd, 11 Community Centre, Panchsheel Park, New Dehli – 110 017, India
Penguin Group (NZ), 67 Apollo Drive, North Shore 0632, New Zealand (a division of Pearson New Zealand Ltd)
Penguin Books (South Africa) (Pty) Ltd, 24 Sturdee Avenue, Rosebank 2196, South Africa

Penguin Books Ltd, Registered Offices: 80 Strand, London WC2R ORL, England

www.penguin.com

First published in the USA by HarperCollins 2010
First published in Great Britain by Allen Lane 2010
1

Printed in the United States of America

ISBN: 978-1-846-14303-8

SDL:

To Jeannette, my soul mate

SJD:

To Ellen, for showing me
how interesting the world can be

WHY AN ILLUSTRATED EDITION?

ONE OF US IS A NUMBERS GUY AND THE OTHER IS A WORD guy, but we both like pictures too. That's why we made this illustrated edition of *SuperFreakonomics*: sometimes numbers and words aren't enough.

By "pictures," we mean a lot of different things—photographs, illustrations, scientific or technical drawings, even panels of data. The idea was simply to add another dimension to the two-dimensional words and numbers we'd already put down on paper. To show, for instance, an actual tracking sheet used to gather data on street prostitution in Chicago (see page 59). To diagram how easy it was to turn a bunch of altruists into a gang of thieves (page 125). To see what the "garden-hose-to-the-sky" scheme to fight global warming might look like (page 210). Because the pages in this edition are larger than those in the original, we also had room to add several stories that hadn't fit, as well an original poem from a climate scientist (pages 228–229) and, perhaps most improbably, an epistolary duel between that same scientist and one of the giants of twentieth-century literature (pages 218–219).

We are greatly indebted to all the people who contributed their photographs, recollections, and sterling ideas, from Allie the high-end call girl (pages 52–58), to the medical futurist Craig Feied (pages 71–78), to the gang of brilliant inventors at Intellectual Ventures (pages 192–221), and to many others.

The main text of the book remains unchanged except for some minor corrections. So if you already own the original edition and want this one as well, you might like to ask someone else to purchase it for you.

This edition was inspired by several readers who wrote to say they'd like to see more of the data behind the stories we tell. That inspiration was amplified by our admiration for Edward Tufte, who has extravagantly expanded the universe for data-centric storytelling. As we got under way, we thought: This is great fun; why isn't *every* book an illustrated book? Then we found out why: because it's a massive amount of work!

Fortunately, we had a corps of amazing comrades to help execute the task. Ryan Hagen was a tireless researcher and writer who also kept track of every logistical detail; you can find a picture of him in the following pages if you look hard enough (hint: he is not a terrorist). And the design firm Number 17 was creative and clever beyond belief. Super-size thanks to Emily Oberman, Bonnie Siegler, Rachel Matts, Naz Sahin, and Jamie Bartolacci. The good ideas and hard work of all these folks, and many more, are evident on every page.

As with childbirth (or so we are told), the pain of creation is quickly forgotten once the fruit of that labor can be held in one's hands. With this edition now complete, we're casting about for other unlikely books that could benefit from an illustrated makeover. Your suggestions are welcome. Next year's federal budget might be interesting . . .

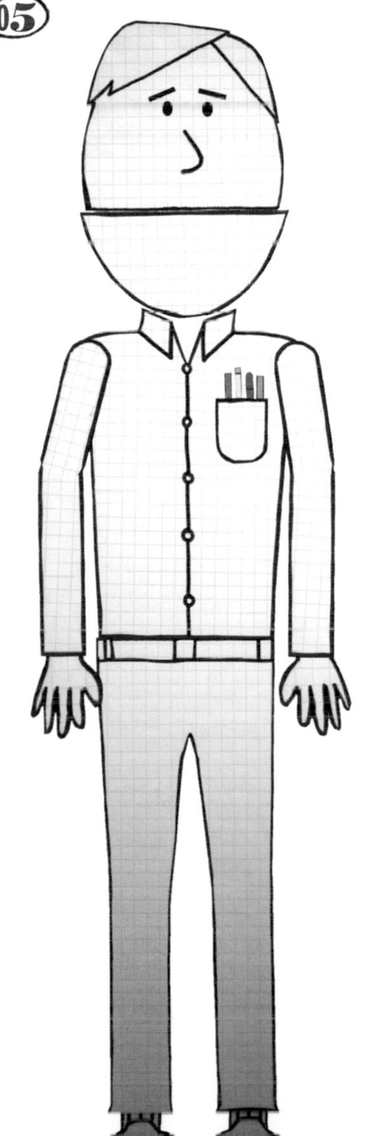

COURTESY LARGEL43 AND OVERHAUL PRODUCTIONS; FROM *FREAKONOMICS: THE MOVIE*

AN EXPLANATORY NOTE

THE TIME HAS COME TO ADMIT THAT IN OUR FIRST BOOK, we lied. Twice.

The first lie appeared in the introduction, where we wrote that the book had no "unifying theme." Here's what happened. Our publishing house—nice people, smart people—read the first draft of our book and cried out in alarm: "This book has no unifying theme!" Instead, the manuscript was a random heap of stories about cheating teachers, self-dealing Realtors, and crack-selling mama's boys. There was no nifty theoretical foundation upon which these stories could be piled to miraculously add up to more than the sum of their parts.

Our publisher's alarm only grew when we proposed a title for this mishmash of a book: *Freakonomics.* Even over the phone, you could hear the sound of palms smacking foreheads: *This pair of bozos just delivered a manuscript with no unifying theme and a nonsensical, made-up title!*

It was duly suggested that in the published book we concede right up front, in the introduction, that we had no unifying theme. And so, in the interest of keeping the peace (and our book advance), that's what we did.

But in truth, the book *did* have a unifying theme, even if it wasn't obvious at the time, even to us. If pressed, you could boil it down to four words: *People respond to incentives.* If you wanted to get more expansive, you might say this: *People respond to incentives, although not necessarily in ways that are predictable or manifest. Therefore, one of the most powerful laws in the universe is the law of unintended consequences. This applies to schoolteachers and Realtors and crack dealers as well as expectant mothers, sumo wrestlers, bagel salesmen, and the Ku Klux Klan.*

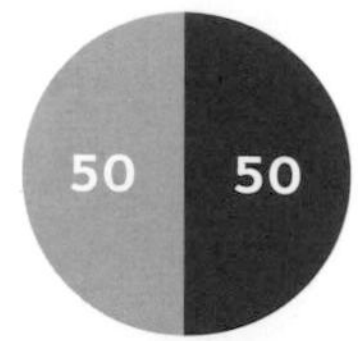

The issue of the book's title, meanwhile, still lay unresolved. After several months and dozens of suggestions, including *Unconventional Wisdom* (eh), *Ain't Necessarily So* (bleh), and *E-Ray Vision* (don't ask), our publisher finally decided that perhaps *Freakonomics* wasn't so bad after all—or, more precisely, it was so bad it might actually be good.

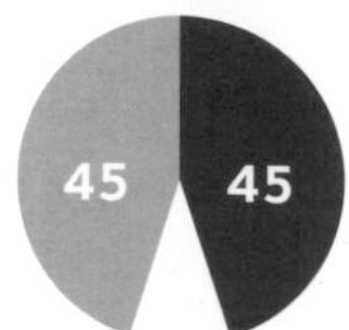

Or maybe they were simply exhausted.

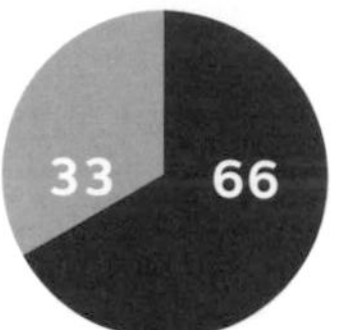

The subtitle promised that the book would explore "the hidden side of everything." This was our second lie. We were sure reasonable people would view such a phrase as intentional hyperbole. But some readers took it literally, complaining that our stories, as motley a collection as they were, did not in fact address "everything." And so, while the subtitle was not intended as a lie, it turned out to be one. We apologize.

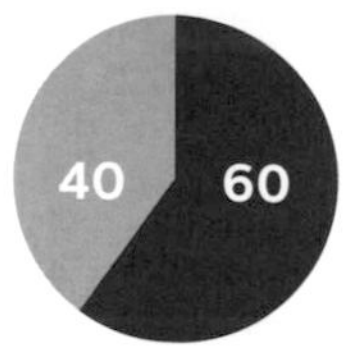

Our failure to include "everything" in the first book, however, had an unintended consequence of its own: it created the need for a second book. But let it be noted straightaway that this second book and the first book combined still do not literally comprise "everything."

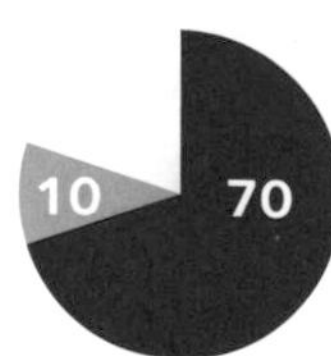

Book covers that, thankfully, never were.

The two of us have now been collaborators for several years. It began when one of us (Dubner, an author and journalist) wrote a magazine article about the other (Levitt, an academic economist). Adversaries in the beginning, albeit civil ones, we joined forces only when several publishers began to offer significant sums of money for a book. (Remember: *people respond to incentives*—and, despite the common perception, economists and journalists are people too.)

We discussed how the money should be divided. Almost immediately we came to an impasse, for each of us insisted on a 60–40 split. Upon realizing that we each thought the *other* guy should get 60 percent, we knew we'd have a good partnership. So we settled on 50–50 and got to work. ◑ We didn't feel much pressure writing that first book because we genuinely thought few people would read it. (Levitt's father agreed and said it was "immoral" to accept even a penny up front.) 💬 These low expectations liberated us to write about any- and everything we found worthwhile. So we had a pretty good time.

We were surprised and thrilled when the book became a hit. As profitable as it might have been to pump out a quick follow-up—think *Freakonomics for Dummies* or *Chicken Soup for the Freakonomics Soul*—we wanted to wait until we had done enough research that we couldn't help but write it all down. So here we finally are, more than four years later, with a second book that we believe is easily better than the first. Of course it is up to you, not us, to say if that is true—or perhaps if it's as bad as some people feared our first book might be.

If nothing else, our publishers have resigned themselves to our unyielding bad taste: when we proposed that this new book be called *SuperFreakonomics*, they didn't even blink.

HOW SOME OTHER PARTNERS HAVE SPLIT THEIR LOOT

ORVILLE and **WILBUR WRIGHT** split their profits straight down the middle, going so far as to divide prize money in half at public events. Such gestures were moot: the brothers shared a bank account.

STEVE JOBS and **STEVE WOZNIAK** launched the Apple Computer Company on April Fools' Day, 1976, with a third partner, Ronald Gerald Wayne. He cashed out his 10 percent stake for $800 less than two weeks later, worried the company might drag him into bankruptcy.

GEORGE WASHINGTON married up when he wed the wealthy widow **MARTHA DANDRIDGE CUSTIS**, receiving one-third of her estate as dowry. He wound up as one of the richest men in America.

LOU COSTELLO reportedly insisted on a 60–40 split in **BUD ABBOTT'S** favor. "Comics are a dime a dozen," Costello said. "Good straight men are hard to find."

COCO CHANEL had more of a head for fashion than for business, retaining only a 10 percent stake in her perfume company. The lion's share went to the financier **PIERRE WERTHEIMER**, with the remainder going to the man who introduced Wertheimer and Chanel.

When Levitt's dad speaks, especially on matters of taste, we listen pretty closely. According to *Discover* magazine, Dr. Michael D. Levitt is "one of the world's leading authorities on the science of flatulence." Like his son, he is fond of attacking conventional wisdom. He did so at length in a 2000 *Salon* article called "Dr. Fart Speaks."

If this book *is* any good, you have yourselves to thank as well. One of the benefits of writing books in an age of such cheap and easy communication is that authors hear directly from their readers, loudly and clearly and in great number. Good feedback is hard to come by, and extremely valuable. Not only did we receive feedback on what we'd already written but also many suggestions for future topics. Some of you who sent e-mails will see your thoughts reflected in this book. Thank you.

The success of *Freakonomics* had one particularly strange by-product: we were regularly invited, together and separately, to give lectures to all sorts of groups. Often we were presented as the very sort of "experts" that in *Freakonomics* we warned you to watch out for—people who enjoy an informational advantage and have an incentive to exploit it. (We tried our best to disabuse audiences of the notion that we are actually expert in anything.)

These encounters also produced material for future writings. During a lecture at UCLA, one of us (Dubner) talked about how people wash their hands after using the bathroom far less often than they admit. Afterward, a gentleman approached the podium, offered his hand, and said he was a urologist. Despite this unappetizing introduction, the urologist had a fascinating story to tell about hand-washing failures in a high-stakes setting—the hospital where he worked—and the creative incentives the hospital used to overcome these failures. You'll find that story in this book, as well as the heroic story of another, long-ago doctor who also fought poor hand hygiene.

At another lecture, to a group of venture capitalists, Levitt discussed some new research he was doing with Sudhir Venkatesh, the sociologist whose adventures with a crack-selling gang were featured in *Freakonomics*. The new research concerned the hour-by-hour activities of street prostitutes in Chicago. As it happened, one of the venture capitalists (we'll call him John) had a date later that evening with a $300-an-hour prostitute (who goes by the name of Allie). When John arrived at Allie's apartment, he saw a copy of *Freakonomics* on her coffee table.

"Where'd you get *that*?" John asked.

Allie said a girlfriend of hers who was also "in the business" had sent it to her.

Hoping to impress Allie—the male instinct to impress the female is apparently strong even when the sex is already bought and paid for—John said he'd attended a lecture that very day by one of the book's authors. As if that weren't coincidence enough, Levitt mentioned he was doing some research on prostitution.

A few days later, this e-mail landed in Levitt's in-box:

From: XXXXXXXXXXXXX.com
Date: Wed 28 Sep 2005 19:03:57
To: s-levitt@uchicago.edu
Subject: Working on a paper about the working girl?

I heard through mutual acquaintances that you are working on a paper about the economics of prostitution, correct?

Since I am not really sure if this is a serious project of yours or if my source was putting me on ... I just thought I would put myself out there and let you know I would love to be of assistance ...am a big fan of Freakanomics and I love the drug studies the book mentions ... Let me know.

Thanks,
Allie

See more info and new pictures at XXXXXXXXXX.com
or call me at XXX-XXX-XXXX

One complication remained: Levitt had to explain to his wife and four kids that he wouldn't be home the following Saturday morning, that instead he'd be having brunch with a prostitute. It was vital, he argued, to meet with her in person to accurately measure the shape of her demand curve. Somehow, they bought it.

And so you will read about Allie in this book as well.

The chain of events that led to her inclusion might be attributed to what economists call *cumulative advantage.* That is, the prominence of our first book produced a series of advantages in writing a second book that a different author may not have enjoyed. Our greatest hope is that we have taken proper advantage of this advantage.

Finally, while writing this book we have tried to rely on a bare minimum of economics jargon, which can be abstruse and unmemorable. So instead of thinking about the Allie affair as an example of *cumulative advantage,* let's just call it . . . well, freaky.

"NOT EVERYTHING": TOPICS THAT NEITHER *FREAKONOMICS* NOR *SUPERFREAKONOMICS* ADDRESSES

The pros and cons of linoleum • Sermons about tithing and their proximity to pastors' mortgage payments • Knitting demographics • A passage from "Heteroskedasticity-Robust Standard Errors for Fixed Effects Panel Data Regression," by James H. Stock and Mark W. Watson • Cost-benefit analysis of leaving cookies out for Santa Claus • Divorce rates among people who got married by a snowman they built in a meadow • A list of Kwanzaa customs, and the derivations thereof • The proper way to scale a fish • Why feng shui benefits are outweighed by desire to leave pants right over there on the floor • Earthquake survival methods • Why U.S. congressmen are more likely to part their hair on the left than on the right • The Milford High School Marching Band trip itinerary • Why the majority of Americans are "doing great," when asked • Philosophy professors and their obligation to talk about *The Matrix* • How even in space, which is awesome, astronauts hate Mondays • Atmospheric reentry strategies • The number of paint colors males identify as "white" • The dietary habits of jellyfish • Variations in strategy employed by East Coast and West Coast peanut vendors, and the rivalries created thereby • Pie recipes • List of failed compliments for your lab partner, including "You look beautiful without goggles" and "I would like to give you this pea plant" • Why cigarette smokers are sexier (until you kiss them) • Whether ex-smokers apply lip balm at disproportionately high rates • Proportion of telephone numbers distributed at bars that are 867-5309 • How professional classical pianists are exceedingly good at tickling! • Causal relationship between writing about swine flu and contracting swine-flu paranoia • Causal relationship between cautiously using your sleeve to touch doorknobs and not contracting any friends • Lost GDP due to misspellings on Craigslist • Why Nigerian shipping heirs are more likely to require help in moving their monies into safe bank accounts than shipping heirs of all other nationalities • The first joke ever told • Why it wasn't funny • Nicest responses to "Do I look fat?" • Introductory principles of astrology • The percentage of bonfires that are bad ideas • How the prevalence of Auto-Tune in recording studios removes incentive to "just do one more take, man, I can feel it this time" • The best possible setting for your thermostat • How to convince your spouse that you have chosen the optimal thermostat setting • The financial benefits of speaking with a British accent in the U.S. • How erroneous interpretation of scripture led to $57 million in losing bets on the Utah Jazz • Migratory patterns of Nebraska retirees • Failed anti-choking measures tried before the Heimlich maneuver was invented • How Oedipus and Freud met one time at a bar and had a really good laugh • Quotes wrongly attributed to Confucius • Quotes wrongly attributed to Mark Twain and Oscar Wilde • Quotes your grandfather claims to have invented, but didn't • Rates of clinical depression among wildlife native to the icy tundra • Average ratio of Facebook friends to real friends • A list of insults that, if used properly by children, will severely diminish other children's self-esteem • Household uses of grapefruit spoons (besides eating grapefruit) • Why steel drummers in the subway outearn guitar players in the subway, regardless of skill level • Steel drum instructions • Ukulele chord fingerings • Risk analysis of using your neighbors' hot tub while they're away • Bernoulli's unfinished crossword puzzles • Ways to achieve eternal life • The secret story of the breakfast-cereal industry's invention of the "snooze" button • How to tie balloon animals • Which balloon animals make children the happiest • Balloon untangling techniques • How to get tangled up in blue • List of medical conditions you couldn't care less about—*until you have one of them* • Modern practical applications for the slide rule • Why the songs you like least are the songs you remember the most • The extraordinary physics of penguin defecation • Why no American has ever fully understood the rules of cricket • How cockle shells and pretty maids all in a row in your garden will get you 25 to life • A list of things you should never do with acid • Salad dressings that never caught on • Salad dressings that caught on, peaked too early, and then faded from memory • Accurate blueprints of Noah's Ark • How the application of Greek sophistry can help make your spouse less angry about your elongated guys' night out • Why the monocle went out of style (and how you can bring it back) • A list of nations in which bribery is not just acceptable but encouraged • List of government officials' home addresses in Venezuela, Angola, Myanmar, and Uzbekistan • Why Levitt feels entitled to eat my Oreos even though they're clearly on my side of the desk • Why Dubner thinks he's *soooo* great that he can ignore the standard office code of conduct for sharing junk food • How to avoid tigers • How short, angry guys suffered from identity crises prior to Napoleon • The actual price of all the tea in China • Why sequels are always worse • *One day while driving my car / I saw that the door was ajar / So I reached in my butt / and I pulled out King Tut / and we sang ancient songs from afar* • Why the Gregory Brothers (of Auto-Tune the News fame) felt compelled to compile this list.

INTRODUCTION

PUTTING THE FREAK IN ECONOMICS

MANY OF LIFE'S DECISIONS ARE HARD. WHAT KIND OF CAREER should you pursue? Does your ailing mother need to be put in a nursing home? You and your spouse already have two kids; should you have a third?

Such decisions are hard for a number of reasons. For one, the stakes are high. There's also a great deal of uncertainty involved. Above all, decisions like these are rare, which means you don't get much practice making them. You've probably gotten pretty good at buying groceries, since you do it so often, but buying your first house is another thing entirely.

Some decisions, meanwhile, are really, really easy.

Imagine you've gone to a party at a friend's house. He lives only a mile away. You have a great time, perhaps because you drank four glasses of wine. Now the party is breaking up. While draining your last glass, you dig out your car keys. Abruptly you conclude this is a bad idea: you are in no condition to drive home.

For the past few decades, we've been rigorously educated about the risks of driving under the influence of alcohol. A drunk driver is thirteen times more likely to cause an accident than a sober one. And yet a lot of people still drive drunk. In the United States, more than 30 percent of all fatal crashes involve at least one driver who has been drinking. During the late-night hours, when alcohol use is greatest, that proportion rises to nearly

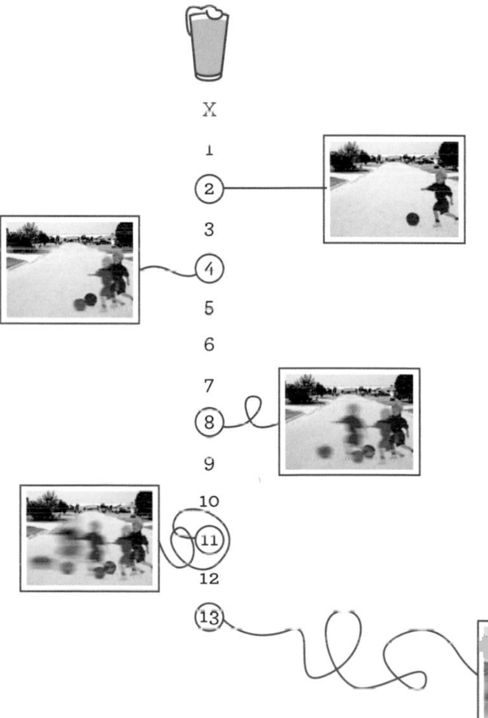

GETTY IMAGES

60 percent. Overall, 1 of every 140 miles is driven drunk, or 21 billion miles each year.

Why do so many people get behind the wheel after drinking? Maybe because—and this could be the most sobering statistic yet—drunk drivers are rarely caught. There is just one arrest for every 27,000 miles driven while drunk. That means you could expect to drive all the way across the country, and then back, and then back and forth three more times, chugging beers all the while, before you got pulled over. As with most bad behaviors, drunk driving could probably be wiped out entirely if a strong-enough incentive were instituted—random roadblocks, for instance, where drunk drivers are executed on the spot—but our society probably doesn't have the appetite for that.

Meanwhile, back at your friend's party, you have made what seems to be the easiest decision in history: instead of driving home, you're going to walk. After all, it's only a mile. You find your friend, thank him for the party, and tell him the plan. He heartily applauds your good judgment.

But should he? We all know that drunk driving is terribly risky, but what about drunk walking? *Is* this decision so easy?

Let's look at some numbers. Each year, more than 1,000 drunk pedestrians die in traffic accidents. They step off sidewalks into city streets; they lie down to rest on country roads; they make mad dashes across busy highways. Compared with the total number of people killed in alcohol-related traffic accidents each year—about 13,000—the number of drunk pedestrians is relatively small. But when you're choosing whether to walk or drive, the overall number isn't what counts. Here's the relevant question: on a per-mile basis, is it more dangerous to drive drunk or walk drunk?

Not all drunk walkers try their best to avoid oncoming traffic. In some parts of the U.S., there is something of a tradition of lying down drunk, at night, in the middle of the road. One five-year stretch claimed 136 such victims in North Carolina alone. "In the end," said a pathologist from the state, "the most sardonic and cynical thing you can say, I suppose, is that we've defined here a baseline of human behavior which no traffic safety measure will ever be able to correct."

The average American walks about a half-mile per day outside the home or workplace. There are some 237 million Americans sixteen and older; all told, that's 43 billion miles walked each year by people of driving age. If we assume that 1 of every 140 of those miles is walked drunk—the same proportion of miles that are driven drunk—then 307 million miles are walked drunk each year.

Doing the math, you find that on a per-mile basis, a drunk walker is *eight times more likely* to get killed than a drunk driver.

There's one important caveat: a drunk walker isn't likely to hurt or kill anyone other than her- or himself. That can't be said of a drunk driver. In fatal accidents involving alcohol, 36 percent of the victims are either passengers, pedestrians, or other drivers. Still, even after factoring in the deaths of those innocents, walking drunk leads to five times as many deaths per mile as driving drunk.

So as you leave your friend's party, the decision should be clear: driving is safer than walking. (It would be even safer, obviously, to drink less, or to call a cab.) The next time you put away four glasses of wine at a party, maybe you'll think through your decision a bit differently. Or, if you're too far gone, maybe your friend will help sort things out. Because friends don't let friends walk drunk.

If you had the option of being born anywhere in the world today, India might not be the wisest choice. Despite its vaunted progress as a major player in the global economy, the country as a whole remains excruciatingly poor. Life expectancy and literacy rates are low; pollution and corruption are high. In the rural areas where more than two-thirds of Indians live, barely half of the households have electricity and only one in four homes has a toilet.

It is especially unlucky to be born female, because many Indian parents express a strong "son preference." Only 10 percent of Indian families with two sons want another child, whereas nearly 40 percent of families with two daughters want to try again. Giving birth to a baby boy is like giving birth to a 401(k) retirement fund. He will grow up to be a wage-earning man who can provide for his parents in their sunset years and, when the time comes, light the funeral pyre. Having a baby girl, meanwhile, means relabeling the retirement fund a dowry fund. Although the dowry system has long been under assault, it is still common for a bride's parents to give the groom or his family cash, cars, or real estate. The bride's family is also expected to pay for the wedding.

The U.S. charity Smile Train, which performs cleft-repair surgery on poor children around the world, recently spent some time in Chennai, India. When one local man was asked how many children he had, he answered "one." The organization later learned that the man did have a son—but he also had five daughters, who apparently didn't warrant a mention. Smile Train also learned that midwives in Chennai were sometimes paid $2.50 to smother a baby girl born with a cleft deformity—and so, putting the lure of incentives to good use, the charity began offering midwives as much as $10 for each baby girl they took to a hospital for cleft surgery.

800 B.C.E.
Greeks are the first recorded practitioners of the dowry, whereby a bride's family sweetens the deal by paying the groom—and, sometimes, giving him a share in the estate of the bride's father.

300 B.C.E.
In the book of Samuel, King Saul demands 100 Philistine foreskins from the would-be king David before allowing him to marry Saul's daughter.

1961
India outlaws dowries, in part because competition over large payments sometimes led to violence. But the practice remains widespread today.

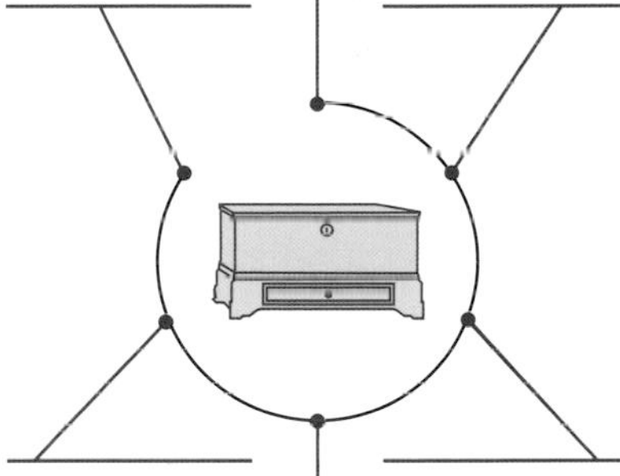

450 C.E.
Attila the Hun, in exchange for marrying the sister of emperor Valentinian III, demands as dowry half of the Roman Empire. When his request is refused, he attempts an invasion.

1772
Thomas Jefferson marries Martha Wayles Skelton, and soon receives an inheritance that includes, among much else, a slave named Betty Hemings. Jefferson is thought to have fathered a son with Betty's daughter Sally.

1662
Catherine of Braganza (Portugal) is married to Charles II of England. Her dowry includes the city of Bombay.

Since 1996 it has been illegal in India to use ultrasound machines for the purpose of revealing the sex of a fetus. General Electric, the top ultrasounds purveyor, even requires its customers to sign an affidavit to that effect. But enforcement of the law is lax: there have been fewer than 500 prosecutions of ultrasound misuse since it was outlawed, with just a handful of convictions.

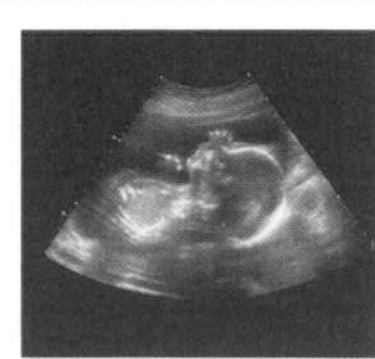

Girls are so undervalued in India that there are roughly 35 million fewer females than males in the population. Most of these "missing women," as the economist Amartya Sen calls them, are presumed dead, either by indirect means (the girl's parents withheld nutrition or medical care, perhaps to the benefit of a brother), direct harm (the baby girl was killed after birth, whether by a midwife or a parent), or, increasingly, a pre-birth decision. Even in India's smallest villages, where electricity might be sporadic and clean water hard to find, a pregnant woman can pay a technician to scan her belly with an ultrasound and, if the fetus is female, have an abortion. In recent years, as these sex-selective abortions have become more common, the male-female ratio in India—as well as in other son-worshipping countries like China—has grown even more lopsided.

A baby Indian girl who does grow into adulthood faces inequality at nearly every turn. She will earn less money than a man, receive worse health care and less education, and perhaps be subjected to daily atrocities. In a national health survey, 51 percent of Indian men said that wife-beating is justified under certain circumstances; more surprisingly, 54 percent of *women* agreed—if, for instance, a wife burns dinner or leaves the house without permission. More than 100,000 young Indian women die in fires every year, many of them "bride burnings" or other instances of domestic abuse.

How do Indian men measure up? While it isn't easy to conduct medical research on penis size, a few international studies do exist. The penis-enlargement company Andromedical compiled the available data and arrived at a ranking (below) that shows average penis size in the countries surveyed. (Yes, several of your favorite countries will be missing.) India indeed ranks toward the low end. For those of you surprised to see France atop the list, it should be noted that the French data were compiled by French scholars.

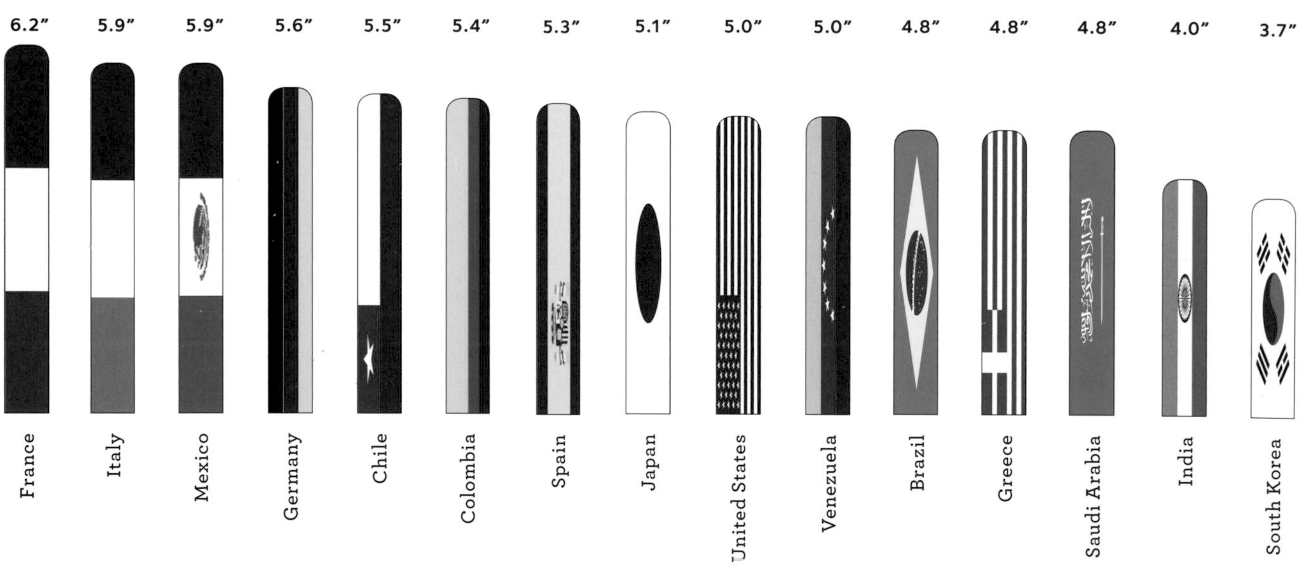

COURTESY EMILY OBERMAN

Take a look at this Indian condom ad. Notice anything unusual? It seems to depict an array of pre-coital couples, but while each woman is different, the man remains the same. Perhaps instead of "People of India," it should have been called "Stud of India."

Indian women also run an outsize risk of unwanted pregnancy and sexually transmitted disease, including a high rate of HIV/AIDS. One cause is that Indian men's condoms malfunction more than 15 percent of the time. Why such a high fail rate? According to the Indian Council of Medical Research, some 60 percent of Indian men have penises too small for the condoms manufactured to fit World Health Organization specs. That was the conclusion of a two-year study in which more than 1,000 Indian men had their penises measured and photographed by scientists. "The condom," declared one of the researchers, "is not optimized for India."

With such a multitude of problems, what should be done to improve the lives of Indian women, especially the majority who live in the countryside?

The government has tried to help by banning dowries and sex-selective abortions, but these laws have largely been ignored. A number of monetary interventions have also been designed for Indian women. These include Apni Beti, Apna Dhan ("My Daughter, My Treasure"), a project that pays rural women not to abort female babies; a vast microcredit industry that makes small-business loans to women; and an array of charitable programs launched by a veritable alphabet soup of international aid agencies.

The Indian government has also vowed to make smaller condoms more readily available.

Unfortunately, most of these projects have proven complicated, costly, and, at best, nominally successful.

A different sort of intervention, meanwhile, *does* seem to have helped. This one, like the ultrasound machine, relies on technology, but it had little to do with women per se and even less to do with baby-making. Nor was it administered by the Indian government or some multinational charity.

JWT, INDIA

EMILY OSTER

Emily Oster has been making mischievous contributions to science since she was two years old. Her parents, a pair of economists, recorded the conversations that Emily held with herself in her crib, and sent the tape to a child psychologist friend of theirs. That tape soon became the touchstone for a series of landmark research papers about early childhood development. Some years later, when she was nine, Emily undertook a study of the gender gap in her Connecticut neighborhood. Here's the report she wrote in the *Everit St. Weekly*:

In fact, it wasn't even designed to help anyone at all, at least not the way we normally think of "help." It was just a plain old entrepreneurial development, called television.

State-run broadcast TV had been around for decades, but poor reception and a dearth of programming meant there simply wasn't much reason to watch. But lately, thanks to a steep fall in the price of equipment and distribution, great swaths of India have been wired for cable and satellite TV. Between 2001 and 2006, some 150 million Indians received cable for the first time, their villages suddenly crackling with the latest game shows and soap operas, newscasts and police procedurals, beamed from the big cities of India and abroad. TV gave many Indian villagers their first good look at the outside world.

But not every village got cable TV, and those that did received it at different times. This staggered introduction produced just the kind of data—a lovely natural experiment—that economists love to exploit. The economists in this case were a pair of young Americans, Emily Oster and Robert Jensen. By measuring the changes in different villages based on whether (and when) each village got cable TV, they were able to tease out the effect of TV on Indian women.

They examined data from a government survey of 2,700 households, most of them rural. Women fifteen and older were asked about their lifestyles, preferences, and familial relationships. As it turned out, the women who recently got cable TV were significantly less willing to tolerate wife-beating, less likely to admit to having a son preference, and more likely to exercise personal autonomy. TV somehow

The Everit St. Weekly

VOL.1 NO.10
MAY 9 1989

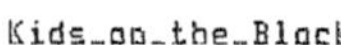

Kids_on_the_Block

Did you ever wonder how many boy verses girls there are on the block? How many kids per house on average or how many kids there are on the block? Well that's exactly what this article is about. It is based only on children living at home.

There are 32 children among our subscribers. To see all the information in pictures look at the graphs below. There are 18 boys and 14 girls. The average number of kids per house is about 1 1/2. There are 9 families that have no children living at home. But only 1 family has no kids at all. The families with the most kids are the Pillsburys and the Levins; they both have 4.

Next week watch for an up date on how old houses on the block are and how long people have lived in them.

Emily Oster

Boys and Girls

Size of Family

Number of kids per family	0	1	2	3	4
Families	9	2	5	4	2

COURTESY EMILY OSTER

seemed to be empowering women in a way that government interventions had not.

What caused these changes? Did rural Indian women become more autonomous after seeing cosmopolitan images on their TV sets—women who dressed as they pleased, handled their own money, and were treated as neither property nor baby-making machines? Or did such programming simply make the rural women feel embarrassed to admit to a government surveyor that they were treated so badly?

There is good reason to be skeptical of data from personal surveys. There is often a vast gulf between how people say they behave and how they actually behave. (In economist-speak, these two behaviors are known as *declared preferences* and *revealed preferences*.) Furthermore, when it costs almost nothing to fib—as in the case of a government survey like this one—a reasonable amount of fibbing is to be expected. The fibs might even be subconscious, with the subject simply saying what she expects the surveyor wants to hear.

But when you can measure the revealed preference, or the actual behavior, then you're getting somewhere. That's where Oster and Jensen found persuasive evidence of real change. Rural Indian families who got cable TV began to have a lower birthrate than families without TV. (In a country like India, a lower birthrate generally means more autonomy for women and fewer health risks.) Families with TV were also more likely to keep their daughters in school, which suggests that girls were seen as more valuable, or at least deserving of equal treatment. (The enrollment rate for boys, notably, didn't change.) These hard numbers made the self-reported survey data more believable. It appears that cable TV really did empower the women of rural India, even to the point of no longer tolerating domestic abuse.

Or maybe their husbands were just too busy watching cricket.

When the world was lurching into the modern era, it grew magnificently more populous, and in a hurry. Most of this expansion took place in urban centers like London, Paris, New York, and Chicago. In the United States alone, cities grew by 30 million residents during the nineteenth century, with half of that gain in just the final twenty years.

But as this swarm of humanity moved itself, and its goods, from place to place, a problem emerged. The main mode of transportation produced

TOP 10 TV SHOWS IN INDIA (2008)

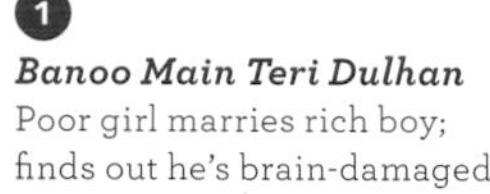

1 ***Banoo Main Teri Dulhan***
Poor girl marries rich boy; finds out he's brain-damaged.

2 ***Kyunki Saas Bhi Kabhi Bahu Thi***
Rich grandson marries poor girl, vexing moneybags grandpa.

3 ***Sa Re Ga Ma Pa***
Little Champs, India's *American Idol*.

4 ***Sapna Babul Ka . . . Bidaai***
Dark-skinned sister, light-skinned sister: who's happier?

5 ***Kahaani Ghar Ghar Ki***
Struggles of a housewife; remarkable for a run of more than 1,700 episodes.

6 ***Saat Phere***
Girl fights prejudice, searches for identity.

7 ***Ghar Ki Lakshmi Betiyann***
A patriarch upholds the status quo, puts down women in his life.

8 ***14th Annual Star Screen Awards***
Bollywood's Oscars.

9 ***Maayka***
Two sisters orphaned by a terrorist attack.

10 ***Kayamath***
A sheltered girl and her two-timing father.

1, 3, 6, 7, 9 ZEE TV; 2, 4, 5, 8, 10: STAR

Firefighting was a dangerous and awe-inspiring business in 19th-century New York City, its many wooden buildings under constant threat of incineration. In 1835, an urban wildfire destroyed most of the downtown area, burning 700 buildings to the ground and bankrupting 23 of the city's 26 fire-insurance companies. A fearful public was looking for a superman to protect them from the ravages of fire. That's when a mythical figure named Big Mose sprang to life. He was based on a real volunteer firefighter named Mose Humphrey, who disappeared in 1838 under mysterious circumstances. In absentia, Mose became a Paul Bunyan-like folk hero who was said to be eight feet tall and able to swim acoss the Hudson in two strokes. If a trolley blocked his fire engine on the way to a blaze, Mose would just lift the trolley over his head to let the engine pass beneath. Mose was also a renowned street fighter, known to uproot a streetlamp to use as a club while swigging beer from a 50-gallon keg tied to his belt. His adventures were regularly featured in Bowery theaters, with Mose fighting trouble in New York, California, and even China.

a slew of the by-products that economists call *negative externalities,* including gridlock, high insurance costs, and far too many traffic fatalities. Crops that would have landed on a family's dinner table were sometimes converted into fuel, driving up food prices and causing shortages. Then there were the air pollutants and toxic emissions, endangering the environment as well as individuals' health.

We are talking about the automobile—aren't we?

No, we're not. We are talking about the horse.

The horse, a versatile and powerful helpmate since the days of antiquity, was put to work in many ways as modern cities expanded: pulling streetcars and private coaches, hauling construction materials, unloading freight from ships and trains, even powering the machines that churned out furniture, rope, beer, and clothing. If your young daughter took gravely ill, the doctor rushed to your home on horseback. When a fire broke out, a team of horses charged through the streets with a pumping truck. ▇ At the turn of the twentieth century, some 200,000 horses lived and worked in New York City, or 1 for every 17 people.

The ASPCA was created in 1866, primarily to care for horses in New York. Founder Henry Bergh chose as its official seal an angel saving a cart-horse from a cruel beating at the hands of its driver. As it happened, the ASPCA was routinely called to put wounded horses to death—which probably made the society the leading horse killer at the time.

But oh, the troubles they caused!

Horse-drawn wagons clogged the streets terribly, and when a horse broke down, it was often put to death on the spot. This caused further delays. Many stable owners held life-insurance policies that, to guard against fraud, stipulated the animal be euthanized by a third party. This meant waiting for the police, a veterinarian, or the ASPCA to arrive. Even death didn't end the gridlock. "Dead horses were extremely unwieldy," writes the transportation scholar Eric Morris. "As a result, street cleaners often waited for the corpses to putrefy so they could more easily be sawed into pieces and carted off."

The noise from iron wagon wheels and horseshoes was so disturbing—it purportedly caused widespread nervous disorders—that some cities banned horse traffic on the streets around hospitals and other sensitive areas.

And it was frighteningly easy to be struck down by a horse or wagon, neither of which is as easy to control as they appear in the movies, especially on slick, crowded city streets. In 1900, horse accidents claimed the lives of 200 New Yorkers, or 1 of every 17,000 residents. In 2007, meanwhile, 274 New Yorkers died in auto accidents, or 1 of every 30,000 residents. This means that a New Yorker was nearly twice as likely to die from a horse accident in 1900 than from a car accident today. (There are unfortunately no statistics available on drunk horse-drivers, but we can assume the number would be menacingly high.)

Worst of all was the dung. The average horse produced about 24 pounds of manure a day. With 200,000 horses, that's nearly 5 million pounds of horse manure. A day. Where did it go?

Decades earlier, when horses were less plentiful in cities, there was a smooth-functioning market for manure, with farmers buying it to truck off (via horse, of course) to their fields. But as the urban equine population exploded, there was a massive glut. In vacant lots, horse manure was piled as high as sixty feet. It lined city streets like banks of snow. In the summertime, it stank to the heavens; when the rains came, a soupy stream of horse manure flooded the crosswalks and seeped into people's basements. Today, when you admire old New York brownstones and their elegant stoops, rising from street level to the second-story parlor, keep in mind that this was a design necessity, allowing a homeowner to rise above the sea of horse manure.

All of this dung was terrifically unhealthy. It was a breeding ground for billions of flies that spread a host of deadly diseases. Rats and other vermin swarmed the mountains of manure to pick out undigested oats and other horse feed—crops that were becoming more costly for human consumption thanks to higher horse demand. No one at the time was worried about global warming, but if they had been, the horse would have been Public Enemy No. 1, for its manure emits methane, a powerful greenhouse gas.

In 1898, New York hosted the first international urban planning conference. The agenda was dominated by horse manure, because cities around the world were experiencing the same crisis. But no solution could be

Dumping 5 MILLION POUNDS of horse manure each day in New York City is roughly equivalent to dumping:

The 2009 Indianapolis Colts
15,750 POUNDS
+
The Statue of Liberty
450,000 POUNDS
+
One blue whale
400,000 POUNDS
+
All the gold mined in a year in South Africa
400,000 POUNDS
+
Air Force One
833,000 POUNDS
+
All the garbage produced in one day in Baltimore, Md.
2,900,000 POUNDS

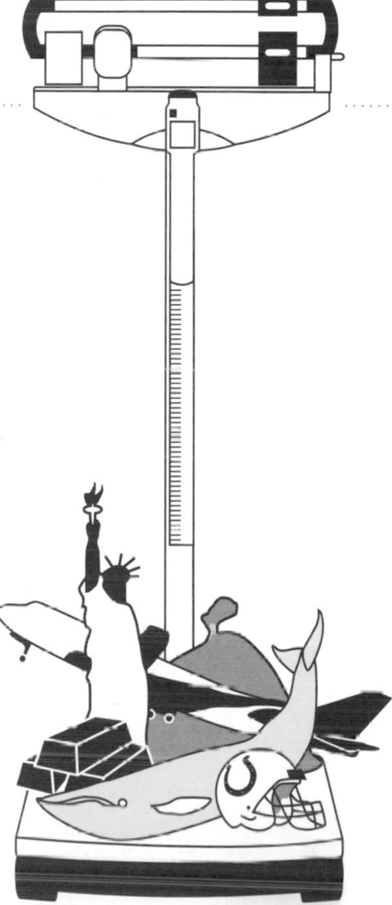

MORTON STREET, CORNER OF BEDFORD, LOOKING TOWARD BLEECKER STREET, MARCH 17, 1893.

Rumor had it that the busy streets of 19th-century New York were paved with gold; in reality, they were paved with horse manure.

found. "Stumped by the crisis," writes Eric Morris, "the urban planning conference declared its work fruitless and broke up in three days instead of the scheduled ten."

The world had seemingly reached the point where its largest cities could not survive without the horse but couldn't survive with it, either.

And then the problem vanished. It was neither government fiat nor divine intervention that did the trick. City dwellers did not rise up in some mass movement of altruism or self-restraint, surrendering all the benefits of horse power. The problem was solved by technological innovation. No, not the invention of a dungless animal. The horse was kicked to the curb by the electric streetcar and the automobile, both of which were extravagantly cleaner and far more efficient. The automobile, cheaper to own and operate than a horse-drawn vehicle, was proclaimed "an environmental savior." Cities around the world were able to take a deep breath—without holding their noses at last—and resume their march of progress.

The story, unfortunately, does not end there. The solutions that saved the twentieth century seem to have imperiled the twenty-first, because the automobile and electric streetcar carried their own negative externalities. The carbon emissions spat out over the past century by more than 1 billion cars and thousands of coal-burning power plants seem to have warmed the earth's atmosphere. Just as equine activity once threatened to stomp out civilization, there is now a fear that human activity will do the same. Martin Weitzman, an environmental economist at Harvard, argues there is a roughly 5 percent chance that global temperatures will rise enough to "effectively destroy planet Earth as we know it." In some quarters—the media, for instance, which never met a potential apocalypse it didn't like—the fatalism runs even stronger.

This is perhaps not very surprising. When the solution to a given problem doesn't lay right before our eyes, it is easy to assume that no solution exists. But history has shown again and again that such assumptions are wrong.

This is not to say the world is perfect. Nor that all progress is always good. Even widespread societal gains inevitably produce losses for some people. That's why the economist Joseph Schumpeter referred to capitalism as "creative destruction."

But humankind has a great capacity for finding technological solutions to seemingly intractable problems, and this will likely be the case for global warming. It isn't that the problem isn't potentially large. It's just that human ingenuity—when given proper incentives—is bound to be larger. Even more encouraging, technological fixes are often far simpler, and therefore cheaper, than the doomsayers could have imagined. Indeed, in the final chapter of this book we'll meet a band of renegade engineers who have developed not one but three global-warming fixes, any of which could be bought for less than the annual sales tally of all the Thoroughbred horses at Keeneland auction house in Kentucky.

The value of horse manure, incidentally, has rebounded, so much so that the owners of one Massachusetts farm recently called the police to stop a neighbor from hauling it away. The neighbor claimed there was a misunderstanding, that he'd been given permission by the farm's previous owner. But the current owner wouldn't back down, demanding $600 for the manure.

Who was this manure-loving neighbor? None other than Martin Weitzman, the economist with the grave global-warming prediction.

"Congratulations," one colleague wrote to Weitzman when the story hit the papers. "Most economists I know are net exporters of horseshit. And you are, it seems, a net importer."

The vanquishing of horse manure . . . the unintended consequences of cable TV . . . the perils of walking while drunk: what does any of this have to do with economics?

Instead of thinking of such stories as "economics," it is better to see them as illustrating "the economic approach." That's a phrase made popular by Gary Becker, the longtime University of Chicago economist who was awarded a Nobel Prize in 1992. In his acceptance lecture, he ex-

In a Sept. 11, 1881, editorial, *The New York Times* called for a solution to the horse.

IN PLACE OF HORSES.

Attempt has been heretofore made in these columns to point out the serious practical objections to the use of horses, especially in large cities.

• • •

Is it possible to devise anything which will do the horse's work, and thus will satisfy all who do not care for the horse himself?

The conditions which must be met are obvious and very severe. The substitute must not be too costly or too bulky; it must develop ample power; must be under easy and safe control; must be simple enough to be manageable in unskilled hands; must be fairly free from accidents and must not get out of order; and it must be economical. Self-propelling carriages have long been sought, but wind is too untrustworthy a motor and steam is too expensive. Experiments with traction engines or road locomotives have been made in the North-west, under stimulus of prizes offered, but the bulk, weight, and cost of the most compact engine and boiler will probably never allow steam to be used, even if the boiler is omitted and the steam taken from a reservoir.

• • •

This may be an advanced view, but to call it chimerical is foolish. In 1824 the idea of being dragged "by a roaring steam engine" was the best of jokes. The first steam ship which crossed the Atlantic carried Dr. LARDNER's essay, proving indubitably that such a thing was impossible. The spark from FRANKLIN's key on a kite-string was curious, but that "spark" is doing wonders now, and seems to have hardly begun. True, no progress has been made in doing without the horse, but the complete answer is that not much effort has been expended to that end; invention has had no stimulus offered it.

To learn how Gary Becker, the Brooklyn kid who loved handball, became Gary Becker, the Nobel Prize–winning economist, see the decision tree on pages 14–15.

CORBIS

plained that the economic approach "does not assume that individuals are motivated solely by selfishness or gain. It is a *method* of analysis, not an assumption about particular motivations. . . . Behavior is driven by a much richer set of values and preferences."

Becker started his career studying topics that weren't typically germane to economics: crime and punishment, drug addiction, the allocation of time, and the costs and benefits of marriage, child rearing, and divorce. Most of his colleagues wouldn't go anywhere near such stuff. "For a long time," he recalled, "my type of work was either ignored or strongly disliked by most of the leading economists. I was considered way out and perhaps not really an economist."

Well, if what Gary Becker was doing was "not really economics," then we want to do it too. Truth be told, what Becker was doing was actually freakonomics—marrying the economic approach to a rogue, freakish curiosity—but the word hadn't yet been invented.

In his Nobel address, Becker suggested that the economic approach is not a subject matter, nor is it a mathematical means of explaining "the economy." Rather, it is a decision to examine the world a bit differently. It is a systematic means of describing how people make decisions and how they change their minds; how they choose someone to love and marry, someone perhaps to hate and even kill; whether, coming upon a pile of money, they will steal from it, leave it alone, or even add to it; why they may fear one thing and yearn for something only slightly different; why they'll punish one sort of behavior while rewarding a similar one.

How do economists describe such decisions? It usually begins by accumulating data, great gobs of it, which may have been generated on purpose or perhaps left behind by accident. A good set of data can go a long way toward describing human behavior as long as the proper questions are asked of it. Our job in this book is to come up with such questions. This will allow us to describe, for instance, how the typical oncologist or terrorist or college student behaves in a given situation, and why.

Some people may feel uneasy about reducing the vagaries of human behavior to cold numerical probabilities. Who among us wants to describe ourselves as "typical"? If, for instance, you added up all the women and men on the planet, you would find that, on average, the typical adult human being has one breast and one testicle—and yet how many people fit that description? If *your* loved one was killed in a drunk-driving accident, what comfort is there in knowing that walking drunk is more dangerous? If *you* are the young Indian bride who is brutalized by her husband, what cheer can be had from learning that cable TV has empowered the *typical* Indian bride?

These objections are good and true. But while there are exceptions to every rule, it's also good to know the rule. In a complex world where people can be *a*typical in an infinite number of ways, there is great value in discovering the baseline. And knowing what happens on average is a good place to start. By so doing, we insulate ourselves from the tendency to build our thinking—our daily decisions, our laws, our governance—on exceptions and anomalies rather than on reality.

When making decisions, people tend to rely on the information they've stored in their memories—which, paradoxically, often resides there not because it is representative but because it's anomalous. This can get us into trouble—when, for instance, a swimmer panics thinking he's seen a shark after watching blanket news coverage of shark attacks. The fact is that far more people are killed by go-karts each year than by sharks.

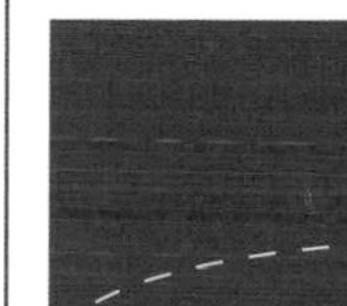

Cast an eye back for a moment to the summer months of 2001, which in the United States came to be known as the Summer of the Shark. The media brought us chilling tales of rampant shark carnage. The prime example was the story of Jessie Arbogast, an eight-year-old boy who was playing in the warm, shallow Gulf waves of Pensacola, Florida, when a bull shark ripped off his right arm and gorged a big piece of his thigh as well. *Time* magazine ran a cover package about shark attacks. Here is the lead of the main article:

> *Sharks come silently, without warning. There are three ways they strike: the hit-and-run, the bump-and-bite and the sneak attack. The hit-and-run is the most common. The shark may see the sole of a swimmer's foot, think it's a fish and take a bite before realizing this isn't its usual prey.*

Scared yet?

A reasonable person might never go near the ocean again. But how many shark attacks do you think actually happened that year?

Take a guess—and then cut your guess in half, and now cut it in half a few more times. During the entire year of 2001, around the world there were just 68 shark attacks, of which 4 were fatal.

Not only are these numbers far lower than the media hysteria implied; they were also no higher than in earlier years or in the years to follow. Between 1995 and 2005, there were on average 60.3 worldwide shark attacks each year, with a high of 79 and a low of 46. There were on average 5.9 fatalities per year, with a high of 11 and a low of 3. In other words, the headlines during the summer of 2001 might just as easily have read

FOLLOW THIS DECISION TREE TO TRACE THE CHOICES THE ECONOMIST GARY BECKER MADE IN HIS LIFE

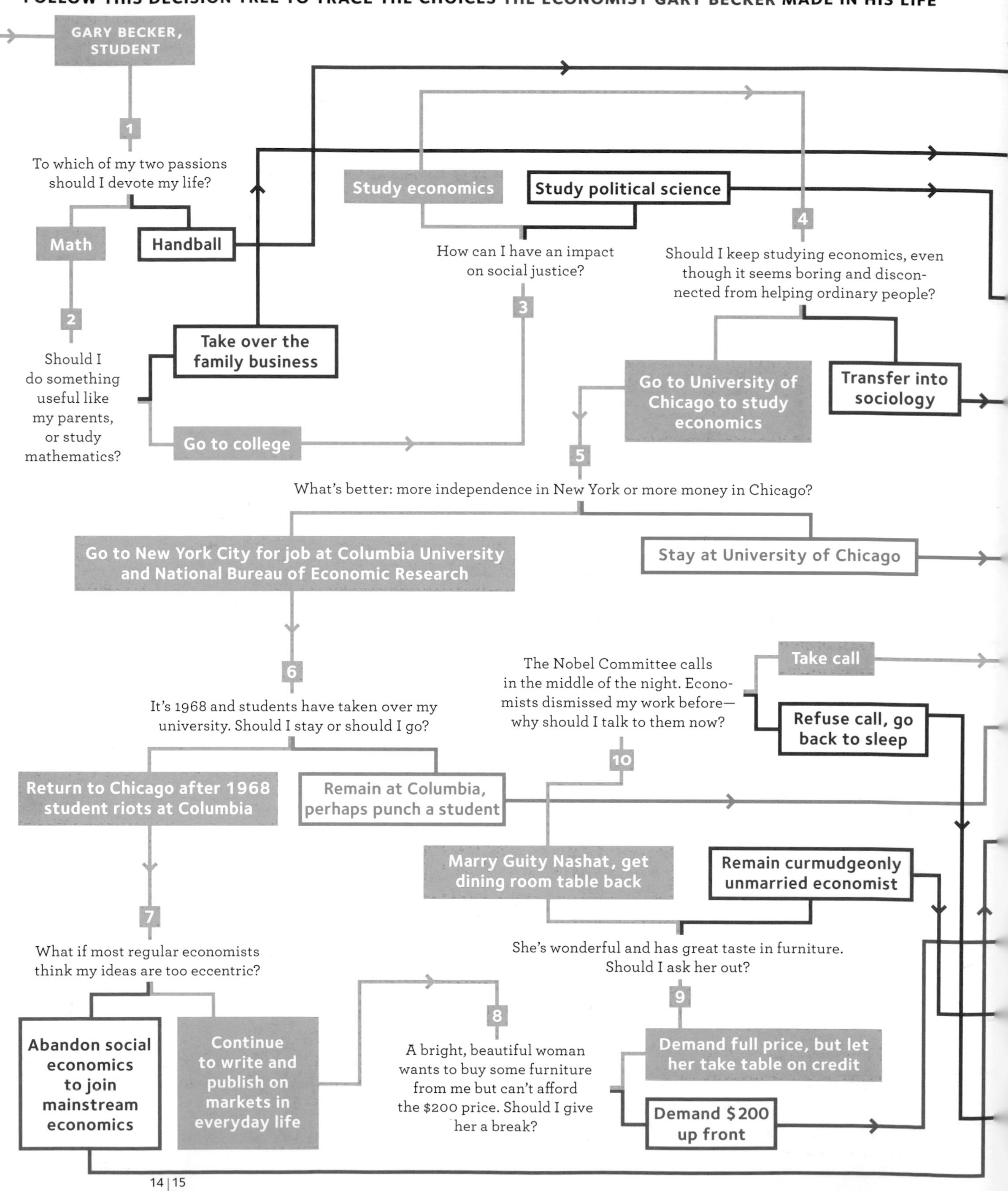

GARY BECKER, STUDENT
1
To which of my two passions should I devote my life?
Math
Handball
2
Should I do something useful like my parents, or study mathematics?
Take over the family business
Go to college
Study economics
Study political science
How can I have an impact on social justice?
3
4
Should I keep studying economics, even though it seems boring and disconnected from helping ordinary people?
Go to University of Chicago to study economics
Transfer into sociology
5
What's better: more independence in New York or more money in Chicago?
Go to New York City for job at Columbia University and National Bureau of Economic Research
Stay at University of Chicago
6
It's 1968 and students have taken over my university. Should I stay or should I go?
Return to Chicago after 1968 student riots at Columbia
Remain at Columbia, perhaps punch a student
7
What if most regular economists think my ideas are too eccentric?
Abandon social economics to join mainstream economics
Continue to write and publish on markets in everyday life
8
A bright, beautiful woman wants to buy some furniture from me but can't afford the $200 price. Should I give her a break?
Demand full price, but let her take table on credit
Demand $200 up front
9
She's wonderful and has great taste in furniture. Should I ask her out?
Marry Guity Nashat, get dining room table back
Remain curmudgeonly unmarried economist
10
The Nobel Committee calls in the middle of the night. Economists dismissed my work before—why should I talk to them now?
Take call
Refuse call, go back to sleep

IN BECKER'S OWN WORDS:

GARY BECKER, WORLD HANDBALL CHAMPION?

GARY BECKER, SMALL-BUSINESS PROPRIETOR

GARY BECKER, NATTERING NABOB

GARY BECKER, SOCIOLOGIST

GARY BECKER, FRUSTRATED ECONOMIST?

GARY BECKER, THE NOBEL PRIZE–WINNING ECONOMIST

GARY BECKER, INMATE 23A2537?

GARY BECKER, REGULAR ECONOMIST

GARY BECKER, HARD-ASS

GARY BECKER, BACHELOR

GARY BECKER, UNGRACIOUS AWARD WINNER

1 "I was a good student, but until age sixteen was more interested in sports. I had to decide between being on the handball and math teams, since they met during the same time period. It was indicative of my shift in priorities that I chose math, although I was better at handball."

2 "My father had left school in Montreal after the eighth grade because he was eager to make money. My mother—whose family emigrated from Eastern Europe to New York City when she was six months old—also left after the eighth grade because girls were not expected to get much education."

3 "We had many lively discussions in the house about politics and justice. By the time I finished high school, my interest in mathematics was beginning to compete with a desire to do something useful for society. These two interests came together during my freshman year at Princeton, when I accidentally took a course in economics and was greatly attracted by the mathematical rigor of a subject that dealt with social organization."

4 "I began to lose interest in economics during my senior (third) year because it did not seem to deal with important social problems. I contemplated transferring to sociology but found that subject too difficult. Fortunately, I decided to go to the University of Chicago for graduate work in economics. My first encounter in 1951 with Milton Friedman's course on microeconomics renewed my excitement."

5 "After my third year of graduate study I became an assistant professor at Chicago. After three years in that position, I turned down a much larger salary from Chicago to take a similar appointment at Columbia combined with one at the National Bureau of Economic Research, then also located in Manhattan. I have always believed this was the correct decision, for I developed greater independence and self-confidence than seems likely if I remained at Chicago."

6 "To provide a better family atmosphere I lived in the suburbs and commuted to Columbia and the Bureau. Eventually, I began to tire of commuting and decided either to move into New York or to leave Columbia for another university. My decision to leave was hastened by the student riots in 1968. I believed that Columbia should take a firm hand and uphold the right to free inquiry without student intimidation. In 1970, I returned to Chicago."

7 "There's no question that initially there was a great deal of skepticism, starting with my first study and book on the economics of racial discrimination. Most of the senior members of the profession at the major institutions were kind of skeptical—or *very* skeptical—about what I was doing. A number of my teachers, like Milton Friedman, were very positive about it. That went with another feeling—it seemed to me very obvious that I was right!"

8 Becker gets a phone call from Guity Nashat, a graduate student in history at the University of Chicago. In her words: "I saw an ad for a table with ten chairs, for only $200. I called the owner later that evening. I was hoping to do some bargaining about the price. When I heard that he was an economics professor, I feared I was facing a stone wall." Becker won't sell for less than $200 but agrees to let Nashat take the table on credit.

9 Guity Nashat: "I began to wonder about what kind of economist this Becker was. He did not know who I was, and he was not willing to come down on the price, yet he would let me take it without paying for it! The following week, I went to his office to pay him. Contrary to the way he sounded on the phone, he seemed quite genial. What surprised me even more was when he asked me to dinner."

10 Woken by his wife, Guity, to take a phone call from Stockholm, Becker learns in 1992 he has won the Nobel Prize. "My work has been getting a lot of attention lately. Perhaps more than it deserves. In the Nobel citation, they mentioned that the work on the family was still controversial. Well, that was 1992. It's less controversial now than it was at that time."

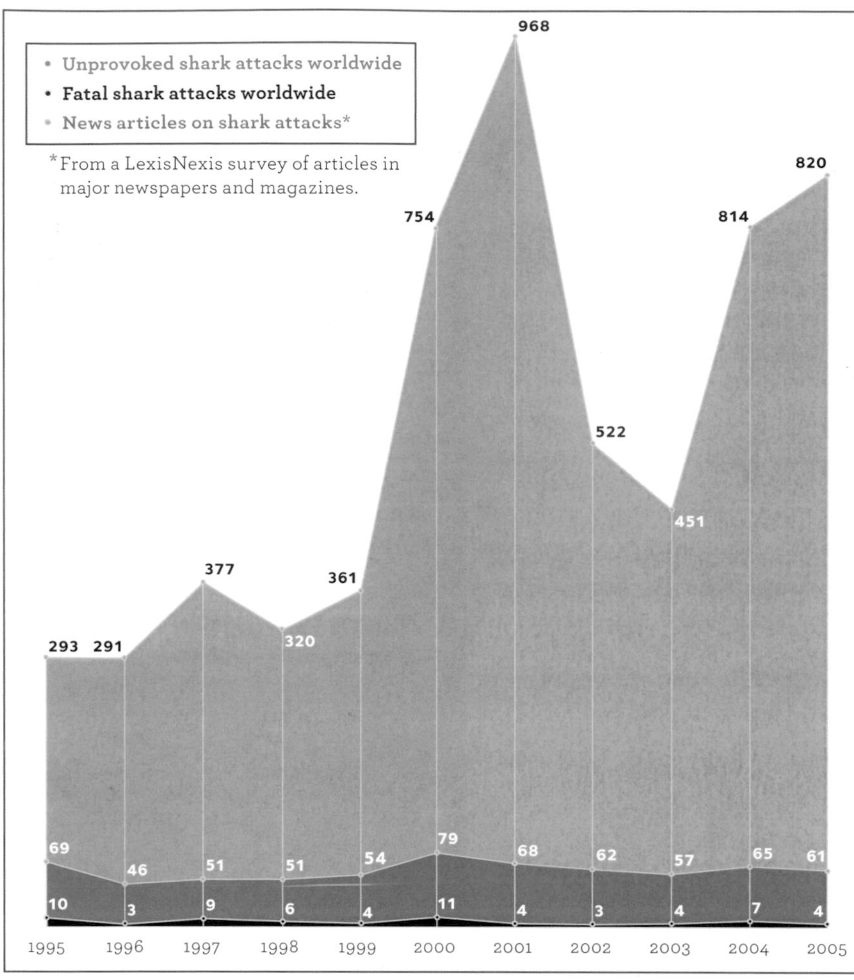

"Shark Attacks About Average This Year." But that probably wouldn't have sold many magazines.

So for a moment, instead of thinking about poor Jessie Arbogast and the tragedy he and his family faced, think of this: in a world with more than 6 billion people, only 4 of them died in 2001 from shark attacks. More people are probably run over each year by TV news vans.

Elephants, meanwhile, kill at least 200 people every year. So why aren't we petrified of them? Probably because most of their victims live in places far from the world's media centers. It may also have something to do with the perceptions we glean from the movies. Friendly, entertaining elephants are a staple of children's films (think *Babar* and *Dumbo*); sharks, meanwhile, are inevitably typecast as villains. If sharks had any legal connections whatsoever, they surely would have sued for an injunction against *Jaws*.

And yet the shark scare played out so relentlessly that summer of 2001, with such full-throated horror, that it didn't quiet down until the terrorist attacks on September 11 at the World Trade Center and the Pentagon. Nearly 3,000 people were killed that day—some 2,500 more than have died from shark attacks since the first records were kept, in the late sixteenth century.

So despite its shortcomings, thinking in terms of the typical does have its advantages. We have therefore done our best to tell stories in this book that rely on accumulated data rather than on individual anecdotes, glaring anomalies, personal opinions, emotional outbursts, or moral leanings. Some people may argue that statistics can be made to say anything, to defend indefensible causes or tell pet lies. But the economic approach aims for the opposite: to address a given topic with neither fear nor favor, letting numbers speak the truth. We don't take sides. The introduction of TV, for instance, has substantially helped the women of rural India. This doesn't mean we accept the power of TV as unerringly positive. As you will read in chapter 3, the introduction of TV in the United States produced a devastating societal change.

The economic approach isn't meant to describe the world as any one of us might *want* it to be, or fear that it is, or pray that it becomes—but rather to explain what it actually is. Most of us want to fix or change the world in some fashion. But to change the world, you first have to understand it.

As of this writing, we are just beginning to stumble out of a financial crisis that began with a subprime-mortgage binge in the United States and spread, like an extremely communicable disease, around the world. There will be hundreds, if not thousands, of books published on the topic.

This is not one of them.

Why? Mainly because the macroeconomy and its multitude of complex, moving parts is simply not our domain. After recent events, one might wonder if the macroeconomy is the domain of *any* economist. Most economists the public encounters are presented as oracles who can tell you, with alluring certainty, where the stock market or inflation or interest rates are heading. But as we've seen lately, such predictions are generally worthless. Economists have a hard enough time explaining the past, much less predicting the future. (They are still arguing over whether Franklin Delano Roosevelt's policy moves quelled the Great Depression or exacerbated it!) They are not alone, of course. It seems to be part of the human condition to believe in our own predictive abilities—and, just as well, to quickly forget how bad our predictions turned out to be.

So we have practically nothing to say in this book about what people call "the economy." Our best defense (slim as it may be) is that the topics we *do* write about, while not directly connected to "the economy," may give some insights into actual human behavior. Believe it or not, if you can understand the incentives that lead a schoolteacher or a sumo wrestler to cheat, you can understand how the subprime-mortgage bubble came to pass.

The stories you will read are set in many realms, from the rarefied corridors of academia to the grimiest street corners. Many are based on

Levitt's recent academic research; others have been inspired by fellow economists as well as engineers and astrophysicists, psychotic killers and emergency-room doctors, amateur historians and transgender neuroscientists. ■ Most of the stories fall into one of two categories: things you always thought you knew but didn't; and things you never knew you wanted to know but do.

Many of our findings may not be all that useful, or even conclusive. But that's all right. We are trying to start a conversation, not have the last word. Which means you may find a few things in the following pages to quarrel with.

In fact, we'd be disappointed if you didn't.

To learn about the underlying research on any given section of the book, please read the endnotes (page 241).

QUARREL FORM

Hey Levitt and Dubner,

I recently picked up your book because I was ____________ and I didn't have any ____________. I was immediately overcome with ____________. I mean, ____________ ____________! Where do you ____________ with this stuff, in the ____________ of your ____________? Have you ever actually ____________ a ____________? Well, I have, and let me tell you, it ____________! (Except for the time I ____________ a ____________, but I was pretty ____________ at the time, so . . .) As for global warming, ____________! Just yesterday, I ____________ a ____________, and the next thing I knew, a ____________ was ____________ me, and I had to ____________ with my ____________. All because of your ____________ book! No wonder your ____________ is so ____________. (By the way, I ____________ for a living, if you ever need help with that.) Anyway, I bet the next book I read is a whole lot ____________ than *SuperFreakonomics*. In the meantime, I'll be ____________ my ____________, and if you get a ____________ in the ____________, it might be from me.

Signed: ____________________

CHAPTER 1

20 | 21

HOW IS A STREET PROSTITUTE LIKE A DEPARTMENT-STORE SANTA?

ONE AFTERNOON NOT LONG AGO, ON A WELCOMING COOL day toward the end of summer, a twenty-nine-year-old woman named LaSheena sat on the hood of an SUV outside the Dearborn Homes, a housing project on the South Side of Chicago. She had a beaten-down look in her eyes but otherwise seemed youthful, her pretty face framed by straightened hair. She was dressed in a baggy black-and-red tracksuit, the kind she'd worn since she was a kid. Her parents rarely had money for new clothes, so she used to get her male cousins' hand-me-downs, and the habit stuck.

LaSheena was talking about how she earns her living. ♣♣ She described four main streams of income: "boosting," "roosting," cutting hair, and turning tricks.

"Boosting," she explained, is shoplifting and selling the swag. "Roosting" means serving as a lookout for the local street gang that sells drugs. She gets $8 for a boy's haircut and $12 for a man's.

Which job is the worst of the four?

"Turning tricks," she says, with no hesitation.

Why?

"'Cause I don't really like men. I guess it bothers me mentally."

And what if prostitution paid twice as much?

"Would I do it more?" she asks. "Yeah!"

Sudhir Venkatesh, a sociologist at Columbia University (you'll meet him more formally on page 29), has spent years studying the underground economy in Chicago's poorest neighborhoods. He found that residents depend on a great variety of off-the-books revenue streams, some illegal and some merely unregulated. Among them:

WOMEN	MEN
Cooking for other families	Selling counterfeit license plates and Social Security cards
Selling food or candy out of an apartment	Fixing cars in a parking lot
Sleeping in a store overnight to deter thieves	Working as freelance janitor
Running a home day care	Gathering scrap metal and aluminum
Preparing taxes	Selling stolen clothes or cigarettes
Taking in boarders	Pirating gas and electricity
Driving people to buy groceries	Running cash bars out of their apartments

Climate scientists now recognize that Europe fell into a "Little Ice Age" that, broadly speaking, lasted from the 14th century until the 19th century. But at the time, foul weather was widely thought to be the work of sinister women who, in partnership with the devil, practiced witchcraft. The economist Emily Oster compared historic data on temperatures and witch trials and found that the persecution of women generally rose when temperatures fell, and vice versa.

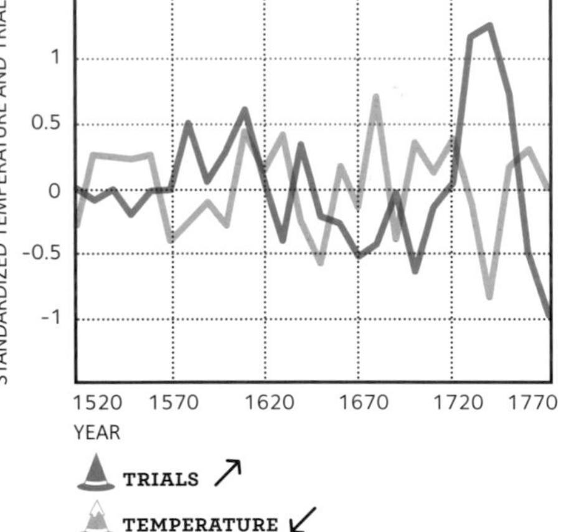

TRIALS ↗

TEMPERATURE ↙

Below is a 16th-century account of a witch burning in Schiltach, Germany. The woman in question "was burned and thirty-six items were read out loud that she confessed to. Most shameful, horrible, and damaging things, how she caused mischief and harm to animals and people. For eighteen years she was working with the Devil, and her own mother herself had taught her."

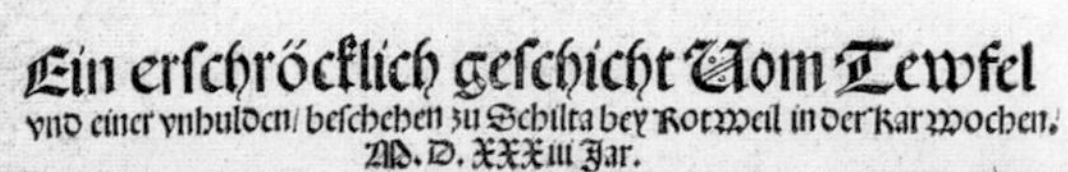

Ein erschröcklich geschicht Vom Tewfel
vnd einer vnhulden/ beschehen zu Schilta bey Rotweil in der Karwochen.
M.D.XXXIII Jar.

Newe zeytung geschehen drey meyl von Rot-
weyl da ist ein Stedlein im Hornberger tal das
hayst Schylta do ist der teufel in das selbig stet
lein in ein Wirts hauß kummen/ist vngefärlich
drey oder vyer tag im selbingen Wirts hauß ge-
wesen/ hat daselbst angefanngen zu Trummen
vñ Pfeyffen in der Stuben vnd allenthalbē im
hauß man hat aber nichts sehen künden sonder
so seltzam ding/der gleichen vor nie/gehö
sind ethlich abeteẅrer kummen vnnd ha
wellen beschweren do hat der Teufel ang

hauß angangen vnnd das gantz Stedtlein biß
on drey kleine heußlein vngefärlich in anderhal
ber stund gar verbrunnē Aber vber die drey heuß
lein/wie sie in der vrgicht bekennt/hat der Teuf
fel kain gewalt gehabt. Die zway sinnd zwayer
armen gesellen gewest vnd das dritt eines dabey
die armen vnnd was sunst niemants hat wellen
beherbergē/herberg gehabt haben. Wie solchs

Throughout history, it has invariably been easier to be male than female. Yes, this is an overgeneralization and yes, there are exceptions, but by any important measure, women have had it rougher than men. Even though men handled most of the warfare, hunting, and brute-force labor, women had a shorter life expectancy. Some deaths were more senseless than others. Between the thirteenth and nineteenth centuries, as many as 1 million European women, most of them poor and many of them widowed, were executed for witchcraft, taking the blame for bad weather that killed crops. ▲▲

Women have finally overtaken men in life expectancy, thanks mainly to medical improvements surrounding childbirth. In many countries, however, being female remains a serious handicap even in the twenty-first century. Young women in Cameroon have their breasts "ironed"—beaten or massaged by a wooden pestle or a heated coconut shell—to make them less sexually tempting. In China, foot binding has finally been done away with (after roughly one thousand years), but females are still far more likely than males to be abandoned after birth, to be illiterate, and to commit suicide. And women in rural India, as we wrote earlier, continue to face discrimination in just about every direction.

But especially in the world's developed nations, women's lives have improved dramatically. There is no comparing the prospects of a girl in twenty-first-century America or Britain or Japan with her counterpart from a century or two earlier. In any arena you look—education, legal and voting rights, career opportunities, and so on—it is far better to be a woman today than at any other point in history. In 1872, the earliest year for which such statistics are available, 21 percent of college students in the United States were female. Today, that number is 58 percent and rising. It has truly been a stunning ascendancy.

And yet there is still a considerable economic price to pay for being a woman. For American women twenty-five and older who hold at least a bachelor's degree and work full-time, the national median income is about $47,000. Similar men, meanwhile, make more than $66,000, a premium of 40 percent. The same is true

STEFAN HAMER AND ERHARD SCHÖN; TRANSLATION: MARTIN BAUMEL AND JOSHUA CLEMENTE BONILLA

One explanation for the steep male-female wage gap is the simple fact that women are far more prominent in lesser-paying professions. Consider the data at right, which reflect earnings of recent college graduates working full-time. It is also true that women earn less than men in every professional field—except for engineering/software/architecture, where a woman actually earns 105 percent of her male coworker's salary. Alas, only 1 in 6 workers in that field is a woman.

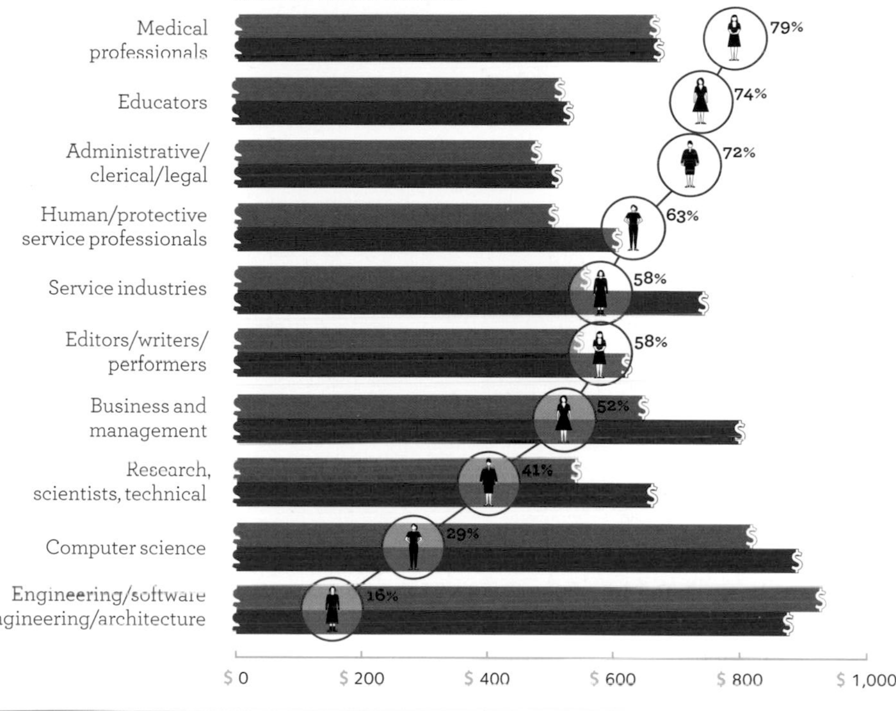

Source: Judy Goldberg Dey and Catherine Hill, "Behind the Pay Gap," AAUW Educational Foundation.

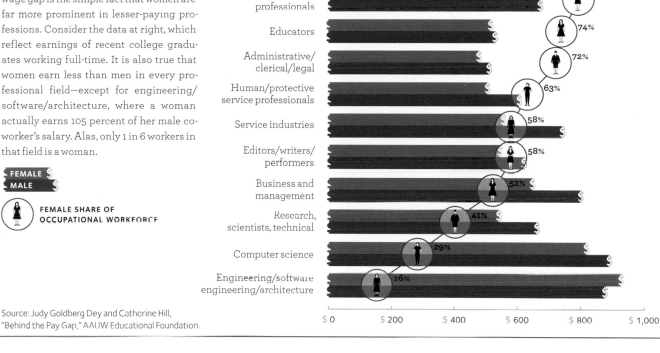

even for women who attend the nation's elite universities. The economists Claudia Goldin and Lawrence Katz found that women who went to Harvard earned *less than half as much* as the average Harvard man. Even when the analysis included only full-time, full-year employees and controlled for college major, profession, and other variables, Goldin and Katz found that the Harvard women still earned about 30 percent less than their male counterparts.

What can possibly account for such a huge wage gap?

There are a variety of factors. Women are more likely to leave the workforce or downshift their careers to raise a family. Even within high-paying occupations like medicine and law, women tend to choose specialties that pay less (general practitioner, for instance, or in-house counsel). And there is likely still a good amount of discrimination. This may range from the overt—denying a woman a promotion purely because she is not a man—to the insidious. A considerable body of research has shown that overweight women suffer a greater wage penalty than overweight men. The same is true for women with bad teeth.

There are some biological wild cards as well. The economists Andrea Ichino and Enrico Moretti, analyzing personnel data from a large Italian bank, found that female employees under forty-five years old tended

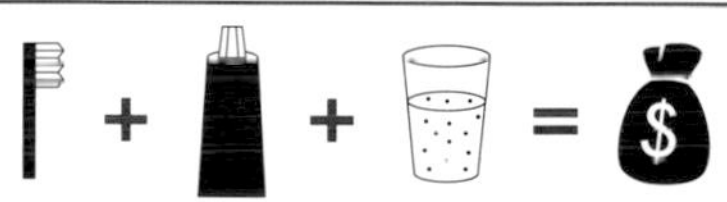

Girls who grow up drinking fluoridated water will earn roughly 4 percent more as adults than those who did not.

The U.S. Army has rejected or refused to deploy recruits with missing teeth.

Good teeth are just one element of a broader "beauty premium" that economists have detected. Daniel Hamermesh and Jeff Biddle found that "above-average-looking" people earn 5 percent more than "average-looking" people, who in turn earn 5 to 10 percent more than "below-average-looking" people.

In the Women's National Basketball Association, men have taken over a lot of the coaching jobs:

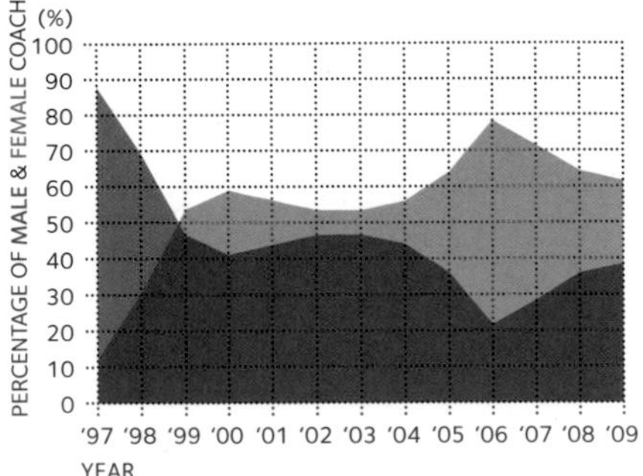

Male coaches have also dominated the winner's circle. Here's a look at the WNBA champions and their coach's gender:

Year	Champion	Coach
1997	Houston Comets	M
1998	Houston Comets	M
1999	Houston Comets	M
2000	Houston Comets	M
2001	Los Angeles Sparks	M
2002	Los Angeles Sparks	M
2003	Detroit Shock	M
2004	Seattle Storm	F
2005	Sacramento Monarchs	M
2006	Detroit Shock	M
2007	Phoenix Mercury	M
2008	Detroit Shock	M
2009	Phoenix Mercury	M

Anne Donovan was the only woman to coach a WNBA team to a championship. In the late 1970s, the six-foot-eight Donovan (she's the one on the left) starred at Paramus Catholic High School in New Jersey and was the nation's top college recruit.

CORBIS

to miss work consistently on twenty-eight-day cycles. Plotting these absences against employee productivity ratings, the economists determined that this menstrual absenteeism accounted for 14 percent of the difference between female and male earnings at the bank.

Or consider the 1972 U.S. law known as Title IX. While broadly designed to prohibit sex discrimination in educational settings, Title IX also required high schools and colleges to bring their women's sports programs up to the level of their men's programs. Millions of young women subsequently joined these new programs, and as the economist Betsey Stevenson discovered, girls who play high-school sports are more likely to attend college and land a solid job, especially in some of the high-skill fields traditionally dominated by men. That's the good news.

But Title IX also brought some bad news for women. When the law was passed, more than 90 percent of college women's sports teams had female head coaches. Title IX boosted the appeal of such jobs: salaries rose and there was more exposure and excitement. Like the lowly peasant food that is "discovered" by the culinary elite and promptly migrates from roadside shacks into high-end restaurants, these jobs were soon snapped up by a new set of customers: men. These days, barely 40 percent of college women's sports teams are coached by women. Among the most visible coaching jobs in women's sports are those in the Women's National Basketball Association (WNBA), founded thirteen years ago as a corollary to the men's NBA. As of 2009, the WNBA had 13 teams and just 6 of them—again, fewer than 50 percent—were coached by women. This is actually an improvement from the league's tenth anniversary season, when only 3 of the 14 coaches were women.

For all the progress women have made in the twenty-first-century labor market, the typical female would come out well ahead if she had simply had the foresight to be born male.

There *is* one labor market women have always dominated: prostitution.

Its business model is built upon a simple premise. Since time immemorial and all over the world, men have wanted more sex than they could get for free. So what inevitably emerges is a supply of women who, for the right price, are willing to satisfy this demand.

Today prostitution is generally illegal in the United States, albeit with

POPULATION.

DISTRIBUTION BY AGE AND SEX OF THE TOTAL POPULATION: 1910.

MALES FEMALES

AGE

HUNDREDS OF THOUSANDS

From the 1910 Census: the women in red were women in red.

a few exceptions and many inconsistencies in enforcement. In the early years of the nation, prostitution was frowned upon but not criminalized. It was during the Progressive Era, roughly from the 1890s to the 1920s, that this leniency ended. There was a public outcry against "white slavery," in which thousands of women were imprisoned against their will to work as prostitutes.

The white slavery problem turned out to be a wild exaggeration. The reality was perhaps scarier: rather than being forced into prostitution, women were choosing it for themselves. In the early 1910s, the Department of Justice conducted a census of 310 cities in 26 states to tally the number of prostitutes in the United States: "We arrive at the conservative figure of approximately 200,000 women in the regular army of vice."

At the time, the American population included 22 million women between the ages of fifteen and forty-four. If the DOJ numbers are to be believed, 1 of every 110 women in that age range was a prostitute. But most prostitutes, about 85 percent, were in their twenties. In that age range, 1 of every *50* American women was a prostitute.

The market was particularly strong in Chicago, which had more than a thousand known brothels. The mayor assembled a blue-ribbon Vice Commission, comprising religious leaders as well as civic, educational, legal, and medical authorities. Once they got their hands dirty, these good people realized they were up against an enemy even more venal than sex: economics.

The "white slavery" panic was fueled in part by books like *The Great War on White Slavery* and *Fighting the Traffic in Young Girls*. The alarmist tone can be seen in the books' illustrations:

Have you a girl to spare? Sixty Thousand White Slaves die every year. *The Vice Resorts cannot run [unless] this number is replaced annually. Are you willing to give your daughter to keep up this terrible business?*

"My God! If only I could get out of here." *The midnight shriek of a young girl in the vice district of a large city, heard by two worthy men, started a crusade which resulted in closing up the dens of shame in that city.*

TOP: CLIFFORD G. ROE, *THE GREAT WAR ON WHITE SLAVERY; OR FIGHTING FOR THE PROTECTION OF OUR GIRLS* (SELF-PUBLISHED, 1911); BOTTOM: ERNEST A. BELL, *FIGHTING THE TRAFFIC IN YOUNG GIRLS, OR WAR ON THE WHITE SLAVE TRADE* (G. S. BALL, 1910)

The results of a survey of 30 Chicago prostitutes "investigated in a most careful and painstak-ing way by a woman intimately connected with the rescue and reform work of the city":

TABLE GIVING DATA REGARDING THIRTY INMATES OF HOUSES OF PROSTITUTION IN CHICAGO.

No.	AGE. Entrance to Life	AGE. Present	Former Occupation	Wages, Week	FAMILY. Brothers	FAMILY. Sisters	Price House	Money, how Spent	Causes for Becoming Prostitute
1	16	29	Saleswoman...	$5.00	1	4	$1.00	Supporting family......	Seduced.
2	28	32	Department Store.......	7.00	3	3	1.00	....	Could not earn enough to live on.
3	20	23	....	....	2	....	....	....	Seduced at 18; reckless after.
4	17	22	Saleswoman...	6.00	Boarded, $4.00.		5.00	Saving to quit.	No money to live on or buy clothes.
5	22	26	Domestic.....	6.00	4	2	5.00	....	Dance halls; tired of drudgery.
6	19	21	Stenographer..	10.00	2	....	5.00	....	Seduced at 18.
7	19	23	Domestic.....	7.00	4	3	1.00	....	Husband deserted her; enticed by older woman.
8	21	24	Waitress......	4.00	1	1	5.00	....	Seduced by married man; family unkind.
9	21	24	Housemaid...	5.00	....	....	5.00	Helping mother.....	Seduced; for need of money.
10	17	24	....	....	....	....	5.00	....	Insufficient education for clerk; domestic work too hard.
11	22	24	Governess and housekeeper.	5.00	1	4	5.00	....	Husband died; could not support child.
12	23	24	Domestic.....	....	Lived with aunt.		5.00	....	No work; no money.
13	20	20	Cigar stand...	6.00	1	2	5.00	....	Seduced; unable to get work.
14	19	24	Waitress, chamber maid.......	3.00	1	4	5.00	For mother and child of 7 years.....	Husband died; to support mother and child.
15	19	25	Never worked.	....	....	....	5.00	....	Naturally bad; immoral at 15 years.
16	17	24	Dressmaker...	2.50	3	2	5.00	....	Tired of drudgery; husband deserted her.
17	18	24	Never worked.	....	2	3	5.00	Lost sight of family......	Seduced at 18; always had nice things.
18	17	24	Housework...	4.00	....	....	1.00	....	Could not make ends meet.
19	19	27	Telephone....	7.00	2	2	1.00	....	Seduced by married man.
20	15	22	Domestic.....	5.00	Orphan.		1.00	....	Seduced by son of family; could not clothe herself.
21	19	21	Ticket seller..	2.50	1	2	1.50	....	Crazy; wanted to; born with devil in her.
22	19	23	Waitress......	4.00	1	1	1.50	....	Wanted to dress like other girls.
23	21	26	Dressmaker; sales.......	5.00	2	1	1.50	....	Low wages; wanted pretty clothes.
24	....	28	....	....	....	3	1.50	....	Could not get on with step-father.
25	22	28	Housework...	3.50	....	....	1.50	....	Not education enough for other work.
26	22	22	Waitress......	5.00	5 Boarded.	2	1.00	Keeps parents.....	Poverty.
27	18	20	Milliner......	Low	1	2	1.00	....	Drink.
28	12	25	Vaudeville....	Uncertain.	....	....	5.00	....	Woman took her into house of prostitution.
29	22	27	Clerk.........	5.00	....	1	Street-walker	....	Drink and bad influence.
30	21	21	Restaurant, factory.....	4.00	2	2	1.00	....	No money and could find no work.

A much larger survey, of prostitutes in a reformatory in Bedford, N.Y., also asked women why they turned to vice. Note that out of the 671 reasons given, only 2 were "white slave."

BEDFORD CASES

CAUSES. REASONS GIVEN BY THE GIRL

A. In connection with her family		
1. Immorality of the parents	15	
2. Incompatibility	39	
3. Neglect and abuse	26	
4. No mother or father or neither	166	
5. Over indulgence	10	
6. Over strictness	35	
7. Poverty	9	
8. Turned out	6	
		306
B. In connection with married life		
1. Death of husband	5	
2. Desertion by husband	8	
3. Immorality (includes cruelty or criminality)	14	
4. Incompatibility	26	
5. Husband put girl on street	2	
		55
C. Personal reasons		
1. Bad company	75	
2. No sex instruction	10	
3. Idle or lonely	5	
4. Sick, needed the money	4	
5. Ruined anyway	10	
6. Lover put girl on the street	10	
7. Previous use of drink or drugs	7	
8. White slave	2	
9. Tired of drudgery	4	
10. "Easy money"	17	
11. Dances	13	
12. Lazy, hated work	20	
13. Stage environment	9	
14. Love of the life	15	
15. Desertion by lover	3	
16. Desire for pleasure (theatre, food, clothes)	48	
17. Desire for money	38	
18. Ashamed to go home after first escapade	1	291
D. Economic reasons		
1. Can't support herself	5	
2. Can't support herself and children	1	
3. Couldn't find work	13	19
TOTAL		671

LEFT: *COMMERCIALIZED PROSTITUTION IN NEW YORK CITY*, GEORGE JACKSON KNEELAND AND KATHARINE BEMENT DAVIS (THE CENTURY CO., 1917), FROM THE COLLECTION OF THE NEW-YORK HISTORICAL SOCIETY; RIGHT: *THE SOCIAL EVIL IN CHICAGO* (VICE COMMISSION OF CHICAGO, 1912)

"Is it any wonder," the commission declared, "that a tempted girl who receives only $6 per week working with her hands sells her body for $25 per week when she learns that there is demand for it and men are willing to pay the price?"

Converted into today's dollars, the $6-per-week shopgirl had an annual salary of only $6,500. The same woman who took up prostitution at $25 a week earned the modern equivalent of more than $25,000 a year. But the Vice Commission acknowledged that $25 per week was at the very low end of what Chicago prostitutes earned. A woman working in a "dollar house" (some brothels charged as little as 50 cents; others charged $5 or $10) took home an average weekly salary of $70, or the modern equivalent of about $76,000 annually.

At the heart of the Levee, the South Side neighborhood that housed block after block of brothels, stood the Everleigh Club, which the Vice Commission described as "the most famous and luxurious house of prostitution in the country." Its customers included business titans, politicians, athletes, entertainers, and even a few anti-prostitution crusaders. The Everleigh's prostitutes, known as "butterfly girls," were not only attractive, hygienic, and trustworthy, but also good conversationalists who could cite classical poetry if that's what floated a particular gentleman's boat. In the book *Sin in the Second City,* Karen Abbott reports that the Everleigh also offered sexual delicacies that weren't available elsewhere—"French" style, for instance, commonly known today as oral sex.

In an age when a nice dinner cost about $12 in today's currency, the Everleigh's customers were willing to pay the equivalent of $250 just to get into the club and $370 for a bottle of champagne. Relatively speaking, the sex was pretty cheap: about $1,250.

Ada and Minna Everleigh, the sisters who ran the brothel, guarded their assets carefully. Butterflies were provided with a healthful diet, excellent medical care, a well-rounded education, and the best wage going: as much as $400 a week, or the modern equivalent of about $430,000 a year.

To be sure, an Everleigh butterfly's wages were off the charts. But why did even a typical Chicago prostitute one hundred years ago earn so much money?

The best answer is that wages are determined in large part by the laws of supply and demand, which are often more powerful than laws made by legislators.

Ada (top) and Minna (bottom) Everleigh, madams—and entrepreneurs—extraordinaire. Their brothel was decked out as ornately as they were.

The Everleigh had 12 soundproofed parlors, each with its own theme; this is the Oriental Music Room. The piano in the Gold Room was covered in gold leaf and cost $15,000, more than $300,000 in today's currency.

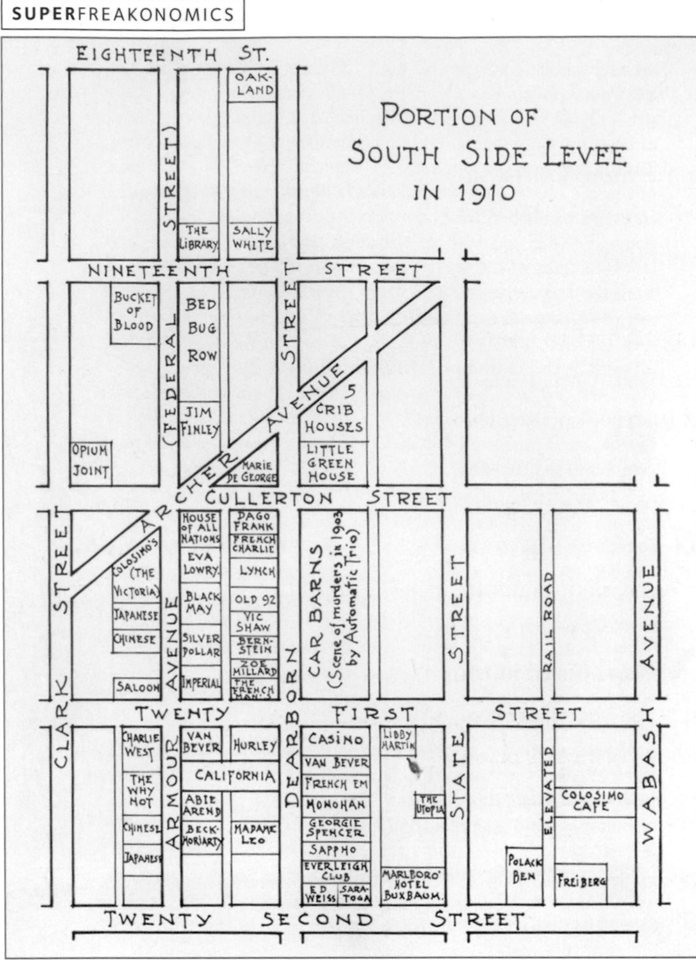

Many of the 1,000-plus brothels in old Chicago were concentrated in the Levee district. The Everleigh Club was on South Dearborn Street just north of Twenty-second Street. Some houses distinguished themselves by offering special services, including Sappho (next door to the Everleigh) and the Japanese and Chinese houses on Armour Avenue.

In a burst of urban renewal in the 1960s, much of this area gave way to the Raymond Hilliard Homes.

LEFT: CHICAGO HISTORICAL SOCIETY; RIGHT: BERTRAND GOLDBERG ASSOCIATES, PHOTOGRAPH BY ORLANDO CABANBAN, COURTESY THE ART INSTITUTE OF CHICAGO

In the United States especially, politics and economics don't mix well. Politicians have all sorts of reasons to pass all sorts of laws that, as well-meaning as they may be, fail to account for the way real people respond to real-world incentives.

When prostitution was criminalized in the United States, most of the policing energy was directed at the prostitutes rather than their customers. This is pretty typical. As with other illicit markets—think about drug dealing or black-market guns—most governments prefer to punish the people who are supplying the goods and services rather than the people who are consuming them.

But when you lock up a supplier, a scarcity is created that inevitably drives the price higher, and that entices more suppliers to enter the market. The U.S. "war on drugs" has been relatively ineffective precisely because it focuses on sellers and not buyers. While drug buyers obviously outnumber drug sellers, more than 90 percent of all prison time for drug convictions is served by dealers.

Why doesn't the public support punishing users? It may seem unfair to punish the little guy, the user, when he can't help himself from partaking in vice. The suppliers, meanwhile, are much easier to demonize.

But if a government really wanted to crack down on illicit goods and services, it would go after the people who demand them. If, for instance, men convicted of hiring a prostitute were sentenced to castration, the market would contract in a hurry.

In Chicago some one hundred years ago, the risk of punishment fell almost entirely on the prostitute. Besides the constant threat of arrest, there was also the deep social stigma of prostitution. Perhaps the greatest penalty was that a woman who worked as a prostitute would never be able to find a suitable husband. Combine these factors and you can see that a prostitute's wages *had* to be high to entice enough women to satisfy the strong demand.

The biggest money, of course, was taken home by the women at the top of the prostitution pyramid. By the time the Everleigh Club was shut down—the Chicago Vice Commission finally got its way—Ada and Minna Everleigh had accumulated, in today's currency, about $22 million.

The mansion that housed the Everleigh Club is long gone. So is the entire Levee district. The very street grid where the Everleigh stood was wiped away in the 1960s, replaced by a high-rise housing project.

But this is still the South Side of Chicago and prostitutes still work there—like LaSheena, in the black-and-red tracksuit—although you can be pretty sure they won't be quoting you any Greek poetry.

LaSheena is one of the many street prostitutes Sudhir Venkatesh has gotten to know lately. Venkatesh, a sociologist at Columbia University in New York, spent his grad-school years in Chicago and still returns there regularly for research.

When he first arrived, he was a naïve, sheltered, Grateful Dead–loving kid who'd grown up in laid-back California, eager to take the temperature of an intense town where race—particularly black and white—played out with great zeal. Being neither black nor white (he was born in India)

Some particulars of Sudhir Venkatesh's Grateful Dead obsession:

Album that got him hooked:
The Closing of Winterland, first heard in 1981, at age 15

First live show:
1984 (Irvine, Calif.)

Last live show:
1995 (Chicago)

Number of live shows seen:
100

Number of bootleg recordings made:
245

Cumulative days spent on the road:
"Three hundred and seventy-three point four, give or take."

Share of miles traveled by VW bus:
100 percent—"except when I flapped my arms and flew."

Average number of traveling companions:
3

Favorite song:
"Saint Stephen"

Songs heard most often:
"Jack Straw," "Estimated Prophet," "Looks Like Rain," "Morning Dew"

Book read most often on the road:
On the Road (5 times)

Number of future academic colleagues he met on the Dead circuit:
0

THIS COUPON ENTITLES BEARER TO
ONE (1) PHOTOCOPIED VERSION
OF
"WHY DO DRUG DEALERS
STILL LIVE WITH THEIR MOMS?"
BASED ON THE RESEARCH OF THE SOCIOLOGIST SUDHIR VENKATESH

You may think we are referring to Sudhir Venkatesh's earlier research on drug dealers simply to entice you to buy our first book. Just to prove that we're not (quite) that greedy, here's an offer: If you are willing to clip out this coupon and mail it with a self-addressed stamped envelope to **"Freakonomics," Parkwest Finance Station, P.O. Box 20197, NY NY 10025,** we will send you a free photocopied version of chapter 3 of *Freakonomics*, "Why Do Drug Dealers Still Live withTheir Moms?"

worked in Venkatesh's favor, letting him slip behind the battle lines of both academia (which was overwhelmingly white) and the South Side ghettos (which were overwhelmingly black). Before long, he had embedded himself with a street gang that practically ran the neighborhood and made most of its money by selling crack cocaine. (Yes, it was Venkatesh's research that figured prominently in the *Freakonomics* chapter about drug dealers, and yes, we are back now for a second helping.) Along the way, he became an authority on the neighborhood's underground economy, and when he was done with the drug dealers he moved on to the prostitutes.

But an interview or two with a woman like LaSheena can reveal only so much. Anyone who wants to really understand the prostitution market needs to accumulate some real data.

That's easier said than done. Because of the illicit nature of the activity, standard data sources (think of census forms or tax rolls) are no help. Even when prostitutes have been surveyed directly in previous studies, the interviews are often conducted long after the fact and by the kind of agency (a drug-rehab center, for instance, or a church shelter) that doesn't necessarily elicit impartial results.

Moreover, earlier research has shown that when people are surveyed about stigmatizing behavior, they either downplay or exaggerate their participation, depending on what's at stake or who is asking.

Consider the Mexican welfare program Oportunidades. To get aid, applicants have to itemize their personal possessions and household goods. Once an applicant is accepted, a caseworker visits his home and learns whether the applicant was telling the truth.

César Martinelli and Susan W. Parker, two economists who analyzed the data from more than 100,000 Oportunidades clients, found that applicants routinely underreported certain items, including cars, trucks, video recorders, satellite TVs, and washing machines. This shouldn't surprise anyone. People hoping to get welfare benefits have an incentive to make it sound like they are poorer than they truly are. But as Martinelli and Parker discovered, applicants *over*reported other items: indoor plumbing, running water, a gas stove, and a concrete floor. Why on earth would welfare applicants say they had these essentials when they didn't?

Martinelli and Parker attribute it to embarrassment. Even people who are poor enough to need welfare apparently don't want to admit to a welfare clerk that they have a dirt floor or live without a toilet.

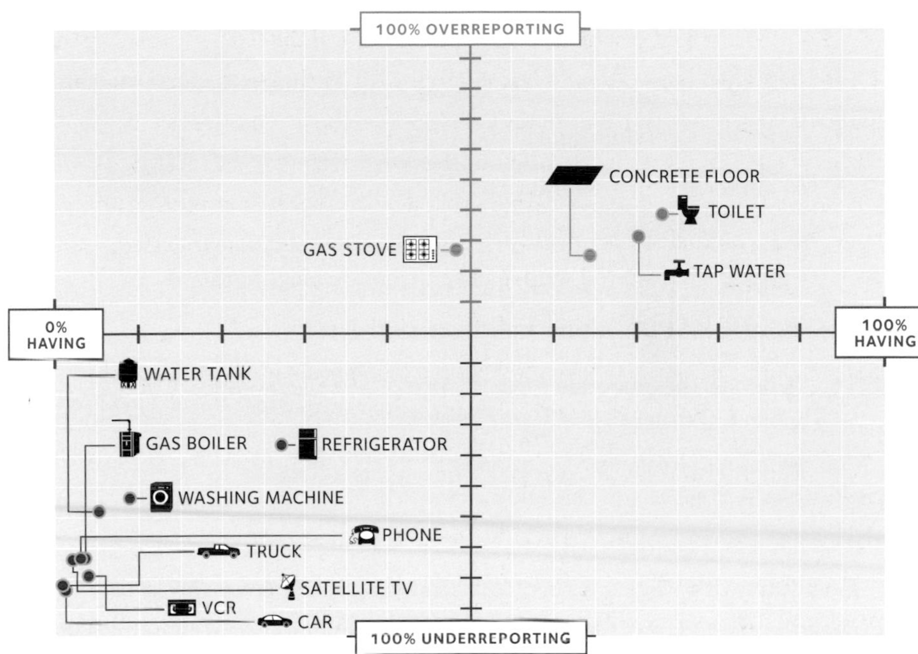

Balancing the stigma of too-little with the curse of too-much: here's a look at the amenities that Mexican welfare applicants reported having in their homes versus what they actually had.

Venkatesh, knowing that traditional survey methods don't necessarily produce reliable results for a sensitive topic like prostitution, tried something different: real-time, on-the-spot data collection. He hired trackers to stand on street corners or sit in brothels with the prostitutes, directly observing some facets of their transactions and gathering more intimate details from the prostitutes as soon as the customers were gone.

Sudhir Venkatesh, a sociologist who is most at home on a city street.

Most of the trackers were former prostitutes—an important credential because such women were more likely to get honest responses. Venkatesh also paid the prostitutes for participating in the study. If they were willing to have sex for money, he reasoned, surely they'd be willing to talk about having sex for money. And they were. Over the course of nearly two years, Venkatesh accumulated data on roughly 160 prostitutes in three separate South Side neighborhoods, logging more than 2,200 sexual transactions.

The tracking sheets recorded a considerable variety of data, including:

- The specific sexual act performed, and the duration of the trick
- Where the act took place (in a car, outdoors, or indoors)
- Amount received in cash
- Amount received in drugs
- The customer's race

- The customer's approximate age
- The customer's attractiveness (10 = sexy, 1 = disgusting)
- Whether a condom was used
- Whether the customer was new or returning
- If it could be determined, whether the customer was married; employed; affiliated with a gang; from the neighborhood
- Whether the prostitute stole from the customer
- Whether the customer gave the prostitute any trouble, violent or otherwise
- Whether the sex act was paid for, or was a "freebie"

So what can these data tell us?

Let's start with wages. It turns out that the typical street prostitute in Chicago works 13 hours a week, performing 10 sex acts during that period, and earns an hourly wage of approximately $27. So her weekly take-home pay is roughly $350. This includes an average of $20 that a prostitute steals from her customers and acknowledges that some prostitutes accept drugs in lieu of cash—usually crack cocaine or heroin, and usually at a discount. Of all the women in Venkatesh's study, 83 percent were drug addicts.

Like LaSheena, many of these women took on other, non-prostitution work, which Venkatesh also tracked. Prostitution paid about four times more than those jobs. But as high as that wage premium may be, it looks pretty meager when you consider the job's downsides. In a given year, a typical prostitute in Venkatesh's study experienced a dozen incidents of violence. At least 3 of the 160 prostitutes who participated died during the course of the study. "Most of the violence by johns is when, for some reason, they can't consummate or can't get erect," says Venkatesh. "Then he's shamed—'I'm too manly for you' or 'You're too ugly for me!' Then the john wants his money back, and you definitely don't want to negotiate with a man who just lost his masculinity."

Moreover, the women's wage premium pales in comparison to the one enjoyed by even the low-rent prostitutes from a hundred years ago. Compared with them, women like LaSheena are working for next to nothing.

Why has the prostitute's wage fallen so far?

Because demand has fallen dramatically. Not the demand for *sex*. That is still robust. But prostitution, like any industry, is vulnerable to competition.

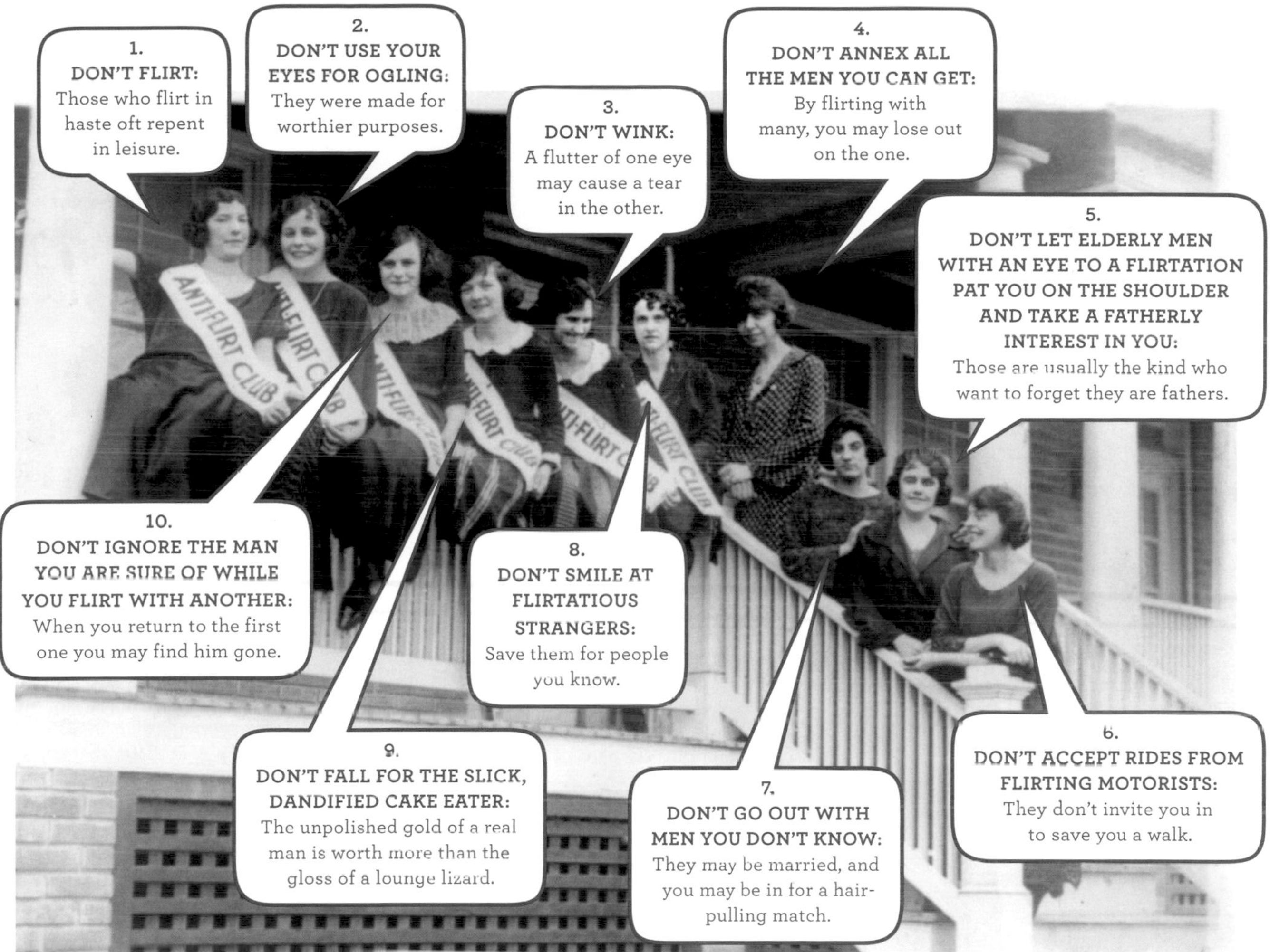

1. DON'T FLIRT: Those who flirt in haste oft repent in leisure.
2. DON'T USE YOUR EYES FOR OGLING: They were made for worthier purposes.
3. DON'T WINK: A flutter of one eye may cause a tear in the other.
4. DON'T ANNEX ALL THE MEN YOU CAN GET: By flirting with many, you may lose out on the one.
5. DON'T LET ELDERLY MEN WITH AN EYE TO A FLIRTATION PAT YOU ON THE SHOULDER AND TAKE A FATHERLY INTEREST IN YOU: Those are usually the kind who want to forget they are fathers.
6. DON'T ACCEPT RIDES FROM FLIRTING MOTORISTS: They don't invite you in to save you a walk.
7. DON'T GO OUT WITH MEN YOU DON'T KNOW: They may be married, and you may be in for a hair-pulling match.
8. DON'T SMILE AT FLIRTATIOUS STRANGERS: Save them for people you know.
9. DON'T FALL FOR THE SLICK, DANDIFIED CAKE EATER: The unpolished gold of a real man is worth more than the gloss of a lounge lizard.
10. DON'T IGNORE THE MAN YOU ARE SURE OF WHILE YOU FLIRT WITH ANOTHER: When you return to the first one you may find him gone.
ANTIFLIRT CLUB

In 1920, a group of young women in Washington, D.C., were so disturbed by the growing forthrightness of the male sex that they formed the Anti-Flirt Club and issued 10 "rules to live by."

Who poses the greatest competition to a prostitute? Simple: any woman who is willing to have sex with a man for free.

It is no secret that sexual mores have evolved substantially in recent decades. The phrase "casual sex" didn't exist a century ago (to say nothing of "friends with benefits"). Sex outside of marriage was much harder to come by and carried significantly higher penalties than it does today.

Imagine a young man, just out of college but not ready to settle down, who wants to have some sex. In decades past, prostitution was a likely option. Although illegal, it was never hard to find, and the risk of arrest was minuscule. While relatively expensive in the short term, it provided good long-term value because it didn't carry the potential costs of an unwanted pregnancy or a marriage commitment. At least 20 percent of American men born between 1933 and 1942 had their first sexual intercourse with a prostitute.

Now imagine that same young man twenty years later. The shift in

Economists are famous for trying to add a bit of humor to their famously dismal science. Some examples:

"Life Among the Econ," by Axel Leijonhufvud, *Western Economic Journal*, 1973.

"The Economics of Brushing Teeth," by Alan S. Blinder, *Journal of Political Economy*, 1974.

"Macroeconomic Policy and the Optimal Destruction of Vampires," by Dennis J. Snower, *Journal of Political Economy*, 1982.

"Chickens, Eggs, and Causality, or Which Came First?" by Walter N. Thurman and Mark E. Fisher, *American Journal of Agricultural Economics*, 1988.

"Cricket versus Baseball as an Engine of Growth," by Howard J. Wall, *Royal Economic Society Newsletter*, 1995.

"Japan's Phillips Curve Looks like Japan," by Gregor W. Smith, *Journal of Money, Credit and Banking*, 2008:

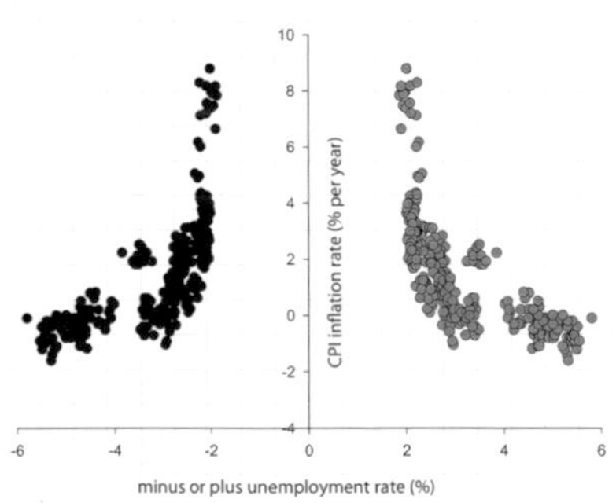

"On the Efficiency of AC/DC: Bon Scott versus Brian Johnson," by Robert J. Oxoby, *Economic Inquiry*, 2009.

"Clerihews in Merry Hues: An A-to-Z of the Lives and Times of Economists in Jolly Rhymes," by S. Subramanian, *Royal Economic Society Newsletter*, 2009.

"The Effect of Prayer on God's Attitude Toward Mankind," by James J. Heckman, *Economic Inquiry*, 2010.

sexual mores has given him a much greater supply of unpaid sex. In his generation, only 5 percent of men lose their virginity to a prostitute. And it's not that he and his friends are saving themselves for marriage. More than 70 percent of the men in his generation have sex before they marry, compared with just 33 percent in the earlier generation.

So premarital sex emerged as a viable substitute for prostitution. And as the demand for paid sex decreased, so too did the wage of the people who provide it.

If prostitution were a typical industry, it might have hired lobbyists to fight against the encroachment of premarital sex. They would have pushed to have premarital sex criminalized or, at the very least, heavily taxed. When the steelmakers and sugar producers of America began to feel the heat of competition—in the form of cheaper goods from Mexico, China, or Brazil—they got the federal government to impose tariffs that protected their homegrown products.

In 2008, the U.S. collected $25.7 billion in tariff revenues. Here are some of the most profitably tariffed goods:

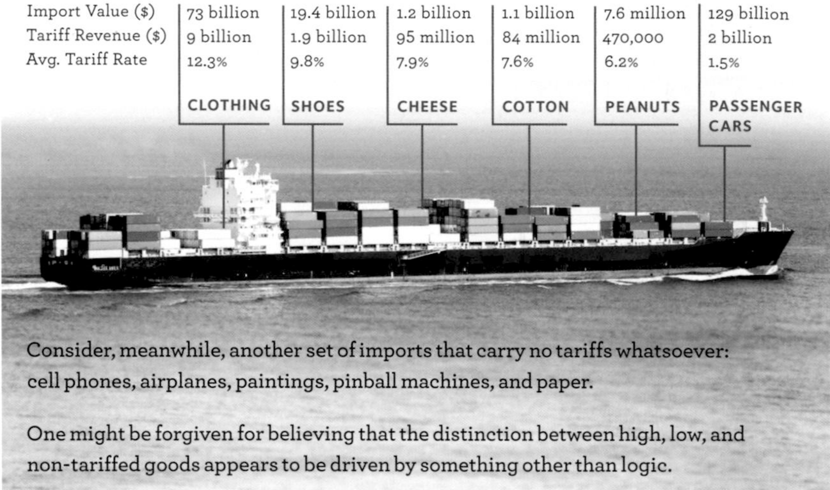

Import Value ($)
Tariff Revenue ($)
Avg. Tariff Rate
73 billion
9 billion
12.3%
CLOTHING
19.4 billion
1.9 billion
9.8%
SHOES
1.2 billion
95 million
7.9%
CHEESE
1.1 billion
84 million
7.6%
COTTON
7.6 million
470,000
6.2%
PEANUTS
129 billion
2 billion
1.5%
PASSENGER CARS

Consider, meanwhile, another set of imports that carry no tariffs whatsoever: cell phones, airplanes, paintings, pinball machines, and paper.

One might be forgiven for believing that the distinction between high, low, and non-tariffed goods appears to be driven by something other than logic.

Such protectionist tendencies are nothing new. More than 150 years ago, the French economist Frédéric Bastiat wrote "The Candlemakers' Petition," said to represent the interests of "the Manufacturers of Candles, Tapers, Lanterns, Candlesticks, Street Lamps, Snuffers, and Extinguishers" as well as "the Producers of Tallow, Oil, Resin, Alcohol, and Generally Everything Connected with Lighting."

These industries, Bastiat complained, "are suffering from the ruinous competition of a foreign rival who apparently works under conditions so far superior to our own for the production of light that he is flooding the domestic market with it at an incredibly low price."

Who was this dastardly foreign rival?

"None other than the sun," wrote Bastiat. He begged the French government to pass a law forbidding all citizens to allow sunlight to enter their homes. (Yes, his petition was a satire; in economists' circles, this is what passes for radical high jinks.)

Alas, the prostitution industry lacks a champion as passionate, even in jest, as Bastiat. And unlike the sugar and steel industries, it holds little sway in Washington's corridors of power—despite, it should be said, its many, many connections with men of high government office. This explains why the industry's fortunes have been so badly buffeted by the naked winds of the free market.

Prostitution is more geographically concentrated than other criminal activity: nearly half of all Chicago prostitution arrests occur in less than one-third of 1 percent of the city's blocks. What do these blocks have in common? They are near train stations and major roads (prostitutes need to be where customers can find them) and have a lot of poor residents—

PROSTITUTION

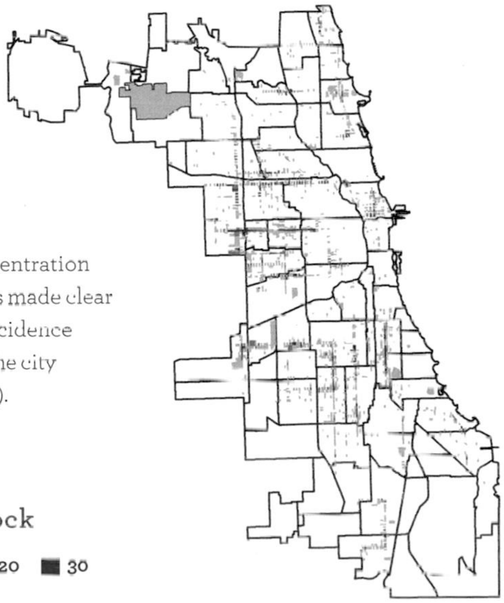

The intense geographic concentration of prostitution in **CHICAGO** is made clear when compared with the incidence of other street crimes in the city (see column at right).

Incidences by Block

0 | 1–5 | 5–10 | 10–20 | 30

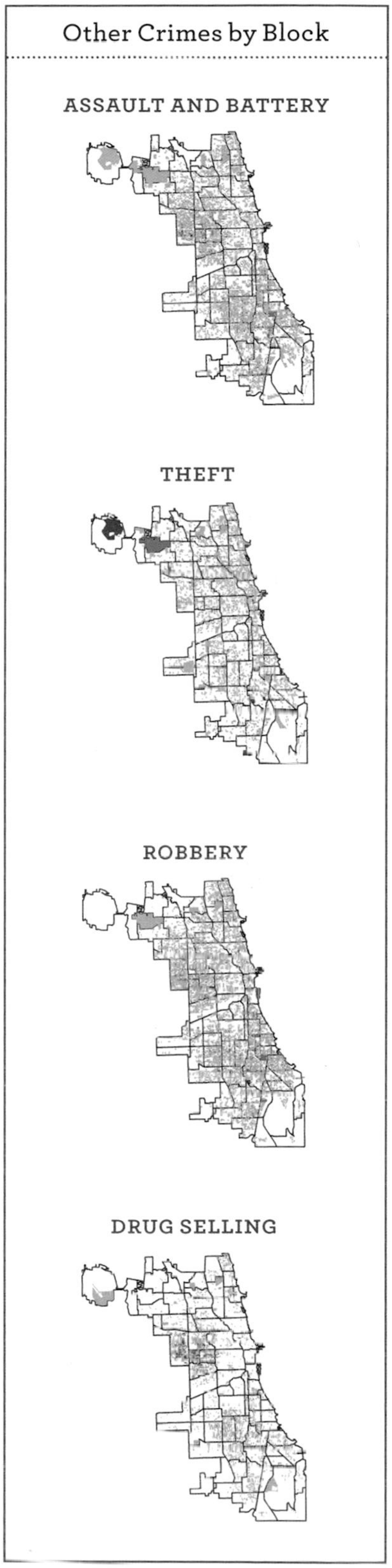

Other Crimes by Block

ASSAULT AND BATTERY

THEFT

ROBBERY

DRUG SELLING

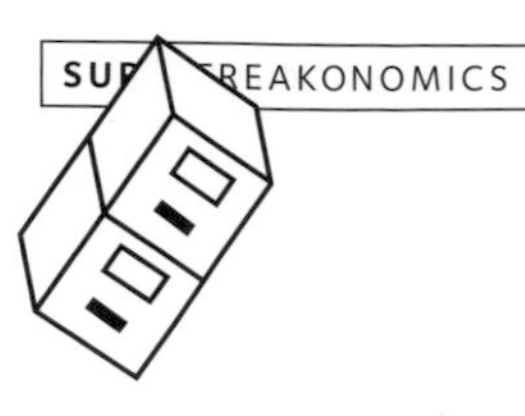

although not, as is common in most poor neighborhoods, an overabundance of female-headed households.

This concentration makes it possible to take Venkatesh's data and merge it with the Chicago Police Department's citywide arrest data to estimate the scope of street prostitution citywide. The conclusion: in any given week, about 4,400 women are working as street prostitutes in Chicago, turning a combined 1.6 million tricks a year for 175,000 different men. That's about the same number of prostitutes who worked in Chicago a hundred years ago. Considering that the city's population has grown by 30 percent since then, the per-capita count of street prostitutes has fallen significantly. One thing that hasn't changed: for the customer at least, prostitution is only barely illegal. The data show that a man who solicits a street prostitute is likely to be arrested about once for every 1,200 visits.

The prostitutes in Venkatesh's study worked in three separate areas of the city: West Pullman, Roseland, and Washington Park. Most of these neighborhoods' residents are African American, as are the prostitutes. West Pullman and Roseland, which adjoin each other, are working-class neighborhoods on the far South Side that used to be almost exclusively white (West Pullman was organized around the Pullman train factory). Washington Park has been a poor black neighborhood for decades. In all three areas, the race of the prostitutes' clientele is mixed.

Monday is easily the slowest night of the week for these prostitutes. Fridays are the busiest, but on Saturday night a prostitute will typically earn about 20 percent more than on Friday.

Why isn't the busiest night also the most profitable? Because the single greatest determinant of a prostitute's price is the specific trick she is hired to perform. And for whatever reason, Saturday customers purchase more expensive services. Consider the four different sexual acts these prostitutes routinely performed, each with its own price tag:

SEXUAL ACT	AVERAGE PRICE
MANUAL STIMULATION	$26.70
ORAL SEX	$37.26
VAGINAL SEX	$80.05
ANAL SEX	$94.13

A john stands just a 1-in-1,200 chance of arrest for visiting a Chicago prostitute. Consider the following events, each of which, according to the Book of Odds, has a similar chance of occurring in a given year:

A high-school marching band will be chosen to perform in the Macy's Thanksgiving Day Parade.

A man in New Hampshire will be diagnosed with chlamydia.

A baby girl will be named Tessa.

An accident involving a desk, shelf, cabinet, or rack will send someone to the emergency room.

A person's accidental death will be caused by falling on ice or snow; or by falling from a tree; or by falling off a cliff.

An Oregon resident 16 or older will be employed at a water or wastewater-treatment plant.

A man will die of lung cancer.

Note: Freebies not included		Whole Sample	Roseland No Pimp	Pullman Pimp	Wash. Park No Pimp
Avg price per trick		$49.45	$43.71	$67.91	$39.70
Percent of tricks:	Manual	14.51%	11.97%	6.31%	28.11%
	Oral	54.81%	57.25%	52.66%	52.49%
	Vaginal	17.24%	15.62%	26.08%	10.85%
	Anal	9.40%	10.38%	11.13%	5.69%
	Other	4.03%	4.77%	3.82%	2.85%
	No condom	79.37%	66.80%	85.32%	96.52%
	condom	20.63%	33.20%	14.68%	3.48%
	Black	56.07%	53.65%	37.21%	82.16%
	White	29.64%	30.62%	42.26%	13.47%
	Hispanic	14.29%	15.73%	20.54%	4.36%
	New customer	52.57%	49.85%	55.59%	54.78%
	Repeat	47.43%	50.15%	44.41%	45.22%
	Customer rated attractive (>5)	27.22%	29.26%	24.88%	25.71%
	Client under 25	25.24%	20.36%	23.79%	36.39%
	Client 25 to 40	31.49%	31.13%	38.97%	24.21%
	Client 41 to 60	18.20%	20.10%	23.94%	8.35%
	Client over 60	11.05%	14.67%	5.16%	10.18%
	Customer paid in drugs	6.04%	8.40%	2.19%	5.51%
Days of the week	Sunday	9.52%	7.10%	6.54%	17.34%
	Monday	8.29%	9.80%	9.80%	4.71%
	Tuesday	12.13%	15.57%	11.76%	5.72%
	Wednesday	16.08%	14.97%	13.07%	21.38%
	Thursday	15.49%	16.25%	17.32%	12.12%
	Friday	21.73%	21.73%	26.65%	17.68%
	Saturday	16.76%	15.06%	15.85%	21.04%

A data panel from "An Empirical Analysis of Street-Level Prostitution," by Levitt and Venkatesh, showing trick-level data.

It's interesting to note that the price of oral sex has plummeted over time relative to "regular" sexual intercourse. In the days of the Everleigh Club, men paid double or triple for oral sex; now it costs less than half the price of intercourse. Why?

True, oral sex imposes a lower cost on the prostitute because it eliminates the possibility of pregnancy and lessens the risk of sexually transmitted disease. (It also offers what one public-health scholar calls "ease of exit," whereby a prostitute can hurriedly escape the police or a threatening customer.) But oral sex *always* had those benefits. What accounted for the price difference in the old days?

The best answer is that oral sex carried a sort of taboo tax. At the time, it was considered a form of perversion, especially by religious-minded folks, since it satisfied the lust requirements of sex without fulfilling the reproductive requirements. The Everleigh Club was of course happy to profit from this taboo. Indeed, the club's physician avidly endorsed oral sex because it meant higher profits for the establishment and less wear and tear on the butterflies.

But as social attitudes changed, the price fell to reflect the new reality. This shift in preferences has not been confined to prostitution. Among U.S. teenagers, oral sex is on the rise while sexual intercourse and pregnancy

The word "taboo" is derived from Pacific languages—either *kapu* or *tapu,* or both; it was brought to the West in 1777 by Captain James Cook. In ancient Hawaii, people who broke religious taboos faced death unless they fled to Pu'uhonua, known as the City of Refuge, where they could seek forgiveness from a priest. In this photo, the sacred spot is guarded by totems of gods.

have fallen. Some might call it coincidence (or worse), but we call it economics at work.

The lower price for oral sex among prostitutes has been met by strong demand. Here is a breakdown of the market share of each sex act performed by the Chicago prostitutes:

SEXUAL ACT	SHARE OF ALL TRICKS
ORAL SEX	55%
VAGINAL SEX	17%
MANUAL STIMULATION	15%
ANAL SEX	9%
OTHER	4%

Included in the "other" category are nude dancing, "just talk" (an extremely rare event, observed only a handful of times over more than two thousand transactions), and a variety of acts that are the complete opposite of "just talk," so far out of bounds that they would tax the imagination of even the most creative reader. If nothing else, such acts suggest a prime reason that a prostitution market still thrives despite the availability of free sex: men hire prostitutes to do things a girlfriend or wife would never be willing to do. (It should also be said, however, that some of the most deviant acts in our sample actually *include* family members, with every conceivable combination of gender and generation.)

Prostitutes do not charge all customers the same price. Black customers, for instance, pay on average about $9 less per trick than white customers, while Hispanic customers are in the middle. Economists have a name for the practice of charging different prices for the same product: *price discrimination.*

In the business world, it isn't always possible to price-discriminate. At least two conditions must be met:

- Some customers must have clearly identifiable traits that place them in the willing-to-pay-more category. (As identifiable traits go, black or white skin is a pretty good one.)

- The seller must be able to prevent resale of the product, thereby destroying any arbitrage opportunities. (In the case of prostitution, resale is pretty much impossible.)

A legendarily vulgar vaudeville joke called "The Aristocrats" may lend some insight into just what happened in some of those "other" sex acts recorded in Sudhir Venkatesh's prostitution study.

The joke varies from comic to comic, but the setup is standard: a family of performers—a husband, wife, and two kids—walk into a talent agent's office and describe their stage act.

This is where each comic has free rein, but the idea is to describe a series of revoltingly transgressive sexual encounters between these self-same family members—as well as, often, a family pet. For instance:

"So the family gets into position together, and

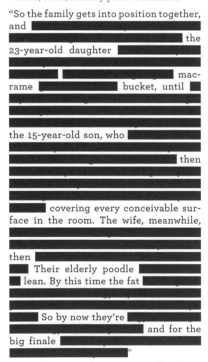

23-year-old daughter
mac-
rame bucket, until
the 15-year-old son, who
then
covering every conceivable surface in the room. The wife, meanwhile,
then
Their elderly poodle
lean. By this time the fat
So by now they're
and for the
big finale

At this point, the agent, utterly aghast, asks the family, "What the heck do you call an act like that?"

Their reply: "The Aristocrats!"

If these circumstances can be met, most firms will profit from price discriminating whenever they can. Business travelers know this all too well, because they routinely pay three times more for a last-minute airline ticket than the vacationer in the next seat. Women who pay for a salon haircut know it too, since they pay twice as much as men for what is pretty much the same haircut. Or consider the online health-care catalog Dr. Leonard's, which sold a Barber Magic hair trimmer for $12.99 and, elsewhere on its site, the Barber Magic Trim-a-Pet hair trimmer for $7.99. The two products appeared to be identical—but Dr. Leonard seemed to think that people will spend more to trim their own hair than their pet's.

How do the Chicago street prostitutes price-discriminate? As Venkatesh learned, they use different pricing strategies for white and black customers. When dealing with blacks, the prostitutes usually name the price outright to discourage any negotiation. (Venkatesh observed that black customers are more likely than whites to haggle—perhaps, he

Price discrimination can hardly be blamed for the entire gap, but American women between 35 and 44 spend more than twice as much per year as their male counterparts on keeping up appearances:

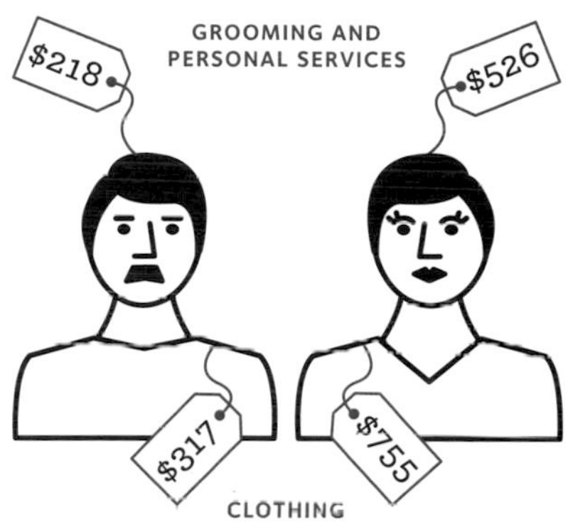

Price discrimination in action:

reasoned, because they're more familiar with the neighborhood and therefore know the market better.) When doing business with white customers, meanwhile, the prostitute makes the *man* name a price, hoping for a generous offer. As evidenced by the black-white price differential in the data, this strategy seems to work pretty well.

Other factors can knock down the price customers pay a Chicago prostitute. For instance:

AVERAGE DISCOUNT	
PROSTITUTE PAID IN DRUGS RATHER THAN CASH	$7.00
SEX ACT PERFORMED OUTDOORS	$6.50
CUSTOMER USES A CONDOM	$2.00

The drug discount isn't much of a shock considering that most of the prostitutes are drug addicts. The outdoors discount is partially a time discount because tricks performed outdoors tend to be faster. But also, prostitutes charge more for an indoor trick because they usually have to pay for

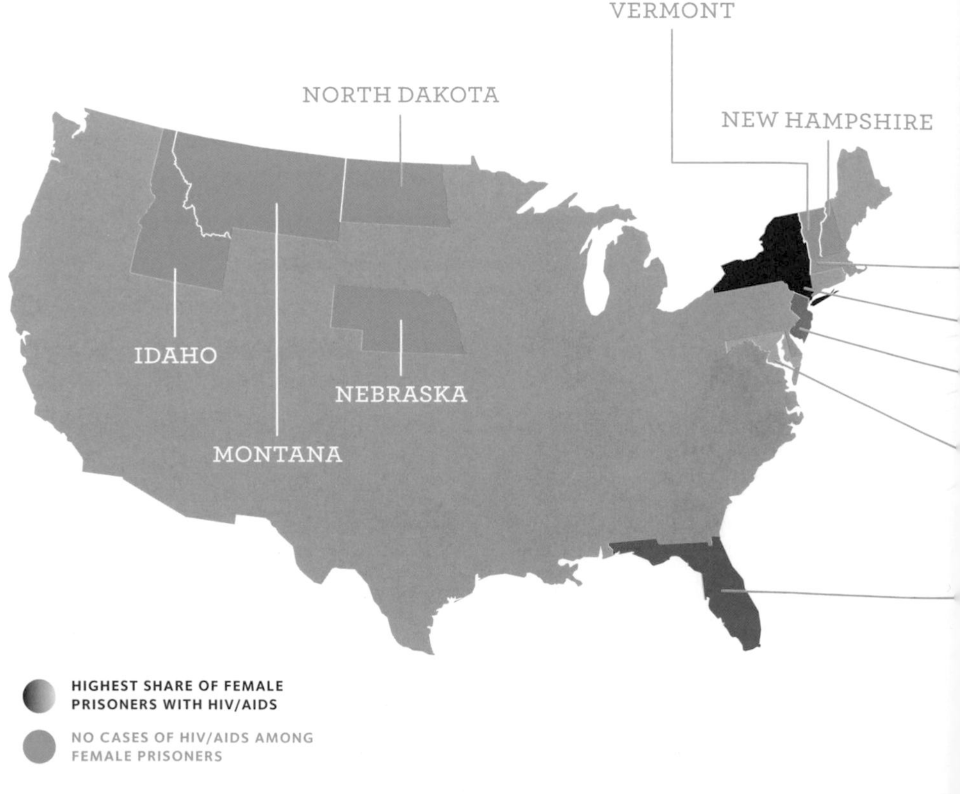

Even though street prostitutes have a relatively low rate of HIV infection, less than 3 percent, that's still roughly 15 times higher than the average rate for U.S. women overall. Another population with an outsize rate of HIV/AIDS: female prisoners, with an overall rate of 2.4 percent. But as these 2006 numbers reveal, there is a wide variance among states.

the indoor space. Some women rent a bedroom in someone's home or keep a mattress in the basement; others use a cheap motel or a dollar store that has closed for the night.

The small discount for condom use *is* surprising. Even more surprising is how seldom condoms are used: less than 25 percent of the time even when counting only vaginal and anal sex. (New customers were more likely to use condoms than repeat customers; black customers were less likely than others.) A typical Chicago street prostitute could expect to have about 300 instances of unprotected sex a year. The good news, according to earlier research, is that men who use street prostitutes have a surprisingly low rate of HIV infection, less than 3 percent. (The same is not true for male customers who hire male prostitutes; their rate is above 35 percent.)

So a lot of factors influence a prostitute's pricing: the act itself, certain customer characteristics, even the location.

But amazingly, prices at a given location are virtually the same from one prostitute to the next. You might think one woman would charge more than another who is less desirable. But that rarely happens. Why?

The only sensible explanation is that most customers view the women as what economists call *perfect substitutes,* or commodities that are easily interchanged. Just as a shopper in a grocery store may see one bunch of bananas as pretty much identical to the rest, the same principle seems to hold true for the men who frequent this market.

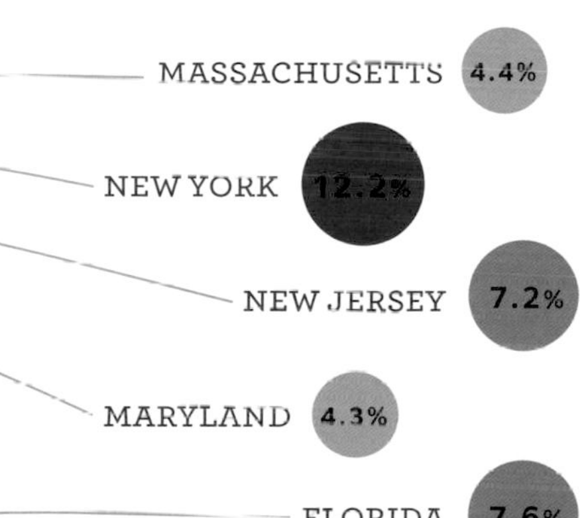

One surefire way for a customer to get a big discount is to hire the prostitute directly rather than dealing with a pimp. If he does, he'll get the same sex act for about $16 less.

This estimate is based on data from the prostitutes in Roseland and West Pullman. The two neighborhoods are located next to each other and are similar in most regards. But in West Pullman, the prostitutes used pimps, whereas those in Roseland did not. West Pullman is slightly more residential, which creates community pressure to keep prostitutes off the streets. Roseland, meanwhile, has more street-gang activity. Even though Chicago's gangs don't typically get involved in pimping, they don't want anyone else horning in on their black-market economy.

This key difference allows us to measure the impact of the pimp (henceforth known as the *pimpact*). But first, here's an important question: how can we be sure the two populations of prostitutes are in fact comparable? Perhaps the prostitutes who work with pimps have different characteristics than the others. Maybe they're savvier or less drug addicted. If that were the case, we'd merely be measuring two different populations of women rather than the pimpact.

But as it happened, many of the women in Venkatesh's study went back and forth between the two neighborhoods, sometimes working with a pimp and sometimes solo. This enabled us to analyze the data in such a way that isolates the pimpact.

As Venkatesh's study progressed, some prostitutes from Roseland who heard about the pimps in West Pullman lobbied Venkatesh for an introduction. There were ultimately more requests than he could accommodate. Venkatesh, showing the best social-science instincts, thought about randomizing the study by creating a lottery whereby some women would be selected to gain access to the pimps while others wouldn't. This would have made our "pimpact" analysis even stronger. Alas, the real world is messier than the laboratory: the women found their way to the West Pullman pimps on their own. So while the pimpact analysis is strong, it isn't the result of a truly randomized study.

As just noted, customers pay about $16 more if they go through a pimp. But the customers who use pimps also tend to buy more expensive services—no manual stimulation for these gents—which further bumps up the women's wages. So even after the pimps take their typical 25 percent commission, the prostitutes earn more money while turning fewer tricks:

PROSTITUTE	WEEKLY SALARY	AVERAGE TRICKS PER WEEK
WORKING SOLO	$ 325	7.8
WITH PIMP	$ 410	6.2

The secret to the pimps' success is that they go after a different clientele than the street prostitutes can get on their own. As Venkatesh learned, the pimps in West Pullman spent a lot of their time recruiting customers, mostly white ones, in downtown strip clubs and the riverboat casinos in nearby Indiana.

But as the data show, the pimpact goes well beyond producing higher wages. A prostitute who works with a pimp is less likely to be beaten up by a customer or forced into giving freebies to gang members.

So if you are a street prostitute in Chicago, using a pimp looks to be all upside. Even after paying the commission, you come out ahead on just about every front. If only every agent in every industry provided this kind of value.

Consider a different sales environment: residential real estate. Just as you can sell your body with or without the aid of a pimp, you can sell your house with or without a Realtor. While Realtors charge a much lower commission than the pimps—about 5 percent versus 25 percent—the Realtor's cut is usually in the tens of thousands of dollars for a single sale.

So do Realtors earn their pay?

Three economists recently analyzed home-sales data in Madison, Wisconsin, which has a thriving for-sale-by-owner market (or FSBO, pronounced "FIZZ-bo"). This revolves around the website FSBOMadison.com, which charges homeowners $150 to list a house, with no commission when the home is sold. By comparing FSBO sales in Madison with Realtor-sold homes in Madison along several dimensions—price, house and neighborhood characteristics, time on market, and so on—the economists were able to gauge the Realtor's impact (or, in the interest of symmetry, the *Rimpact*).

What did they find?

The homes sold on FSBOMadison.com typically fetched about the same price as the homes sold by Realtors. That doesn't make the Realtors look very good. Using a Realtor to sell a $400,000 house means paying a commission of about $20,000—versus just $150 to FSBOMadison.com. (Another recent study, meanwhile, found that flat-fee real-estate agents, who typically charge about $500 to list a house, also get about the same price as full-fee Realtors.)

But there are some important caveats. In exchange for the 5 percent commission, someone else does all the work for you. For some home sellers, that's well worth the price. It's also hard to say if the Madison results would hold true in other cities. Furthermore, the study took place during a strong housing market, which probably makes it easier to sell a home yourself. Also, the kind of people who choose to sell their houses without a Realtor may have a better business head to start with. Finally, even though the FSBO homes sold for the same average price as those sold by Realtors, they took twenty days longer to sell. But most people would probably consider it worth $20,000 to live in their old home for an extra twenty days.

A Realtor and a pimp perform the same primary service: marketing your product to potential customers. As this study shows, the Internet is proving to be a pretty powerful substitute for the Realtor. But if you're trying to sell street prostitution, the Internet isn't very good—not yet, at least—at matching sellers to buyers.

What do home sellers think will attract buyers—and what do prostitutes think will do the same? Here's a look at the 10 most common adjectives used by homeowners in a random selection of FSBOMadison.com listings and an equivalent list gleaned from Craigslist "adult services" ads for the Madison area. There is no overlap between the two lists, although it doesn't take much imagination to see how there might be.

SEXY REAL
BEAUTIFUL MATURE
BLONDE SHY
AVAILABLE BLUE SATISFIED
NICE

So once you consider the value you get for each of these two agents, it seems clear that a pimp's services are considerably more valuable than a Realtor's. Or, for those who prefer their conclusions rendered mathematically:

PIMPACT > RIMPACT

During Venkatesh's study, six pimps managed the prostitution in West Pullman, and he got to know each of them. They were all men. In the old days, prostitution rings in even the poorest Chicago neighborhoods were usually run by women. But men, attracted by the high wages, eventually took over—yet another example in the long history of men stepping in to outearn women.

Real-world pimps may work hard to not stand out in a crowd. The general public, meanwhile, has a different idea. A recent eBay search of "pimp hat" turned up nearly 200 items for sale, including these:

RED VELVET HOT PLAYA

GANGSTER

VELVET BIG POPPA

SLICK PLAYER

BLACK FUNKY FUZZY

FLAME

These six pimps ranged in age from their early thirties to their late forties and "were doing pretty well," Venkatesh says, making roughly $50,000 a year. Some also held legit jobs—car mechanic or store manager—and most owned their homes. None were drug addicts.

One of their most important roles was handling the police. Venkatesh learned that the pimps had a good working relationship with the police, particularly with one officer, named Charles. When he was new on the beat, Charles harassed and arrested the pimps. But this backfired. "When you arrest the pimps, there'll just be fighting to replace them," Venkatesh says, "and the violence is worse than the prostitution."

So instead, Charles extracted some compromises. The pimps agreed to stay away from the park when kids were playing there, and to keep the prostitution hidden. In return, the police would leave the pimps alone—and, importantly, they wouldn't arrest the prostitutes either. Over the course of Venkatesh's study, there was only one official arrest of a prostitute in an area controlled by pimps. Of all the advantages a prostitute gained by using a pimp, not getting arrested was one of the biggest.

But you don't necessarily need a pimp to stay out of jail. The average prostitute in Chicago will turn 450 tricks before she is arrested, and only 1 in 10 arrests leads to a prison sentence.

It's not that the police don't know where the prostitutes are. Nor have the police brass or mayor made a conscious decision to let prostitution thrive. Rather, this is a graphic example of what economists call *the principal-agent problem*. That's what happens when two parties in a given undertaking seem to have the same incentives but in fact may not.

In this case, you could think of the police chief as the principal. He would like to curtail street prostitution. The cop on the street, meanwhile, is the agent. He may also want to curtail prostitution, at least in theory, but he doesn't have a very strong incentive to actually make arrests. As some officers see it, the prostitutes offer something far more appealing than just another arrest tally: sex.

This shows up loud and clear in Venkatesh's study. Of all the tricks turned by the prostitutes he tracked, roughly 3 percent were freebies given to police officers.

The data don't lie: a Chicago street prostitute is more likely to have sex with a cop than to be arrested by one.

It would be hard to overemphasize how undesirable it is to be a street prostitute—the degradation, the risk of disease, the nearly constant threat of violence.

Nowhere were the conditions as bad as in Washington Park, the third neighborhood in Venkatesh's study, which lies about six miles north of Roseland and West Pullman. It is more economically depressed and less accessible to outsiders, especially whites. The prostitution is centered around four locations: two large apartment buildings, a five-block stretch of busy commercial street, and in the park itself, a 372-acre landmark designed in the 1870s by Frederick Law Olmsted and Calvert Vaux. The prostitutes in Washington Park work without pimps, and they earn the lowest wages of any prostitutes in Venkatesh's study.

This might lead you to think that such women would rather be doing anything else but turning tricks. But one feature of a market economy is that prices tend to find a level whereby even the worst conceivable job is worth doing. As bad off as these women are, they would seem to be worse off without prostitution.

Sound absurd?

The strongest evidence for this argument comes from an unlikely source: the long-loved American tradition known as the family reunion. Every summer around the Fourth of July holiday, Washington Park is thronged with families and other large groups who get together for cookouts and parties. For some of these visitors, catching up with Aunt Ida over lemonade isn't quite stimulating enough. It turns out that the demand

Prostitution is not the only crime to benefit from the principal-agent problem: the George Mason University economist Peter Leeson argues that it fueled sea piracy in the 1700s. Since sailors didn't have a personal stake in their cargo, they didn't have much incentive to safeguard a ship from pirates. Furthermore, pirates were sometimes known to treat captured sailors better than they'd been treated by their own captains—which gave sailors an extra incentive to surrender rather than fight as soon as they spotted the Jolly Roger on an approaching ship.

PETER LEESON

Among the pirate-happy economist's writings on the topic: a book called *The Invisible Hook: The Hidden Economics of Pirates* and a research paper called "An-*arrgh*-chy: The Law and Economics of Pirate Organization."

LIYA PALAGASHVILI

Prostitution increases during the Chicago summertime, as do other crimes. Here, according to Chicago Police Department data from 1999 to 2009, is the monthly incidence of **murder, sexual assault,** and **battery**:

CRIMES PER MONTH

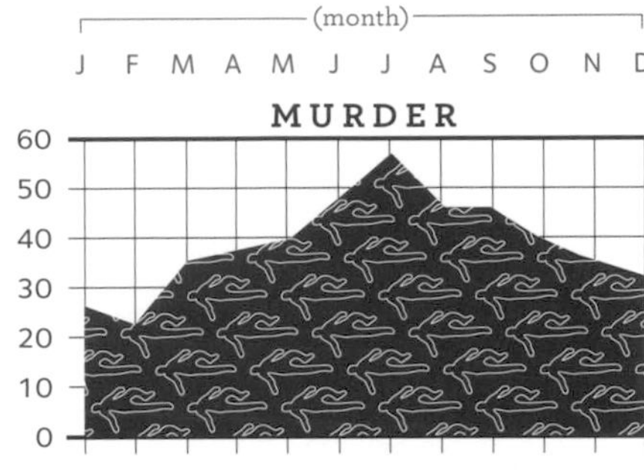

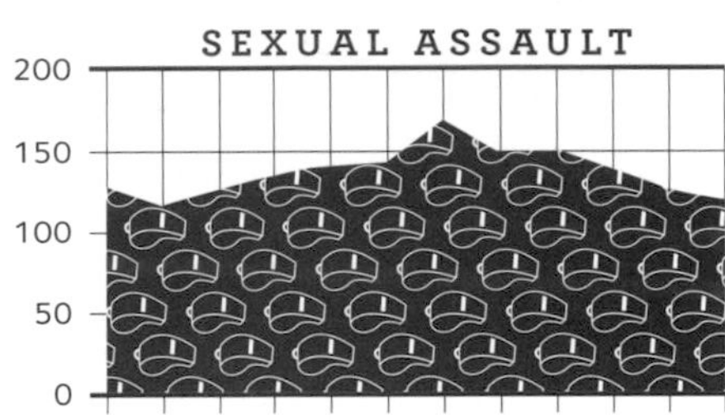

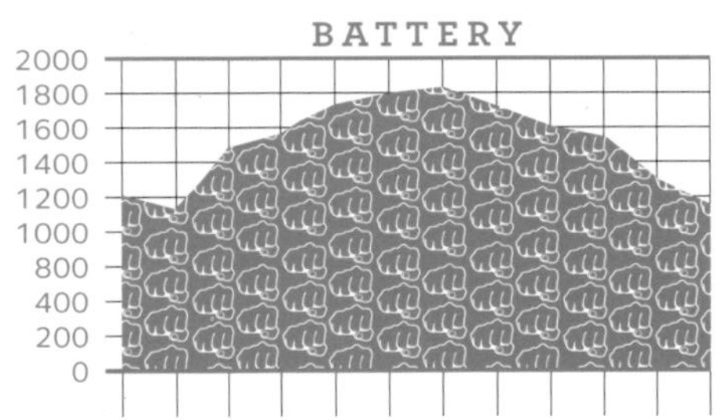

Car theft, on the other hand, is more of a year-round pursuit:

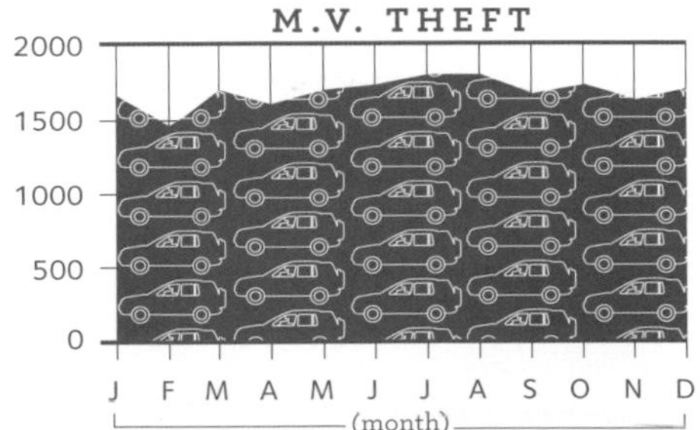

for prostitutes in Washington Park skyrockets every year during this period.

And the prostitutes do what any good entrepreneur would do: they raise prices by about 30 percent and work as much overtime as they can handle.

Most interestingly, this surge in demand attracts a special kind of worker—a woman who steers clear of prostitution all year long but, during this busy season, drops her other work and starts turning tricks. Most of these part-time prostitutes have children and take care of their households; they aren't drug addicts. But like prospectors at a gold rush or Realtors during a housing boom, they see the chance to cash in and jump at it.

As for the question posed in this chapter's title—*How is a street prostitute like a department-store Santa?*—the answer should be obvious: they both take advantage of short-term job opportunities brought about by holiday spikes in demand.

We've already established that demand for prostitutes is far lower today than it was sixty years ago (if offset a bit by holiday surges), in large part because of the feminist revolution.

If you found that surprising, consider an even more unlikely victim of the feminist revolution: schoolchildren.

Teaching has traditionally been dominated by women. A hundred years ago, it was one of the few jobs available to women that didn't involve cooking, cleaning, or other menial labor. (Nursing was another such profession, but teaching was far more prominent, with six teachers for every nurse.) At the time, nearly 6 percent of the female workforce were teachers, trailing only laborers (19 percent), servants (16 percent), and laundresses (6.5 percent). And by a large margin it was the job of choice among college graduates. As of 1940, an astonishing 55 percent of all college-educated female workers in their early thirties were employed as teachers.

Soon after, however, opportunities for smart women began to multiply. The Equal Pay Act of 1963 and the Civil Rights Act of 1964 were contributing factors, as was the societal shift in the perception of women's roles. As more girls went off to college, more women emerged ready to join the workforce, especially in the desirable professions that had been largely off-limits: law, medicine, business, finance, and so on. (One of the unsung

AORBS members gather in New York City in late 2009 to recommend swine flu vaccinations for all Santas. Back row, left to right: **John Hauck**, **Thomas Guilliams**, **Robert Miller**; front row, left to right: **Robert Flemming**, **Nicholas Trolli** (AORBS president), and **Jack Satter**.

ASSOCIATED PRESS

heroes of this revolution was the widespread use of baby formula, which allowed new mothers to get right back to work.)

These demanding, competitive professions offered high wages and attracted the best and brightest women available. No doubt many of these women would have become schoolteachers had they been born a generation earlier.

But they didn't. As a consequence, the schoolteacher corps began to experience a brain drain. In 1960, about 40 percent of female teachers scored in the top quintile of IQ and other aptitude tests, with only 8 percent in the bottom. Twenty years later, fewer than half as many were in

While most Santas are blatant opportunists, donning a fake beard in December to rake in a little holiday cash, there exists a Santa subset whose facial hair is real and who find regular, year round work. In 1994, they formed a guild to promote their interests, the Amalgamated Order of Real Bearded Santas (AORBS), which provided discounts on Santa gear and liability insurance. In 2007, rocked by a financial scandal, the group split into three factions: AORBS Inc., The Fraternal Order of Real Bearded Santas (FORBS), and the Red Suit Society.

One pushback against the teacher brain drain has been Teach for America (TFA), a program that since 1990 has sent more than 17,000 graduates of top colleges to teach in low-income schools. Some TFA facts worth knowing:

TFA teachers who return after their first year of teaching:
92%

Non-TFA teachers in the same districts who return after first year:
83%

TFA participants still in the classroom:
31%

All U.S. teachers who are TFA alums:
0.16%

New teachers in TFA-affiliated districts who are TFA teachers:
10–30%

TFA is extraordinarily popular at many top colleges. Consider the schools at which a particularly large share of the class of 2009 applied for TFA:

Spelman:* **25%**

Yale: **16%**

Princeton, Wellesley: **15%**

Brown,* University of Chicago, Haverford: **14%**

Bowdoin, Harvard: **13%**

Columbia, Cornell, Duke, Georgetown,* Swarthmore: **11%**

Amherst, Notre Dame, Tulane,* Vanderbilt, William & Mary: **10%**

TFA is, in general, heavily oversubscribed. In 2009, even though it accepted a record-high 5,277 new teachers, that represented only 15 percent of the applicants. Which means it is harder to get into TFA than it is to get into some of the Ivy League schools that produce so many TFA teachers. Cornell, for instance, has an acceptance rate of 19 percent.

*TFA is the top employer of students graduating from this institution.

the top quintile, with more than twice as many in the bottom. It hardly helped that teachers' wages were falling significantly in relation to those of other jobs. "The quality of teachers has been declining for decades," the chancellor of New York City's public schools declared in 2000, "and no one wants to talk about it."

This isn't to say that there aren't still a lot of great teachers. Of course there are. But overall teacher skill declined during these years, and with it the quality of classroom instruction. Between 1967 and 1980, U.S. test scores fell by about 1.25 grade-level equivalents. The education researcher John Bishop called this decline "historically unprecedented," arguing that it put a serious drag on national productivity that would continue well into the twenty-first century.

But at least things worked out well for the women who went into other professions, right?

Well, sort of. As we wrote earlier, even the best-educated women earn less than their male counterparts. This is especially true in the high-flying financial and corporate sectors—where, moreover, women are vastly underrepresented. The number of female CEOs has increased roughly eightfold in recent years, but women still hold less than 1.5 percent of all CEO positions. Among the top fifteen hundred companies in the United States, only about 2.5 percent of the highest-paying executive positions are held by women. This is especially surprising given that women have earned more than 30 percent of all the master's in business administration (MBA) degrees at the nation's top colleges over the past twenty-five years. Their share today is at its highest yet, 43 percent.

The economists Marianne Bertrand, Claudia Goldin, and Lawrence

JANE BURWELL

MAUREEN CAMPBELL

CHRISTINA HAYWARD

PAIGE PERSAK JAMES

BARBARA LANCASTER

PHOTOS COURTESY OF THE TEACHERS

Katz tried to solve this wage-gap puzzle by analyzing the career outcomes of more than 2,000 male and female MBAs from the University of Chicago.

Their conclusion: while gender discrimination may be a minor contributor to the male-female wage differential, it is desire—or the lack thereof—that accounts for most of the wage gap. The economists identified three main factors:

- Women have slightly lower GPAs than men and, perhaps more important, they take fewer finance courses. All else being equal, there is a strong correlation between a finance background and career earnings.
- Women work fewer hours than men. Ten years after completing their MBAs, women in the study were working 52 hours a week versus 58 hours a week for the men.
- Women take more career interruptions than men. After ten years in the workforce, only 10 percent of male MBAs went for six months or more without working, compared with 40 percent of female MBAs.

The big issue seems to be that many women, even those with MBAs, love kids. The average female MBA with no children works only 3 percent fewer hours than the average male MBA. But female MBAs *with* children work 24 percent less. "The pecuniary penalties from shorter hours and any job discontinuity among MBAs are enormous," the three economists write. "It appears that many MBA mothers, especially those with well-off spouses, decided to slow down within a few years following their first birth."

This is a strange twist. Many of the best and brightest women in the

MARYANN MAZZACARO

JOAN ROSEN

BETTY RUSSELL

KRISTIN SMITH

LINDA LAPORTE TORRES

Some of the excellent (female) teachers our own children have had over the years.

Could it be that the male appetite for money is just one facet of a heightened appetite for competition itself?

In a 2002 experiment, the economists Uri Gneezy and Aldo Rustichini had 140 fourth-grade boys and girls run a series of footraces on a school track in Ra'anana, Israel.

In the first race, each child ran alone. Then they ran in pairs: some boy-boy, some girl-girl, and some boy-girl.

The result?

Most of the boys ran faster when competing, and even faster when competing against girls. The girls, meanwhile, ran slower during competition, especially when racing other girls. As Gneezy and Rustichini concluded, this male-female dynamic is likely not limited to footraces: "Girls who are as talented as boys will end up performing worse just because they are not as competitive, and will not achieve as high scores in examinations as boys."

United States get an MBA so they can earn high wages, but they end up marrying the best and brightest men, who *also* earn high wages—which affords these women the luxury of not having to work so much.

Does this mean the women's investment of time and money in pursuing an MBA was poorly spent? Maybe not. Perhaps they never would have *met* such husbands if they hadn't gone to business school.

There's one more angle to consider when examining the male-female wage gap. Rather than interpreting women's lower wages as a failure, perhaps it should be seen as a sign that a higher wage simply isn't as meaningful an incentive for women as it is for men. Could it be that men have a weakness for money just as women have a weakness for children?

Consider a recent pair of experiments in which young men and women were recruited to take an SAT-style math test with twenty questions. In one version, every participant was paid a flat rate, $5 for showing up and another $15 for completing the test. In the second version, participants were paid the $5 show-up fee and another $2 for each correct answer.

How'd they do?

In the flat-rate version, the men performed only slightly better, getting 1 more correct answer out of 20 than the women. But in the cash-incentive version, the men blew away the women. The women's performance barely budged when compared with the flat-rate version, whereas the average man scored an extra 2 correct questions out of the 20.

Economists do the best they can by assembling data and using complex statistical techniques to tease out the reasons why women earn less than men. The fundamental difficulty, however, is that men and women differ in so many ways. What an economist would *really* like to do is perform an experiment, something like this: take a bunch of women and clone male versions of them; do the reverse for a bunch of men; now sit back and watch. By measuring the labor outcomes of each gender group against their own clones, you could likely gain some real insights.

Or, if cloning weren't an option, you could take a bunch of women, randomly select half of them, and magically switch their gender to male, leaving everything else about them the same, and do the opposite with a bunch of men.

Unfortunately, economists aren't allowed to conduct such experiments.

(Yet.) But individuals can if they want to. It's called a sex-change operation.

So what happens when a man decides to employ surgery and hormone therapy to live as a woman (a so-called MTF, or male-to-female transgender) or when a woman decides to live as a man (an FTM, or female-to-male)?

Ben Barres, a Stanford neurobiologist, was born Barbara Barres and became a man in 1997, at the age of forty-two. Neurobiology, like most math and science disciplines, is heavily populated by men. His decision "came as a surprise to my colleagues and students," he notes, but they "have all been terrific about it." Indeed, his intellectual stature seems to have increased. Once, after Barres gave a seminar, a fellow scientist turned to a friend of Barres's in the audience and issued this left-handed compliment: "Ben Barres's work is much better than his sister's." But Barres doesn't have a sister; the commenter was slighting Barres's former, female self.

"It is much harder for men to transition to women than for women to transition to men," Barres admits. The problem, he says, is that males are presumed to be competent in certain fields—especially areas like science and finance—while females are not.

On the other hand, consider Deirdre McCloskey, a prominent economist at the University of Illinois at Chicago. She was born a male, Donald, and decided to become a woman in 1995, at the age of fifty-three. Economics, like neuroscience, is a heavily male field. "I was prepared to move to Spokane and become a secretary in a grain elevator," she says. That proved unnecessary, but McCloskey did "detect a queerness penalty toward me in some of the economics profession. I reckon I'd make a little more money now if I were still Donald."

McCloskey and Barres are just two data points. A pair of researchers named Kristen Schilt and Matthew Wiswall wanted to systematically examine what happens to the salaries of people who switched gender as adults. It is not quite the experiment we proposed above—after all, the set of folks who switch gender aren't exactly a random sample, nor are they the typical woman or man before or after—but still, the results are intriguing. Schilt and Wiswall found that women who become men earn slightly more money after their gender transitions, while men who become women make, on average, nearly one-third less than their previous wage.

Their conclusion comes with a number of caveats. For starters, the sample set was very small: just fourteen MTFs and twenty-four FTMs.

Not all transgendered people are willing to share pre-switch pictures of themselves. The Stanford neurobiologist Ben Barres is a bit less shy. The photo on the left shows him as Barbara, in the late 1980s, at his sister's wedding. "I was a bridesmaid," he says, "and I recall vividly the agony of having to wear that dress. Not to mention high heels and makeup, something I hardly ever did unless it was really essential." The other photo was taken a few years ago in Barres's lab at Stanford and was staged by a university photographer. "Since I never actually personally do any of the experiments anymore, my colleagues always have a good laugh when they see me holding that empty pipette."

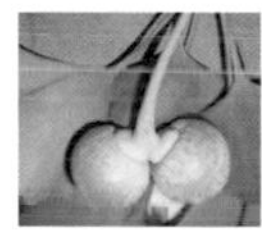

How is a transgendered person like a ginkgo tree? Their sex doesn't emerge until maturity. Few plant species come in male and female versions. But ginkgo trees do, a fact that has caused problems for urban planners. Ginkgos, which thrive on city streets, were planted all over Manhattan in the early 1900s. But the female tree—indistinguishable from the male until a tree is 20 to 30 years old—produces a small, cherrylike fleshy seed that gives off a strong odor. As the seed ripens and falls, it is squashed underfoot by thousands of New York pedestrians, generating a vomitlike stench that can carry for blocks.

TOP: BOTH COURTESY BEN BARRES; BOTTOM: COURTESY DENNIS STEVENSON, NEW YORK BOTANICAL GARDEN

Furthermore, the people they studied were mainly recruited at transgender conferences. That puts them in the category of what Deirdre McCloskey calls "professional gender crossers," who aren't necessarily representative.

"One could easily believe," she says, "that people who do not just become women and then get on with their lives, but keep looking back, are not going to be the most successful people in the workplace." (She may have changed gender, but once an economist, always an economist.)

Back in Chicago, in a chic neighborhood just a few miles from where the street prostitutes work, lives someone who was born female, stayed that way, and makes more money than she ever thought possible.

She grew up in a large and largely dysfunctional family in Texas and left home to join the military. She trained in electronics and worked in research and development on navigation systems. When she rejoined the civilian world seven years later, she took a job in computer programming with one of the world's largest corporations. She made a solid five-figure salary and married a man who earned well into six figures as a mortgage broker. Her life was a success, but it was also—well, it was boring.

She got divorced (the couple had no children) and moved back to Texas, in part to help care for a sick relative. Working once again as a computer programmer, she remarried but this marriage also failed.

Her career wasn't going much better. She was smart, capable, technically sophisticated, and she also happened to be physically attractive, a curvaceous and friendly blonde whose attributes were always well appreciated in her corporate setting. But she just didn't like working all that hard. So she became an entrepreneur, launching a one-woman business that enabled her to work just ten or fifteen hours a week and earn five times her old salary. Her name is Allie, and she is a prostitute.

She fell into the profession by accident, or at least on a lark. Her family was devout Southern Baptist, and Allie had grown up "very straitlaced," she says. As an adult, she was the same. "You know, yard-of-the-month in the suburbs, no more than two beers a night and *never* before seven." But as a young divorcée, she started visiting online dating sites—she liked men, and she liked sex—and just for fun listed "escort" on her profile. "I mean, it was so instantaneous," she recalls. "I just thought I'd put it up and see what happens."

Her computer was instantly flooded with replies. "I started hitting *minimize, minimize, minimize,* just so I could keep up!"

She arranged to meet a man at two o'clock on a weekday afternoon at a hotel, in the southwest corner of its parking lot. He'd be driving a black Mercedes. Allie had no idea what to charge. She was thinking about $50.

He was a dentist—physically unintimidating, married, and perfectly kind. Once inside the room, Allie undressed nervously. She can no longer recall the particulars of the sex ("it's all a big blur by this point," she says) but does remember that "it was nothing really kinky or anything."

When they were done, the man put some money on the dresser. "You've never done this before, have you?" he asked.

Allie tried to fib, but it was useless.

"Okay," he said, "this is what you need to do." He began to lecture her. She had to be more careful; she shouldn't be willing to meet a stranger in a parking lot; she needed to know something in advance about her clients.

"He was the perfect first date," Allie says. "To this day, I remain grateful."

Once he left the room, Allie counted the cash on the dresser: $200. "I'd been giving it away for years, and so the fact that someone was going to give me even a penny—well, that was shocking."

She was immediately tempted to take up prostitution full-time, but she was worried her family and friends would find out. So she eased into it, booking mainly out-of-town liaisons. She curtailed her programming hours but even so found the job stultifying. That's when she decided to move to Chicago.

Yes, it was a big city, which Allie found intimidating, but unlike New York or Los Angeles, it was civil enough to make a southern girl feel at home. She built a website (those computer skills came in handy) and, through intensive trial and error, determined which erotic-services sites would help her attract the right kind of client and which ones would waste her ad dollars. (The winners were Eros.com and BigDoggie.net.)

Running a one-woman operation held several advantages, the main one being that she didn't have to share her revenues with anyone. In the old days, Allie probably would have worked for someone like the Everleigh sisters, who paid their girls handsomely but took enough off the top to make themselves truly rich. The Internet let Allie be her own madam and accumulate the riches for herself. Much has been said of the Internet's awesome ability to "disintermediate"—to cut out the agent or middleman—in

This is what Allie's face looks like, sort of. The photos on the following pages show her body for real.

THE ALLIE TALLY

Years worked as an escort:
8

Total number of clients:
1,000+

Total number of hours spent with clients:
4,800+

Number of sets of lingerie purchased:
100+

Average cost per set:
$75

ALL ALLIE PHOTOS COURTESY ALLIE

Number of clients Allie knew for 5 years or more:
14

Average age of clients:
40

Busiest day of the week:
FRIDAY

Most common appointment time:
NOON

Average number of showers per day:
3

Average number of nights worked per week:
2

Average number of weekends worked per year:
1

Most common sex act requested:
ORAL

Average amount spent on advertising each month:
$500

industries like travel, real estate, insurance, and the sale of stocks and bonds. But it is hard to think of a market more naturally suited to disintermediation than high-end prostitution.

The downside was that Allie had no one but herself to screen potential clients and ensure they wouldn't beat her up or rip her off. She hit upon a solution that was as simple as it was smart. When a new client contacted her online, she wouldn't book an appointment until she had secured his real name and his work telephone number. Then she'd call him the morning of their date, ostensibly just to say how excited she was to meet him.

But the call also acknowledged that she could reach him at will and, if something were to go wrong, she could storm his office. "Nobody wants to see the 'crazy ho' routine," she says with a smile. To date, Allie has resorted to this tactic only once, after a client paid her in counterfeit cash. When Allie visited his office, he promptly located some real money.

She saw clients in her apartment, mainly during the day. Most of them were middle-aged white men, 80 percent of whom were married, and they found it easier to slip off during work hours than explain an evening absence. Allie loved having her evenings free to read, go to the movies, or just relax. She set her fee at $300 an hour—that's what most other women of her caliber seemed to be charging—with a few discount options: $500 for two hours or $2,400 for a twelve-hour sleepover. About 60 percent of her appointments were for a single hour.

Her bedroom—"my office," she calls it with a laugh—is dominated by a massive Victorian four-poster, its carved mahogany pillars draped with an off-white silk crepe. It is not the easiest bed to mount. When asked if any of her clients have difficulty doing so, she confesses that one portly gentleman actually broke the bed not long ago.

What did Allie do?

"I told him that the damn thing was already broken, and I was sorry I hadn't gotten it fixed."

She is the kind of person who sees something good in everyone—and this, she believes, has contributed to her entrepreneurial success. She genuinely likes the men who come to her, and the men therefore like Allie even beyond the fact that she will have sex with them. Often, they bring gifts: a $100 gift certificate from Amazon.com; a nice bottle of wine (she Googles the label afterward to determine the value); and, once, a new MacBook. The men sweet-talk her, and compliment her looks or the decor. They treat her, in many ways, as men are expected to treat their wives but often don't.

Most women of Allie's pay grade call themselves "escorts." When Allie discusses her friends in the business, she simply calls them "girls." But she isn't fussy. "I like *hooker,* I like *whore,* I like them all," she says. "Come on, I know what I do, so I'm not trying to butter it up." Allie mentions one friend whose fee is $500 an hour. "She thinks she's nothing like the girls on the street giving blow jobs for $100, and I'm like, 'Yes, honey, you're the same damn thing.'"

About this, Allie is likely wrong. Although she views herself as similar to a street prostitute, she has less in common with that kind of woman than she does with a trophy wife. Allie is essentially a trophy wife who is rented by the hour. She isn't really selling sex, or at least not sex alone. She sells men the opportunity to trade in their existing wives for a younger, more sexually adventurous version—without the trouble and long-term expense of actually having to go through with it. For an hour or two, she represents the ideal wife: beautiful, attentive, smart, laughing at your jokes and satisfying your lust. She is happy to see you every time you show up at her door. Your favorite music is already playing and your favorite beverage is on ice. She will never ask you to take out the trash.

Allie says she is "a little more liberal" than some prostitutes when it comes to satisfying a client's unusual request. There was, for instance, the fellow back in Texas who still flew her in regularly and asked her to incorporate some devices he kept in a briefcase in a session most people wouldn't even recognize as sex per se. But she categorically insists that her clients wear a condom.

What if a client offered her $1 million to have sex without a condom?

Allie pauses to consider this question. Then, exhibiting a keen understanding of what economists call *adverse selection,* she declares that she still wouldn't do it—because any client crazy enough to offer $1 million for a single round of unprotected sex must be so crazy that he should be avoided at all costs.

When she started out in Chicago, at $300 an hour, the demand was nearly overwhelming. She took on as many clients as she could physically accommodate, working roughly thirty hours a week. She kept that up for a while, but once she paid off her car and built up some cash reserves, she scaled back to fifteen hours a week.

Top concerns when meeting a new client:
SAFETY
HYGIENE
PUNCTUALITY

Number of clients who showed up for an appointment but whom Allie sent away:
7

Number of clients who showed up but decided not to go through with it:
4

As the story goes: An economist, away from home for a conference, visits the hotel bar and spots an attractive woman. "I'll give you $1 million to have sex with me tonight," he tells her.

The woman is flabbergasted. But she looks him over and, despite what she sees, accepts the offer. One million dollars is a lot of money! "I've changed my mind," the economist says. "Instead of $1 million, I'll pay you $100." The woman is incensed. "What do you think I am, a prostitute?" "Well, we've already established that," the economist replies. "Now we're just negotiating on price."

Number of paying customers with whom Allie never had sex:
6

Number of women who approached Allie:
4

Number of women with whom she followed through:
0

Number of couples who approached Allie:
3

Number of couples with whom she followed through:
3

Most common professions of clients:
LAWYER
REAL-ESTATE DEVELOPER
ENTREPRENEUR
COLLEGE PROFESSOR
DOCTOR

Most common topics of conversation with clients:
WEATHER
TRAVEL
WEEKEND PLANS
SPORTS
CURRENT EVENTS

Clients' favorite beverages, stocked by Allie:
SCOTCH
RED WINE
WHITE WINE
VODKA

Even so, she began to wonder if one hour of her time was more valuable to her than another $300. As it was, a fifteen-hour workload generated more than $200,000 a year in cash.

Eventually she raised her fee to $350 an hour. She expected demand to fall, but it didn't. So a few months later, she raised it to $400. Again, there was no discernible drop-off in demand. Allie was a bit peeved with herself. Plainly she had been charging too little the whole time. But at least she was able to strategically exploit her fee change by engaging in a little price discrimination. She grandfathered in her favorite clients at the old rate but told her less-favorite clients that an hour now cost $400—and if they balked, she had a handy excuse to cut them loose. There were always more where they came from.

It wasn't long before she raised her fee again, to $450 an hour, and a few months later to $500. In the space of a couple of years, Allie had increased her price by 67 percent, and yet she saw practically no decrease in demand.

Her price hikes revealed another surprise: the more she charged, the less actual sex she was having. At $300 an hour, she had a string of one-hour appointments with each man wanting to get in as much action as he could. But charging $500 an hour, she was often wined and dined—"a four-hour dinner date that ends with a twenty-minute sexual encounter," she says, "even though I was the same girl, dressed the same, and had the same conversations as when I charged $300."

She figured she may have just been profiting from a strong economy. This was during 2006 and 2007, which were go-go years for many of the bankers, lawyers, and real-estate developers she saw. But Allie had found that most people who bought her services were, in the language of economics, *price insensitive*. Demand for sex seemed relatively uncoupled from the broader economy.

Our best estimate is that there are fewer than one thousand prostitutes like Allie in Chicago, either working solo or for an escort service. Street prostitutes like LaSheena might have the worst job in America. But for elite prostitutes like Allie, the circumstances are completely different: high wages, flexible hours, and relatively little risk of violence or arrest. So the real puzzle isn't why someone like Allie becomes a prostitute, but rather why *more* women don't choose this career.

Certainly, prostitution isn't for every woman. You have to like sex enough, and be willing to make some sacrifices, like not having a husband (unless he is very understanding, or very greedy). Still, these negatives just might not seem that important when the wage is $500 an hour. Indeed, when Allie confided to one longtime friend that she had become a prostitute and described her new life, it was only a few weeks before the friend joined Allie in the business.

Allie has never had any trouble with the police, and doesn't expect to. The truth is that she would be distraught if prostitution were legalized, because her stratospherically high wage stems from the fact that the service she provides *cannot* be gotten legally.

Allie had mastered her domain. She was a shrewd entrepreneur who kept her overhead low, maintained quality control, learned to price-discriminate, and understood well the market forces of supply and demand. She also enjoyed her work.

But all that said, Allie began looking for an exit strategy. She was in her early thirties by now and, while still attractive, she understood that her commodity was perishable. She felt sorry for older prostitutes who, like aging athletes, didn't know when to quit. (One such athlete, a future Hall of Fame baseball player, had propositioned Allie while she was vacationing in South America, not knowing that she was a professional. Allie declined, uninterested in a busman's holiday.)

She had also grown tired of living a secret life. Her family and friends didn't know she was a prostitute, and the constant deception wore her out. The only people with whom she could be unguarded were other girls in the business, and they weren't her closest friends.

She had saved money but not enough to retire. So she began casting about for her next career. She got her real-estate license. The housing boom was in full swing, and it seemed pretty simple to transition out of her old job and into the new, since both allowed a flexible schedule. But too many other people had the same idea. The barrier to entry for real-estate agents is so low that every boom inevitably attracts a swarm of new agents—in the previous ten years, membership in the National Association of Realtors had risen 75 percent—which has the effect of depressing their median income. And Allie was aghast when she realized she'd have to give half of her commission to the agency that employed her. That was a steeper cut than any pimp would dare take!

Most common gift from clients:
FLOWERS

Allie's preferred gift:
CASH

Percentage of gifts Allie kept:
100

For dinner dates, most common meal:
FISH (Allie)
STEAK (clients)

Most profitable convention:
RADIOLOGICAL SOCIETY OF NORTH AMERICA

Most commonly booked hotel in Chicago:
PENINSULA

Cities most commonly visited for out-of-town work:
NEW YORK
WASHINGTON, D.C.
LOS ANGELES
BOSTON
DALLAS

Favorite vacation spot:
MEXICO

Number of people who knew both Allie's true identity and her escort identity:
6

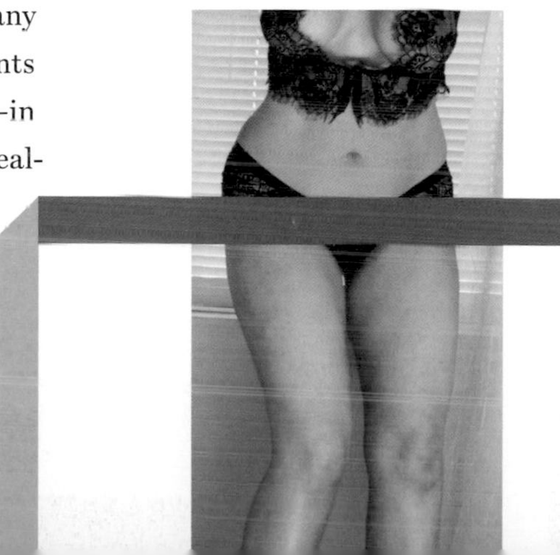

Number of other escorts with whom Allie sometimes conferred:
50+

Number of
"escort networking parties" Allie attended:
3

Total number of run-ins with a client's wife:
2
(Allie: "Ouch!")

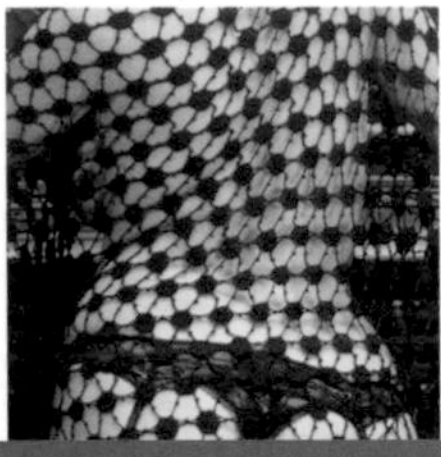

THE END

Finally Allie realized what she really wanted to do: go back to college. She would build on everything she'd learned by running her own business and, if all went well, apply this newfound knowledge to some profession that would pay an insanely high wage without relying on her own physical labor.

Her chosen field of study? Economics, of course.

12

(Friday)

EVENT TRACKING SHEET

Date: ________ Location: ________ Recorder: ________

Woman's Name	Time trick starts:	ends:	Trick/Event: (circle all that apply)	Used a condom	Amount paid in cash ($)	Amount paid in drugs	Where done	Race of customer	Approx. age of customer	Was customer new or repeat?	How attractive is the customer (10 = sexy, 1 = disgusting)	Was it a freebie?	Any trouble?	Did you steal from John?
1			Blow Job Vaginal Sex Anal Sex Other Sex act Arrest	yes no	60	20	Car Outside Inside	Black White Hispanic Other	under 25 25 - 40 41 - 60 over 60	new repeat	1 2 3 4 5 6 7 8 9 10	yes no If yes: who to:	yes no If yes: explain below	yes no if yes: cash ($): drugs:
Notes:														
2			Blow Job Vaginal Sex Anal Sex Other Sex act Arrest	yes no	75		Car Outside Inside	Black White Hispanic Other	under 25 25 - 40 41 - 60 over 60	new repeat	1 2 3 4 5 6 7 8 9 10	yes no If yes: who to:	yes no If yes: explain below	yes no if yes: cash ($): drugs:
Notes: 2 gang members; inside client's house														
3			Blow Job Vaginal Sex Anal Sex Other Sex act Arrest	yes no	—	—	Car Outside Inside	Black White Hispanic Other	under 25 25 - 40 41 - 60 over 60	new repeat	1 2 3 4 5 6 7 8 9 10	yes no If yes: who to:	yes no If yes: explain below	yes no if yes: cash ($): drugs:
Notes: * COP; agreed not to arrest her for B.S.O.B.														
4			Blow Job Vaginal Sex Anal Sex Other Sex act Arrest	yes no	100		Car Outside Inside	Black White Hispanic Other	under 25 25 - 40 41 - 60 over 60	new repeat	1 2 3 4 5 6 7 8 9 10	yes no If yes: who to:	yes no If yes: explain below	yes no If yes: cash ($): drugs:
Notes:														
5			Blow Job Vaginal Sex Anal Sex Other Sex act Arrest	yes no	100		Car Outside Inside	Black White Hispanic Other	under 25 25 - 40 41 - 60 over 60	new repeat	1 2 3 4 5 6 7 8 9 10	yes no If yes: who to:	yes no If yes: explain below	yes no if yes: cash ($): drugs:
Notes: father & son; inside client's house while mother watched														

Other relevant observations by recorder:

A SAMPLE TRACKING SHEET FROM VENKATESH'S PROSTITUTION STUDY.

CHAPTER 2

WHY SHOULD SUICIDE BOMBERS BUY LIFE INSURANCE?

IF YOU KNOW SOMEONE IN SOUTHEASTERN UGANDA WHO is having a baby next year, you should hope with all your heart that the baby isn't born in May. If so, it will be roughly 20 percent more likely to have visual, hearing, or learning disabilities as an adult.

Three years from now, however, May would be a fine month to have a baby. But the danger will have only shifted, not disappeared; April would now be the cruelest month.

What can possibly account for this bizarre pattern? Before you answer, consider this: the same pattern has been identified halfway across the world, in Michigan. In fact, a May birth in Michigan might carry an even greater risk than in Uganda.

The economists Douglas Almond and Bhashkar Mazumder have a simple answer for this strange and troubling phenomenon: Ramadan.

Some parts of Michigan have a substantial Muslim population, as does southeastern Uganda. Islam calls for a daytime fast from food and drink for the entire month of Ramadan. Most Muslim women participate even while pregnant; it's not a round-the-clock fast, after all. Still, as Almond and Mazumder found by analyzing years' worth of natality data, babies that were in utero during Ramadan are more likely to exhibit developmental aftereffects. The magnitude of these effects depends on

Muslims traditionally break the daylong Ramadan fast by first eating a date, followed by the *iftar*, or break-fast meal. Here, a boy readies the *iftar* at a mosque in Karachi, Pakistan, on the first day of Ramadan in 2008.

REUTERS

For those who wish to plan against the prenatal effect of Ramadan fasting, here are the dates for the beginning of the month in the coming 10 years:

AUGUST 1, 2011
JULY 20, 2012
JULY 9, 2013
JUNE 28, 2014
JUNE 18, 2015
JUNE 6, 2016
MAY 27, 2017
MAY 16, 2018
MAY 6, 2019
APRIL 24, 2020
APRIL 13, 2021

which month of gestation the baby is in when Ramadan falls. The effects are strongest when fasting coincides with the first month of pregnancy, but they can occur if the mother fasts at any time up to the eighth month.

Islam follows a lunar calendar, so the month of Ramadan begins eleven days earlier each year. In 2010, it ran from August 11 to September 9, which made May 2011 the unluckiest month in which to be born. Three years later, with Ramadan beginning on July 9, April would be the riskiest birth month. The risk is magnified when Ramadan falls during summertime because there are more daylight hours—and, therefore, longer periods without food and drink. That's why the birth effects can be stronger in Michigan, which has fifteen hours of daylight during summer, than in Uganda, which sits at the equator and therefore has roughly equal daylight hours year-round.

It is no exaggeration to say that a person's entire life can be greatly influenced by the fluke of his or her birth, whether the fluke is one of time, place, or circumstance. Even animals are susceptible to this natal roulette. Kentucky, the capital of Thoroughbred horse breeding, was hit by a mysterious disease in 2001 that left 500 foals stillborn and resulted in about 3,000 early fetal losses. In 2004, as this diminished cohort of three-year-olds came of age, two of the three Triple Crown races were won by Smarty Jones, a colt whose dam was impregnated in Kentucky but returned home to Pennsylvania before she could be afflicted.

Levitt's undergraduate thesis was called "Rational Bubbles in Thoroughbred Horse Breeding." From the abstract:

This paper broadens the scope of rational bubble research by focusing on a very specific asset: the thoroughbred horse. A model of thoroughbred pricing is developed which is shown to be consistent with rational bubbles. After demonstrating that the model of market fundamentals is unable to explain the path of observed prices, the paper looks for evidence of rational bubbles. The verdict on rational bubbles is uncertain. A specification test developed by West strongly supports the rational bubble hypothesis, but other approaches, such as examining ex-post returns, do not.

Levitt is hardly the only person with a dual interest in economics and racing. Consider some of the theme-named horses in recent years:

HORSE	YEAR OF BIRTH	LIFETIME EARNINGS
ASSET ALLOCATION	1994	$ 93,743
MARKET FORECAST	1997	$ 30,455
NASDEK MAYHEM	1999	$ 50,075
ECONOMIST AT LAST	2001	$ 147,740
GREENSPAN SPEAKS	2001	$ 3,835
RATIONALEXUBERANCE	2002	$ 41,058
LEVERAGE RISK	2004	$ 15,190
LEADING INDICATOR	2007	$ 12,465

Does it pay to give your horse an econ-theme name? Probably not. Nevertheless:
Average lifetime earnings for the econ-named horses in this sample: **$49,320**.
Average lifetime earnings for all horses: **$15,000**.

Such birth effects aren't as rare as you might think. Douglas Almond, examining U.S. Census data from 1960 to 1980, found one group of people whose terrible luck persisted over their whole lives. They had more physical ailments and lower lifetime income than people who'd been born just a few months earlier or a few months later. They stood out in the census record like a layer of volcanic ash stands out in the archaeological record, a thin stripe of ominous sediment nestled between two thick bands of normalcy.

What happened?

These people were in utero during the "Spanish flu" pandemic of 1918. It was a grisly plague, killing more than half a million Americans in just a few months—a casualty toll, as Almond notes, greater than all U.S. combat deaths during all the wars fought in the twentieth century.

More than *25 million* Americans, meanwhile, contracted the flu but survived. This included one of every three women of childbearing age. The infected women who were pregnant during the pandemic had babies who, like the Ramadan babies, ran the risk of carrying lifelong scars from being in their mothers' bellies at the wrong time.

Other birth effects, while not nearly as dire, can exert a significant pull on one's future. It is common practice, especially among economists, to co-write academic papers and list the authors alphabetically by last name. What does this mean for an economist who happened to be born Albert Zyzmor instead of, say, Albert Aab? Two (real) economists addressed this question and found that, all else being equal, Dr. Aab would be more likely to gain tenure at a top university, become a fellow in the Econometric Society (hooray!), and even win the Nobel Prize.

"Indeed," the two economists concluded, "one of us is currently contemplating dropping the first letter of her surname." The offending name: Yariv.

Or consider this: if you visit the locker room of a world-class soccer team early in the calendar year, you are more likely to interrupt a birthday celebration than if you arrive later in the year. A recent tally of the British national youth leagues, for instance, shows that fully half of the players were born between January and March, with the other half spread out over the nine remaining months. On a similar German team, 52 elite players were born between January and March, with just 4 players born between October and December.

The birthdate bulge is evident in the high-est levels of youth soccer all over western Europe. Take a look at the birth months of 763 players on the national youth teams of 10 European countries, in the under-15 to under-18 age brackets. Overall, 43 percent of the players were born in the first 3 months; only 9 percent were born in the final 3.

CLOCKWISE FROM JANUARY:

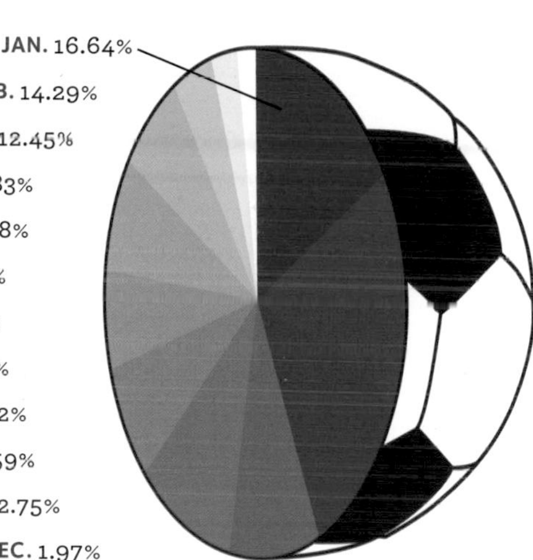

It's important to note that the relative-age effect fades considerably as players get older. Consider the birthdate data for European tournaments in the under-16 (U-16) and under-21 (U-21) brackets:

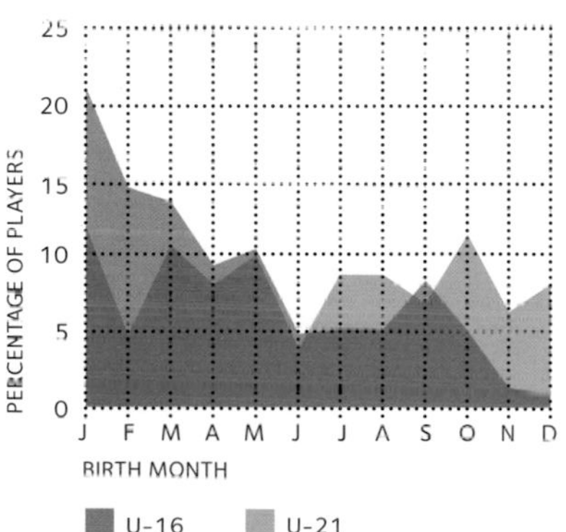

Care to guess which of these men is the "en-thusiastic, bearded, and burly Swede" K. Anders Ericsson? (You'll find the answer on page 66.)

Why such a severe birthdate bulge?

Most elite athletes begin playing their sports when they are quite young. Since youth sports are organized by age, the leagues naturally impose a cutoff birthdate. The youth soccer leagues in Europe, like many such leagues, use December 31 as the cutoff date.

Imagine now that you coach in a league for seven-year-old boys and are assessing two players. The first one (his name is Jan) was born on January 1, while the second one (his name is Tomas) was born 364 days later, on December 31. So even though they are both technically seven-year-olds, Jan is a year older than Tomas—which, at this tender age, confers substantial advantages. Jan is likely to be bigger, faster, and more mature than Tomas.

So while you may be seeing maturity rather than raw ability, it doesn't much matter if your goal is to pick the best players for your team. It probably isn't in a coach's interest to play the scrawny younger kid who, if he only had another year of development, might be a star.

And thus the cycle begins. Year after year, the bigger boys like Jan are selected, encouraged, and given feedback and playing time, while boys like Tomas eventually fall away. This "relative-age effect," as it has come to be known, is so strong in many sports that its advantages last all the way through to the professional ranks.

K. Anders Ericsson, an enthusiastic, bearded, and burly Swede, is the ringleader of a merry band of relative-age scholars scattered across the globe. He is now a professor of psychology at Florida State University, where he uses empirical research to learn what share of talent is "natural" and how the rest of it is acquired. His conclusion: the trait we commonly call "raw talent" is vastly overrated. "A lot of people believe there are some inherent limits they were born with," he says. "But there is surprisingly little hard evidence that anyone could attain any kind of exceptional performance without spending a lot of time perfecting it." Or, put another way, expert performers—whether in soccer or piano playing, surgery or computer programming—are nearly always made, not born.

And yes, just as your grandmother always told you, practice does make

A few years ago, we wrote a *New York Times* *Magazine* column called "A Star Is Made," about the birthdate bulge and Ericsson's talent research. We planned to expand upon it for a chapter in this book. Alas, we ended up discarding that chapter, half-written, for the field became suddenly crowded with other books (and very good ones!) that highlighted Ericsson's research. Among them: *Outliers*, by Malcolm Gladwell; *The Talent Code*, by Daniel Coyle, and *Talent Is Overrated* by Geoff Colvin. Interestingly, all three of these writers argued that

PHOTO CREDITS ON PAGE 66 SO YOU CAN'T CHEAT

perfect. But not just willy-nilly practice. Mastery arrives through what Ericsson calls "deliberate practice." This entails more than simply playing a C-minor scale a hundred times or hitting tennis serves until your shoulder pops out of its socket. Deliberate practice has three key components: setting specific goals; obtaining immediate feedback; and concentrating as much on technique as on outcome.

The people who become excellent at a given thing aren't necessarily the same ones who seemed to be "gifted" at a young age. This suggests that when it comes to choosing a life path, people should do what they love—yes, your nana told you this too—because if you don't love what you're doing, you are unlikely to work hard enough to get very good at it.

Once you start to look, birthdate bulges are everywhere. Consider the case of Major League Baseball players. Most youth leagues in the United States have a July 31 cutoff date. As it turns out, a U.S.-born boy is roughly 50 percent more likely to make the majors if he is born in August instead of July. Unless you are a big, big believer in astrology, it is hard to argue that someone is 50 percent better at hitting a big-league curveball simply because he is a Leo rather than a Cancer.

But as prevalent as birth effects are, it would be wrong to overemphasize their pull. Birth timing may push a marginal child over the edge, but other forces are far, far more powerful. If you want your child to play Major League Baseball, the most important thing you can do—infinitely more important than timing an August delivery date—is make sure the baby isn't born with two X chromosomes. Now that you've got a son instead of a daughter, you should know about a single factor that makes him *eight hundred times* more likely to play in the majors than a random boy.

What could possibly have such a mighty influence?

Having a father who also played Major League Baseball. So if your son doesn't make the majors, you have

Mozart, while commonly viewed as a pure example of the "raw talent" argument, was in fact a poster boy for the "deliberate practice" theory. From the books:

"Even Mozart—the greatest musical prodigy of all time—couldn't hit his stride until he had his ten thousand hours [of practice] in. Dr. Michael Howe of Exeter University estimates that Mozart, by his sixth birthday, had studied 3,500 hours of music with his instructor-father, a fact that places his musical memory in the realm of impressive but obtainable skill. *The New Yorker*'s music critic, Alex Ross, sums up much of the recent scholarship on the Miracle of Salzburg: 'Ambitious parents who are currently playing the "Baby Mozart" video for their toddlers may be disappointed to learn that Mozart became Mozart by working furiously hard.'"

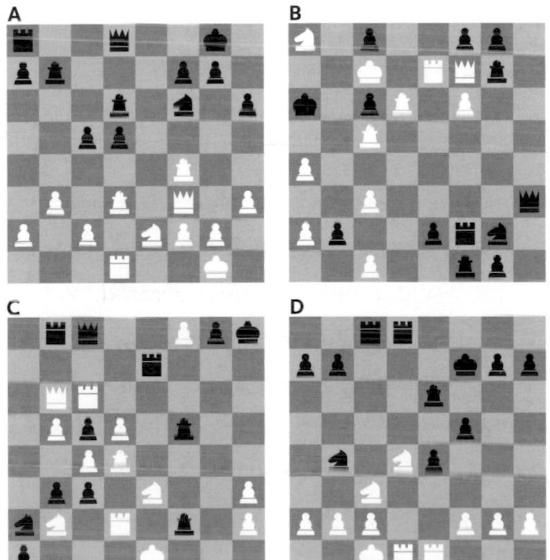

ANSWER KEY: REAL: A, D; RANDOM: B, C

In one talent experiment, expert and novice chess players were shown images of chess games in progress and asked to re-create from memory what they'd seen.

But there was a hitch: some boards represented real games, while others were gibberish, their pieces placed at random. With the real games, the expert players crushed the novices in re-creating the board. But the experts' advantage vanished on the gibberish boards, suggesting that their abilities were more the product of deliberate practice than raw talent.

Try it yourself with these boards, some real, some gibberish. The more chess you've played, the easier it should be to accurately re-create the real boards.

To date, Anders Ericsson has studied pianists, violinists, chess and Scrabble players, crossword solvers and spelling-bee contestants, soccer and dart players, rhythmic gymnasts, golfers, and memory champions.

Asked what kind of experiments he'd *really* like to do, Ericsson suggested the following:

- Choose at random a set of Olympic athletes and prevent them from practicing at all before the games. Allow another set to practice just half their usual amount. "It would even be interesting to have some athletes practice 150 percent of what they normally do," Ericsson says. "No coach and athlete would ever be willing to engage in such an experiment willingly."

- Randomly choose a set of elite athletes, make them switch sports, and see how quickly they can become as skilled as their new teammates. Ericsson wonders: "How rapidly could someone attain a high level of performance in chess if they started training at age 60?"

- Track in minute detail the lives of thousands of children from birth to age 20 or 25, using video, tests, and brain scans, and hope at least one of them grows up to be an elite performer. Then study their results. "It is very rare that someone starts acquiring skills after age 30," says Ericsson.

no one to blame but yourself: you should have practiced harder when you were a kid.

Some families produce baseball players. Others produce terrorists.

Conventional wisdom holds that the typical terrorist comes from a poor family and is himself poorly educated. This seems sensible. Children who are born into low-income, low-education families are far more likely than average to become criminals, so wouldn't the same be true for terrorists?

To find out, the economist Alan Krueger combed through a Hezbollah newsletter called *Al-Ahd* (*The Oath*) and compiled biographical details on 129 dead *shahids* (martyrs). He then compared them with men from the same age bracket in the general populace of Lebanon. The terrorists, he found, were *less* likely to come from a poor family (28 percent versus 33 percent) and *more* likely to have at least a high-school education (47 percent versus 38 percent).

A similar analysis of Palestinian suicide bombers by Claude Berrebi found that only 16 percent came from impoverished families, versus more than 30 percent of male Palestinians overall. More than 60 percent of the bombers, meanwhile, had gone beyond high school, versus 15 percent of the populace.

In general, Krueger found, "terrorists tend to be drawn from well-educated, middle-class or high-income families." Despite a few exceptions—the Irish Republican Army and perhaps the Tamil Tigers of Sri Lanka (there isn't enough evidence to say)—the trend holds true around the world, from Latin American terrorist groups to the al Qaeda members who carried out the September 11 attacks in the United States.

How can this be explained?

It may be that when you're hungry, you've got better things to worry about than blowing yourself up. It may be that terrorist leaders place a high value on competence, since a terrorist attack requires more orchestration than a typical crime.

When the sociologists Diego Gambetta and Steffen Hertog analyzed the educational background of 284 Islamic terrorists from the Arab world and Southeast Asia, they, too, found a hugely disproportionate share of them, 196, had attended college. One particular wrinkle caught their eye: engineering was far and away the most popular academic concentration:

ENGINEERING	78
ISLAMIC STUDIES	34
MEDICINE	14
BUSINESS/ECONOMICS	12
SCIENCES	7
EDUCATION	5
OTHER	28
UNKNOWN	18
TOTAL	196

Indeed, several recent notable terrorist attacks show this concentration of engineers:

ATTACK	NUMBER OF TERRORISTS	SHARE OF ENGINEERS AMONG THOSE WHOSE AREA OF STUDY IS KNOWN
WORLD TRADE CENTER BOMBING, 1993	12	41.7%
AFRICAN EMBASSY BOMBINGS, 1998	16	42.9%
SEPTEMBER 11 ATTACKS, 2001	25	57.1%
BALI NIGHTCLUB BOMBING, 2002	23	66.7%

Gambetta and Hertog weren't sure why engineers were so profoundly overrepresented, but think economics may have something to do with it. In countries where the professional prospects for engineers were unusually low, the share of engineer-terrorists was unusually high, and vice versa. It has also been noted that engineering skills can be particularly useful for carrying out terrorist acts—suggesting, perhaps, that some would-be terrorists pursue engineering for that very purpose.

Furthermore, as Krueger points out, crime is primarily driven by personal gain, whereas terrorism is fundamentally a political act. In his analysis, the kind of person most likely to become a terrorist is similar to the kind of person most likely to . . . vote. Think of terrorism as civic passion on steroids.

Anyone who has read some history will recognize that Krueger's terrorist profile sounds quite a bit like the typical revolutionary. Fidel Castro and Che Guevara, Ho Chi Minh, Mohandas Gandhi, Leon Trotsky and Vladimir Lenin, Simón Bolívar, and Maximilien Robespierre—you won't find a single lower-class, uneducated lad among them.

What mark has the well-educated middle class left on terrorism? The world's first ammonium-nitrate car bomb—the design is still in common use today—was detonated in 1970 by an anti–Vietnam War group that included University of Wisconsin students. The explosion severely damaged a campus building and killed a researcher who'd been conducting an experiment in low-temperature physics; his young son, by chance, became friends with Steve Levitt when both attended Harvard.

Investigators look over the remains of the exploded van. The same basic formula of ammonium nitrate and fuel oil was used in the truck bomb that destroyed the Alfred P. Murrah Federal Building in Oklahoma City in 1995.

Bombed-out cars and rubble outside Sterling Hall on the University of Wisconsin–Madison campus.

The trunk of the blue Chevy Caprice that was turned into a sniper's nest. In the frame just above the license plate is the hole from which the shots were fired. Below, the Bushmaster .223 rifle used in the shootings.

The Beltway snipers left behind tarot cards like this one at several of the shooting scenes.

But a revolutionary and a terrorist have different goals. Revolutionaries want to overthrow and replace a government. Terrorists want to—well, it isn't always clear. As one sociologist puts it, they might wish to remake the world in their own dystopian image; religious terrorists may want to cripple the secular institutions they despise. Krueger cites more than one hundred different scholarly definitions of terrorism. "At a conference in 2002," he writes, "foreign ministers from over 50 Islamic states agreed to condemn terrorism but could not agree on a definition of what it was that they had condemned."

What makes terrorism particularly maddening is that killing isn't even the main point. Rather, it is a means by which to scare the pants off the living and fracture their normal lives. Terrorism is therefore devilishly efficient, exerting far more leverage than an equal amount of nonterrorist violence.

In October 2002, the Washington, D.C., metropolitan area experienced fifty murders, a fairly typical number. But ten of these murders were different. Rather than the typical domestic disputes or gang killings, these were random and inexplicable shootings. Ordinary people minding their own business were shot while pumping gas or leaving the store or mowing the lawn. After the first few killings, panic set in. As they continued, the region was virtually paralyzed. Schools were closed, outdoor events canceled, and many people wouldn't leave their homes at all.

What kind of sophisticated and well-funded organization had wrought such terror?

Just two people, it turned out: a forty-one-year-old man and his teenage accomplice, firing a Bushmaster .223-caliber rifle from an old Chevy sedan, its roomy trunk converted into a sniper's nest. So simple, so cheap, and so effective: that is the leverage of terror. Imagine that the nineteen hijackers from September 11, rather than going to the trouble of hijacking airplanes and flying them into buildings, had instead spread themselves around the country, nineteen men with nineteen rifles in nineteen cars, each of them driving to a new spot every day and shooting random people at gas stations and schools and restaurants. Had the nineteen of them synchronized their actions, they would have effectively set off a nationwide time bomb every day. They would have been hard to catch, and even if one of them was caught, the other eighteen would carry on. The entire country would have been brought to its knees.

ASSOCIATED PRESS

Terrorism is effective because it imposes costs on everyone, not just its direct victims. The most substantial of these indirect costs is fear of a future attack, even though such fear is grossly misplaced. The probability that an average American will die in a given year from a terrorist attack is roughly 1 in 5 million; he is 575 times more likely to commit suicide.

Consider the less obvious costs, too, like the loss of time and liberty. Think about the last time you went through an airport security line and were forced to remove your shoes, shuffle through the metal detector in stocking feet, and then hobble about while gathering up your belongings.

The beauty of terrorism—if you're a terrorist—is that you can succeed even by failing. We perform this shoe routine thanks to a bumbling British national named Richard Reid, who, even though he couldn't ignite his shoe bomb, exacted a huge price. Let's say it takes an average of one minute to remove and replace your shoes in the airport security line. In the United States alone, this procedure happens roughly 560 million times per year. Five hundred and sixty million minutes equals more than 1,065 years—which, divided by 77.8 years (the average U.S. life expectancy at birth), yields a total of nearly 14 person-lives. So even though Richard Reid failed to kill a single person, he levied a tax that is the time equivalent of 14 lives per year.

The direct costs of the September 11 attacks were massive—nearly three thousand lives and economic losses as high as $300 billion—as were the costs of the wars in Afghanistan and Iraq that the United States launched in response. But consider the collateral costs as well. In just the three months following the attacks, there were one thousand extra traffic deaths in the United States. Why?

One contributing factor is that people stopped flying and drove instead. Per mile, driving is much more dangerous than flying. Interestingly, however, the data show that most of these extra traffic deaths occurred not on interstates but on local roads, and they were concentrated in the Northeast, close to the terrorist attacks. Furthermore, these fatalities were more likely than usual to involve drunken and reckless driving. These facts, along with myriad psychological studies of terrorism's aftereffects, suggest that the September 11 attacks led to a spike in alcohol abuse and post-traumatic stress that translated into, among other things, extra driving deaths.

HOW INFLATED IS OUR FEAR OF TERRORISM? CONSIDER THE FOLLOWING MORTALITY ODDS FOR THE AVERAGE AMERICAN (OVER A LIFETIME):

HEART DISEASE
1 IN 4

CANCER (ALL FORMS)
1 IN 7

PNEUMONIA
1 IN 57

MOTOR VEHICLE ACCIDENT
1 IN 88

SUICIDE
1 IN 120

CRIMINAL HOMICIDE
1 IN 240

ON-THE-JOB ACCIDENT
1 IN 620

ACCIDENTAL ELECTROCUTION
1 IN 4,000

LIGHTNING STRIKE
1 IN 39,000

COMMERCIAL AIRCRAFT ACCIDENT
1 IN 40,000

TERRORISM
1 IN 69,000

1,000X

PLAGUE
1 IN 240,000

ANTHRAX
1 IN 730,000

PASSENGER TRAIN ACCIDENT
1 IN 920,000

SHARK ATTACK
1 IN 3,700,000

The likelihood of airline terrorism is even smaller. Between 1999 and 2009, six U.S or U.S.-bound aircraft were attacked by terrorists. The statistician Nate Silver looked at Bureau of Transportation Statistics data for that period and found there were a total of 99,320,309 flights within the U.S., including international flights that either originated or terminated here. On average, a terrorist struck one of these flights for every:

16,553,385 DEPARTURES
27,221,877 HOURS AIRBORNE
11,569,297,667 MILES FLOWN

Such trickle-down effects are nearly endless. Thousands of foreign-born university students and professors were kept out of the United States because of new visa restrictions after the September 11 attacks. At least 140 U.S. corporations exploited the ensuing stock-market decline by illegally back-dating stock options. In New York City, so many police resources were shifted to terrorism that other areas—the Cold Case Squad, for one, as well as anti-Mafia units—were neglected. A similar pattern was repeated on the national level. Money and manpower that otherwise would have been spent chasing financial scoundrels were instead diverted to chasing terrorists—perhaps contributing to, or at least exacerbating, the recent financial meltdown.

Not all of the September 11 aftereffects were harmful. Thanks to decreased airline traffic, influenza—which travels well on planes—was slower to spread and less dangerous. In Washington, D.C., crime fell whenever the federal terror-alert level went up (thanks to extra police flooding the city). And an increase in border security was a boon to some California farmers—who, as Mexican and Canadian imports declined, grew and sold so much marijuana that it became one of the state's most valuable crops.

When one of the four airplanes hijacked on September 11 crashed into the Pentagon, all of the seriously injured victims, most of whom suffered burns, were taken to Washington Hospital Center, the largest hospital in the city. There were only a handful of patients—corpses were more plentiful—but even so, the burn unit was nearly overwhelmed. Like most hospitals, WHC routinely operated at about 95 percent of capacity, so even a small surge of patients stressed the system. Worse yet, the hospital's phone lines went down, as did local cell service, so anyone needing to make a call had to jump in a car and drive a few miles away.

All things considered, WHC performed well. But for Craig Feied (pronounced *FEE-ed*), an emergency-medicine specialist there, the incident confirmed his greatest fears. If the hospital nearly went haywire with just a few extra burn patients, what would happen during a major disaster?

Even before September 11, Feied had spent thousands of hours thinking such grim thoughts. He was the chief architect of a federally funded pilot program called ER One, which was meant to drag the emergency room into the modern era.

In this concept sketch for ER One, the "emergency room of the future," the entrance is configured like an airport terminal so as to take in a lot of patients quickly in the event of a wide-scale emergency. ER One was designed for Washington, D.C. "One of the more convincing arguments for funding," notes Craig Feied, "was that members of Congress might find themselves personally in need of ER One in the event of a disaster in the nation's capital."

COURTESY CRAIG FEIED

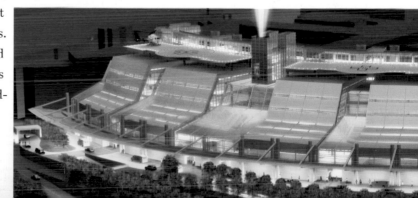

Until the 1960s, hospitals simply weren't designed to treat emergencies. "If you brought someone to a hospital at night," Feied says, "the doors would be locked. You'd ring the bell, a nurse would come down to see what you wanted. She might let you in, then she'd call the doctor at home, and he might or might not come in." Ambulances were often run by the local mortuary. It is hard to think of a better example of misaligned incentives: a funeral director who is put in charge of helping a patient not die!

Today, emergency medicine ranks as the seventh-largest physician specialty (out of thirty-eight), with a fivefold increase in practitioners since 1980. It is a master-of-all-trades endeavor, performed at lightning speed, and the emergency room has become the linchpin of public health. In a given year, there are roughly 115 million ER visits in the United States. Excluding pregnancies, 56 percent of all people admitted to U.S. hospitals come through the ER, up from 46 percent in 1993. And yet, Feied says, "you could drive a truck through the gaps in our protocols."

September 11 brought home the point that emergency rooms are painfully limited in their surge capacity. If there had been a thousand victims at WHC, would they even have gotten inside?

Such a prospect makes Feied grimace. Most ERs have an ambulance bay that can fit only a few vehicles at a time. The docks are also built too high—"because the people who designed them were used to building loading docks," Feied says. Rooftop helipads are similarly problematic because of the time and space constraints of a single elevator. Feied's idea for getting rid of such bottlenecks is to design an ER more like an airport, with a large convex intake area that could accommodate a multitude of ambulances, buses, or even helicopters.

Washington Hospital Center's ambulance bay could accommodate only four ambulances at once, and they had to be parked and unloaded backwards:

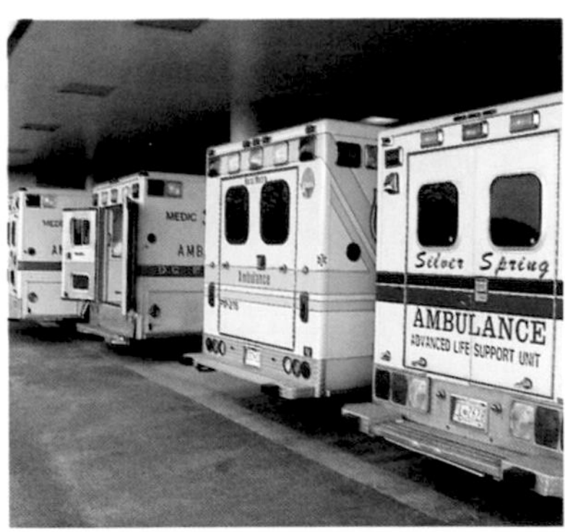

But these intake issues aren't what worry Feied the most. A hospital that gets hit with something serious and communicable—SARS or anthrax or Ebola or a new strain of lethal influenza—would soon cripple itself. Like most buildings, hospitals recirculate their air, which means that one sick patient could infect hundreds. "You don't want to go to the hospital for a broken ankle and get SARS," Feied says.

Craig Feied's dream of a more perfect ambulance bay, built to resemble an airport:

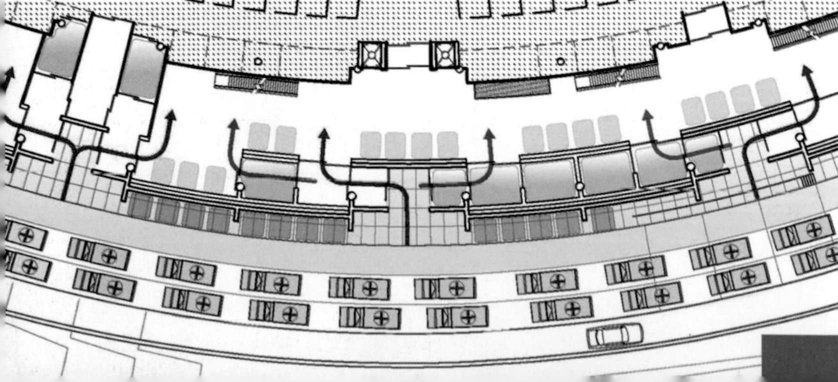

COURTESY CRAIG FEIED

The answer is to build hospitals, and especially ERs, with rooms designed for isolation and zero air recirculation. But most hospitals, Feied notes, don't want to spend money on such unsexy, non-revenue-generating features. "There were some nice emergency departments built in 2001, state-of-the-art, and they're completely obsolete today. They were built with open bays, divided by curtains, but if you have a SARS patient in Bed 4, there's not a patient or doctor in the world who will want to go into Bed 5."

And don't even get Feied started on all the hospital patients who die from a cause *other* than what brought them to the hospital: wrong diagnoses (the result of carelessness, hubris, or cognitive bias); medication errors (based, far too often, on sloppy handwriting); technical complications (reading an X-ray backward, for instance); and bacterial infections (the deadliest and most pervasive problem).

"The state of current medical practice is *so* bad right now that there's not very much worth protecting about the old ways of doing things," Feied says. "Nobody in medicine wants to admit this but it's the truth."

In 1995, a Texas cardiologist named Ramachandra Kolluru prescribed Isordil, an angina medication, for his patient Ramon Vasquez. But the pharmacist misread Kolluru's handwritten "Isordil" as "Plendil," a drug for high blood pressure. Vasquez took that drug at what turned out to be eight times the recommended dose, and soon suffered a fatal heart attack. A jury found the doctor and the pharmacist equally negligent, ordering them each to pay $225,000 in damages to Vasquez's family.

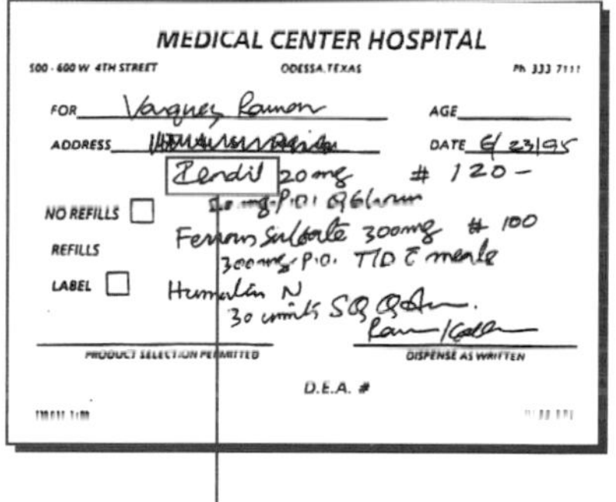
MEDICAL CENTER HOSPITAL

ODESSA, TEXAS

FOR Vasquez Ramon AGE

ADDRESS DATE 6/23/95

NO REFILLS

REFILLS

LABEL

PRODUCT SELECTION PERMITTED

DISPENSE AS WRITTEN

D.E.A. #

Plendil

Feied grew up in Berkeley, California, during the very raucous 1960s, and he fit right in. He skateboarded everywhere; he occasionally jammed on drums with a local band called the Grateful Dead. He had an aptitude for mechanics, taking apart and reassembling whatever looked interesting, and he was enterprising: by eighteen, he had founded a small technology company. He studied biophysics and mathematics before going into medicine. He became a doctor, he says, because of "the lure of secret knowledge," a desire to understand the human body as well as he understood machines.

Still, you sense that machines remain his first love. He is a fervent early adopter—he put a fax machine in the ER and started riding a Segway when both were novelties—and he excitedly recalls hearing a lecture by the computer scientist Alan Kay more than thirty-five years ago on object-oriented programming. Kay's idea—to encapsulate each chunk of code with logic that enabled it to interact with any other piece—was a miracle of streamlining, making programmers' lives easier and helping turn computers into more robust and flexible tools.

Feied arrived at Washington Hospital Center in 1995, recruited by his longtime colleague Mark Smith to help fix its emergency department. (Smith was also a true believer in technology. He had a master's degree in computer

During the 1960s, Craig Feied regularly purloined rock-concert posters from all over the Bay Area. Some of the jewels of his collection are laid out here in his Washington, D.C., living room, which has morphed into a full-time music space.

Even in relatively high-tech ERs, the flow of patient information was until quite recently charted primarily on whiteboards. This one, at George Washington University Hospital—that's Craig Feied with his back to the camera—contained basic information on every patient in the ER: their arrival time, condition, who'd been treating them, and which orders needed to be carried out next. Sometimes, Feied says, the order called for the records department to pull a stack of old charts—a process that could take hours.

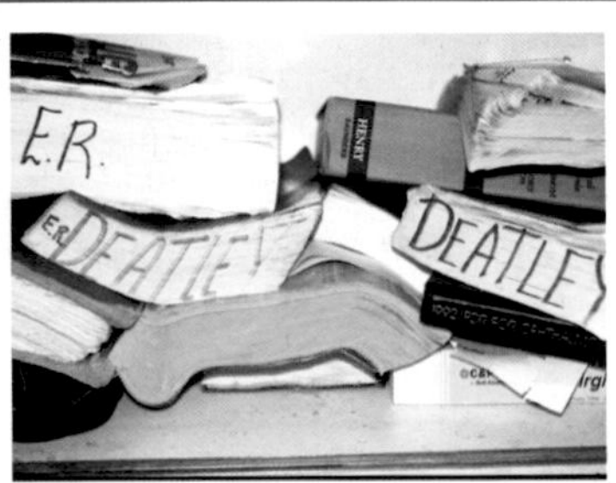

Feied and Smith's survey was conducted in the early days of the Internet, before the advent of the Web. Feied took this photo in the early 1990s in the medical-reference library at George Washington University Hospital. "The books marked 'DEATLEY' were out-of-date cast-offs donated by Craig DeAtley, who ran our paramedic training program, after he purchased current versions," Feied recalls. "Most were missing critical pages, including index pages. From an information-access point of view, the state of patient charts was just as bad."

science from Stanford, where his thesis adviser was none other than Alan Kay.) Although some of WHC's specialty departments were well regarded, the ER consistently ranked last in the D.C. area. It was crowded, slow, and disorganized; it ran through a new director every year or so, and the hospital's own medical director called the ER "a pretty undesirable place."

By this time, Feied and Smith had between them treated more than a hundred thousand patients in various emergency rooms. They found one commodity was always in short supply: information. A patient would come in—conscious or unconscious, cooperative or not, sober or high, with a limitless array of potential problems—and the doctor had to decide quickly how to treat him. But there were usually more questions than answers: Was the patient on medication? What was his medical history? Did a low blood count mean acute internal bleeding or just chronic anemia? And where was the CT scan that was supposedly done two hours ago?

"For years, I treated patients with no more information than the patients could tell me," Feied says. "Any other information took too long, so you couldn't factor it in. We often knew what information we needed, and even knew where it was, but it just wasn't available in time. The critical piece of data might have been two hours away or two weeks away. In a busy emergency department, even two *minutes* away is too much. You can't do that when you have forty patients and half of them are trying to die."

The problem agitated Feied so badly that he turned himself into the world's first emergency-medicine informaticist. (He made up the phrase, based on the European term for computer science.) He believed that the best way to improve clinical care in the ER was to improve the flow of information.

Even before taking over at WHC, Feied and Smith hired a bunch of medical students to follow doctors and nurses around the ER and pepper them with questions. Much like Sudhir Venkatesh hired trackers to interview Chicago street prostitutes, they wanted to gather reliable, real-time data that were otherwise hard to get. Here are some of the questions the students asked:

Since I last talked to you, what information did you need?

How long did it take to get it?

What was the source: Did you make a phone call? Use a reference book? Talk to a medical librarian?

Did you get a satisfactory answer to your query?

TOP: JON HANDLER; BOTTOM: CRAIG FEIED

Did you make a medical decision based on that answer?

How did that decision impact patient care?

What was the financial impact of that decision on the hospital?

The diagnosis was clear: the WHC emergency department had a severe case of "datapenia," or low data counts. (Feied invented this word as well, stealing the suffix from "leucopenia," or low white-blood-cell counts.) Doctors were spending about 60 percent of their time on "information management," and only 15 percent on direct patient care. This was a sickening ratio. "Emergency medicine is a specialty defined not by an organ of the body or by an age group but by time," says Mark Smith. "It's about what you do in the first sixty minutes."

Smith and Feied discovered more than three hundred data sources in the hospital that didn't talk to one another, including a mainframe system, handwritten notes, scanned images, lab results, streaming video from cardiac angiograms, and an infection-control tracking system that lived on one person's computer on an Excel spreadsheet. "And if *she* went on vacation, God help you if you're trying to track a TB outbreak," says Feied.

To give the ER doctors and nurses what they really needed, a computer system had to be built from the ground up. It had to be encyclopedic (one missing piece of key data would defeat the purpose); it had to be muscular (a single MRI, for instance, ate up a massive amount of data capacity); and it had to be flexible (a system that couldn't incorporate any data from any department in any hospital in the past, present, or future was useless).

It also had to be really, really fast. Not only because slowness kills in an ER but because, as Feied had learned from the scientific literature, a person using a computer experiences "cognitive drift" if more than one second elapses between clicking the mouse and seeing new data on the screen. If ten seconds pass, the person's mind is somewhere else entirely. That's how medical errors are made.

To build this fast, flexible, muscular, encyclopedic system, Feied and Smith turned to their old crush: object-oriented programming. They set to work using a new architecture that they called "data-centric" and "data-atomic." Their system would deconstruct each piece of data from every department and store it in a way that allowed it to interact with any other single piece of data, or any other 1 billion pieces.

Alas, not everyone at WHC was enthusiastic. Institutions are by nature

Even in the early days of computing, researchers understood the importance of quick response time. In a landmark 1968 paper, IBM researcher Robert Miller argued that computers should behave as attentively as two people do while speaking to each other. "In conversation of any kind between humans," Miller wrote, "silences of more than four seconds become embarrassing because they imply a breaking of the thread of communication."

Response time became ever more important as computers began to perform more complicated tasks. Consider the gowned-and-gloved surgeon below, who is preparing to take a brain biopsy at Washington Hospital Center. He is using a gesture-recognition system that lets him manipulate an MRI image of the patient's brain without having to touch the non-sterile screen. He expects the computer to respond instantaneously as he moves his hand. With even a brief delay, cognitive drift might set in—and you don't want that happening to a man with a scalpel in his hand.

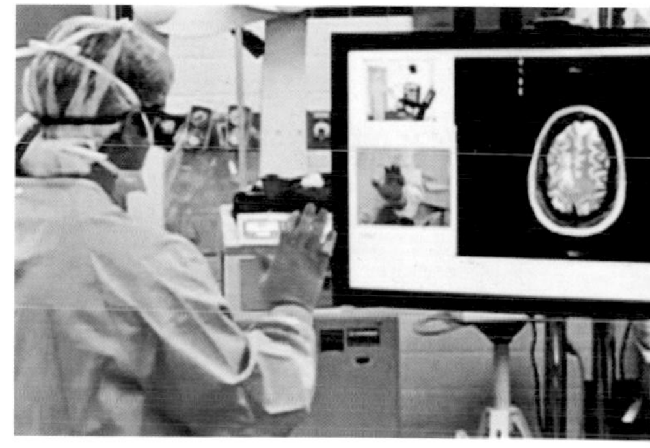

COURTESY CRAIG FEIED

Craig Feied, at right, and Mark Smith, his longtime collaborator, riding their Segways down the main corridor of Washington Hospital Center in 2002.

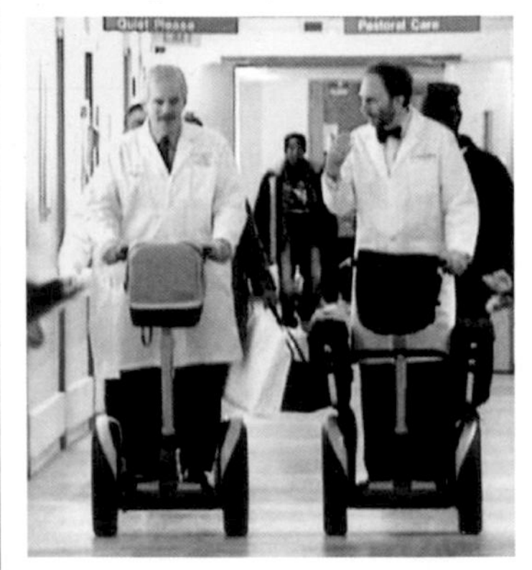

large and inflexible beasts with fiefdoms that must be protected and rules that must not be broken. Some departments considered their data proprietary and wouldn't surrender it. The hospital's strict purchasing codes wouldn't let Feied and Smith buy the computer equipment they needed. One top administrator "hated us," Feied recalls, "and missed no opportunity to try to stonewall and prevent people from working with us. He used to go into the service-request system at night and delete our service requests."

It probably didn't help that Feied was such an odd duck—the contrarianism, the Segway, the original Miró prints on his office wall—or that, when challenged, he wouldn't rest until he found a way to charm or, if need be, threaten his way to victory. Even the name he gave his new computer system seemed grandiose: Azyxxi (*uh-ZICK-see*), which he told people came from the Phoenician for "one who is capable of seeing far"—but which really, he admits with a laugh, "we just made up."

In the end, Feied won—or, really, the data won. Azyxxi went live on a single desktop computer in the WHC emergency room. Feied put a sign on the monitor, warning doctors to not use this beta-testing system. (No one ever said he wasn't clever.) Like so many Adams and Eves, doctors and nurses began to peck at the forbidden fruit and found it nothing short of miraculous. In a few seconds they could locate practically any information they needed. Within a week, the Azyxxi computer had a waiting line. And it wasn't just ER docs: they came from all over the hospital to drink up the data. At first glance, it seemed like the product of genius. But no, says Feied. It was "a triumph of doggedness."

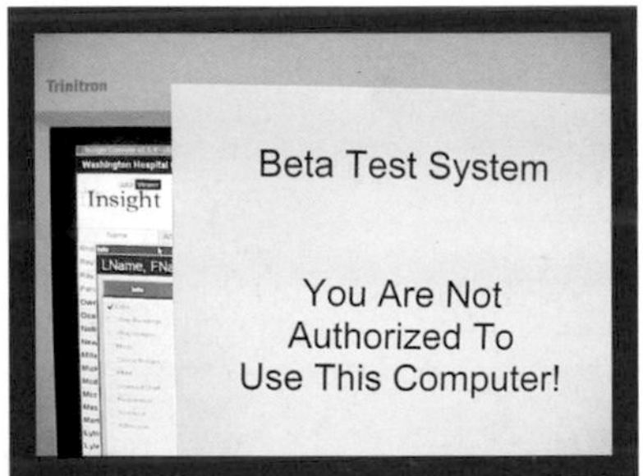

Azyxxi's forbidden fruit: what better way to get doctors to use it?

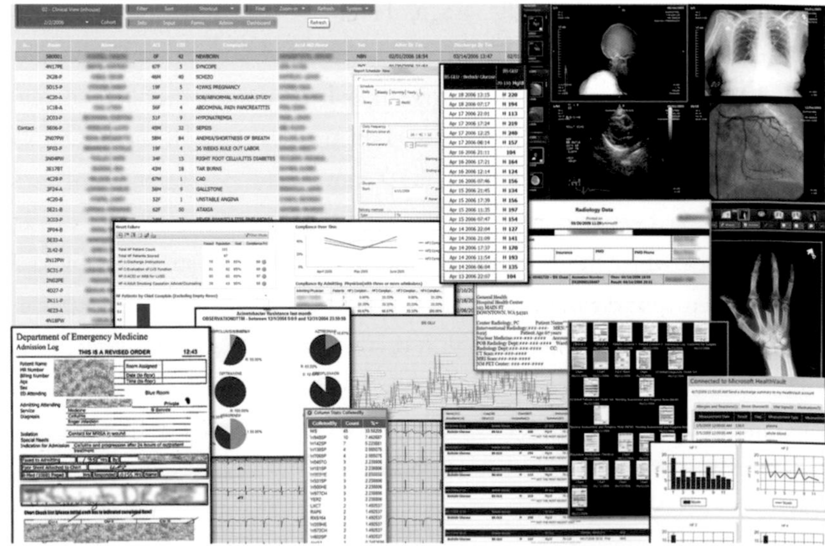

A screenshot of Amalga, the successor to Azyxxi, demonstrating the different kinds of patient information that can be displayed. It's a bit more advanced than the old ER whiteboard.

TOP: JULIE FEIED; MIDDLE AND BOTTOM: COURTESY CRAIG FEIED

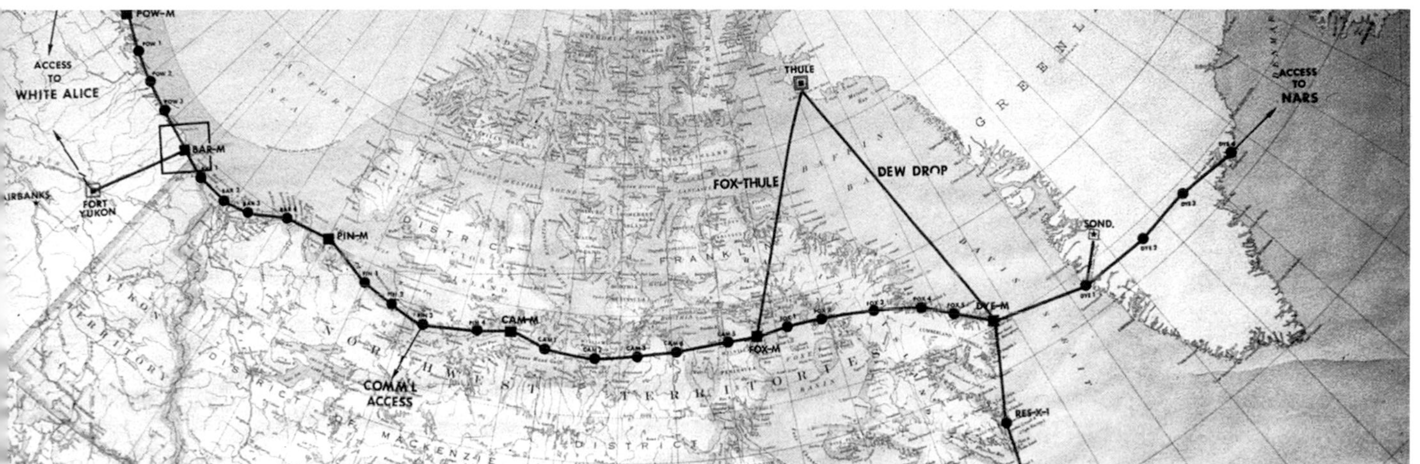

The original Distant Early Warning Line, in the 1950s, was a 3,600-mile string of radar stations across the northern coast of Alaska and Canada, and into Greenland, meant to detect Soviet bombers that might be headed toward the U.S. over the Arctic Circle.

Within a few years, the WHC emergency department went from worst to first in the Washington region. Even though Azyxxi quadrupled the amount of information that was actually being seen, doctors were spending 25 percent less time on "information management," and more than twice as much time directly treating patients. The old ER wait time averaged eight hours; now, 60 percent of patients were in and out in less than two hours. Patient outcomes were better and doctors were happier (and less error-prone). Annual patient volume doubled, from 40,000 to 80,000, with only a 30 percent increase in staffing. Efficiencies abounded, and this was good for the hospital's bottom line.

As Azyxxi's benefits became clear, many other hospitals came calling. So did, eventually, Microsoft, which bought it, Craig Feied and all. Microsoft renamed it Amalga and, within the first year, installed the system in fourteen major hospitals, including Johns Hopkins, New York–Presbyterian, and the Mayo Clinic. Although it was developed in an ER, more than 90 percent of its use is currently in other hospital departments. As of this writing, Amalga covers roughly 10 million patients at 350 care sites; for those of you keeping score at home, that's more than 150 terabytes of data.

It would have been enough if Amalga merely improved patient outcomes and made doctors more efficient. But such a massive accumulation of data creates other opportunities. It lets doctors seek out markers for diseases in patients who haven't been diagnosed. It makes billing more efficient. It makes the dream of electronic medical records a straightforward reality. And, because it collects data in real time from all over the country, the system can serve as a Distant Early Warning Line for disease outbreaks or even bioterrorism.

A DEW communications site at Boswell Bay, Alaska, now deactivated; photographed in June 1987 by Rob Stapleton for the Historic American Engineering Record project.

TOP: U.S. AIR FORCE TECH. SGT. DONALD L. WETTERMAN

The psychologist Anders Ericsson and his fellow talent researchers have tried to explore doctor skill by subjecting physicians to a variety of job-related tests. Their findings were unsettling: in most cases, the longer a doctor had been out of medical school, the worse he or she performed on these tests. Why? Because medical school was the last time they got fast and reliable feedback on their decisions. Ever since, there has been a lot more guesswork—as when a doctor reads a mammogram, for instance. With such a sloppy feedback loop, Ericsson and his colleagues argue, a doctor's ability deteriorates over time. One notable exception to this rule: surgeons, who get nearly instantaneous feedback on their work.

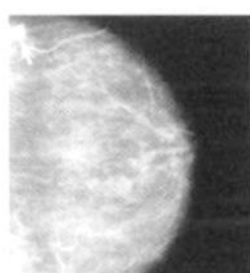

It also allows other, non-medical people—people like us, for instance—to repurpose its data to answer other kinds of questions, such as: who are the best and worst doctors in the ER?

For a variety of reasons, measuring doctor skill is a tricky affair.

The first is selection bias: patients aren't randomly assigned to doctors. Two cardiologists will have two sets of clientele who may differ on many dimensions. The better doctor's patients may even have a *higher* death rate. Why? Perhaps the sicker patients seek out the best cardiologist, so even if he does a good job, his patients are more likely to die than the other doctor's.

It can therefore be misleading to measure doctor skill solely by looking at patient outcomes. That is generally what doctor "report cards" do and, though the idea has obvious appeal, it can produce some undesirable consequences. A doctor who knows he is being graded on patient outcomes may "cream-skim," turning down the high-risk patients who most need treatment so as to not tarnish his score. Indeed, studies have shown that hospital report cards have actually hurt patients precisely because of this kind of perverse physician incentive.

Measuring doctor skill is also tricky because the impact of a doctor's decisions may not be detectable until long after the patient is treated. When a doctor reads a mammogram, for instance, she can't be sure if there is breast cancer or not. She may find out weeks later, if a biopsy is ordered—or, if she missed a tumor that later kills the patient, she may *never* find out. Even when a doctor gets a diagnosis just right and forestalls a potentially serious problem, it's hard to make sure the patient follows directions. Did he take the prescribed medication? Did he change his diet and exercise program as directed? Did he stop scarfing down entire bags of pork rinds?

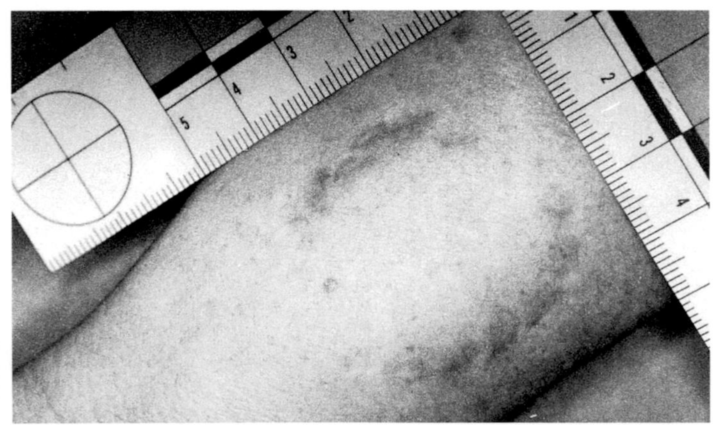

This photo was taken as evidence in a domestic-violence case. The measuring scale, created by the American Board of Forensic Odontology, shows the bite to be about 3.5 centimeters in diameter. The same scale is sometimes used to measure fingerprints and blood.

The data culled by Craig Feied's team from the WHC emergency room turn out to be just the thing to answer some questions about doctor skill. For starters, the data set is huge, re-

TOP: NATIONAL CANCER INSTITUTE; BOTTOM: MICHAEL F. LAFORTE AND EAGLE CRIME SCENES, INC.

cording some 620,000 visits by roughly 240,000 different patients over nearly eight years, and the more than 300 doctors who treated them.

It contains everything you might want to know about a given patient—anonymized, of course, for our analysis—from the moment she walks, rolls, or is carried through the ER door until the time she leaves the hospital, alive or otherwise. The data include demographic information; the patient's complaint upon entering the ER; how long it took to see a doctor; how the patient was diagnosed and treated; whether the patient was admitted to the hospital, and the length of stay; whether the patient was later readmitted; the total cost of the treatment; and if or when the patient died. (Even if the patient died two years later outside the hospital, the death would still be included in our analysis as a result of cross-linking the hospital data with the Social Security Death Index.)

The data also show which doctor treated which patients, and we know a good bit about each doctor as well, including age, gender, medical school attended, hospital where residency was served, and years of experience.

When most people think of ERs, they envision a steady stream of gunshot wounds and accident victims. In reality, dramatic incidents like these represent a tiny fraction of ER traffic and, because WHC has a separate Level I trauma center, such cases are especially rare in our ER data. That said, the main emergency room has an extraordinary array of patient complaints, from the life-threatening to the entirely imaginary.

On average, about 160 patients showed up each day. The busiest day is Monday, and weekend days are the slowest. (This is a good clue that many ailments aren't so serious that they can't wait until the weekend's activities are over.) The peak hour is 11:00 A.M., which is five times busier than the slowest hour, which is 5:00 A.M. Six of every ten patients are female; the average age is forty-seven.

The first thing a patient does upon arrival is tell the triage nurse what's wrong. Some complaints are common: "shortness of breath," "chest pains," "dehydration," "flulike symptoms." Others are far less so: "fish bone stuck in throat," "hit over the head with book," and a variety of bites, including a good number of dog bites (about 300) and insect or spider bites (200). Interestingly, there are more human bites (65) than rat bites and cat bites combined (30), including 1 instance of being "bitten by client at work." (Alas, the intake form didn't reveal the nature of this patient's job.)

THE APPROXIMATE BITE FORCE, RENDERED IN NEWTONS, OF 10 SELECTED ANIMALS

*Tyrannosaurus rex**:
13,300

(Alligator mississippiensis)
AMERICAN ALLIGATOR:
9,400

(Crocuta crocuta)
SPOTTED HYENA:
4,500

(Panthera leo)
AFRICAN LION:
4,250

*Allosaurus fragilis**:
2,000

(Pongo pygmaeus)
ORANGUTAN:
1,900

(Carcharhinus obscurus)
DUSKY SHARK:
1,500

(Canis lupus)
GRAY WOLF:
1,450

(Homo sapiens)
HUMAN:
750

(Canis familiaris)
LABRADOR DOG:
700

*Extinct

In 2007, at a zoo in Kaohsiung, in southern Taiwan, a crocodile bit off the forearm of the veterinarian who'd been treating it. While zoo employees worked to free the forearm from the crocodile's mouth, the vet was taken to a hospital, where after several hours he was surgically reunited with his lost limb.

CORBIS

Why do people think there are so many deaths in the ER? Perhaps because that's how it looks on television. For a research paper called "If You Must Be Hospitalized, Television Is Not the Place," the Israeli communications scholar Amir Hetsroni analyzed one season's worth of the U.S. hospital dramas *ER, Chicago Hope,* and *Grey's Anatomy*. It turned out that TV patients were drastically more likely to die in the hospital than real-life patients. They were also more likely to be young, seriously injured white men (preferably good-looking ones). Consider some details:

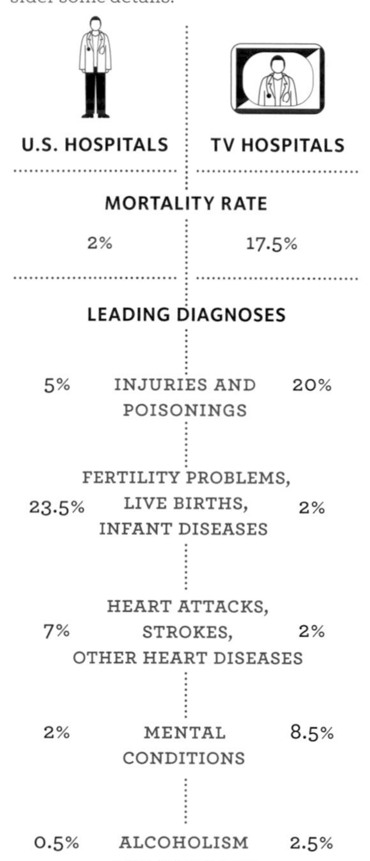

The vast majority of patients who come to the ER leave alive. Only 1 of every 250 patients dies within a week; 1 percent die within a month, and about 5 percent die within a year. But knowing whether a condition is life-threatening or not isn't always obvious (especially to the patients themselves). Imagine you're an ER doc with eight patients in the waiting room, one each with one of the following eight common complaints. Four of these conditions have a relatively high death rate while the other four are low. Can you tell which ones are which?

COMPLAINTS	
NUMBNESS	PSYCHIATRIC
CHEST PAINS	SHORTNESS OF BREATH
FEVER	INFECTION
DIZZINESS	CLOT

Here's the answer, based on the likelihood of a patient dying within twelve months:

HIGH-RISK CONDITIONS	LOW-RISK CONDITIONS
CLOT	CHEST PAINS
FEVER	DIZZINESS
INFECTION	NUMBNESS
SHORTNESS OF BREATH	PSYCHIATRIC

Shortness of breath is by far the most common high-risk condition. (It is usually notated as "SOB," so if someday you see that abbreviation on your chart, don't think the doctor hates you.) To many patients, SOB might seem less scary than something like chest pains. But here's what the data say:

HIGH-RISK CONDITIONS	SOB	CHEST PAINS
AVERAGE AGE OF PATIENT	54.5	51.4
SHARE OF ER PATIENTS WITH COMPLAINT	7.4%	12.1%
ADMITTED TO HOSPITAL	51.3%	41.9%
1-MONTH MORTALITY RATE	2.9%	1.2%
1-YEAR MORTALITY RATE	12.9%	5.3%

These and other death rates are *risk-adjusted* death rates, controlling for age, other symptoms, etc.

So a patient with chest pains is no more likely than the average ER patient to die within a year, whereas shortness of breath more than doubles the death risk. Similarly, roughly 1 in 10 patients who show up with a clot, a fever, or an infection will be dead within a year; but if a patient is dizzy, is numb, or has a psychiatric condition, the risk of dying is only one-third as high.

With all this in mind, let's get back to the question at hand: given all these data, how do we measure the efficacy of each doctor?

The most obvious course would be to simply look at the raw data for differences in patient outcomes across doctors. Indeed, this method would show radical differences among doctors. If these results were trustworthy, there would be few factors in your life as important as the identity of the doctor who happens to draw your case when you show up at the ER.

But for the same reasons you shouldn't put much faith in doctor report cards, a comparison like this is highly deceptive. Two doctors in the same ER are likely to treat very different pools of patients. The average patient at noon, for instance, is about ten years older than one who comes in the middle of the night. Even two doctors working the same shift might see very different patients, based on their skills and interests. It is the triage nurse's job to match patients and doctors as best as possible. One doc may therefore get all the psychiatric cases on a shift, or all the elderly patients. Because an old person with shortness of breath is much more likely to die than a thirty-year-old with the same condition, we have to be careful not to penalize the doctor who happens to be good with old people.

What you'd *really* like to do is run a randomized, controlled trial so that when patients arrive they are randomly assigned to a doctor, even if that doctor is overwhelmed with other patients or not well equipped to handle a particular ailment.

But we are dealing with one set of real, live human beings who are trying to keep another set of real, live human beings from dying, so this kind of experiment isn't going to happen, and for good reason.

Since we can't do a true randomization, and if simply looking at patient outcomes in the raw data will be misleading, what's the best way to measure doctor skill?

Thanks to the nature of the emergency room, there is another sort of de facto, accidental randomization that can lead us to the truth. The

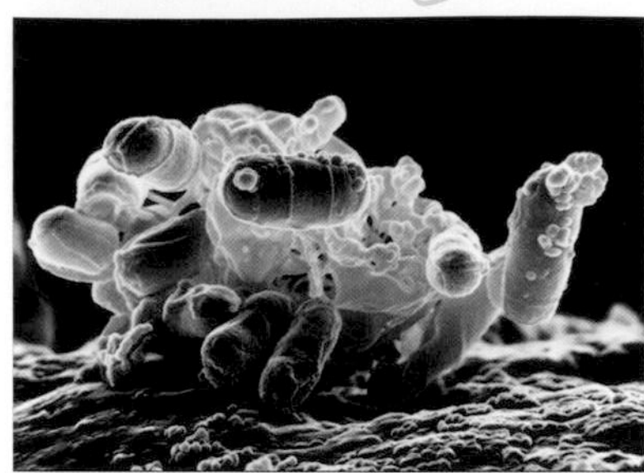

E. coli bacteria are the brown, oblong shapes shown above. Most strains of *E. coli* are harmless, and some are even helpful. But other strains secrete a substance called Shiga toxin, which in humans can cause stomach cramps, severe diarrhea, and even seizures, organ failure, and death. These toxin-producing strains are almost always the culprits in widespread food-poisoning outbreaks. The bacteria live in the fecal matter of cattle and are most often consumed in contaminated hamburger meat, though two notable outbreaks in the 2000s came from *E. coli* on spinach and lettuce.

ERIC ERBE; COLORIZATION: CHRISTOPHER POOLEY; COURTESY U.S. DEPT. OF AGRICULTURE

key is that patients generally have no idea which doctors will be working when they arrive at the ER. Therefore, the patients who show up between 2:00 and 3:00 P.M. on one Thursday in October are, on average, likely to be similar to the patients who show up the following Thursday, or the Thursday after that. But the *doctors* working on those three Thursdays will probably be different. So if the patients who came on the first Thursday have worse outcomes than the patients who came on the second or third Thursday, one likely explanation is that the doctors on that shift weren't as good. (In this ER, there were usually two or three doctors per shift.)

There could be other explanations, of course, like bad luck or bad weather or an *E. coli* outbreak. But if you look at a particular doctor's record across hundreds of shifts and see that the patients on those shifts have worse outcomes than is typical, you have a pretty strong indication that the doctor is at the root of the problem.

One last note on methodology: while we exploit information about which doctors are working on a shift, we *don't* factor in which doctor actually treats a particular patient. Why? Because we know that the triage nurse's job is to match patients with doctors, which makes the selection far from random. It might seem counterintuitive—wasteful, even—to ignore the specific doctor-patient match in our analysis. But in scenarios where selection is a problem, the only way to get a true answer is, paradoxically, to *throw away* what at first seems to be valuable information.

So, applying this approach to Craig Feied's massively informative data set, what can we learn about doctor skill?

Or, put another way: if you land in an emergency room with a serious condition, how much does your survival depend on the particular doctor you draw?

The short answer is . . . not all that much. Most of what looks like doctor skill in the raw data is in fact the luck of the draw, the result of some doctors getting more patients with less-threatening ailments.

This isn't to say there's *no* difference between the best and worst doctors in the ER. (And no, we're not going to name them.) In a given year, an excellent ER doctor's patients will have a twelve-month death rate that is nearly 10 percent lower than the average. This may not sound like much, but in a busy ER with tens of thousands of patients, an excellent doctor might save six or seven lives a year relative to the worst doctor.

Interestingly, health outcomes are largely uncorrelated to spending. This means the best doctors don't spend any more money—for tests, hospital admittance, and so on—than the lesser doctors. This is worth pondering in an era when higher health-care spending is widely thought to produce better health-care outcomes. In the United States, the health-care sector accounts for more than 16 percent of GDP, up from 5 percent in 1960, and is projected to reach 20 percent by 2015.

As U.S. health care continues to grow more expensive, have you ever wondered which medical conditions consume the most resources? Here's a look at personal health-care spending by category in recent years:

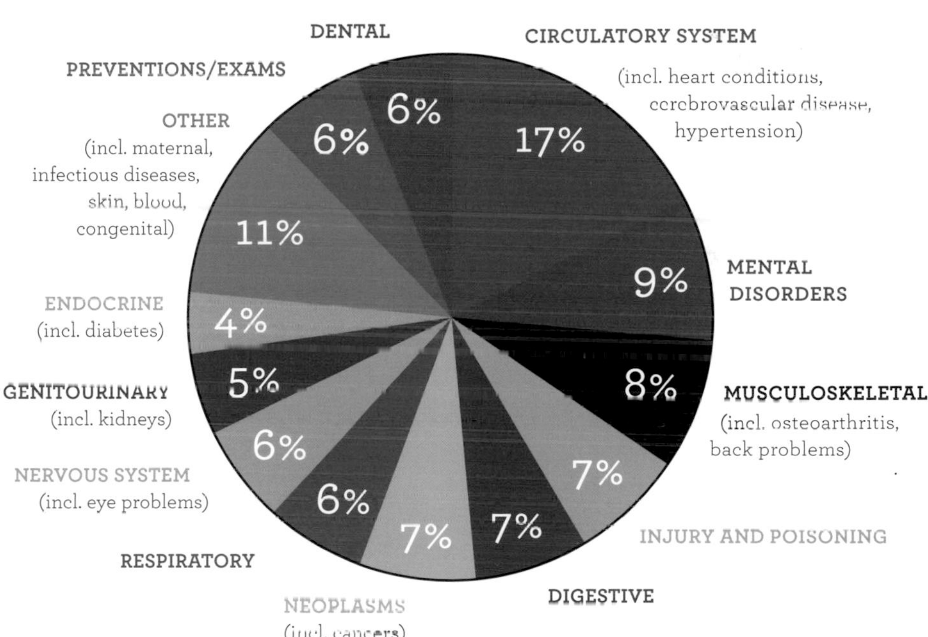

So what are the characteristics of the best doctors?

For the most part, our findings aren't very surprising. An excellent doctor is disproportionately likely to have attended a top-ranked medical school and served a residency at a prestigious hospital. More experience is also valuable: an extra ten years on the job yields the same benefit as having served a residency at a top hospital.

And oh yes: you also want your ER doctor to be a woman. It may have been bad for America's schoolchildren when so many smart women passed up teaching jobs to go to medical school, but it's good to know that, in our analysis at least, such women are slightly better than their male counterparts at keeping people alive.

One factor that *doesn't* seem to matter is whether a doctor is highly rated by his or her colleagues. We asked Feied and the other head physicians at WHC to name the best docs in the ER. The ones they chose turned out to be no better than average at lowering death rates. They were, however, good at spending less money per patient.

So the particular doctor you draw in the ER does matter—but, in the broader scheme of things, not nearly as much as other factors: your ailment, your gender (women are much less likely than men to die within a year of visiting the ER), or your income level (poor patients are much more likely to die than rich ones).

For those wishing to cut down on their interactions with doctors, here's a list of some home remedies some people believe may be of some help.

ANAL ITCHING
Place a warm tea bag on the area of irritation.
STINKY FEET
Human urine (i.e., pee on yourself).
DANDRUFF
Snake gourd juice or selenium.
STUFFY NOSE
Pour salt water into one nostril and let it drain out the other; repeat. To be done over a sink.

The medical establishment, meanwhile, has long warned against home remedies, as seen in this 1945 poster from the U.S. Public Health Service.

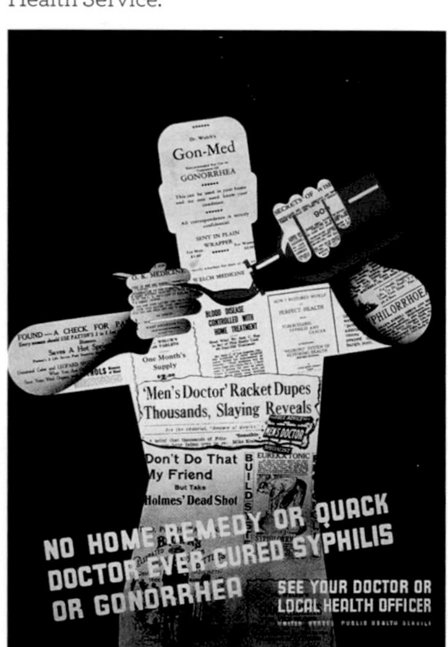

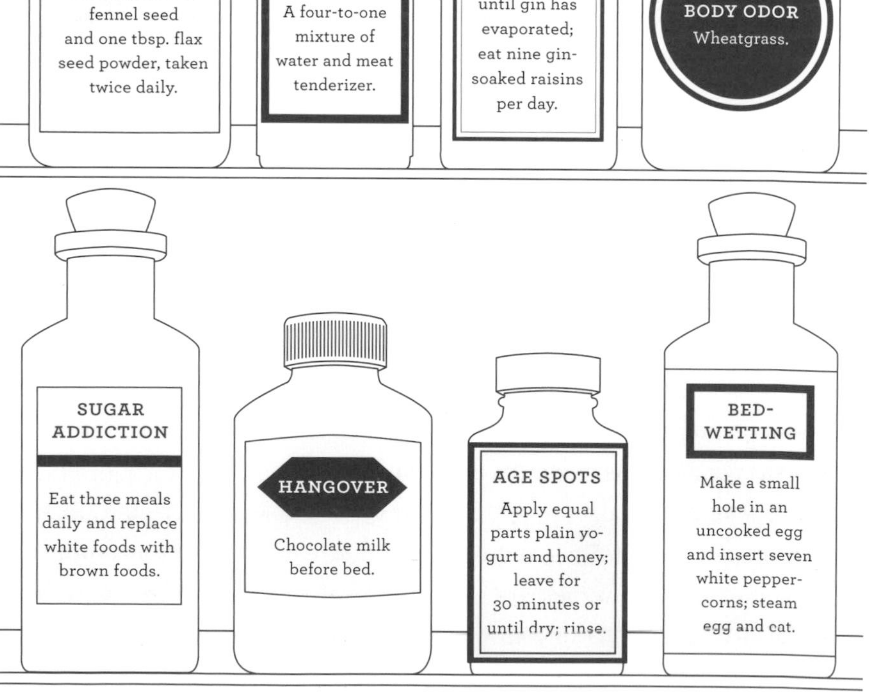

FLATULENCE
Two capsules of fennel seed and one tbsp. flax seed powder, taken twice daily.
BEE STING
A four-to-one mixture of water and meat tenderizer.
ARTHRITIS
Soak raisins in gin for one week or until gin has evaporated; eat nine gin-soaked raisins per day.
BODY ODOR
Wheatgrass.
SUGAR ADDICTION
Eat three meals daily and replace white foods with brown foods.
HANGOVER
Chocolate milk before bed.
AGE SPOTS
Apply equal parts plain yogurt and honey; leave for 30 minutes or until dry; rinse.
BED-WETTING
Make a small hole in an uncooked egg and insert seven white peppercorns; steam egg and eat.

LEONARD KARSAKOV

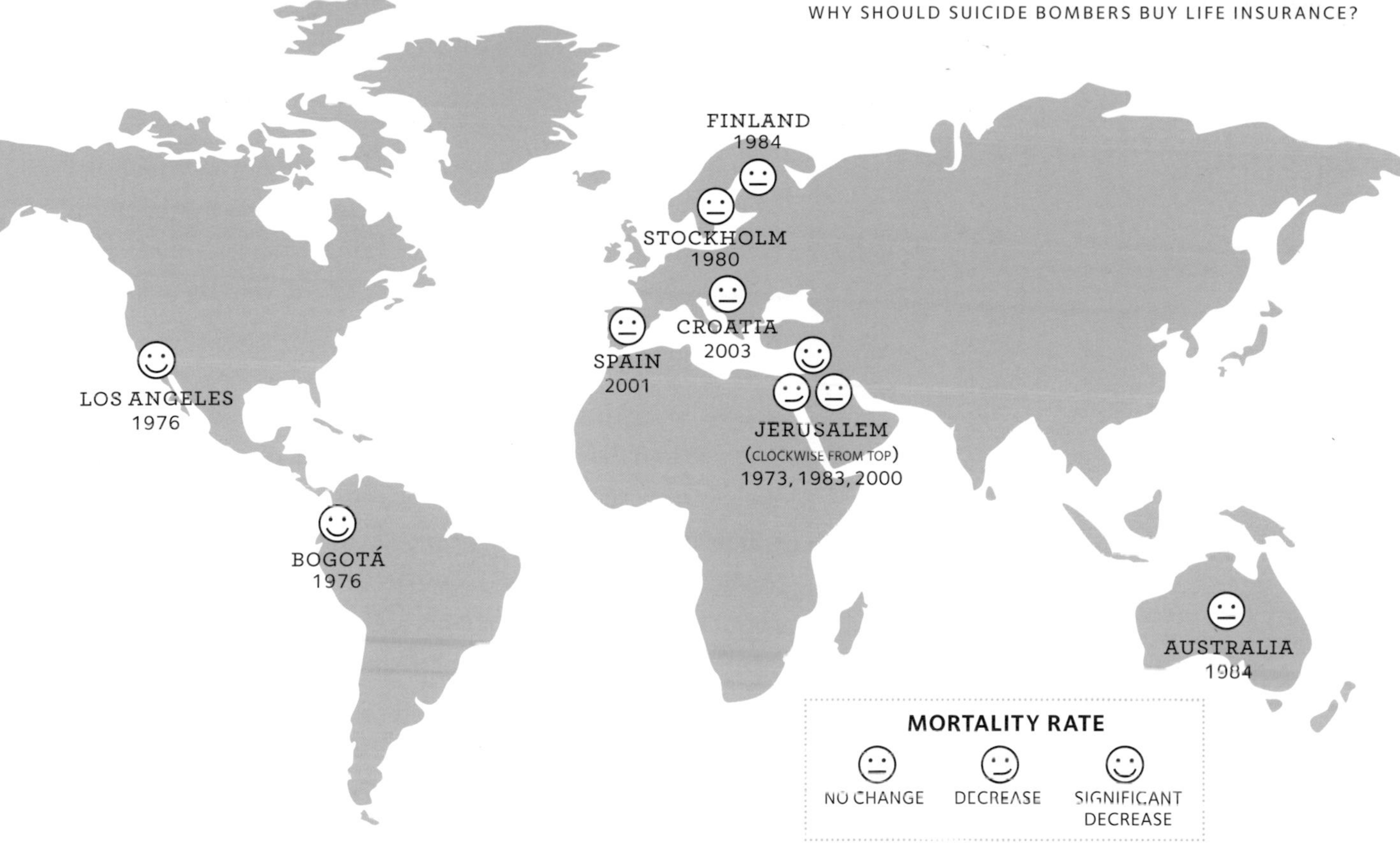

The best news is that most people who are rushed to the ER and think they are going to die are in little danger of dying at all, at least not any time soon.

In fact, they might have been better off if they simply stayed at home. Consider the evidence from a series of widespread doctor strikes in Los Angeles, Israel, and Colombia. It turns out that the death rate dropped significantly in those places, anywhere from 18 percent to 50 percent, when the doctors stopped working! ☺

The evidence is hardly strong enough to warrant getting rid of all the doctors, but here's a look at what happens to the mortality rate when doctors go on strike.

This effect might be partially explained by patients' putting off elective surgery during the strike. That's what Craig Feied first thought when he read the literature. But he had a chance to observe a similar phenomenon firsthand when a lot of Washington doctors left town at the same time for a medical convention. The result: an across-the-board drop in mortality.

"When there are too many physician-patient interactions, the amplitude gets turned up on everything," he says. "More people with non-fatal problems are taking more medications and having more procedures, many of which are not really helpful and a few of which are harmful, while the people with really fatal illnesses are rarely cured and ultimately die anyway."

How will the vagaries of life unspool? That eternal question was turned into the Checkered Game of Life in 1860 by the Milton Bradley Company.

So it may be that going to the hospital slightly increases your odds of surviving if you've got a serious problem but increases your odds of dying if you don't. Such are the vagaries of life.

Meanwhile, there *are* some ways to extend your life span that have nothing to do with going to the hospital. You could, for instance, win a Nobel Prize. An analysis covering fifty years of the Nobels in chemistry and physics found that the winners lived longer than those who were merely nominated. (So much for the Hollywood wisdom of "It's an honor just to be nominated.") Nor was the winners' longevity a function of the Nobel Prize money. "Status seems to work a kind of health-giving magic," says Andrew Oswald, one of the study's authors. "Walking across that platform in Stockholm apparently adds about two years to a scientist's life span."

You could also get elected to the Baseball Hall of Fame. A similar analysis shows that men who are voted into the Hall outlive those who are narrowly omitted.

But what about those of us who aren't exceptional at science or sport? Well, you could purchase an annuity, a contract that pays off a set amount of income each year but only as long as you stay alive. People who buy annuities, it turns out, live longer than people who don't, and not because the people who buy annuities are healthier to start with. The evidence suggests that an annuity's steady payout provides a little extra incentive to keep chugging along.

Religion also seems to help. A study of more than 2,800 elderly Christians and Jews found that they were more likely to die in the thirty days after their respective major holidays than in the thirty days before. (One piece of evidence proving a causal link: Jews had no aversion to dying in the thirty days before a *Christian* holiday, nor did Christians disproportionately outlast the Jewish holidays.) In a similar vein, longtime friends and rivals Thomas Jefferson and John Adams each valiantly struggled to forestall death until they'd reached an important landmark. They expired within fifteen hours of each other on July 4, 1826, the fiftieth anniversary of the ratification of the Declaration of Independence.

John Adams's final letter to Thomas Jefferson refers to Jefferson's previous missive to him. "Your letter," Adams wrote, "is one of the most beautiful and delightful I have ever received." The two former presidents died a few months later on the same historic day.

Your letter is one of the most beautiful and delightful I have ever received

Holding off death by even a single day can sometimes be worth millions of dollars. Consider the estate tax, which is imposed on the taxable estate of a person upon his or her death. In the United States, the rate in recent years was 45 percent, with an exemption for the first $2 million. In 2009, however, the exemption jumped to $3.5 million—which meant that the heirs of a rich, dying parent had about 1.5 million reasons to console themselves if said parent died on the first day of 2009 rather than the last day of 2008. With this incentive, it's not hard to imagine such heirs giving their parent the best medical care money could buy, at least through the end of the year. Indeed, two Australian scholars found that when their nation abolished its inheritance tax in 1979, a disproportionately high number of people died in the week after the abolition as compared with the week before.

For a time, it looked as if the U.S. estate tax would be temporarily abolished for one year, in 2010. (This was the product of a bipartisan hissy fit in Washington, which, as of this writing, appears to have been resolved.) If the tax *had* been suspended, a parent worth $100 million who died in 2010 could have passed along all $100 million to his or her heirs. But, with a scheduled resumption of the tax in 2011, such heirs would have surrendered more than $40 million if their parent had the temerity to die even one day too late. Perhaps the bickering politicians decided to smooth out the tax law when they realized how many assisted suicides they might have been responsible for during the waning weeks of 2010.

Most people want to fend off death no matter the cost. More than $40 billion is spent worldwide each year on cancer drugs. In the United States, they constitute the second-largest category of pharmaceutical sales, after heart drugs, and are growing twice as fast as the rest of the market. The bulk of this spending goes to chemotherapy, **606** which is used in a variety of ways and has proven effective on some cancers, including leukemia, lymphoma, Hodgkin's disease, and testicular cancer, especially if these cancers are detected early.

But in most other cases, chemotherapy is remarkably *in*effective. An exhaustive analysis of cancer treatment in the United States and Australia showed that the five-year survival rate for all patients was about 63 percent but that chemotherapy contributed barely 2 percent to this result. There is a long list of cancers for which chemotherapy had *zero* discernible effect, including multiple myeloma, soft-tissue sarcoma, melanoma of the skin, and cancers of the pancreas, uterus, prostate, bladder, and kidney.

The first chemotherapy drug was invented in 1909 by the German doctor Paul Ehrlich, as a cure for syphilis. It was known as Salvarsan, arsphenamine, and "606"—for it was reportedly the 606th chemical compound that Ehrlich had tried.

DOCTORS HAVE FAITH IN EHRLICH'S '606'

Danger, All Admit, Attends Faulty Technique in Using the Blood Cure.

IT MUST ENTER THE VEINS

Fatalities Have Resulted Only Where Salvarsan Has Been Introduced Into Muscular Tissues.

THE NEW YORK TIMES

Ever since cigarette smoking was designated the leading cause of lung cancer, many people have tried many ways to discourage smoking. The favorite tool of governments? Make cigarettes more expensive through taxation. Between 1970 and 2007, the U.S. government increased cigarette taxes from 8 to 39 cents per pack, and the average state tax went from $.10 to $1.07. Consider the long-term trends in cigarette consumption and price. →

U.S. CIGARETTE PRICES VS. CONSUMPTION 1970–2007

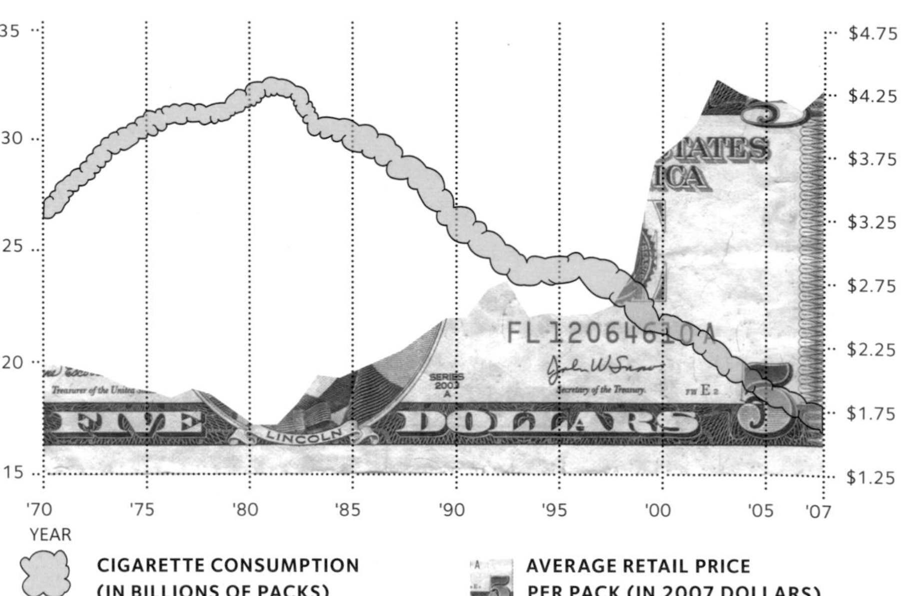

And here's a look at cigarette prices (in 2008 U.S. dollars, adjusted for purchasing power parity) and smoking rates around the world:

SEYCHELLES	$15.00	28 / 3
SINGAPORE	$11.00	34 / 5
U.K.	$ 8.00	26 / 24
NORWAY	$ 7.00	30 / 30
AUSTRALIA	$ 6.50	22 / 19
GERMANY	$ 5.50	37 / 26
INDIA	$ 5.00	28 / 1
U.S.	$ 4.50	25 / 19
GREECE	$ 4.25	63 / 39
SOUTH AFRICA	$ 4.15	27 / 8
SPAIN	$ 3.90	37 / 27
MEXICO	$ 3.75	36 / 12
JAPAN	$ 2.75	42 / 13
BRAZIL	$ 1.75	19 / 12
EGYPT	$ 1.50	24 / 1
CHINA	$ 1.50	59 / 4
RUSSIA	$ 1.00	70 / 28

PRICE OF MOST POPULAR BRAND

PERCENTAGE OF MALES/ FEMALES WHO SMOKE

Consider lung cancer, by far the most prevalent fatal cancer, killing more than 150,000 people a year in the United States. → A typical chemotherapy regime for non-small-cell lung cancer costs more than $40,000 but helps extend a patient's life by an average of just two months. Thomas J. Smith, a highly regarded oncology researcher and clinician at Virginia Commonwealth University, examined a promising new chemotherapy treatment for metastasized breast cancer and found that each additional year of healthy life gained from it costs $360,000—if such a gain could actually be had. Unfortunately, it couldn't: the new treatment typically extended a patient's life by less than two months.

Costs like these put a tremendous strain on the entire health-care system. Smith points out that cancer patients make up 20 percent of Medicare cases but consume 40 percent of the Medicare drug budget.

Some oncologists argue that the benefits of chemotherapy aren't necessarily captured in the mortality data, and that while chemotherapy may not help nine out of ten patients, it may do wonders for the tenth. Still, considering its expense, its frequent lack of efficacy, and its toxicity—nearly 30 percent of the lung-cancer patients on one protocol stopped treatment rather than live with its brutal side effects—why is chemotherapy so widely administered?

The profit motive is certainly a factor. Doctors are, after all, human beings who respond to incentives. Oncologists are among the highest-paid doctors, their salaries increasing faster than any other specialists', and they typically derive more than half of their income from selling and administering chemotherapy drugs. Chemotherapy can also help oncologists inflate their survival-rate data. It may not seem all that valuable to give a late-stage victim of lung cancer an extra two months to live, but perhaps the patient was only expected to live four months anyway. On paper, this will look like an impressive feat: the doctor extended the patient's remaining life by 50 percent.

President Richard Nixon signing the National Cancer Act on Dec. 23, 1971, officially declaring war on cancer. "I hope in the years ahead we will look back on this action today as the most significant action taken during my Administration," he said.

LINDA BARTLETT

Tom Smith doesn't discount either of these reasons, but he provides two more.

It is tempting, he says, for oncologists to overstate—or perhaps over*believe* in—the efficacy of chemotherapy. "If your slogan is 'We're winning the war on cancer,' that gets you press and charitable donations and money from Congress," he says. "If your slogan is 'We're still getting our butts kicked by cancer but not as bad as we used to,' that's a different sell. The reality is that for most people with solid tumors—brain, breast, prostate, lung—we aren't getting our butts kicked as badly, but we haven't made much progress."

There's also the fact that oncologists are, once again, human beings who have to tell other human beings they are dying and that, sadly, there isn't much to be done about it. "Doctors like me find it incredibly hard to tell people the very bad news," Smith says, "and how ineffective our medicines sometimes are."

If this task is so hard for doctors, surely it must also be hard for the politicians and insurance executives who subsidize the widespread use of chemotherapy. Despite the mountain of negative evidence, chemotherapy seems to afford cancer patients their last, best hope to nurse what Smith calls "the deep and abiding desire not to be dead." Still, it is easy to envision a point in the future, perhaps fifty years from now, when we col-

Tom Smith offered this quotation from memory, attributing it to his colleague Thomas Finucane, who had written a *Journal of the American Medical Association* article called "How Gravely Ill Becomes Dying: A Key to End-of-Life Care." But Smith had, in his memory, slightly improved Finucane's original words, which were "the widespread and deeply held desire not to be dead."

Many medical practices from the past have been abandoned. Among the most dramatic is trepanning (or trephining), in which a section of skull is scraped, hacked, or drilled away to expose the dura mater, the fibrous membrane that encases the brain. Evidence of trepanning goes back to the Stone Age; it was used to treat everything from migraines to depression. A similar procedure, known as a craniotomy, is sometimes still used to treat brain hematomas and remove brain tumors, among other things.

In the Anthropological Laboratory at the National Museum (now the Smithsonian's National Museum of Natural History), chief preparator William H. Egberts examines trepanned skulls.

A trepanning procedural from a 17th-century medical text, illustrated by Jonas Arnold. Given that anesthetics were not commonly used in surgery until the mid-19th century, we should probably consider the patient's calm demeanor a wishful fiction on the part of the artist.

lectively look back at the early twenty-first century's cutting-edge cancer treatments and say: We were giving our patients *what*?

The age-adjusted mortality rate for cancer is essentially unchanged over the past half-century, at about 200 deaths per 100,000 people. This is despite President Nixon's declaration of a "war on cancer" more than thirty years ago, which led to a dramatic increase in funding and public awareness.

Believe it or not, this flat mortality rate actually hides some good news. Over the same period, age-adjusted mortality from cardiovascular disease has plummeted, from nearly 600 people per 100,000 to well beneath 300. What does this mean?

Many people who in previous generations would have died from heart disease are now *living long enough to die from cancer* instead. Indeed, nearly 90 percent of newly diagnosed lung-cancer victims are fifty-five or older; the median age is seventy-one.

The flat cancer death rate obscures another hopeful trend. For people twenty and younger, mortality has fallen by more than 50 percent, while people aged twenty to forty have seen a decline of 20 percent. These gains are real and heartening—all the more so because the *incidence* of cancer among those age groups has been increasing. (The reasons for this increase aren't yet clear, but among the suspects are diet, behaviors, and environmental factors.)

With cancer killing fewer people under forty, fighting two wars must surely be driving the death toll higher for young people, no?

From 2002 to 2008, the United States was fighting bloody wars in Afghanistan and Iraq; among active military personnel, there were an average 1,643 fatalities per year. But over the same stretch of time in the early 1980s, with the United States fighting no major wars, there were more than 2,100 military deaths per year. How can this possibly be?

For one, the military used to be much larger: 2.1 million on active duty in 1988 versus 1.4 million in 2008. But even the *rate* of death in 2008 was lower than in certain peacetime years. Some of this improvement is likely due to better medical care. But a surprising fact is that the accidental death rate for soldiers in the early 1980s was higher than the death rate by hostile fire for every year the United States has been fighting in Afghanistan and Iraq. It seems that practicing to fight a war can be just about as dangerous as really fighting one.

And, to further put things in perspective, think about this: since 1982, some 42,000 active U.S. military personnel have been killed—roughly the same number of Americans who die in traffic accidents in a single year.

If someone smokes two packs of cigarettes a day for thirty years and dies of emphysema, at least you can say he brought it on himself and got to enjoy a lifetime of smoking.

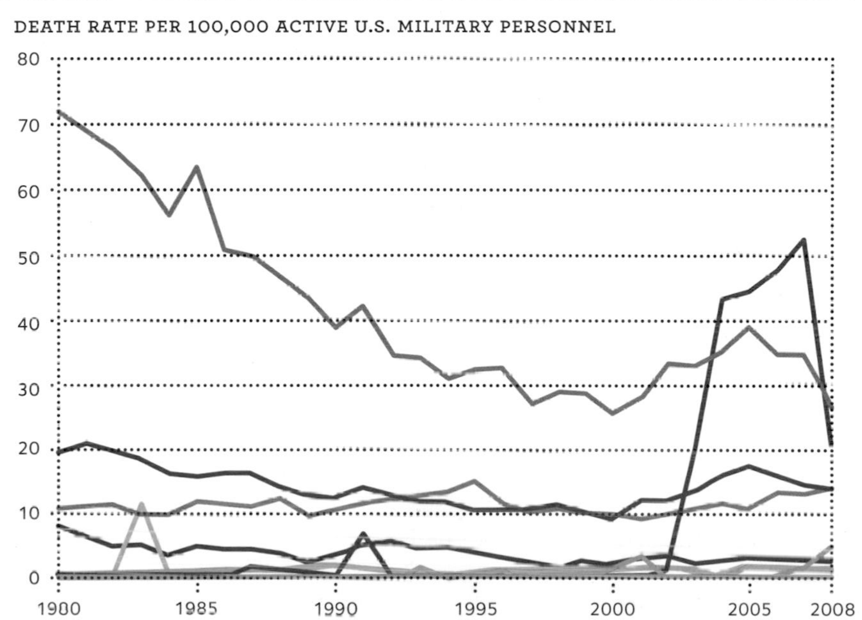

For the past several years, with the U.S. at war in Afghanistan and Iraq, military deaths due to hostile action have skyrocketed. But note the historic decline in accidental deaths. Note also that in the military, as in civilian life, suicide is far more common than homicide. That said, homicide generally gets a lot more media coverage and is therefore perceived to be more prevalent.

In the fall of 2001, letters containing anthrax spores were sent to U.S. politicians and news organizations, killing five people and prompting a nationwide postal scare. The FBI eventually concluded the letters had been sent by an Army microbiologist named Bruce Ivins. His incentive? Ivins's life work was devoted to an anthrax vaccine program that seemed headed for cancellation; the FBI speculated he sent the letters to revive interest in his program. For a while, it worked. But in 2006, investigators began to suspect Ivins, and he committed suicide in 2008.

There is no such consolation for the victim of a terrorist attack. Not only is your demise sudden and violent but you did nothing to earn it. You are collateral damage; the people who killed you neither knew nor cared a whit about your life, your accomplishments, your loved ones. Your death was a prop.

Terrorism is all the more frustrating because it is so hard to prevent, since terrorists have a virtually unlimited menu of methods and targets. Bombs on a train. An airplane crashed into a skyscraper. Anthrax sent through the mail. After an attack like 9/11 in the United States or 7/7 in London, a massive amount of resources is inevitably deployed to shield the most precious targets, but there is a Sisyphean element to such a task. Rather than walling off every target a terrorist may attack, what you'd really like to do is figure out who the terrorists are *before* they strike and throw them in jail.

The good news is there aren't many terrorists. This is a natural conclusion if you consider the relative ease of carrying out a terrorist attack and the relative scarcity of such attacks. There has been a near absence of terrorism on U.S. soil since September 11; in the United Kingdom, terrorists are probably more prevalent but still exceedingly rare.

The bad news is the scarcity of terrorists makes them hard to find before they do damage. Anti-terror efforts are traditionally built around three activities: gathering human intelligence, which is difficult and dangerous; monitoring electronic "chatter," which can be like trying to sip from a fire hose; and following the international money trail—which, considering the trillions of dollars sloshing around the world's banks every day, is like trying to sift the entire beach for a few particular grains of sand. The nineteen men behind the September 11 attacks funded their entire operation with $303,671.62, or less than $16,000 per person.

Might there be a fourth tactic that could help find terrorists?

Ian Horsley believes there may. He doesn't work in law enforcement, or in government or the military, nor does anything in his background or manner suggest he might be the least bit heroic. He grew up in the

This name is, for reasons that will soon become apparent, a pseudonym. All other facts about him are real.

TOP: COURTESY FBI

heart of England, the son of an electrical engineer, and is now well into middle age. He still lives happily far from the maddening thrum of London. While perfectly affable, he isn't outgoing or jolly by any measure; Horsley is, in his own words, "completely average and utterly forgettable."

Growing up, he thought he might like to be an accountant. But he left school when his girlfriend's father helped him get a job as a bank cashier. He took on new positions at the bank as they arose, none of them particularly interesting or profitable. One job, in computer programming, turned out to be a bit more intriguing because it gave him "a fundamental understanding of the underlying database that the bank operates on," he says.

Horsley proved to be diligent, a keen observer of human behavior, and a man who plainly knew right from wrong. Eventually he was asked to sniff out fraud among bank employees, and in time he graduated to consumer fraud, which was a far wider threat to the bank. U.K. banks lose about $1.5 billion annually to such fraud. In recent years, it had been facilitated by two forces: the rise of online banking and the fierce competition among banks to snag new business.

For a time, money was so cheap and credit so easy that anyone with a pulse, regardless of employment or citizenship or creditworthiness, could walk into a British bank and walk out with a debit card. (In truth, even a pulse wasn't necessary: fraudsters were happy to use the identities of dead and fictional people as well.) Horsley learned the customs of various subgroups. West African immigrants were master check washers, while Eastern Europeans were the best identity thieves. Such fraudsters were relentless and creative: they would track down a bank's call center and linger outside until an employee exited, offering a bribe for customers' information.

Horsley built a team of data analysts and profilers who wrote computer programs that could crawl through the bank's database and detect fraudulent activity. The programmers were good. The fraudsters were also good, and nimble too, devising new scams as soon as old ones were compromised. These rapid mutations sharpened Horsley's ability to think like a fraudster. Even in his sleep, his mind cruised through billions upon billions of bank data points, seeking out patterns that might betray wrongdoing. His algorithms got tighter and tighter.

We had the good fortune to meet Ian Horsley at about this time and, jointly, we began to wonder: if his algorithms could sift through an end-

Card skimming is one particularly clever scam. Here's how it works. A fraudster selects an ATM machine and, usually late at night, installs a card skimmer over the slot where you normally dip your card. The transaction goes off as usual, but the skimmer records the data from your card's magnetic strip; your PIN is also recorded, either by a pinhole camera or a plate placed over the keyboard. Armed with your data and PIN, a fraudster can easily clone your card.

This card skimmer was recovered by police from a Citibank ATM near Los Angeles in late 2009. In the first photo, the skimmer fits snugly over the original card reader slot. But as can be seen in the second photo, an ATM user would never see the telltale cutout.

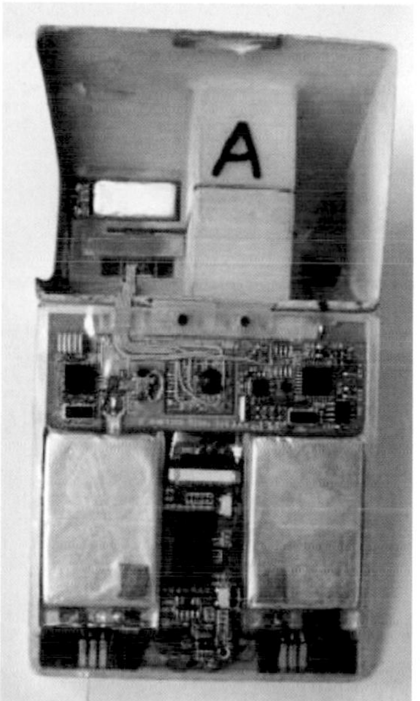

A rear view of the skimmer shows its circuitry, which may have been cannibalized from an MP3 player.

less stream of retail banking data and successfully detect fraudsters, might the same data be coaxed to identify other bad guys, like would-be terrorists?

This hunch was supported by the data trail from the September 11 attacks. The banking histories of those nineteen terrorists revealed some behaviors that, in the aggregate, distinguished them from the typical bank customer:

- They opened their U.S. accounts with cash or cash equivalents, in the average amount of roughly $4,000, usually at a branch of a large, well-known bank.
- They typically used a P.O. box as an address, and the addresses changed frequently.
- Some of them regularly sent and received wire transfers to and from other countries, but these transactions were always below the limit that triggered the bank's reporting requirements.
- They tended to make one large deposit and then withdraw cash in small amounts over time.
- Their banking didn't reflect normal living expenses like rent, utilities, auto payments, insurance, and so on.
- There was no typical monthly consistency in the timing of their deposits or withdrawals.
- They didn't use savings accounts or safe-deposit boxes.
- The ratio of cash withdrawals to checks written was unusually high.

It is obviously easier to retroactively create a banking profile of a proven terrorist than to build one that would identify a terrorist before he acts. Nor would a profile of these nineteen men—foreign nationals living in the United States who were training to hijack jetliners—necessarily fit the profile of, say, a homegrown suicide bomber in London.

Furthermore, when data have been used in the past to identify wrongdoing—like the cheating schoolteachers and collusive sumo wrestlers we wrote about in *Freakonomics*—there was a relatively high prevalence of fraud among a targeted population. But in this case, the population was gigantic (Horsley's bank alone had many millions of customers) while the number of potential terrorists was very small.

COURTESY BRIAN KREBS, KREBSONSECURITY.COM

Let's say, however, you *could* develop a banking algorithm that was 99 percent accurate. We'll assume the United Kingdom has 500 terrorists. The algorithm would correctly identify 495 of them, or 99 percent. But there are roughly 50 million adults in the United Kingdom who have nothing to do with terrorism, and the algorithm would also wrongly identify 1 percent of *them*, or 500,000 people. At the end of the day, this wonderful, 99-percent-accurate algorithm spits out too many false positives—half a million people who would be rightly indignant when they were hauled in by the authorities on suspicion of terrorism.

Nor, of course, could the authorities handle the workload.

This is a common problem in health care. A review of a recent cancer-screening trial showed that 50 percent of the 68,000 participants got at least 1 false-positive result after undergoing 14 tests. So although health-care advocates may urge universal screening for all sorts of maladies, the reality is that the system would be overwhelmed by false positives and the sick would be crowded out. The baseball player Mike Lowell, a recent World Series MVP, underscored a related problem while discussing a plan to test every ballplayer in the league for human growth hormone. "If it's 99 percent accurate, that's going to be 7 false positives," Lowell said. "What if one of the false positives is Cal Ripken? Doesn't it put a black mark on his career?"

Similarly, if you want to hunt terrorists, 99 percent accurate is not even close to good enough.

On July 7, 2005, four Islamic suicide bombers struck in London, one on a crowded bus and three in the Underground. The murder toll was fifty-two. "Personally, I was devastated by it," Horsley recalls. "We were just starting to work on identifying terrorists and I thought maybe, just maybe, if we had started a couple years earlier, would we have stopped it?"

The 7/7 bombers left behind some banking data, but not much. In the coming months, however, a flock of suspicious characters accommodated our terrorist-detection project by getting themselves arrested by the British police. Granted, none of these men were *proven* terrorists; most of them would

When the 19 terrorists who hijacked American jetliners on Sept. 11, 2001, entered the U.S., several of them opened checking accounts. Here's a look at their total inflows and outflows.

TOTALS FOR 19 HIJACKERS

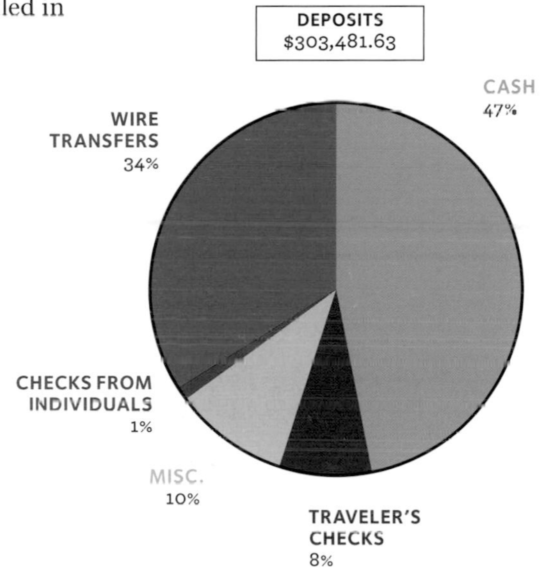

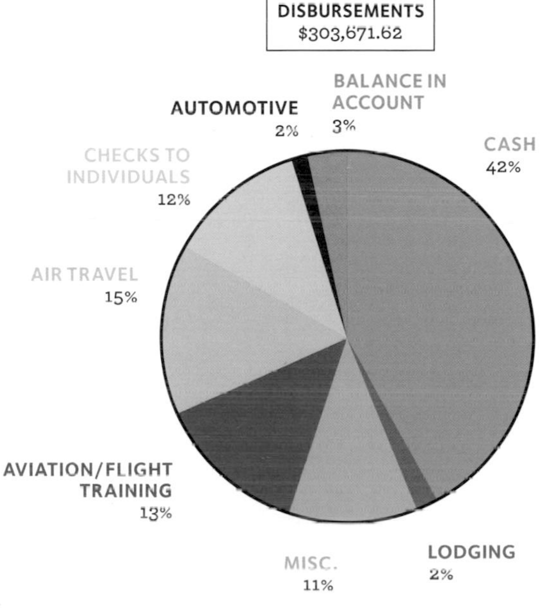

The British government and law enforcement agencies have been proactive in asking banks (and their customers) to look out for terrorists, as seen on this poster, issued by the Metropolitan Police.

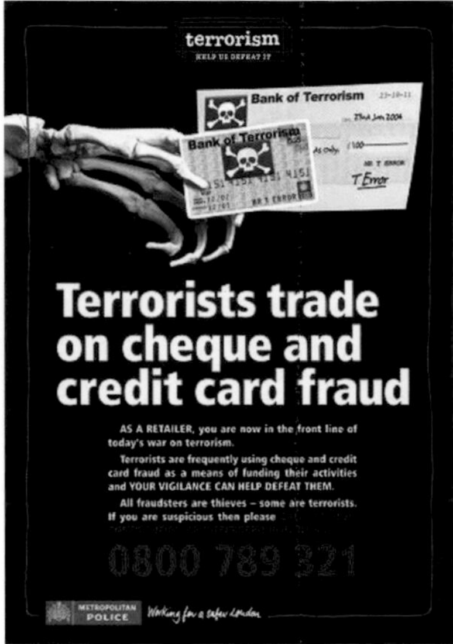

never be convicted of anything. But if they resembled a terrorist closely enough to get arrested, perhaps their banking habits could be mined to create a useful algorithm. As luck would have it, more than a hundred of these suspects were customers at Horsley's bank.

The procedure would require two steps. First, assemble all the available data on these hundred-plus suspects and create an algorithm based on the patterns that set these men apart from the general population. Once the algorithm was successfully fine-tuned, it could be used to dredge through the bank's database to identify other potential bad guys.

Given that the United Kingdom was battling Islamic fundamentalists and no longer, for instance, Irish militants, the arrested suspects invariably had Muslim names. This would turn out to be one of the strongest demographic markers for the algorithm. A person with neither a first nor a last Muslim name stood only a 1 in 500,000 chance of being a suspected terrorist. The likelihood for a person with a first *or* a last Muslim name was 1 in 30,000. For a person with first *and* last Muslim names, however, the likelihood jumped to 1 in 2,000.

The likely terrorists were predominately men, most commonly between the ages of twenty-six and thirty-five. Furthermore, they were disproportionately likely to:

- Own a mobile phone
- Be a student
- Rent, rather than own, a home

These traits, on their own, would hardly be grounds for arrest. (They describe just about every research assistant the two of us have ever had, and we are pretty sure none of them are terrorists.) But, when stacked atop the Muslim-name markers, even these common traits began to add power to the algorithm.

Once the preceding factors were taken into account, several other characteristics proved fundamentally neutral, not identifying terrorists one way or another. They included:

- Employment status
- Marital status
- Living in close proximity to a mosque

A poster in support of the (Provisional) Irish Republican Army (IRA). From 1916 through 1997, various Irish revolutionaries carried out attacks aimed at removing British troops from Northern Ireland and establishing a united Irish state.

BOTTOM: UNIVERSITY OF ULSTER

So contrary to common perception, a single, unemployed, twenty-six-year-old man who lived next door to a mosque was no more likely to be a terrorist than another twenty-six-year-old who had a wife, a job, and lived five miles from the mosque.

There were also some prominent negative indicators. The data showed that a would-be terrorist was disproportionately *un*likely to:

- Have a savings account
- Withdraw money from an ATM on a Friday afternoon
- Buy life insurance

The no-ATM-on-Friday metric would seem to be a proxy for a Muslim who attends that day's mandatory prayer service. The life insurance marker is a bit more interesting. Let's say you're a twenty-six-year-old man, married with two young children. It probably makes sense to buy some life insurance so your family can survive if you happen to die young. But an insurance company may not pay out if the policyholder commits a suicide bombing. So a twenty-six-year-old family man who suspects he may one day blow himself up may not waste money on life insurance.

This all suggests that if a budding terrorist wants to cover his tracks, he should go down to the bank and change the name on his account to something very un-Muslim (Ian, perhaps). It also wouldn't hurt to buy some life insurance. Horsley's own bank offers starter policies for just a few quid per month.

All these metrics, once combined, did a pretty good job of creating an algorithm that could distill the bank's entire customer base into a relatively small group of potential terrorists.

It was a tight net but not yet tight enough. What finally made it work was one last metric that dramatically sharpened the algorithm. In the interest of national security, we have been asked to not disclose the particulars; we'll call it Variable X.

What makes Variable X so special? For one, it is a behavioral metric, not a demographic one. The dream of anti-terrorist authorities everywhere is to somehow become a fly on the wall in a roomful of terrorists. In one

Some of the research assistants we've had in recent years. Despite their demographic markers, you would be hard-pressed to find a terrorist among them (we hope). Left to right, top to bottom: Ryan Hagen, Dana Chandler, Adam Castor, Jeff Picel, Steve Cicala, Ethan Lieber, Kris Hult, Dimitrios Batzilis, Massimo Young, Nick Simmons, David Greis, and Trevor Gallen.

HEADSHOTS COURTESY OF THE RESEARCH ASSISTANTS

How valuable would it be to actually have a fly on the wall in a terrorist lair? "Their ears wouldn't be able to hear a conversation the way humans do," says Michael Dickinson, a fly-obsessed bioengineer at Caltech. "They couldn't hear something unless it was said very nearby." But they could see quite well—as long as the room's occupants were moving. "Fly vision is based on motion," Dickinson says. "So if nothing was moving in the room, it would slowly fade to a nothingness that we cannot understand. Of course the fly could itself move, and then it would get an image. They also have exquisite noses, so they could smell what was being drunk in the room. They could smell pretty much anything, depending on the type of fly, but it could be as innocuous as water vapor." Or as dangerous as explosive powder.

small, important way, Variable X accomplishes that. Unlike most other metrics in the algorithm, which produce a yes or no answer, Variable X measures the *intensity* of a particular banking activity. While not unusual in low intensities among the general population, this behavior occurs in high intensities much more frequently among those who have other terrorist markers.

This ultimately gave the algorithm great predictive power. Starting with a database of millions of bank customers, Horsley was able to generate a list of about 30 highly suspicious individuals. According to his rather conservative estimate, at least 5 of those 30 are almost certainly involved in terrorist activities. Five out of 30 isn't perfect—the algorithm misses many terrorists and still falsely identifies some innocents—but it sure beats 495 out of 500,495.

As of this writing, Horsley has handed off the list of 30 to his superiors, who in turn have handed it off to the proper authorities. Horsley has done his work; now it is time for them to do theirs. Given the nature of the problem, Horsley may never know for certain if he was successful. And you, the reader, are even less likely to see direct evidence of his success because it would be invisible, manifesting itself in terrorist attacks that never happen.

But perhaps you'll find yourself in a British pub some distant day, one stool away from an unassuming, slightly standoffish stranger. You have a pint with him, and then another and a third. With his tongue loosened a bit, he mentions, almost sheepishly, that he has recently gained an honorific: he is now known as Sir Ian Horsley. He's not at liberty to discuss the deeds that led to his knighthood, but it has something to do with protecting civil society from those who would do it great harm. You thank him profusely for the great service he has performed, and buy him another pint, and then a few more. When the pub at last closes, the two of you stumble outside. And then, just as he is about to set off on foot down a darkened lane, you think of a very small way to repay his service. You push him back onto the curb, hail a taxi, and stuff him inside. Because, remember, friends don't let friends walk drunk.

CHAPTER 3

UNBELIEVABLE STORIES ABOUT APATHY AND ALTRUISM

IN MARCH 1964, LATE ON A COLD AND DAMP THURSDAY night, something terrible happened in New York City, something suggesting that human beings are the most brutally selfish animals to ever roam the planet.

A twenty-eight-year-old woman named Kitty Genovese drove home from work and parked, as usual, in the lot at the Long Island Rail Road station. She lived in Kew Gardens, Queens, roughly twenty minutes by train from Manhattan. It was a nice neighborhood, with tidy homes on shaded lots, a handful of apartment buildings, and a small commercial district.

Genovese lived above a row of shops that fronted Austin Street. The entrance to her apartment was around the rear. She got out of her car and locked it; almost immediately, a man started chasing her and stabbed her in the back. Genovese screamed. The assault took place on the sidewalk in front of the Austin Street shops and across the street from a ten-story apartment building called the Mowbray.

The assailant, whose name was Winston Moseley, retreated to his car, a white Corvair parked at the curb some sixty yards away. He put the car in reverse and backed it down the block, passing out of view.

Genovese, meanwhile, staggered to her feet and made her way around to the back of her building. But in a short time Moseley returned. He sexually

NEW YORK DAILY NEWS

Kitty Genovese in a photo likely taken at Ev's Eleventh Hour, the Queens tavern where she worked.

assaulted her and stabbed her again, leaving Genovese to die. Then he got back in his car and drove home. Like Genovese, he was young, twenty-nine years old, and he too lived in Queens. His wife was a registered nurse; they had two children. On the drive home, Moseley noticed another car stopped at a red light, its driver asleep at the wheel. Moseley got out and woke the man. He didn't hurt or rob him. The next morning, Moseley went to work as usual.

The crime soon became infamous. But not because Moseley was a psychopath—a seemingly normal family man who, although he had no criminal record, turned out to have a history of grotesque sexual violence. And it wasn't because Genovese was a colorful character herself, a tavern manager who happened to be a lesbian and had a prior gambling arrest. Nor was it because Genovese was white and Moseley was black.

The Kitty Genovese murder became infamous because of an article published on the front page of *The New York Times*. It began like this:

> *For more than half an hour 38 respectable, law-abiding citizens in Queens watched a killer stalk and stab a woman in three separate attacks in Kew Gardens.... Not one person telephoned the police during the assault; one witness called after the woman was dead.*

The murder took about thirty-five minutes from start to finish. "If we had been called when he first attacked," said a police inspector, "the woman might not be dead now."

The police had interviewed Genovese's neighbors the morning after the murder, and the *Times*'s reporter reinterviewed some of them. When asked why they hadn't intervened or at least called the police, they offered a variety of excuses:

"We thought it was a lovers' quarrel."

"We went to the window to see what was happening but the light from our bedroom made it difficult to see the street."

"I was tired. I went back to bed."

The article wasn't very long—barely fourteen hundred words—but its impact was immediate and explosive. There seemed to be general agreement that the thirty-eight witnesses in Kew Gardens represented a new low in human civilization. Politicians, theologians, and editorial writers lambasted the neighbors for their apathy. Some even called for the neighbors' addresses to be published so justice could be done.

Winston Moseley, arriving at Queens Criminal Court for his arraignment on charges of murdering Kitty Genovese.

TOM GALLAGHER/*NEW YORK DAILY NEWS*

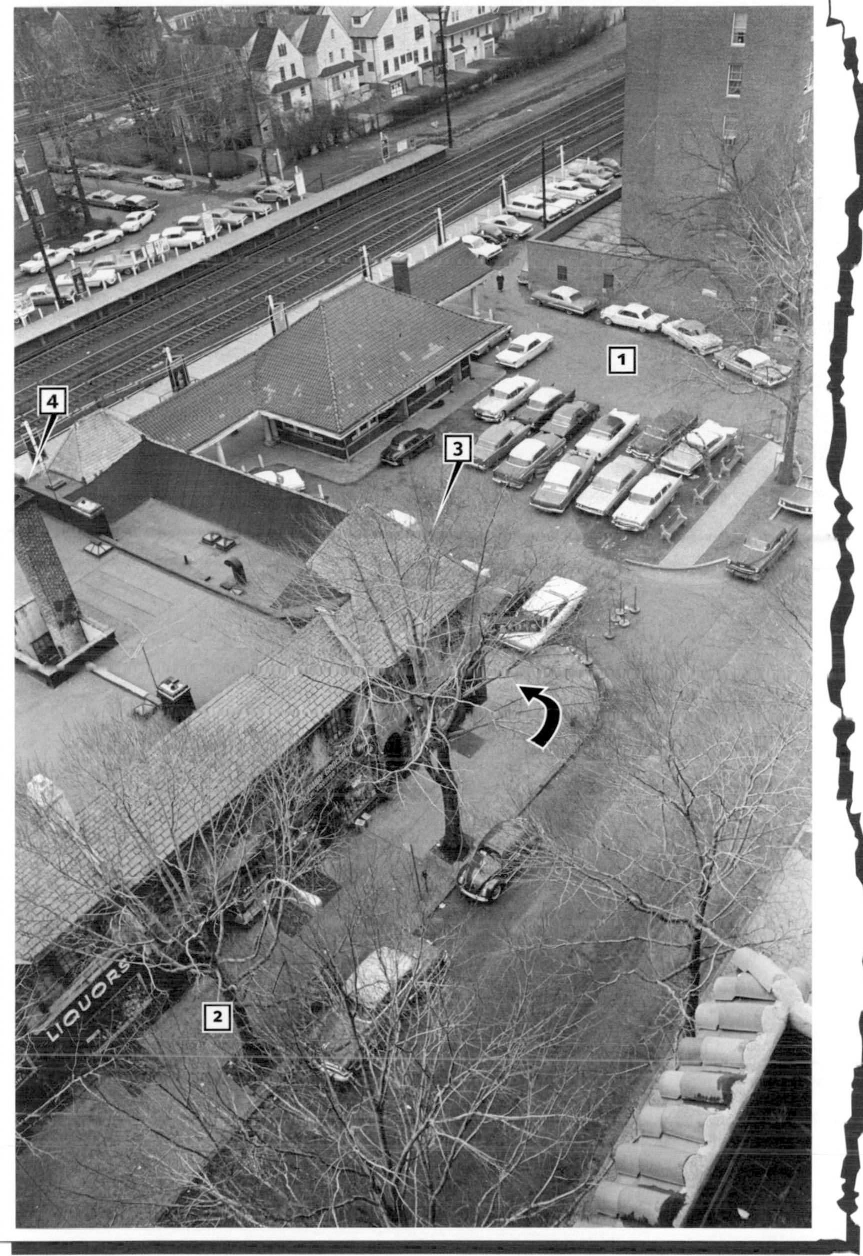

The annotated photo that ran with the *Times*'s report of Kitty Genovese's murder. The caption read:

> *At 3:20 A.M. on March 13, Miss Catherine Genovese drove into the parking lot at Kew Gardens railroad station and parked (1). Noticing a man in [the] lot, she became nervous and headed along Austin Street toward a police telephone box. The man caught and attacked her (2) with a knife. She got away, but he attacked her again (3) and again (4).*

The incident so deeply shook the nation that over the next twenty years, it inspired more academic research on bystander apathy than the Holocaust.

To mark the thirtieth anniversary, President Bill Clinton visited New York City and spoke about the crime: "It sent a chilling message about what had happened at that time in a society, suggesting that we were each of us not simply in danger but fundamentally alone."

More than thirty-five years later, the horror lived on in *The Tipping*

Point, Malcolm Gladwell's groundbreaking book about social behavior, as an example of the "bystander effect," whereby the presence of multiple witnesses at a tragedy can actually *inhibit* intervention.

Today, more than forty years later, the Kitty Genovese saga appears in all ten of the top-selling undergraduate textbooks for social psychology. One text describes the witnesses remaining "at their windows in fascination for the 30 minutes it took her assailant to complete his grisly deed, during which he returned for three separate attacks."

How on earth could thirty-eight people stand by and watch as their neighbor was brutalized? Yes, economists always talk about how self-interested we are, but doesn't this demonstration of self-interest practically defy logic? Does our apathy really run so deep?

The Genovese murder, coming just a few months after President John F. Kennedy's assassination, seemed to signal a sort of social apocalypse. Crime was exploding in cities all across the United States, and no one seemed capable of stopping it.

For decades, the rate of violent and property crimes in the United States had been steady and relatively low. But levels began to rise in the mid-1950s. By 1960, the crime rate was 50 percent higher than it had been in 1950; by 1970, the rate had *quadrupled.*

Why?

It was hard to say. So many changes were simultaneously rippling through American society in the 1960s—a population explosion, a growing anti-authoritarian sentiment, the expansion of civil rights, a wholesale shift in popular culture—that it wasn't easy to isolate the factors driving crime.

Imagine, for instance, you want to know whether putting more people in prison really lowers the crime rate. This question isn't as obvious as it may

Sensational crimes often come to stand for some broader social fear. Consider a few lowlights of the past century:

1920S

© CORBIS

LEOPOLD AND LOEB

Two young men from elite Chicago families murdered a local teenager for sport, seemingly demonstrating the corrupting power of idle wealth.

seem. Perhaps the resources devoted to catching and jailing criminals could have been used more productively. Perhaps every time a bad guy is put away, another criminal rises up to take his place.

To answer this question with some kind of scientific certainty, what you'd really like to do is conduct an experiment. Pretend you could randomly select a group of states and command each of them to release 10,000 prisoners. At the same time, you could randomly select a different group of states and have them lock up 10,000 people, misdemeanor offenders perhaps, who otherwise wouldn't have gone to prison. Now sit back, wait a few years, and measure the crime rate in those two sets of states. Voilà! You've just run the kind of randomized, controlled experiment that lets you determine the relationship between variables.

Unfortunately, the governors of those random states probably wouldn't take too kindly to your experiment. Nor would the people you sent to prison in some states or the next-door neighbors of the prisoners you freed in others. So your chances of actually conducting this experiment are zero.

That's why researchers often rely on what is known as a *natural experiment,* a set of conditions that mimic the experiment you want to conduct but, for whatever reason, cannot. In this instance, what you want is a radical change in the prison population of various states for reasons that have nothing to do with the amount of crime in those states.

Happily, the American Civil Liberties Union was good enough to create just such an experiment. In recent decades, the ACLU has filed lawsuits against dozens of states to protest overcrowded prisons. Granted, the choice of states is hardly random. The ACLU sues where prisons are most crowded and where it has the best chance of winning. But the crime trends in states sued by the ACLU look very similar to trends in other states.

The ACLU wins virtually all of these cases, after which the state is or-

THOMAS TRUMBLE

1930s

LINDBERGH KIDNAPPING

The infant son of aviation hero Charles Lindbergh was kidnapped and murdered, the butcher's bill for a culture delirious with celebrity obsession.

1940s

THE BLACK DAHLIA

The mutilation and murder of Elizabeth Short, a 22-year-old woman who'd recently moved to Los Angeles, came to represent the deepening dark side of Hollywood in the heyday of postwar noir.

dered to reduce overcrowding by letting some prisoners free. In the three years after such court decisions, the prison population in these states falls by 15 percent relative to the rest of the country.

What do those freed prisoners do? A whole lot of crime. In the three years after the ACLU wins a case, violent crime rises by 10 percent and property crime by 5 percent in the affected states.

So it takes some work, but using indirect approaches like natural experiments can help us look back at the dramatic crime increase of the 1960s and find some explanations.

One major factor was the criminal-justice system itself. The ratio of arrests per crime fell dramatically during the 1960s, for both property and violent crime. But not only were the police catching a smaller share of the criminals; the courts were less likely to lock up those who were caught. In 1970, a criminal could expect to spend an astonishing 60 percent less time behind bars than he would have for the same crime committed a decade earlier. Overall, the decrease in punishment during the 1960s seems to be responsible for roughly 30 percent of the rise in crime.

The postwar baby boom was another factor. Between 1960 and 1980, the fraction of the U.S. population between the ages of fifteen and twenty-four rose by nearly 40 percent, an unprecedented surge in the age group most at risk for criminal involvement. But even such a radical demographic shift can only account for about 10 percent of the increase in crime.

Most states try to ensure that freed prisoners have a bit of money in their pockets to get started on the outside. This usually comes in the form of prisoner account funds, noninterest-bearing bank accounts funded by wages earned or money received from outsiders during incarceration. Here's what the state of Virginia provides its prisoners upon release:

$25 PLUS PRISONER ACCOUNT FUNDS

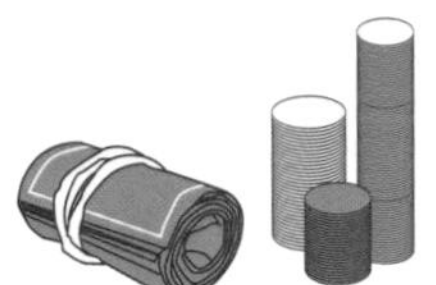

BUS TICKET TO ANYWHERE IN VIRGINIA

PICTURE ID

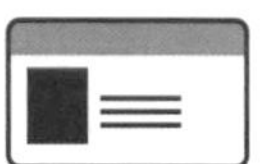

CLOTHING (IF NECESSARY)

PERSONAL PROPERTY

30-DAY SUPPLY OF ANY NECESSARY MEDICATION

1950s

THE CLUTTER MURDERS

A pair of young men burst into a Kansas farmhouse and, in cold blood, murdered Herbert and Bonnie Clutter and their two teenage children, shattering the illusion of heartland neighborliness.

1960s

KITTY GENOVESE

Was the big city so callous that a woman's neighbors could simply stand around and watch as she was murdered?

ASSOCIATED PRESS

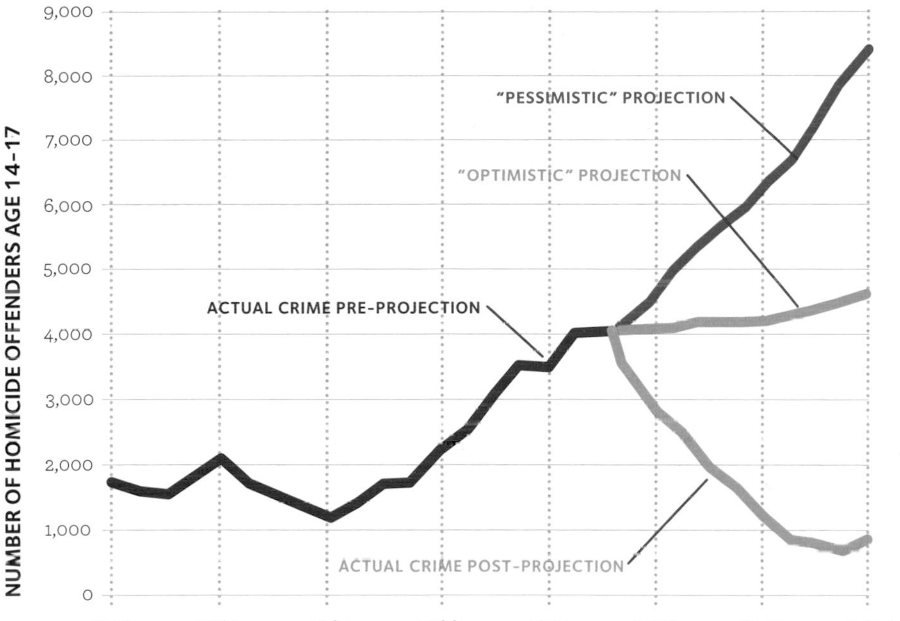

If criminologists were perplexed about the surging crime rate of the 1960s, they were baffled by the sudden drop in crime a few decades later. In a mid-1990s report to the Department of Justice, the well-regarded criminologist James Alan Fox predicted a possible doubling of teenage killers by 2004. But in reality the trend moved in exactly the opposite direction.

What led to such a sudden and unexpected crime drop? In *Freakonomics*, we examined the reasons most commonly cited in the media: innovative policing strategies; increased reliance on prisons; changes in crack and other drug markets; aging of the population; tougher gun-control laws; a strong economy; increased number of police; and capital punishment. As it turned out, only three of these factors—more police, more prisons, and a waning crack market—contributed to the falling crime rate. There was, however, one major contributing factor that didn't even make it onto the list: the legalization of abortion. As abortion became widely available, the number of unwanted children—who would be disproportionately likely to become criminals—substantially fell.

So together, the baby boom and the declining rate of imprisonment explain less than half of the crime spike. Although a host of other hypotheses have been advanced—including the great migration of African Americans from the rural South to northern cities and the return of Vietnam vets scarred by war—all of them combined still cannot explain the crime surge. Decades later, most criminologists remain perplexed.

The answer might be right in front of our faces, literally: television. Maybe Beaver Cleaver and his picture-perfect TV family weren't just a casualty of the changing times (*Leave It to Beaver* was canceled in 1963, the same year Kennedy was assassinated). Maybe they were actually a *cause* of the problem.

People have long posited that violent TV shows lead to violent behavior, but that claim is not supported by data. We are making an entirely different argument here. Our claim is that children who grew up watching a

1970S

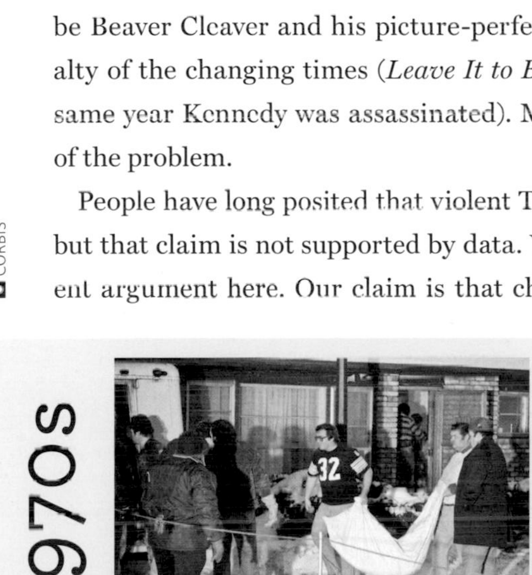

JOHN WAYNE GACY

Having tortured, raped, and murdered at least 33 men and boys, Gacy put a twisted exclamation point on the sexual turbulence of the 1970s.

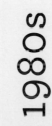

1980S

CENTRAL PARK JOGGER

The violent rape of a young woman—at first attributed to a "wolf pack" of teenagers—confirmed fears that a generation of superpredator was upon us.

lot of TV, even the most innocuous family-friendly shows, were more likely to engage in crime when they got older.

Testing this hypothesis isn't easy. You can't just compare a random bunch of kids who watched a lot of TV with those who didn't. The ones who were glued to the TV are sure to differ from the other children in countless ways beyond their viewing habits.

A more believable strategy might be to compare cities that got TV early with those that got it much later.

We wrote earlier that cable TV came to different parts of India at different times, a staggered effect that made it possible to measure TV's impact on rural Indian women. The initial rollout of TV in the United States was even bumpier. This was mainly due to a four-year interruption, from 1948 to 1952, when the Federal Communications Commission declared a moratorium on new stations so the broadcast spectrum could be reconfigured.

Some places in the United States started receiving signals in the mid-1940s while others had no TV until a decade later. As it turns out, there is a stark difference in crime trends between cities that got TV early and those that got it late. These two sets of cities had similar rates of violent crime before the introduction of TV. But by 1970, violent crime was twice as high in the cities that got TV early relative to those that got it late.

What's on TV tonight? Highlights from a long-ago viewing day:

WEDNESDAY, DECEMBER 14, 1955

3-4—Matinee Theatre: "This One Is Different," John Conte in romantic comedy about two bachelors (Color)—(4).

7:30-8:30—Disneyland: "Davy Crockett and the River Pirates," with Fess Parker, Buddy Ebsen, Jeff York, others—(7).

7:30-9, 10-11:30—Film: Million Dollar Movie: "The Intruder," with Jack Hawkins, Dennis Price, Susanne Shaw; story of a man's journey into the past—(9).

8-9—Arthur Godfrey and His Friends: Janette Davis, Frank Parker, others—(2).

8-8:30—Screen Directors Playhouse: "Lincoln's Doctor's Dog," Robert Ryan as Lincoln; Charles Bickford as Dr. Stone; Richard Long as Presidential aide; story of a light note supplied by puppy in critical time—(4).

8:30-9—Father Knows Best: With Robert Young, Jane Wyatt, Billy Gray, Lee Erickson, others, in "Bad Influence"—(4).

8:30-9—M-G-M Parade: George Murphy, host; scene from "Mutiny on the Bounty," other motion pictures; Howard Keel, guest—(7).

9-10—Television Theatre: "A Nugget From the Sunrise," with Elizabeth Ross, Henry Jones, Jane Rose, Harry Townes, John McGiver; comedy of a young woman who tries to win an eligible bachelor in a Nevada ghost town—(4).

9-9:30—Hollywood Preview: Scenes from new motion pictures; Conrad Nagel host to Jayne Mansfield, Frank Borzage—(5).

9-9:30—Masquerade Party: Disguised celebrities; Peter Donald host to Mary Healy, Ilka Chase, Ogden Nash, Bobby Sherwood—(7).

9—Basketball: Fordham vs. Rhode Island—(13).

9:30—I've Got a Secret: Garry Moore, host; panelists are Bill Cullen, Henry Morgan, Jayne Meadows and guest—(2).

9:30-10—Break the Bank: Bert Parks host in audience participation quiz—(7).

10-11—Play: "Miracle on 34th Street," with Macdonald Carey, Teresa Wright, Thomas Mitchell; comedy about a Santa Claus in a New York City department store—(2).

10—Boxing: Gil Turner vs. Jackie LaBua in ten-round middleweight bout, Syracuse—(7).

10-10:30—I Led Three Lives: Richard Carlson as F. B. I. counterspy—(11).

10:30-11—Douglas Fairbanks Jr. Presents: "The Immigrant," with Andre Morell; story of intrigue on a Polish ship—(4).

11:15-1—Film: Late Show: "The Long Night," with Henry Fonda, Barbara Bel Geddes; story of a man who kills his rival for the affections of a girl—(2).

11:20-1—Tonight—Steve Allen: Guests are Robert Maxwell, harpist; Anna Russell, singing comedienne—(4).

1990s

O. J. SIMPSON

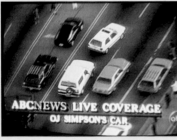

The ex-football star's flight from police and his ensuing murder trial triggered an era of obsessional media coverage whenever any famous person did anything vaguely infamous.

2000s

LACI PETERSON

When a 27-year-old pregnant woman was murdered by her husband, it reminded a country shaken by a devastating terrorist attack that psychotic violence could still strike at home.

For property crime, the early-TV cities started with much *lower* rates in the 1940s than the late-TV cities, but ended up with much higher rates.

One of the earliest mentions of TV as an "electronic babysitter" came in May 1950 from an NBC programming executive named Judith Waller. "We should all realize that the child parked in front of a television or radio set is not just under the care of an electronic babysitter," she told a gathering of 3,000 delegates to the National Congress of Parents and Teachers. And yet, she argued, the blessings of TV and radio "far outnumber their curses, and some of their curses are disguised as blessings."

There may of course be other differences between the early-TV cities and the late-TV cities. To get around that, we can compare children born in the *same* city in, say, 1950 and 1955. So in a city that got TV in 1954, we are comparing one age group that had no TV for the first four years of life with another that had TV the entire time. Because of the staggered introduction of TV, the cutoff between the age groups that grew up with and without TV in their early years varies widely across cities. This leads to specific predictions about which cities will see crime rise earlier than others—as well as the age of the criminals doing the crimes.

So did the introduction of TV have any discernible effect on a given city's crime rate?

The answer seems to be yes, indeed. For every extra year a young person was exposed to TV in his first 15 years, we see a 4 percent increase in the number of property-crime arrests later in life and a 2 percent increase in violent-crime arrests. According to our analysis, the total impact of TV on crime in the 1960s was an increase of 50 percent in property crimes and 25 percent in violent crimes.

Why did TV have this dramatic effect?

Our data offer no firm answers. The effect is largest for children who had extra TV exposure from birth to age four. Since most four-year-olds weren't watching violent shows, it's hard to argue that content was the problem.

A white student in Little Rock, Ark., being educated via television while the city closed its schools to avoid integration.

TOP: ESTHER BUBLEY, U.S. CHILDREN'S BUREAU, COURTESY WESLEYAN UNIVERSITY PRESS; BOTTOM: LIBRARY OF CONGRESS

It may be that kids who watched a lot of TV never got properly socialized, or never learned to entertain themselves. Perhaps TV made the have-nots want the things the haves had, even if it meant stealing them. Or maybe it had nothing to do with the kids at all; maybe Mom and Dad became derelict when they discovered that watching TV was a lot more entertaining than taking care of the kids.

Or maybe early TV programs somehow *encouraged* criminal behavior. *The Andy Griffith Show,* a huge hit that debuted in 1960, featured a friendly sheriff who didn't carry a gun and his extravagantly inept dep-

A selection of Gary Becker's research papers reveals his unusual worldview:

"Crime and Punishment: An Economic Approach," *Journal of Political Economy*, 1968.

"The Forces Determining Discrimination in the Marketplace," in *The Economics of Discrimination*, 1971.

"On the Interaction Between the Quantity and Quality of Children," with H. Gregg Lewis, *Journal of Political Economy*, 1971.

"An Economic Analysis of Marital Instability," with Elisabeth M. Landes and Robert T. Michael, *Journal of Political Economy*, 1977.

"Altruism in the Family and Selfishness in the Market Place," *Economica*, 1981.

"Human Capital, Effort, and the Sexual Division of Labor," *Journal of Labor Economics*, 1985.

"A Theory of Rational Addiction," with Kevin Murphy, *Journal of Political Economy*, 1988.

"Status, Lotteries and Inequality," with Kevin Murphy and Iván Werning, working paper, 2000.

"Suicide: An Economic Approach," with Richard A. Posner, working paper, 2004.

"On the Economics of Capital Punishment," *Economists' Voice*, 2006.

"Evolutionary Efficiency and Happiness," with Luis Rayo, *Journal of Political Economy*, 2007.

"Introducing Incentives in the Market for Live and Cadaveric Organ Donations," with Julio Jorge Elías, *Journal of Economic Perspectives*, 2007.

Gary Becker, the University of Chicago's resident iconoclast.

COURTESY UNIVERSITY OF CHICAGO

uty, named Barney Fife. Could it be that all the would-be criminals who watched this pair on TV concluded that the police simply weren't worth being afraid of?

As a society, we've come to accept that some bad apples will commit crimes. But that still doesn't explain why none of Kitty Genovese's neighbors—regular people, good people—stepped in to help. We all witness acts of altruism, large and small, just about every day. (We may even commit some ourselves.) So why didn't a single person exhibit altruism on that night in Queens?

A question like this may seem to fall beyond the realm of economics. Sure, liquidity crunches and oil prices and even collateralized debt obligations—but social behaviors like altruism? Is that really what economists do?

For hundreds of years, the answer was no. But around the time of the Genovese murder, a few renegade economists had begun to care deeply about such things. Chief among them was Gary Becker, whom we met earlier, in this book's introduction. Not satisfied with just measuring the economic choices people make, Becker tried to incorporate the sentiments they attached to such choices.

Some of Becker's most compelling research concerned altruism. He argued, for instance, that the same person who might be purely selfish in business could be exceedingly altruistic among people he knew—although, importantly (Becker *is* an economist, after all), he predicted that altruism even within a family would have a strategic element. Years later, the economists Doug Bernheim, Andrei Shleifer, and Larry Summers empirically demonstrated Becker's point. Using data from a U.S. government longitudinal study, they showed that an elderly parent in a retirement home is more likely to be visited by his grown children if they are expecting a sizable inheritance.

But wait, you say: maybe the offspring of wealthy families are simply more caring toward their elderly parents?

A reasonable conjecture—in which case you'd expect an only child of wealthy parents to be especially dutiful. But the data show no increase in retirement-home visits if a wealthy family has only one grown child; there need to be at least two. This suggests that the visits increase because of competition between siblings for the parent's estate. What might look like good old-fashioned intrafamilial altruism may be a sort of prepaid inheritance tax.

Some governments, wise to the ways of the world, have gone so far as to legally require grown children to visit or support their aging moms and dads. In Singapore, the law is known as the Maintenance of Parents Act.

Still, people appear to be extraordinarily altruistic, and not just within their own families. Americans in particular are famously generous, donating about $300 billion a year to charity, more than 2 percent of the nation's GDP. Just think back to the last hurricane or earthquake that killed

The Maintenance of Parents Act stipulates that any Singapore citizen "who is of or above 60 years of age and who is unable to maintain himself adequately... may apply to the Tribunal for an order that one or more of his children pay him a monthly allowance or any other periodical payment or a lump sum for his maintenance." The Tribunal, composed of at least three government appointees, may fine an offending child up to $5,000 and/or imprison him for up to six months. Above: Singaporeans Lam Kien Seak, 90, a retired pawnshop worker, and his wife, Ho Show Lan, 84, outside their home. The photo was taken by their granddaughter Lynette Lan, who would be nice to them even if the law did not require it.

The economist Andrei Shleifer with his son Danny, the middle of three children. What sort of devotion should aging parents expect from their offspring? *The Memoirs of Glückel of Hameln,* a centuries-old story of a German-Jewish widow with fourteen children, contains one answer:

A bird once set out to cross a windy sea with its three fledglings. The sea was so wide and the wind so strong, the father bird was forced to carry his young, one by one, in his strong claws. When he was halfway across with the first fledgling the wind turned to a gale, and he said, "My child, look how I am struggling and risking my life in your behalf. When you are grown up, will you do as much for me and provide for my old age?"

The fledgling replied, "Only bring me to safety, and when you are old I shall do everything you ask of me." Whereat the father bird dropped his child into the sea and it drowned, and he said, "So shall it be done to such a liar as you."

Then the father bird returned to shore, set forth with his second fledgling, asked the same question, and receiving the same answer, drowned the second child with the cry, "You, too, are a liar!"

Finally he set out with the third fledgling, and when he asked the same question, the third and last fledgling replied, "My dear father, it is true you are struggling mightily and risking your life in my behalf, and I shall be wrong not to repay you when you are old, but I cannot bind myself. This though I can promise: when I am grown up and have children of my own, I shall do as much for them as you have done for me."

Whereupon the father bird said, "Well-spoken, my child, and wisely; your life I will spare and I will carry you to shore in safety."

TOP: LYNETTE LAN. FLICKR.COM/LYNETTELAN; BOTTOM: NANCY ZIMMERMAN; *THE MEMOIRS OF GLÜCKEL OF HAMELN,* TRANSLATED BY MARVIN LOWENTHAL, COURTESY SCHOCKEN BOOKS

An early-twentieth-century barn raising in what is now North York City Centre, Toronto. It typically took one day to put up a new barn: the men did the building and the women kept them fed.

a lot of people, and recall how Good Samaritans rushed forward with their money and time.

But why?

Economists have traditionally assumed that the typical person makes rational decisions in line with his own self-interest. So why should this rational fellow—*Homo economicus,* he is usually called—give away some of his hard-earned cash to someone he doesn't know in a place he can't pronounce in return for nothing more than a warm, fuzzy glow?

Building on Gary Becker's work, a new generation of economists decided it was time to understand altruism in the world at large. But how? How can we know whether an act is altruistic or self-serving? If you help rebuild a neighbor's barn, is it because you're a moral person or because you know your own barn might burn down someday? When a donor gives millions to his alma mater, is it because he cares about the pursuit of knowledge or because he gets his name plastered on the football stadium?

Sorting out such things in the real world is extremely hard. While it is easy to observe actions—or, in the Kitty Genovese case, *in*action—it is much harder to understand the intentions behind an action.

Is it possible to use natural experiments, like the ACLU-prison scenario, to measure altruism? You might consider, for instance, looking at a series of calamities to see how much charitable contribution they produce. But with so many variables, it would be hard to tease out the altruism from everything else. A crippling earthquake in China is not the same as a scorching drought in Africa, which is not the same as a devastating hurricane in New Orleans. Each disaster has its own sort of "appeal"—and, just as important, donations are heavily influenced by media coverage. One recent academic study found that a given disaster received an 18 percent spike in charitable aid for each seven-hundred-word newspaper article and a 13 percent spike for every sixty seconds of TV news coverage. (Anyone hoping to raise money for a Third World disaster had better hope it happens on a slow news day.) And such disasters are by their nature anomalies—especially noisy ones, like shark attacks—that probably don't have much to say about our baseline altruism.

In the wake of a natural disaster, what exactly does the media cover? Scholars have found that most victims help one another out, but the media tends to focus on whatever desperate or violent people can be found—looters, for instance. When looting images dominated the news coverage of a Chilean earthquake in early 2010, some Chileans barricaded their neighborhoods—an action of "collective psychosis," as one resident told *The New York Times.* "People begin imagining things and making themselves afraid," he said, "but it's not real."

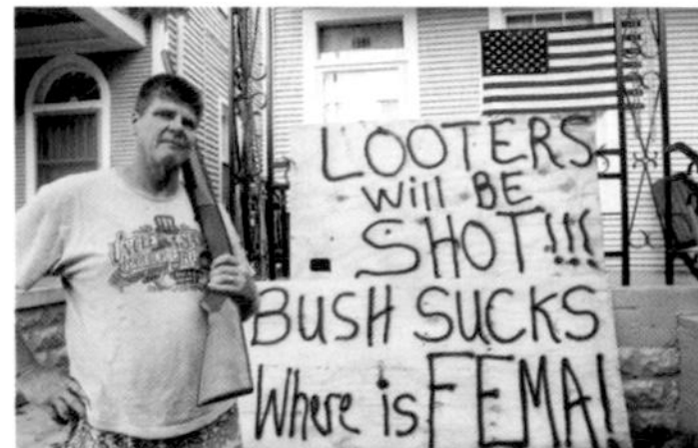

In New Orleans, Chris Horrigan protects his property after Hurricane Katrina struck in 2005.

TOP: ALEXANDER W. GALBRAITH, COURTESY CITY OF TORONTO ARCHIVES; BOTTOM: Q. SAKAMAKI

In time, those renegade economists took a different approach: since altruism is so hard to measure in the real world, why not peel away all the real world's inherent complexities by bringing the subject into the laboratory?

Laboratory experiments are of course a pillar of the physical sciences and have been since Galileo Galilei rolled a bronze ball down a length of wooden molding to test his theory of acceleration. Galileo believed—correctly, as it turned out—that a small creation like his could lead to a better understanding of the greatest creations known to humankind: the earth's forces, the order of the skies, the workings of human life itself.

More than three centuries later, the physicist Richard Feynman reasserted the primacy of this belief. "The test of all knowledge is experiment," he said. "Experiment is the sole judge of scientific 'truth.'" The electricity you use, the cholesterol drug you swallow, the page or screen or speaker from which you are consuming these very words—they are all the product of a great deal of experimentation.

Economists, however, have never been as reliant on the lab. Most of the problems they traditionally worry about—the effect of tax increases, for instance, or the causes of inflation—are difficult to capture there. But if the lab could unravel the scientific mysteries of the universe, surely it could help figure out something as benign as altruism.

These new experiments typically took the form of a game, run by college professors and played by their students. This path had been paved by the beautiful mind of John Nash and other economists who, in the 1950s, experimented broadly with the Prisoner's Dilemma, a game-theory problem that came to be seen as a classic test of strategic cooperation. (It was invented to glean insights about the nuclear standoff between the United States and the Soviet Union.)

By the early 1980s, the Prisoner's Dilemma had inspired a lab game called Ultimatum, which works as follows. Two players, who remain anonymous to each other, have a onetime chance to split a sum of money. Player 1 (let's call her Annika) is given $20 and is instructed to offer any amount, from $0 to $20, to Player 2 (we'll call her Zelda).

Richard Feynman, who won a Nobel Prize in 1965 for his work in quantum physics, was also an avid bongo player, lock picker, and enthusiast of the Tuvan art of throat singing. In 1986, he made headlines for the experiment he performed as part of a presidential commission investigating the explosion of the U.S. space shuttle *Challenger*. Dunking an O-ring seal into a glass of ice water and then compressing it in a clamp, Feynman demonstrated that the shuttle's O-rings were prone to fail under pressure in cold temperatures—a fatal flaw that led to the explosion of the shuttle.

BETTMANN/CORBIS

ULTIMATUM!
AVOID REJECTION! BE A WINNER!
ULTIMATUM! AVOID REJECTION! BE A WINNER!

The play-at-home versions.

Zelda must decide whether to accept or reject Annika's offer. If she accepts, they split the money according to Annika's offer. But if she rejects, they both go home empty-handed. Both players know all these rules coming into the game.

To an economist, the strategy is obvious. Since even a penny is more valuable than nothing, it makes sense for Zelda to accept an offer as low as a penny—and, therefore, it makes sense for Annika to *offer* just a penny, keeping $19.99 for herself.

But, economists be damned, that's not how normal people played the game. The Zeldas usually rejected offers below $3. They were apparently so disgusted by a lowball offer that they were willing to pay to express their disgust. Not that lowball offers happened very often. On average, the Annikas offered the Zeldas more than $6. Given how the game works, an offer this large was clearly meant to ward off rejection. But still, an average of $6—almost a third of the total amount—seemed pretty generous.

Does that make it altruism?

Maybe, but probably not. The Ultimatum player making the offer has something to gain—the avoidance of rejection—by giving more generously. As often happens in the real world, seemingly kind behaviors in Ultimatum are inextricably tied in with potentially selfish motivations.

Enter, therefore, a new and ingenious variant of Ultimatum, this one called Dictator. Once again, a small pool of money is divided between two people. But in this case, only one person gets to make a decision. (Thus the name: the "dictator" is the only player who matters.)

The original Dictator experiment went like this. Annika was given $20 and told she could split the money with some anonymous Zelda in one of two ways: (1) right down the middle, with each person getting $10; or (2) with Annika keeping $18 and giving Zelda just $2.

Smile Train, a charity that performs cleft-palate surgery on poor children around the world, works hard to shatter the anonymity that might discourage giving. For the photographs that potential donors will see, the child looks directly at the camera. Photos taken before the operation tend to show a sad child; afterward, a happy child. The idea is to establish a personal connection to an otherwise abstract problem, which research shows can increase altruism. Below, a Smile Train beneficiary named Juliana, before and after her cleft-palate surgery.

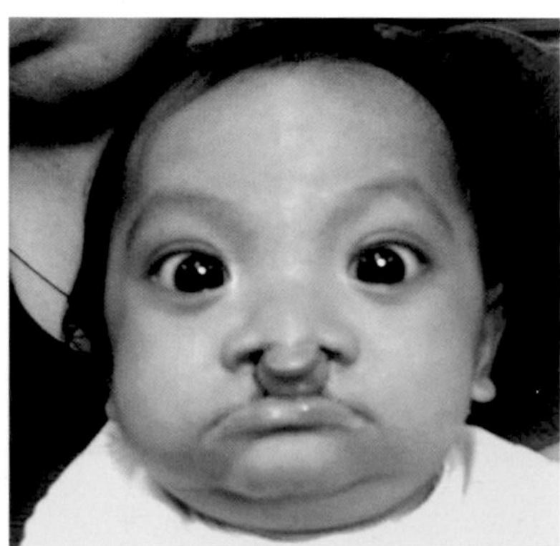

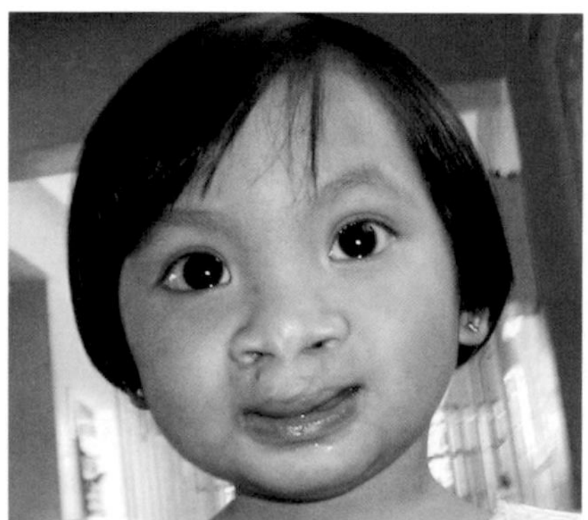

COURTESY SMILE TRAIN

Dictator was brilliant in its simplicity. As a one-shot game between two anonymous parties, it seemed to strip out all the complicating factors of real-world altruism. Generosity could not be rewarded, nor could selfishness be punished, because the second player (the one who wasn't the dictator) had no recourse to punish the dictator if the dictator acted selfishly. The anonymity, meanwhile, eliminated whatever personal feeling the donor might have for the recipient. The typical American, for instance, is bound to feel different toward the victims of Hurricane Katrina than the victims of a Chinese earthquake or an African drought. She is also likely to feel different about a hurricane victim and an AIDS victim.

So the Dictator game seemed to go straight to the core of our altruistic impulse. How would *you* play it? Imagine that you're the dictator, faced with the choice of giving away half of your $20 or giving just $2.

The odds are you would . . . divide the money evenly. That's what three of every four participants did in the first Dictator experiments. Amazing!

Dictator and Ultimatum yielded such compelling results that the games soon caught fire in the academic community. They were conducted hundreds of times in myriad versions and settings, by economists as well as psychologists, sociologists, and anthropologists. In a landmark study published in book form as *Foundations of Human Sociality,* a group of preeminent scholars traveled the world to test altruism in fifteen small-scale societies, including Tanzanian hunter-gatherers, the Ache Indians of Paraguay, and Mongols and Kazakhs in western Mongolia.

As it turns out, it didn't matter if the experiment was run in western Mongolia or the South Side of Chicago: people gave. By now the game was usually configured so that the dictator could give any amount (from $0 to $20), rather than being limited to the original two options ($2 or $10). Under this construct, people gave on average about $4, or 20 percent of their money.

The message couldn't have been much clearer: human beings indeed seemed to be hardwired for altruism. Not only was this conclusion uplifting—at the very least, it seemed to indicate that Kitty Genovese's neighbors were nothing but a nasty anomaly—but it rocked the very foundation of traditional economics. "Over the past decade," *Foundations of Human Sociality* claimed, "research in experimental economics has emphatically falsified the textbook representation of *Homo economicus.*"

Non-economists could be forgiven if they felt like crowing with satisfaction. *Homo economicus,* that hyper-rational, self-interested creature that dismal scientists had embraced since the beginning of time, was dead (if he ever really existed). Hallelujah!

Even non-humans seem to practice some-thing that resembles altruism. The psychologist Marc Hauser and the economist Keith Chen ran a series of experiments with cotton-top tamarins in which the monkeys faced each other in adjoining cages, each equipped with a lever that would release a marshmallow into the other monkey's cage. The only way for one monkey to get a marshmallow was for the other monkey to pull its own lever. So pulling the lever was to some degree an act of altruism, or at least of strategic cooperation.

The tamarins were fairly cooperative but still showed a healthy amount of self-interest: over repeated encounters with fellow monkeys, the typical tamarin pulled the lever about 40 percent of the time. Then Hauser and Chen heightened the drama, conditioning one tamarin to always pull the lever (thus creating an altruistic stooge) and another to never pull the lever (thus creating a selfish jerk). The stooge and the jerk were then sent to play the game with the other tamarins. The stooge blithely pulled her lever over and over, never failing to dump a marshmallow into the other monkey's cage. Initially, the other monkeys responded in kind, pulling their own levers 50 percent of the time. But once they figured out that their partner was a pushover, their rate of reciprocation dropped to 30 percent—lower than the original average rate. The selfish jerk, meanwhile, was punished even worse. Once her reputation was established, Chen recalls, the other tamarins "would just go nuts" whenever she was led into the experimenting chamber.

MARC HAUSER

If this new paradigm—*Homo altruisticus*?—was bad news for traditional economists, it looked good to nearly everyone else. The philanthropy and disaster-relief sectors in particular had reason to cheer. But there were far broader implications. Anyone from a high government official down to a parent hoping to raise civic-minded children had to gain inspiration from the Dictator findings—for if people are innately altruistic, then society should be able to rely on its altruism to solve even the most vexing problems.

Consider the case of organ transplantation. The first successful kidney transplant was performed in 1954. To the layperson, it looked rather like a miracle: someone who would surely have died of kidney failure could now live on by having a replacement organ plunked inside him.

Where did this new kidney come from? The most convenient source was a fresh cadaver, the victim of an automobile accident perhaps or some other type of death that left behind healthy organs. The fact that one person's death saved the life of another only heightened the sense of the miraculous.

But over time, transplantation became a victim of its own success. The normal supply of cadavers couldn't keep up with the demand for organs. In the United States, the rate of traffic fatalities was declining, which was great news for drivers but bad news for patients awaiting a lifesaving kidney. (At least motorcycle deaths kept up, thanks in part to many

Between 1994 and 2007, six states repealed laws that required all motorcyclists to wear helmets. Here's a look at per-capita organ donations from male victims of motor-vehicle crashes in those states versus all other states.

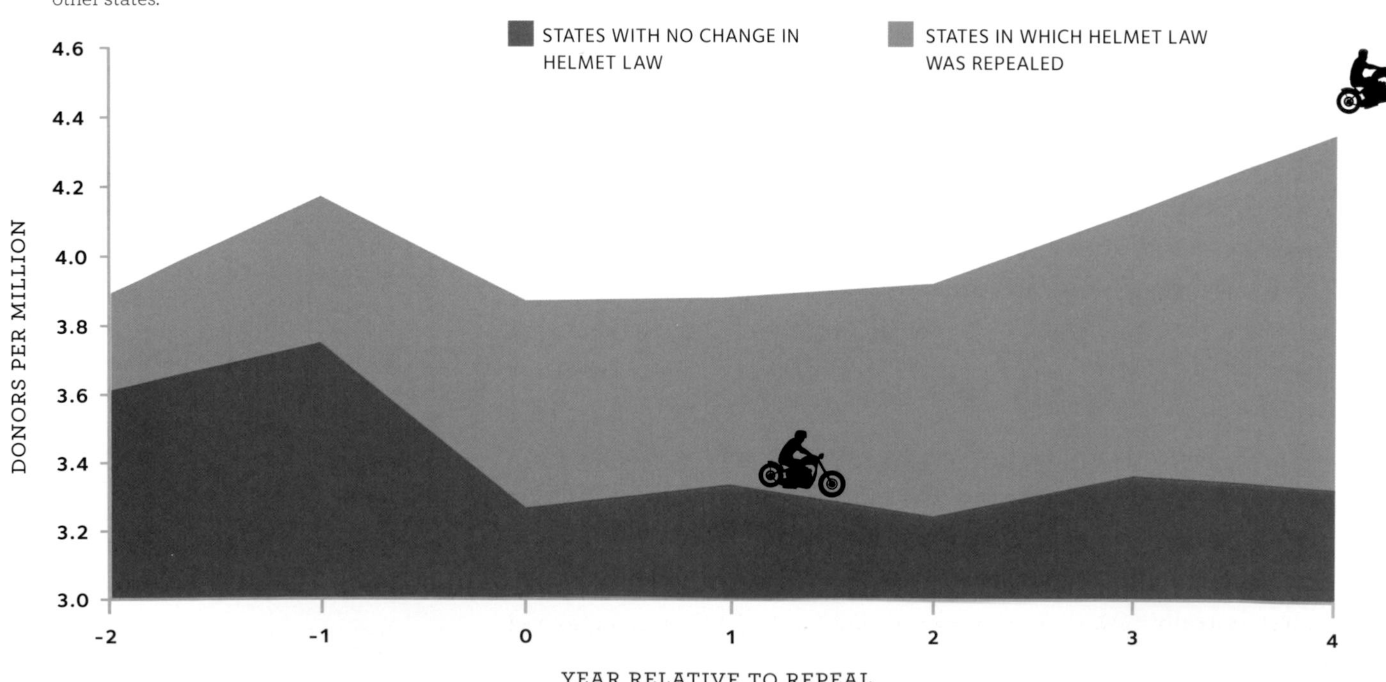

state laws allowing motorcyclists—or, as transplant surgeons call them, "donorcyclists"—to ride without helmets.) In Europe, some countries passed laws of "presumed consent"; rather than requesting that a person donate his organs in the event of an accident, the state assumed the right to harvest his organs unless he or his family specifically opted out. But even so, there were never enough kidneys to go around.

Fortunately, cadavers aren't the only source of organs. We are born with two kidneys but need only one to live—the second kidney is a happy evolutionary artifact—which means that a living donor can surrender one kidney to save someone's life and still carry on a normal life himself. Talk about altruism!

Stories abounded of one spouse giving a kidney to the other, a brother coming through for his sister, a grown woman for her aging parent, even kidneys donated between long-ago playground friends. But what if you were dying and didn't have a friend or relative willing to give you a kidney?

One country, Iran, was so worried about the kidney shortage that it enacted a program many other nations would consider barbaric. It sounded like the kind of idea some economist might have dreamed up, drunk on his belief in *Homo economicus:* the Iranian government would *pay* people to give up a kidney, roughly $1,200, with an additional sum paid by the kidney recipient.

In the United States, meanwhile, during a 1983 congressional hearing, an enterprising doctor named Barry Jacobs described his own pay-for-organs plan. His company, International Kidney Exchange, Ltd., would bring Third World citizens to the United States, remove one of their kidneys, give them some money, and send them back home. Jacobs was savaged for even raising the idea. His most vigorous critic was a young Tennessee congressman named Al Gore, who wondered if these kidney harvestees "might be willing to give you a cut-rate price just for the chance to see the Statue of Liberty or the Capitol or something."

Congress promptly passed the National Organ Transplant Act, which made it illegal "for any person to knowingly acquire, receive, or otherwise transfer any human organ for valuable consideration for use in human transplantation."

Sure, a country like Iran might let people buy and sell human organs as if they were live chickens at a market. But surely the United States had

There's an added twist to organ donation: what if you want it back? In 2001, Richard Batista, a 41-year-old surgeon at Nassau University Medical Center on Long Island, N.Y., gave a kidney to his wife, Dawnell, who was suffering renal failure after a long illness. Leading up to the donation, the Batistas' marriage had been strained. "My first priority was to save her life," Richard told reporters. "The second bonus was to turn the marriage around." Dawnell recovered, but, alas, the marriage did not. In 2005, Dawnell filed for divorce, leading Richard to demand in court that Dawnell return his kidney—or pay him $1.5 million. A judge ultimately rejected Richard's claim on the grounds that an organ donation is an irrevocable gift, and that Richard's demand "inappropriately equates human organs with commodities."

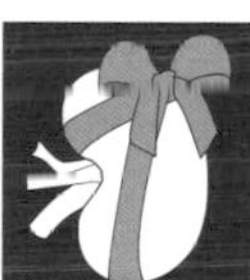

The economist John List is not to be confused with the more notorious John List, a New Jersey accountant who in 1971 killed his mother, wife, and three children, and then, eluding a national manhunt, vanished. Using an assumed name, he stayed in hiding so long that the police lost track of what he looked like. So they hired a forensic sculptor named Frank Bender to create a bust of List as he might look after 18 years on the run. The bust was televised on *America's Most Wanted*. A woman in Richmond, Va., called the police to say the bust looked just like her neighbor, right down to his horn-rimmed glasses. List was promptly arrested and sentenced to five life terms in prison, where he died in 2008.

Left: John List before the crime. **Right:** Bender's bust, which projected List's aging.

Below: List shortly before his death in 2008.

neither the stomach nor the need for such a desperate maneuver. After all, some of the nation's most brilliant academic researchers had scientifically established that human beings are altruistic by their very nature. Perhaps this altruism was just an ancient evolutionary leftover, like that second kidney. But who cared *why* it existed? The United States would lead the way, a light unto the nations, relying proudly on our innate altruism to procure enough donated kidneys to save tens of thousands of lives every year.

The Ultimatum and Dictator games inspired a boom in experimental economics, which in turn inspired a new subfield called behavioral economics. A blend of traditional economics and psychology, it sought to capture the elusive and often puzzling human motivations Gary Becker had been thinking about for decades.

With their experiments, behavioral economists continued to sully the reputation of *Homo economicus*. He was starting to look less self-interested every day—and if you had a problem with that conclusion, well, just look at the latest lab results on altruism, cooperation, and fairness.

One of the most prolific experimental economists among the new generation was a native of Sun Prairie, Wisconsin, named John List. He became an economist by accident and had a far less polished academic

Future economist John List, golfing for Sun Prairie (Wisc.) High School in 1985.

TOP LEFT: COURTESY FRANK BENDER; TOP RIGHT: NEW JERSEY DEPARTMENT OF CORRECTIONS; BOTTOM: *SUN PRAIRIE (WISC.) STAR*

pedigree than his peers and elders. He came from a family of truckers. "My grandfather moved here from Germany, and he was a farmer," List says. "Then he saw that truckers were making more money than he was just to take his grain to the mill, so he decided to sell everything and buy one truck."

The Lists were a smart, hardworking, athletic family, but academics were not of paramount importance. John's father started driving trucks when he was twelve, and John too was expected to join the family business. But he rebelled by going to college. This happened only because he earned a partial golf and academic scholarship to the University of Wisconsin-Stevens Point. During school breaks he'd help his father unload calf feed or haul a load of paper goods down to Chicago, three and a half hours away.

During golf practice at Stevens Point, List noticed a group of professors who had time to play golf just about every afternoon. They taught economics. That's when List decided to become an economics professor too. (It helped that he liked the subject.)

For graduate school he chose the University of Wyoming. It was hardly a top-tier program, but even so he felt overmatched. On the first day, when students went around the classroom and gave a bit of personal background, List felt everyone staring at him when he said he'd graduated from Stevens Point. They had all gone to places like Columbia and the University of Virginia. He decided his only chance was to outwork them. Over the next few years, he wrote more papers and took more qualifying exams than anyone else—and, like many young economists, started to dabble with lab experiments.

When it was time to apply for a teaching job, List sent out 150 applications. The response was, shall we say, muted. He did land a job at the University of Central Florida, in Orlando, where he took on a heavy teaching load and also coached the men's and women's waterskiing teams. He was a blue-collar economist if ever there was one. He was still writing paper after paper and running lots of experiments; his water-skiers even qualified for the national championships.

After a few years, List was invited to join Vernon Smith, the godfather of economic lab experiments, at the University of Arizona. The job would pay $63,000, considerably more than his UCF salary. Out of loyalty, List presented the offer to his dean, expecting UCF to at least match the offer.

"For $63,000," he was told, "we think we can replace you."

Another notable economist-golfer was John Maynard Keynes (below), who played the game whenever he had a spare moment. Not that he was very good. The economic historian C. R. Fay, an occasional partner, called Keynes one of the two worst golfers he ever knew. Still, Keynes meticulously recorded his scores in diaries—along with other minutiae, including his sexual escapades. The names of his carnal partners (most of whom were male) were written in code ("Auburn haired of Marble Arch," for example, and "Lift boy of Vauxhall"). The golf scores were, sadly, not in code.

CORBIS

His stay at Arizona was brief, for he was soon recruited by the University of Maryland. While teaching there, he also served on the President's Council of Economic Advisors; List was the lone economist on a forty-two-person U.S. delegation to India to help negotiate the Kyoto Protocol.

He was by now firmly at the center of experimental economics, a field that had never been hotter. In 2002, the Nobel Prize for economics was shared by Vernon Smith and Daniel Kahneman, a psychologist whose research on decision-making laid the groundwork for behavioral economics. These men and others of their generation had built a canon of research that fundamentally challenged the status quo of classical economics, and List was following firmly in their footsteps, running variants of Dictator and other behavioralist lab games.

But since his days at Stevens Point, he had also been conducting quirky field experiments—studies where the participants didn't know an experiment was going on—and found that the lab findings didn't always hold up in the real world. (Economists are known to admire theoretical proofs; thus the old quip: *Sure, it works in practice, but does it work in theory?*)

Some of his most interesting experiments took place at a baseball-card show in Virginia. List had been attending such shows for years. As an undergrad, he sold sports cards to earn cash, driving as far as Des Moines, Chicago, or Minneapolis, wherever there was a good market.

In Virginia, List cruised the trading floor and randomly recruited customers and dealers, asking them to step into a back room for an economics experiment. It went like this. A customer would state how much he was willing to pay for a single baseball card, choosing from one of five prices that List established. These offers ranged from lowball ($4) to premium ($50). Then the dealer would give the customer a card that was supposed to correspond to the offered price. Every customer and dealer did five such transactions, though with a different partner for each round.

When the customer has to name his price first—like the white men who visit Chicago street prostitutes—the dealer is plainly in a position to cheat, by giving a card that's worth less than the offer. The dealer is also in a better position to know each card's true worth. But the buyers had some leverage, too: if they thought the sellers *would* cheat, they could simply make a lowball offer each round.

So what happened? On average, the customers made fairly high offers and the dealers offered cards of commensurate value. This suggests

VERNON SMITH

A child of the Depression, Vernon Smith grew up in rural Kansas and attended a one-room schoolhouse. After losing their farm, his family moved to Wichita, where Smith checked out a library book that said the best college in the country was the California Institute of Technology. That's where he set his sights, despite mediocre grades; he wound up acing the entrance exam and discovering his love for economics at Caltech. In 2002, he won the Nobel Memorial Prize in Economic Sciences for his work in experimental economics. In his Nobel autobiography, he recalled his college days: "[It] was a meat grinder like I could never have imagined. I studied night, day, weekends and survived hundreds of problems, but what a joy to take freshman chemistry from Linus Pauling [and] hear physics lectures by J. Robert Oppenheimer."

COURTESY VERNON SMITH

that the buyers trusted the sellers and the buyers' trust was rewarded fairly.

This didn't surprise List. He had simply demonstrated that the results you get in a lab with college students could be replicated outside the lab with sport-card traders, at least when the participants know a researcher is carefully recording their actions.

Then he ran a different experiment, out on the real trading floor. Once again, he recruited random customers. But this time he had them approach dealers at their booths, and the dealers didn't know they were being watched.

The most extensive collection of American trading cards, known as the Jefferson R. Burdick Collection, is held at the Metropolitan Museum of Art in New York. Burdick, a Syracuse electrician who died in 1963, collected nearly every baseball card printed between 1887 and 1959 (his collection holds some 30,000 cards), including the famous Honus Wagner T206 card. It was distributed by the American Tobacco Company in 1909 without Wagner's permission. Wagner reportedly hated smoking and objected to the use of his image, and the card was pulled from the market. Fewer than 100 Wagner T206s are thought to exist today. In 2007, a near-mint Wagner T206 was sold for $2.8 million.

The protocol was simple. A customer would make a dealer one of two offers: "Give me the best Frank Thomas card you can for $20" or "Give me the best Frank Thomas card you can for $65."

What happened?

Unlike their scrupulous behavior in the back room, the dealers consistently ripped off the customers, giving them lower-quality cards than the offer warranted. This was true for both the $20 offer and the $65 offer. In the data, List found an interesting split: the out-of-town dealers cheated more often than the locals. This made sense. A local dealer was probably more concerned with protecting his reputation. He might even have been worried about retribution—a baseball bat upside the head, perhaps, after

John List, right, with his father, Augie, outside of List Trucking, the company Augie still runs in Sun Prairie, Wisc.

a customer went home, got online, and found out he'd been hustled.

The trade-floor cheating made List wonder if perhaps all the "trust" and "fairness" he'd witnessed in the back room weren't trust and fairness at all. What if they were just a product of the experimenter's scrutiny? And what if the same was true for altruism?

Despite all the lab evidence of altruism collected by his peers and elders, List was skeptical. His own field experiments pointed in a different direction, as did his personal experience. Back when he was nineteen years old, he delivered a load of paper goods to Chicago. His girlfriend, Jennifer, came along for the ride. (They'd later marry and have five kids.) When they got to the warehouse, four men were in the loading bay, sitting on a couch. It was the dead of summer and punishingly hot. One man said they were on break.

List asked how long the break would last.

"Well, we don't know," the man said, "so why don't you just start unloading yourself."

It was customary for warehouse workers to unload a trucker's truck, or at least help. Plainly that wasn't going to happen.

"Well, if you guys don't want to help, that's fine," List said. "Just give me the keys to the forklift."

They laughed and told him the keys were lost.

So List, along with Jennifer, began unloading the truck, box by box. Drenched in sweat and thoroughly miserable, they labored under the mocking eyes of the four workmen. Finally only a few boxes were left. One of the workmen suddenly found the keys to the forklift and drove it over to List's truck.

Encounters like this had made John List seriously question whether altruism truly runs wild through the veins of humankind, as Dictator and other lab experiments argued.

Yes, that research had won much acclaim, including a Nobel Prize. But the more List thought about it, the more he wondered if perhaps those findings were simply—well, wrong.

In 2005, thanks largely to his field experiments, List was offered a tenured professor position at the University of Chicago, perhaps the most storied economics program in the world. This wasn't supposed to happen. It is a nearly inexorable law of academia that when a professor lands a tenured job, he does so at an institution less prestigious than the one where he began teaching, and also less prestigious than where he received his Ph.D. John List, meanwhile, was like a salmon who swam downstream to spawn, into the open water. Back in Wisconsin, his family was unimpressed. "They wonder why I've failed so miserably," he says, "why I'm not still in Orlando, where the weather is really great, instead of Chicago, where the crime is really high."

By now he knew the literature on altruism experiments as well as anyone. And he knew the real world a bit better. "What is puzzling," he wrote, "is that neither I nor any of my family or friends (or their families or friends) have ever received an anonymous envelope stuffed with cash. How can this be, given that scores of students around the world have outwardly exhibited their preferences [illegible] for giving in laboratory experiments by sending anonymous cash gifts to anonymous souls?"

So List set out to definitively determine if people are altruistic by nature. His weapon of choice was Dictator, the same tool that created the conventional wisdom. But List had a few modifications up his sleeve. This meant recruiting a whole bunch of student volunteers and running a few different versions of the experiment.

He began with classic Dictator. The first player (whom we'll call Annika once again) was given some cash and had to decide whether to give none, some, or even all of it to some anonymous Zelda. List found that 71 percent of the Annikas gave some money to Zelda,

Economists like John List are keen to measure people's *preferences*, both declared preferences (how people say they'll behave) and revealed preferences (their actual behavior). Americans in particular are not shy about declaring their preferences in public. One time-honored tradition: the bumper sticker. And what does such an overt declaration of preference reveal about its declarer? According to William Szlemko, a social psychologist at Colorado State University, drivers with bumper stickers—even those with pacifist messages—are more likely than other drivers to exhibit road rage. Visualize whirled peas indeed.

MARK SARDELLA

and the average "donation" was about 25 percent of the total. This result was perfectly in line with the typical Dictator findings, and perfectly consistent with altruism.

In the second version, List gave Annika another option: she could still give Zelda any amount of her money but, if she preferred, she could instead *take* $1 from Zelda. If the dictators were altruistic, this tweak to the game shouldn't matter at all; it should only affect the people who otherwise would have given nothing. All List did was expand the dictator's "choice set" in a way that was irrelevant for all but the stingiest of players.

But only 35 percent of the Annikas in this modified, steal-a-dollar-if-you-want version gave any money to Zelda. That was just half the number who gave in the original Dictator. Forty-three percent, meanwhile, didn't give a penny, while the remaining 22 percent *took* a dollar from Zelda.

Hey, what happened to all the altruism?

But List didn't stop there. In the third version, Annika was told that Zelda had been given the same amount of money that she, Annika, was given. And Annika could steal Zelda's entire payment—or, if she preferred, she could give Zelda any portion of her own money.

What happened? Now only 10 percent of the Annikas gave Zelda any money, while 60 percent of the Annikas took from Zelda. More than 40 percent of the Annikas took *all* of Zelda's money. Under List's guidance, a band of altruists had suddenly—and quite easily—been turned into a gang of thieves.

The fourth and final version of List's experiment was identical to the third—the dictator could steal the other player's entire pile of money—but with one simple twist. Instead of being handed some money to play the game, as is standard in such lab experiments, Annika and Zelda first had to work for it. (List needed some envelopes stuffed for another experiment, and with limited research funds he was killing two birds with one stone.)

After they worked, it was time to play. Annika still had the option of taking Zelda's money, as 60 percent of the Annikas did in the previous version. But now, with both players having earned their money, only 28 percent of the Annikas took from Zelda. Fully two-thirds of the Annikas neither gave nor took a penny.

So what had John List done, and what does it mean?

He upended the conventional wisdom on altruism by introducing new elements to a clever lab experiment to make it look a bit more like the real

John List's four variations on the Dictator game showed that a bunch of seeming altruists could easily be manipulated into acting like a gang of thieves. He had the students play the following versions of the game, with "Annika" as the Dictator and "Zelda" as the beneficiary.

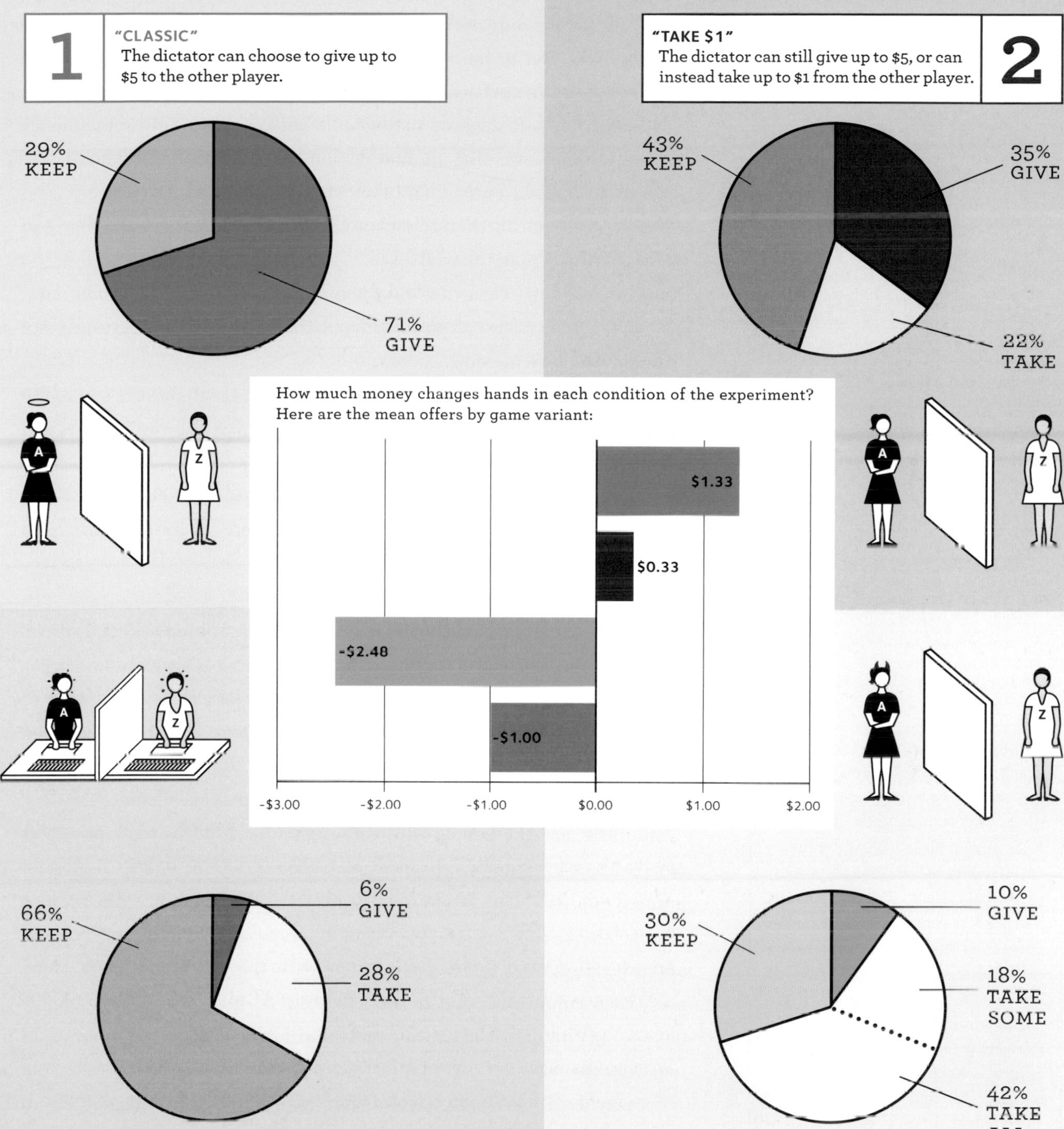

1
"CLASSIC"
The dictator can choose to give up to $5 to the other player.
29% KEEP
71% GIVE
"TAKE $1"
The dictator can still give up to $5, or can instead take up to $1 from the other player.
2
43% KEEP
35% GIVE
22% TAKE
How much money changes hands in each condition of the experiment? Here are the mean offers by game variant:
$1.33
$0.33
-$2.48
-$1.00
-$3.00
-$2.00
-$1.00
$0.00
$1.00
$2.00
A
Z
66% KEEP
6% GIVE
28% TAKE
30% KEEP
10% GIVE
18% TAKE SOME
42% TAKE ALL
4
"EARNINGS"
The dictator can give or take up to $5, but the players have both worked beforehand to earn their money.
"TAKE $5"
The dictator can still give up to $5, or can instead take up to $5 from the other player.
3

NICHOLAS BARDSLEY

It should be noted that at least one other economist was conducting similar experiments at the same time. Nicholas Bardsley, at the University of Southampton in the U.K., in his 2005 paper "Altruism or Artefact? A Note on Dictator Game Giving," reached conclusions much like List's. In another paper, Bardsley argued that no economics lab experiment, no matter how well designed, could escape the artificial taint of the lab, and the results of such experiments shouldn't stand as descriptions of how humans behave in the real world.

world. If your only option in the lab is to give away some money, you probably will. But in the real world, that is rarely your only option. The final version of his experiment, with the envelope-stuffing, was perhaps most compelling. It suggests that when a person comes into some money honestly and believes that another person has done the same, she neither gives away what she earned nor takes what doesn't belong to her.

But what about all the prizewinning behavioral economists who had identified altruism in the wild?

"I think it's pretty clear that most people are misinterpreting their data," List says. "To me, these experiments put the knife in it. It's certainly not altruism we've been seeing."

List had painstakingly worked his way up from truck driver's son to the center of an elite group of scholars who were rewriting the rules of economic behavior. Now, in order to stay true to his scientific principles, he had to betray them. As word of his findings began to trickle out, he suddenly became, as he puts it, "clearly the most hated guy in the field."

List can at least be consoled by knowing that he is almost certainly correct. Let's consider some of the forces that make such lab stories unbelievable.

The first is selection bias. Think back to the tricky nature of doctor report cards. The best cardiologist in town probably attracts the sickest and most desperate patients. So if you're keeping score solely by death rate, that doctor may get a failing grade even though he is excellent.

Similarly, are the people who volunteer to play Dictator more cooperative than average? Quite likely yes. Scholars long before John List pointed out that behavioral experiments in a college lab are "the science of just those sophomores who volunteer to participate in research and who also keep their appointment with the investigator." Moreover, such volunteers tend to be "scientific do-gooders" who "typically have . . . [a] higher need for approval and lower authoritarianism than non-volunteers."

Or maybe, if you're *not* a do-gooder, you simply don't participate in this kind of experiment. That's what List observed during his baseball-card study. When he was recruiting volunteers for the first round, which he clearly identified as an economics experiment, he made note of which dealers declined to participate. In the second round, when List dispatched

Sophomore volunteers who happen to be female may pose an additional challenge to those who wish to design unbiased lab experiments. A University of San Francisco study found that menstruating women were less likely to volunteer for research experiments. The authors therefore concluded that "many experiments that use female volunteers test a disproportionate number whose hormonal status is skewed from that of the normal female population." At right, Doris Clausen, a sophomore at Iowa State College during a physiology class in May 1942.

TOP: ECONOMIC AND SOCIAL RESEARCH COUNCIL; BOTTOM: LIBRARY OF CONGRESS

customers to see if unwitting dealers would rip them off, he found that the dealers who declined to participate in the first round were, on average, the biggest cheaters.

Another factor that pollutes laboratory experiments is scrutiny. When a scientist brings a lump of uranium into a lab, or a mealworm or a colony of bacteria, that object isn't likely to change its behavior just because it's being watched by someone in a white lab coat.

For human beings, however, scrutiny has a powerful effect. Do you run a red light when there's a police car—or, increasingly these days, a mounted camera—at the intersection? Thought not. Are you more likely to wash your hands in the office restroom if your boss is already washing hers? Thought so.

Our behavior can be changed by even subtler levels of scrutiny. At the University of Newcastle upon Tyne in England, a psychology professor named Melissa Bateson surreptitiously ran an experiment in her own department's break room. Customarily, faculty members paid for coffee and other drinks by dropping money into an "honesty box." Each week, Bateson posted a new price list. The prices never changed, but the small photograph atop the list did. On odd weeks, there was a picture of flowers; on even weeks, a pair of human eyes. When the eyes were watching, Bateson's colleagues left *nearly three times as much* money in the honesty box. So the next time you laugh when a bird is frightened off by a silly scarecrow, remember that scarecrows work on human beings too.

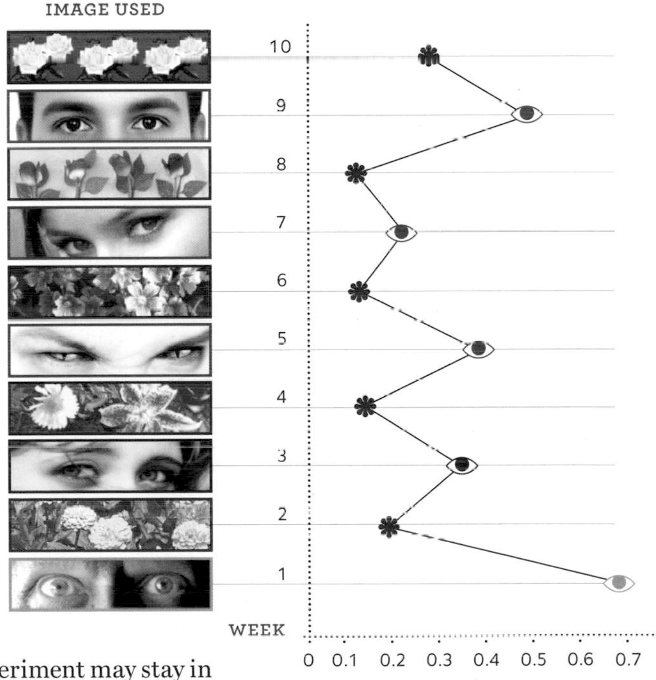

Here are the photos posted in the honesty-box experiment at the University of Newcastle upon Tyne. The researchers used milk consumption as the primary measure of overall tea and coffee consumption.

How does scrutiny affect the Dictator game? Imagine you're a student—a sophomore, probably—who volunteered to play. The professor running the experiment may stay in the background, but he's plainly there to record which choices the participants are making. Keep in mind that the stakes are relatively low, just $20. Keep in mind also that you got the $20 just for showing up, so you didn't work for the money.

Now you are asked if you'd like to give some of your money to an anonymous student who *didn't* get $20 for free. You didn't really want to keep all that money, did you? You may not like this particular professor; you might even actively dislike him—but no one wants to look cheap in front of somebody else. *What the heck*, you decide, *I'll give away a few of my dollars*. But even a cockeyed optimist wouldn't call that altruism.

In addition to scrutiny and selection bias, there's one more factor to consider. Human behavior is influenced by a dazzlingly complex set of incentives, social norms, framing references, and the lessons gleaned from past experience—in a word, context. We act as we do because, given the choices and incentives at play in a particular circumstance, it seems most productive to act that way. This is also known as rational behavior, which is what economics is all about.

Martin Orne, who died at 72 in 2000, specialized in hypnosis and brainwashing. The founder of the University of Pennsylvania's experimental psychiatry unit, Orne was the poet Anne Sexton's therapist in the mid-1960s and earned considerable ire decades later when, at the request of Sexton's daughter, he released taped interviews of Sexton to her biographer. Orne also testified on behalf of Patricia Hearst in her 1976 bank-robbery trial, saying that Hearst had truly been brainwashed by her Symbionese Liberation Army captors and feared death if she disobeyed.

Martin Orne, center, with F. Lee Bailey, Patricia Hearst's defense attorney, and Hearst's sister, Anne, in Feb. 1976, outside the San Francisco courtroom where the newspaper heiress was being tried for bank robbery.

BETTMANN/CORBIS

It isn't that the Dictator participants didn't behave in context. They did. But the lab context is unavoidably artificial. As one academic researcher wrote more than a century ago, lab experiments have the power to turn a person into "a stupid automaton" who may exhibit a "cheerful willingness to assist the investigator in every possible way by reporting to him those very things which he is most eager to find." The psychiatrist Martin Orne warned that the lab encouraged what might best be called forced cooperation. "Just about any request which could conceivably be asked of the subject by a reputable investigator," he wrote, "is legitimized by the quasi-magical phrase 'This is an experiment.'"

Orne's point was borne out rather spectacularly by at least two infamous lab experiments. In a 1961–62 study designed to understand why Nazi officers obeyed their superiors' brutal orders, the Yale psychologist Stanley Milgram got volunteers to follow his instructions and administer a series of increasingly painful electric shocks—at least they *thought* the shocks were painful; the whole thing was a setup—to unseen lab partners. In 1971, the Stanford psychologist Philip Zimbardo conducted a prison experiment, with some volunteers playing guards and others playing inmates. The guards started behaving so sadistically that Zimbardo had to shut down the experiment.

When you consider what Zimbardo and Milgram got their lab volunteers to do, it is no wonder that the esteemed researchers who ran the Dictator game, with its innocuous goal of transferring a few dollars from one undergrad to another, could, as List puts it, "induce almost any level of giving they desire."

The surge in demand for donated organs (about 80% of which is for kidneys) can be seen in these wait-list data from the United Network for Organ Sharing:

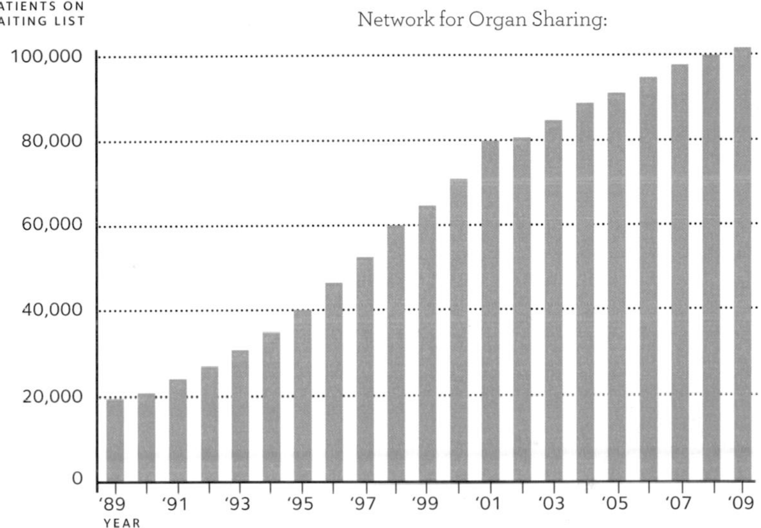

When you look at the world through the eyes of an economist like John List, you realize that many seemingly altruistic acts no longer seem so altruistic.

It may appear altruistic when you donate $100 to your local public-radio station, but in exchange you get a year of guilt-free listening (and, if you're lucky, a canvas tote bag). U.S. citizens are easily the world's leaders in per-capita charitable contributions, but the U.S. tax code is among the most generous in allowing deductions for those contributions.

Most giving is, as economists call it, *impure altruism* or *warm-glow altruism*. You give not only because you want to help but because it makes you look good, or feel good, or perhaps feel less bad.

Consider the panhandler. Gary Becker once wrote that most people who give money to panhandlers do so only because "the unpleasant appearance or persuasive appeal of beggars makes them feel uncomfortable or guilty." That's why people often cross the street to avoid a panhandler but rarely cross over to visit one.

But the supply of donated kidneys isn't nearly large enough to meet the demand:

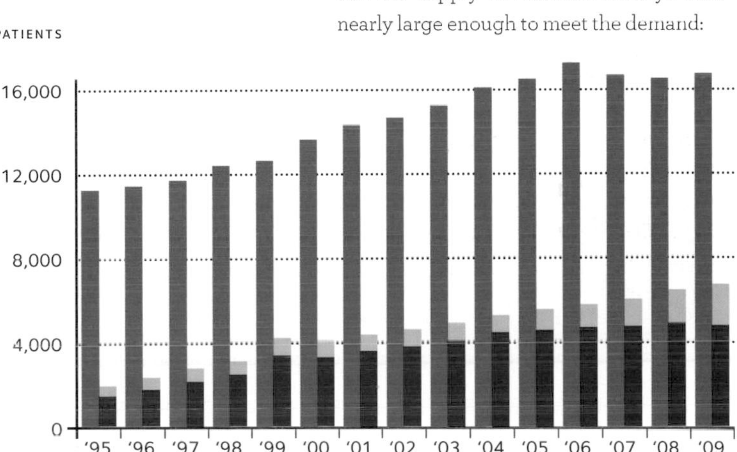

And what about U.S. organ-donation policy, based on its unyielding belief that altruism will satisfy the demand for organs—how has that worked out?

Not so well. There are currently 80,000 people in the United States on a waiting list for a new kidney, but only some 16,000 transplants will be performed this year. This gap grows larger every year. More than 50,000 people on the list have died over the past twenty years, with at least 13,000 more falling off the list as they became too ill to have the operation.

If altruism were the answer, this demand for kidneys would have been met by a ready supply of donors. But it hasn't been. This has led some

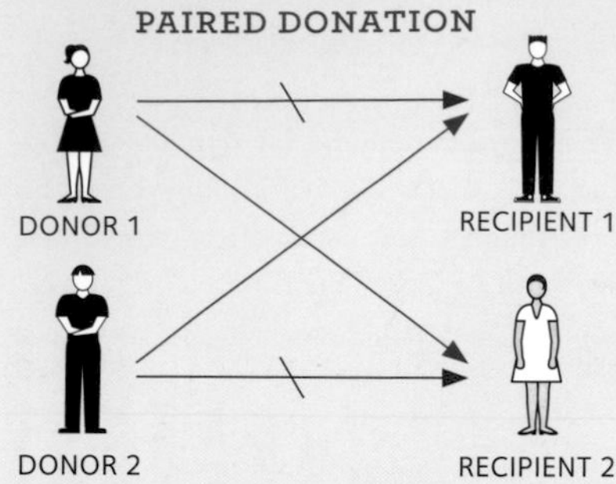

The Harvard economist Alvin E. Roth, a specialist in market design, helped invent a "paired donation" organ exchange that finds matches for compatible organ donors. Here's how it works:

A willing donor enters the exchange along with a person she wants to give an organ to (her husband, for instance) but with whom she is biologically incompatible. This pair is matched with a similar pair of people so that each pair's donor is compatible with the other pair's recipient. Although this organ-for-organ transaction is in fact a sort of market, it doesn't provoke the repugnance of a cash exchange. With this kind of exchange in mind, consider how the repugnance barrier has shifted over time, in one direction or the other:

ONCE REPUGNANT, NOW ACCEPTED:

Adoption
Abortion
Birth control
Cadavers, for dissection and as a source of body parts
Currency speculation
Interest on loans
Life insurance
Surrogate motherhood, egg and sperm donation
Volunteer armies

ONCE ACCEPTED, NOW REPUGNANT:

Discrimination based on race or gender
Dowry
Dwarf tossing
Mercenary soldiers
Performance-enhancing drugs in sports
Polygamy
Prostitution
Sale of indulgences
Slavery and indentured servitude

people—including, not surprisingly, Gary Becker—to call for a well-regulated market in human organs, whereby a person who surrenders an organ would be compensated in cash, a college scholarship, a tax break, or some other form. This proposal has so far been greeted with widespread repugnance and seems for now politically untenable.

Recall, meanwhile, that Iran established a similar market nearly thirty years ago. Although this market has its flaws, anyone in Iran needing a kidney transplant does not have to go on a waiting list. The demand for transplantable kidneys is being fully met. The average American may not consider Iran the most forward-thinking nation in the world, but surely some credit should go to the only country that has recognized altruism for what it is—and, importantly, what it's not.

If John List's research proves anything, it's that a question like "Are people innately altruistic?" is the wrong kind of question to ask. People aren't "good" or "bad." People are people, and they respond to incentives. They can nearly always be manipulated—for good *or* ill—if only you find the right levers.

So are human beings capable of generous, selfless, even heroic behavior? Absolutely. Are they also capable of heartless acts of apathy? Absolutely.

The thirty-eight witnesses who watched Kitty Genovese's brutal murder come to mind. What's so puzzling about this case is how little altruism was required for someone to have called the police from the safety of his or her home. That's why the same question—how could those people have acted so horribly?—has lingered all these years.

But perhaps there's a better question: *did* they act so horribly?

The foundation for nearly everything ever written or said about Genovese's murder was that provocative *New York Times* article, which wasn't published until two weeks after the crime. It had been conceived at a lunch between two men: A.M. Rosenthal, the paper's metro editor, and Michael Joseph Murphy, the city's police commissioner.

Genovese's killer, Winston Moseley, was already under arrest and had confessed to the crime. The story wasn't big news, especially in the *Times*. It was just another murder, way out in Queens, not the kind of thing the paper of record gave much space.

Strangely, though, Moseley also confessed to a second murder even though the police had already arrested a different man for that crime.

FIVE DEGREES OF KEVIN BACON:

By 1971, A.M. ROSENTHAL [1] had become *The New York Times's* managing editor, once again playing a central role in a legendary chapter of journalism—the *Times's* publication of the Pentagon Papers. The top-secret study documenting U.S. military involvement in Vietnam was leaked by the military analyst DANIEL ELLSBERG [2]. In the 2003 TV movie *The Pentagon Papers*, Ellsberg was portrayed by JAMES SPADER [3], who in 1992 had appeared in *Bob Roberts* with DAVID STRATHAIRN [4], who, two years later, appeared in *The River Wild* with KEVIN BACON [5].

"What about that double confession out in Queens?" Rosenthal asked Murphy at lunch. "What's that story all about anyway?"

Instead of answering, Murphy changed the subject.

"That Queens story is something else," he said, and then told Rosenthal that thirty-eight people had watched Kitty Genovese be murdered without calling the police.

"Thirty-eight?" 38 Rosenthal asked.

"Yes, thirty-eight," Murphy said. "I've been in this business a long time, but this beats everything."

Rosenthal, as he later wrote, "was sure that the Commissioner was exaggerating." If so, Murphy may have had sufficient incentive. A story about two men arrested for the same murder clearly had the potential to embarrass the police. Furthermore, given the prolonged and brutal nature of the Genovese murder, the police may have been touchy about who caught the blame. Why *hadn't* they been able to stop it?

Despite Rosenthal's skepticism, he sent Martin Gansberg, a longtime copy editor who'd recently become a reporter, to Kew Gardens. Four days later, one of the most indelible first sentences in newspaper history appeared on the *Times's* front page:

> *For more than half an hour 38 respectable, law-abiding citizens in Queens watched a killer stalk and stab a woman in three separate attacks in Kew Gardens.*

The number 38 is also:

The total number of surviving plays by Shakespeare.

The number of pockets in an American roulette wheel—1 through 36, along with 0 and 00. European wheels, which don't have the 00, have only 37 pockets.

The latitudinal line that once demarcated North Korea from South Korea.

The ranking of John Lennon on *Rolling Stone's* "100 Greatest Artists of All Time" list. (The Beatles are No. 1.)

The number of days a Smith & Wesson chairman served in 2004 before resigning, after it was revealed that he was once convicted of armed robbery.

The atomic number of strontium, a radioactive element used as a cancer treatment.

The approximate length, in minutes, of Great Britain's war with Zanzibar, on August 27, 1896.

The percentage of people not actually entitled to their opinions, according to the satirical newspaper *The Onion*.

For a brand-new reporter like Gansberg and an ambitious editor like Rosenthal—he later wrote a book, *Thirty-Eight Witnesses*, about the case and became the *Times*'s top editor—it was an unqualified blockbuster. It isn't often that a pair of lowly newspapermen can tell a tale that will set the public agenda, for decades hence, on a topic as heady as civic apathy. So *they* certainly had strong incentives to tell the story.

One of us (Dubner) had the opportunity to work with Rosenthal as the latter's days at the *Times* expired. Even toward the end of his life (he died in 2006), Rosenthal remained a forceful journalist and an exceedingly sharp-opinioned man who didn't suffer fools or, as some have argued, dissenting opinions. In 2004, Rosenthal participated in a symposium at Fordham University in New York to mark the fortieth anniversary of the Genovese murder. He offered a singular explanation for his obsession with the case: "Why did the Genovese incident move me so deeply? I tell you this. I had five sisters, and I was the youngest. What loving and magnificent sisters I had. But one of my sisters was murdered. Young Bess was returning home two nights before New Year's through a path in Van Cortlandt Park, when a sexual pervert jumped out of the bushes and exposed himself to her. In shock, she escaped, and ran home one mile, sweaty in the chill weather. Within two days, Bess fell ill and died. I still miss our darling Bess, and feel Bess was murdered by this criminal who took her life away, no less than the monster who killed Kitty Genovese."

But was it true?

The Genovese murder led some pundits to dust off a famous remark uttered by Edmund Burke two centuries earlier: "The only thing necessary for the triumph of evil is for good men to do nothing." It seemed to perfectly sum up what happened that night in Queens. But Fred Shapiro, editor of *The Yale Book of Quotations*, could never locate the quotation in Burke's writings. Which means that this famous line—along with, seemingly, half the quotations attributed to Oscar Wilde and Mark Twain—appears to lie within the realm of apocrypha, or at least exaggeration, not unlike the event it was trotted out to describe.

The best person to answer that question may be Joseph De May Jr., a sixty-year-old maritime lawyer who lives in Kew Gardens. He has an open face, thinning black hair, hazel eyes, and a hearty disposition. On a brisk Sunday morning not long ago, he gave us a tour of the neighborhood.

"Now the first attack occurred roughly in here," he said, pausing on the sidewalk in front of a small shop on Austin Street. "And Kitty parked her car over there, in the train station parking lot," he said, gesturing to an area perhaps thirty-five yards away.

The neighborhood has changed little since the crime. The buildings, streets, sidewalks, and parking areas remain as they were. The Mowbray, a well-kept brick apartment house, still stands across the street from the scene of the first attack.

De May moved to the neighborhood in 1974, a decade after Genovese was killed. The murder wasn't something he thought about much. Several years ago, De May, a member of the local historical society, built a website devoted to Kew Gardens history. After a time, he felt he should add a section about the Genovese murder, since it was the only reason Kew Gardens was known to the outside world, if it was known at all.

As he gathered old photographs and news clippings, he began to find

From left: Burke, Wilde, and Twain.

discrepancies with the official Genovese history. The more intently he reconstructed the crime, chasing down legal documents and interviewing old-timers, the more convinced he became that the legendary story of the thirty-eight apathetic witnesses was—well, a bit too heavy on legend. Like the lawyer he is, De May dissected the *Times* article and identified six factual errors in the first paragraph alone.

Joseph De May in 2008, at the scene of the first attack on Kitty Genovese.

The legend held that thirty-eight people "remained at their windows in fascination" and "watched a killer stalk and stab a woman in three separate attacks" but "not one person telephoned the police during the assault."

The real story, according to De May, went more like this:

The first attack occurred at about 3:20 A.M., when most people were asleep. Genovese cried out for help when Moseley stabbed her in the back. This awoke some Mowbray tenants, who rushed to their windows.

The sidewalk was not well lit, so it may have been hard to make sense of what was happening. As Moseley later testified, "[I]t was late at night and I was pretty sure that nobody could see that well out of the window." What someone likely *would* have seen at that point was a man standing over a woman on the ground.

The entrance to Kitty Genovese's apart- ment, right, as it looks today.

At least one Mowbray tenant, a man, shouted out the window: "Leave that girl alone!" This prompted Moseley to run back to his car, which was parked less than a block away. "I could see that she had gotten up and wasn't dead," Moseley testified. He backed his car down the street, he said, to obscure his license plate.

Genovese struggled to her feet and slowly made her way around to the back of the building, toward her apartment's entrance. ■ But she didn't make it all the way, collapsing inside the vestibule of a neighboring apartment.

■ BOTH: STEPHEN J. DUBNER

Roughly ten minutes after the first attack, Moseley returned. It is unclear how he tracked her in the dark; he may have followed a trail of blood. He attacked her again inside the vestibule, then fled for good.

The *Times* article, as with most crime articles, especially of that era, relied heavily on information given by the police. At first the police said Moseley attacked Genovese three separate times, so that is what the newspaper published. But only two attacks occurred. (The police eventually corrected this but, as in a game of Telephone, the error took on a life of its own.)

So the first attack, which was brief, occurred in the middle of the night on a darkened sidewalk. And the second attack occurred some time later, in an enclosed vestibule, out of view of anyone who might have seen the first attack.

Who, then, were "the thirty-eight witnesses"?

That number, also supplied by the police, was apparently a whopping overstatement. "We only found half a dozen that saw what was going on, that we could use," one of the prosecutors later recalled. This included one neighbor who, according to De May, may have witnessed part of the sec-

This diagram of the Kitty Genovese murder scene is based on one created by Joseph De May. Witnesses in the Mowbray who might have seen the first attack could not have seen the second attack.

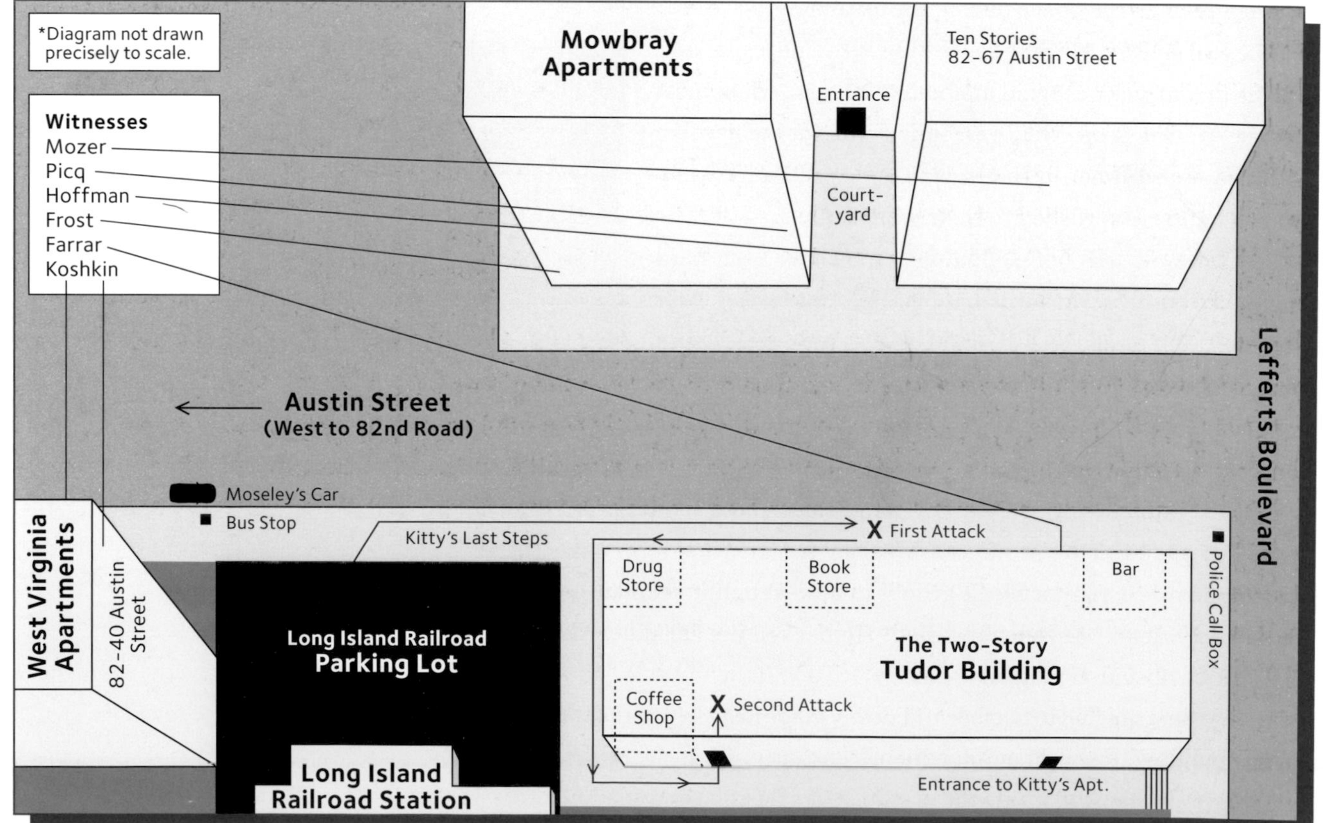

ond attack, but was apparently so drunk that he was reluctant to phone the police.

But still: even if the murder was not a bloody and prolonged spectacle that took place in full view of dozens of neighbors, why didn't anyone call the police for help?

Even that part of the legend may be false. When De May's website went live, one reader who found it was named Mike Hoffman. He was just shy of fifteen years old when Genovese was murdered, and he lived on the Mowbray's second floor.

As Hoffman recalls, he was awakened by a commotion on the street. He opened his bedroom window but still couldn't make out what was being said. He thought perhaps it was a lovers' quarrel and, more angry than concerned, he "yelled for them to 'Shut the fuck up!'"

Hoffman says he heard other people shouting, and when he looked out the window, he saw a man run away. To keep the man in view, Hoffman went to the other window in his room, but the figure faded into the darkness. Hoffman returned to the first window and saw a woman on the sidewalk stagger to her feet. "That's when my dad came in my room and yelled at me for yelling and waking *him* up."

Hoffman told his father what happened. "This guy just beat up a lady and ran away!" Hoffman and his father watched as the woman, walking with great difficulty, rounded the corner. Then everything was quiet. "Dad called the police in case she was hurt badly and needed medical attention," Hoffman says. "In those days, there was no 9-1-1. We had to dial the operator and wait for the eventual connection to the police operator. It took several minutes to get connected to the police and my father told them what we had seen and heard, and that she did walk away but appeared dazed. At that point we couldn't see or hear anything else and we all went back to sleep."

It wasn't until morning that the Hoffmans found out what happened.

"We were interviewed by detectives and learned that she had went around the back of the building across the street, and the guy came back to finish her off," Hoffman says. "I remember my dad saying to them that if they had come when we called them, she'd probably still be alive."

Hoffman believes the police response was slow because the situation his father described was not a murder in progress but rather a domestic disturbance—which, by the looks of it, had concluded. The attacker had fled and the victim had walked off, if shakily, under her own power. With a low-priority call like that, Hoffman says, "the cops don't put down the donuts as fast as if it were to come across as a homicide call."

The police acknowledged that someone did call after the second attack, in the vestibule, and they arrived shortly thereafter. But Hoffman believes their response may have been based on his father's original call. Or, perhaps, there was more than one call: Joseph De May has heard from other Mowbray tenants who claim to have phoned the police after the first attack.

It is hard to say how reliable Hoffman's memory of the events may be. (He did write and sign an affidavit of his recollections.) It is also hard to say if De May's revisionist history is fully accurate. (To his credit, he points out that "an undetermined number of ear witnesses reacted badly" that night, and perhaps could have done more to help; he is also reluctant to cast himself as the infallible source on all things Genovese.)

Selections from Mike Hoffman's affidavit about the Genovese murder:

> We then waited by the Austin Street window of my bedroom to see if the police or ambulance arrived so we could call out to them the direction she was headed in the last we saw her. After about 2 minutes, dad said he was tired and he went back to bed. At this point everything was quiet and dark. Nothing was happening. My teenage curiosity wanted me to stay up, but my bed was at that window. I was on the bed and I propped my pillow up so I could see out the window for when the cops arrived. That's the last I remember, which is why I missed them getting there.

• • •

> The newspapers said that a few minutes after the first attack on Austin Street, Kitty was attacked again on the parking lot side of the 2 story Tudor Building, and that she screamed for help. Although we could not see her on that side of the building, we probably would have heard her if she screamed again from that location. We did not hear anything once she turned the corner by the drugstore. At the time, neither my dad nor I ever thought for a second that this was an attempted murder, or that the man I saw run away would return, find Kitty, and kill her.

• • •

> I worked as a New York City policeman out of the 112nd Precinct although that was years after Kitty was killed. While stationed at the 112, I met an old timer (it's been way too many years to remember his name) who was almost ready to retire. He told me he was on duty in the 102nd Precinct that night and heard the first call go out as a simple assault. It wasn't even put out as "in progress". The dispatcher sent out a second call escalating the situation after Kitty was found lying in the hallway.

• • •

> Signature of Affiant: [signature]
>
> MICHAEL HOFFMAN
>
> Sworn to (or affirmed) and subscribed before me this 15 day of July, 2003 by Michael Hoffman

De May and Hoffman both have an incentive to exonerate their neighborhood from the black eye the Genovese murder gave it. That said, De May strives hard to not be an apologist, and Hoffman seems to be a pretty good witness—a man who, now in his late fifties and living in Florida, spent twenty years as a New York City policeman and retired as a lieutenant.

Now, considering the various incentives at play, which is more unbelievable: the De May–Hoffman version of events or the conventional wisdom that a whole neighborhood of people stood around and watched, refusing to help, as a man murdered a woman?

Before you answer, consider also the circumstances under which Winston Moseley was ultimately arrested. It happened a few days after the Genovese murder. At about three o'clock in the afternoon in Corona, another Queens neighborhood, Moseley was seen carrying a television out of a home belonging to a family named Bannister and loading it into his car.

A neighbor approached and asked what he was doing. Moseley said he was helping the Bannisters move. The neighbor went back in his house and phoned another neighbor to ask if the Bannisters were really moving.

"Absolutely not," said the second neighbor. He called the police while the first neighbor went back outside and loosened the distributor cap on Moseley's car.

When Moseley returned to his car and found it wouldn't start, he fled on foot but was soon chased down by a policeman. Under interrogation, he freely admitted to killing Kitty Genovese a few nights earlier.

Which means that a man who became infamous because he murdered a woman whose neighbors failed to intervene was ultimately captured because of . . . a neighbor's intervention.

As dangerous as Winston Moseley was, the car he drove—a Corvair—was more so. With a rear-mounted engine, it was back-heavy in a way most Americans weren't used to. As race-car driver and author Denise McCluggage put it, "The classic Corvair accident is a quick spin in a turn and *swoosh!*—off the road backwards." In his 1965 book *Unsafe at Any Speed*, Ralph Nader called the Corvair fatally unstable, a charge that spurred General Motors to discontinue the car.

A 1960 Corvair.

"Cardboard signs are for amateurs, people going for a quick fix," says James McWilliams, a historian at Texas State University–San Marcos. "The rainproof signs are indications of experience." McWilliams is a connoisseur of panhandlers' signs. While driving around Austin, he has bought more than 100 of them from men—they are always men—on the street. Offering to buy the signs rather than simply giving them money "radically transforms the interaction," he says. "A one-way street becomes two ways. Empathy yields to the (admittedly provisional) logic of market exchange and, as a result, both parties seem happier. Only once did a panhandler refuse to sell his sign. I offered him $3. Then $6. Then $9. I stopped at $20, and asked why not, to which he replied that he'd had the sign for three years and it had served him well. A remarkable assessment, I thought, given that he was still—well, panhandling." Williams says that most of the transactions are necessarily brief. "Lights change. People honk. There's usually little time for negotiation. This is clearly to my economic advantage, although one time—with my cash at the ready in my shirt pocket—I realized after I drove off that I accidentally handed over the $385 check I was taking to the bank. I swung around the highway underpass and the man was there, waiting for me, holding my check."

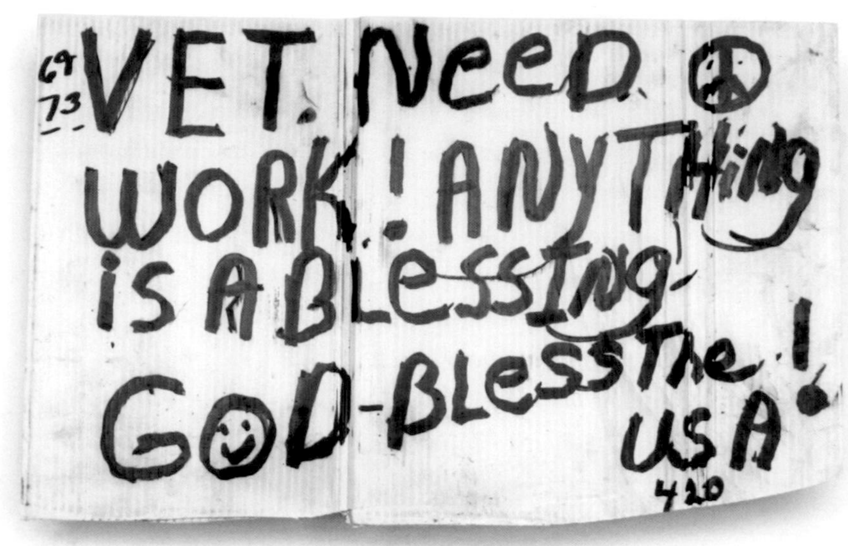

I, PROLETARIAT,
OWN NOTHING
BUT MY LABOR.
MY LABOR IS
FOR SALE.
CAPITAISM
SUX!

I AM Michael!
U.S.A.F. Veteran-VIET-NAM
Sure could use A Little help!
Thankyou!! Any! Any! Act of Kindness
is greatly Appreciated God Bless
Thank-you

WHY LIE
I NEED
BEER

HUNGRY!
TENGO HAMBRE!

CHAPTER 4

THE FIX IS IN— AND IT'S CHEAP AND SIMPLE

IT IS A FACT OF LIFE THAT PEOPLE LOVE TO COMPLAIN, particularly about how terrible the modern world is compared with the past.

They are nearly always wrong. On just about any dimension you can think of—warfare, crime, income, education, transportation, worker safety, health—the twenty-first century is far more hospitable to the average human than any earlier time.

Consider childbirth. In industrialized nations, the current rate of maternal death during childbirth is 9 women per 100,000 births. Just one hundred years ago, the rate was *more than fifty times* higher.

One of the gravest threats of childbearing was a condition known as puerperal fever, which was often fatal to both mother and child. During the 1840s, some of the best hospitals in Europe—the London General Lying-in Hospital, the Paris Maternité, the Dresden Maternity Hospital—were plagued by it. Women would arrive healthy at the hospital to deliver a baby and then, shortly

Around the turn of the 20th century, U.S. women who gave birth in hospitals—they were still in the minority—were subjected to excessive and unhygienic interventions by doctors: bacterial infections alone accounted for 40 percent of maternal deaths. But in short course, the adoption of sterile practices and the use of antibiotics made hospitals much safer. The rate of maternal death plunged as the rate of hospital births rose.

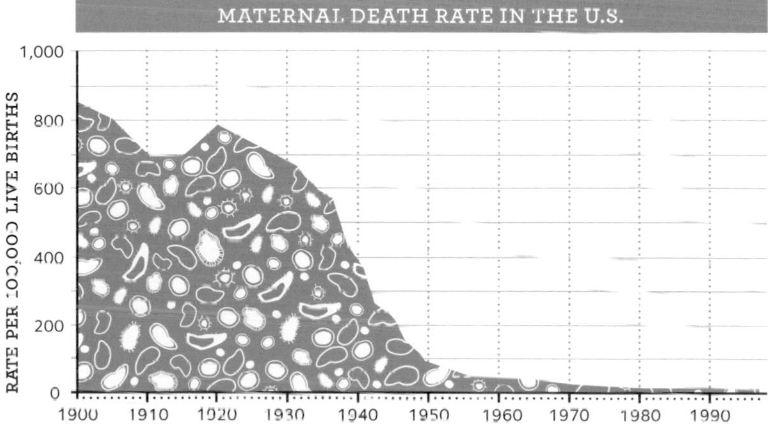

Occupying a complex of buildings originally designed as a poorhouse, Vienna General Hospital opened in 1784 and became one of the largest lying-in hospitals in the world.

thereafter, contract a raging fever and die.

Perhaps the finest hospital at the time was the Allgemeine Krankenhaus, or General Hospital, in Vienna. Between 1841 and 1846, doctors there delivered more than 20,000 babies; nearly 2,000 of the mothers, or 1 of every 10, died. In 1847, the situation worsened: *1 of every 6* mothers died from puerperal fever.

That was the year Ignatz Semmelweis, a young Hungarian-born doctor, became assistant to the director of Vienna General's maternity clinic. Semmelweis was a sensitive man, very much attuned to the suffering of others, and he was so distraught by the rampant loss of life that he became obsessed with stopping it.

Unlike many sensitive people, Semmelweis was able to put aside emotion and focus on the facts, known and unknown.

The first smart thing he did was acknowledge that doctors really had no idea what caused puerperal fever. They might *say* they knew, but the exorbitant death rate argued otherwise. A look back at the suspected causes of the fever reveals an array of wild guesses:

- "[M]isconduct in the early part of pregnancy, such as tight stays and petticoat bindings, which, together with the weight of the uterus, detain the faeces in the intestines, the thin putrid parts of which are taken up into the blood."
- "[A]n atmosphere, a miasma, or . . . by milk metastasis, lochial suppression, cosmo-telluric influences, personal predisposition . . ."
- Foul air in the delivery wards.
- The presence of male doctors, which perhaps "wounded the modesty of parturient mothers, leading to the pathological change."
- "Catching a chill, errors in diet, rising in the labor room too soon after delivery in order to walk back to bed."

IGNATZ SEMMELWEIS

The fifth of nine children in a prosperous family, Ignatz Semmelweis was a graduate of the University of Vienna's medical school. It was only after being rejected for two jobs in pathology that he turned to obstetrics, a field that wasn't held in particularly high regard at the time. Obstetrics would become the main passion of Semmelweis's life.

It is interesting to note that the women were generally held to blame. This may have had something to do with the fact that all doctors at the time were male. Although nineteenth-century medicine may seem primitive today, doctors were considered nearly godlike in their wisdom and authority. And yet puerperal fever presented a troubling contradiction: when women delivered babies at home with a midwife, as was still common, they were at least sixty times *less* likely to die of puerperal fever than if they delivered in a hospital.

The very male faculty of the Vienna Medical School in 1853. Four years earlier, Elizabeth Blackwell had become the first woman to earn a medical degree, from Geneva Medical College in upstate New York. But widespread acceptance of female doctors was slow. As the historian Martha Clevenger points out, as late as 1871, "American Medical Association President Alfred Stille held that women were morally unfit to practice medicine, claiming them to be ignorant, inexact, untrustworthy, unbusinesslike, lacking in sense and mental perception, and contemptuous of logic."

NATIONAL LIBRARY OF MEDICINE

How could it be more dangerous to have a baby in a modern hospital with the best-trained doctors than on a lumpy mattress at home with a village midwife?

To solve this puzzle, Semmelweis became a data detective. Gathering statistics on the death rate at his own hospital, he discovered a bizarre pattern. The hospital had two separate wards, one staffed by male doctors and trainees, the other by female midwives and trainees. There was a huge gap between the two wards' death rates:

	DOCTORS' WARD			MIDWIVES' WARD		
YEAR	BIRTHS	DEATHS	RATE	BIRTHS	DEATHS	RATE
1841	3,036	237	7.8%	2,442	86	3.5%
1842	3,287	518	15.8%	2,659	202	7.6%
1843	3,060	274	9.0%	2,739	164	6.0%
1844	3,157	260	8.2%	2,956	68	2.3%
1845	3,492	241	6.9%	3,241	66	2.0%
1846	4,010	459	11.4%	3,754	105	2.8%
TOTAL	20,042	1,989		17,791	691	
AVERAGE RATE			9.9%			3.9%

Why on earth was the death rate in the doctors' ward more than twice as high?

On Dec. 9, 1980, New York City's chief medi-cal examiner Elliot M. Gross discussed the autopsy carried out on John Lennon. But this was not the most noteworthy aspect of Dr. Gross's tenure.

Starting in 1981, New York's suicide rate began to plummet. In surrounding areas, meanwhile, people kept killing themselves with the expected frequency. Why?

According to "Where Did the Bodies Go?," a 2006 paper by the sociologist Hugh P. Whitt, the medical examiner's office under Gross's tenure had serious administrative and budgetary problems. The average processing time for an autopsy report doubled; lawyers and pathologists deemed the office's findings unreliable. One wrinkle: a lot of likely suicides were misclassified as accidents.

From a medical examiner's perspective, a false positive in a suicide declaration is a bigger problem than a false negative. With a possible suicide, an overworked medical examiner might spare himself the work of proving suicidal intent and convincing bereaved relatives to accept a suicide classification. Instead, he would declare the death an accident due to a fall or poisoning or a bathtub electrocution.

In 1987, Dr. Gross was dismissed from his post. By 1989, the number of reported suicides in New York had more than doubled, returning to the normal range.

Semmelweis wondered if the women patients admitted to the doctors' ward were sicker, weaker, or in some other way compromised.

No, that couldn't be it. Patients were assigned to the wards in alternating twenty-four-hour cycles, depending on the day of the week they arrived. Given the nature of pregnancy, an expectant mother came to the hospital when it was time to have the baby, not on a day that was convenient. This assignment methodology wasn't quite as rigorous as a randomized, controlled trial, but for Semmelweis's purpose it did suggest that the divergent death rates weren't the result of a difference in patient populations.

So perhaps one of the wild guesses listed above *was* correct: did the very presence of men in such a delicate feminine enterprise somehow kill the mothers?

Semmelweis concluded that this too was improbable. After examining the death rate for *newborns* in the two wards, he again found that the doctors' ward was far more lethal than the midwives': 7.6 percent versus 3.7 percent. Nor was there any difference in the death rate of male babies versus females. As Semmelweis noted, it was unlikely that newborns would "be offended by having been delivered in the presence of men." So it was unreasonable to suspect that male presence was responsible for the mothers' deaths.

There was also a theory that patients admitted to the doctors' ward, having heard of its high death rate, were "so frightened that they contract the disease." Semmelweis didn't buy this explanation either: "We can assume that many soldiers engaged in murderous battle must also fear death. However, these soldiers do not contract childbed fever."

No, some other factor unique to the doctors' ward had to figure in the fever.

Semmelweis had by now established a few facts:

- Even the poorest women who delivered their babies on the street and *then* came to the hospital did not get the fever.
- Women who were dilated for more than twenty-four hours "almost invariably became ill."
- Doctors did not contract the disease from the women or newborns, so it was almost certainly not contagious.

Still, he remained puzzled. "Everything was in question; everything seemed inexplicable; everything was doubtful," he wrote. "Only the large number of deaths was an unquestionable reality."

The answer finally came to him in the wake of a tragedy. An older professor whom Semmelweis admired died quite suddenly after a mishap. He had been leading a student through an autopsy when the student's knife slipped and cut the professor's finger. The maladies he suffered before dying—bilateral pleurisy, pericarditis, peritonitis, and meningitis—were, Semmelweis observed, "identical to that from which so many hundred maternity patients had also died."

The professor's case held little mystery. He died from "cadaverous particles that were introduced into his vascular system," Semmelweis noted. Were the dying women also getting such particles in their bloodstream?

Of course!

In recent years, Vienna General and other first-rate teaching hospitals had become increasingly devoted to understanding anatomy. The ultimate teaching tool was the autopsy. What better way for a medical student to limn the contours of illness than to hold in his hands the failed organs, to sift for clues in the blood and urine and bile? At Vienna General, every single deceased patient—including the women who died of puerperal fever—was taken directly to the autopsy room.

But doctors and students often went to the maternity ward straight from the autopsy table with, at best, a cursory cleansing of their hands. Although it would be another decade or two before the medical community accepted germ theory—which established that many diseases are caused by living microorganisms and not animal spirits or stale air or too-tight corsets—Semmelweis understood what was going on. It was the *doctors* who were responsible for puerperal fever, transferring "cadaverous particles" from the dead bodies to the women giving birth.

This explained why the death rate in the doctors' ward was so much higher than in the midwives' ward. It also explained why women in the doctors' ward died more often than women who gave birth at home or even in the streets, and why women in a longer state of dilation were more susceptible to the fever: the longer a woman lay in that state, the more often

As germ theory gained currency in the 1870s, much of the credit went to the French chemist Louis Pasteur. His experiments proved that fermentation and putrefaction were caused by microscopic organisms, thus providing an underpinning for the idea that disease was caused by bacteria and viruses. Pasteur's experiments led to the process now known as pasteurization, whereby a liquid is preserved by heating it (to kill the bacteria) and then sealing it (against contamination by the outside air). Pasteur also developed vaccines for rabies and anthrax. His work made him an international hero.

Louis Pasteur and his granddaughter, Camille Vallery-Radot, in a 1912 reproduction of an 1886 portrait by Léon Bonnat.

NATIONAL LIBRARY OF MEDICINE

her uterus was poked and prodded by a gaggle of doctors and medical students, their hands still dripping with the remnants of their latest autopsy.

"None of us knew," as Semmelweis later lamented, "that *we* were causing the numerous deaths."

Thanks to him, the plague could finally be halted. He ordered all doctors and students to disinfect their hands in a chlorinated wash after performing autopsies. The death rate in the doctors' maternity ward fell to barely 1 percent. Over the next twelve months, Semmelweis's intervention saved the lives of 300 mothers and 250 babies—and that was just in a single maternity ward in a single hospital.

To confirm his suspicion that autopsies were somehow causing the high death rate in Vienna General's maternity ward, Ignatz Semmelweis compared the Vienna statistics with those of a maternity hospital in Dublin, where doctors did not perform autopsies. The results were striking:

■ **VIENNA DEATH RATE**

■ DUBLIN DEATH RATE

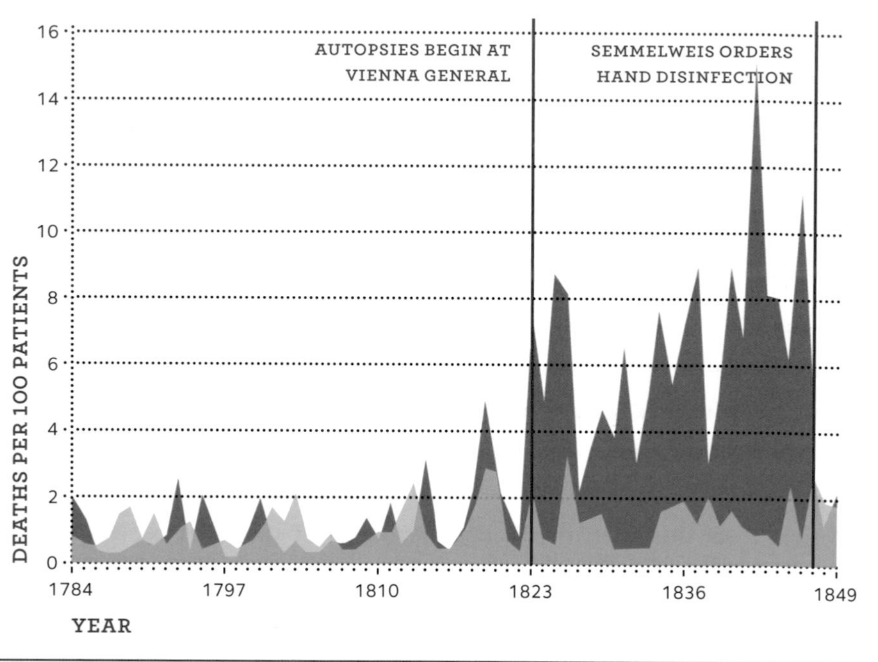

As we wrote earlier, the law of unintended consequences is among the most potent laws in existence. Governments, for instance, often enact legislation meant to protect their most vulnerable charges but that instead ends up hurting them.

Consider the Americans with Disabilities Act (ADA), which was intended to safeguard disabled workers from discrimination. A noble intention, yes? Absolutely—but the data convincingly show that the net result was *fewer* jobs for Americans with disabilities. Why? After the ADA became law, employers were so worried they wouldn't be able to discipline or fire bad workers who had a disability that they avoided hiring such workers in the first place.

The Endangered Species Act created a similarly perverse incentive. When landowners fear their property is an attractive habitat for an endangered animal, or even an animal that is being considered for such status, they rush to cut down trees to make it less attractive. Among the recent victims of such shenanigans are the cactus ferruginous pygmy owl and the red-cockaded woodpecker. Some environmental economists have argued that "the Endangered Species Act is actually endangering, rather than protecting, species."

Politicians sometimes try to think like economists and use price to encourage good behavior. In recent years, many governments have started to base their trash-pickup fees on volume. If people have to pay for each extra bag of garbage, the thinking goes, they'll have a strong incentive to produce less of it.

But this new way of pricing also gives people an incentive to stuff their bags ever fuller (a tactic now known by trash officers the world around as the "Seattle Stomp") or just dump their trash in the woods (which is what happened in Charlottesville, Virginia). In Germany, trash-tax avoiders flushed so much uneaten food down the toilet that the sewers became infested with rats. A new garbage tax in Ireland generated a spike in backyard trash burning—which was bad not only for the environment but for public health too: St. James's Hospital in Dublin recorded a near tripling of patients who'd set themselves on fire while burning trash.

In a beautiful irony, the German town that recently made headlines for its rat infestation was Hamelin, where according to legend the Pied Piper saved the town from a plague of rats by luring them into the river with his magic pipe. (When the residents refused to pay the piper for his services, he led their children away with the same tune.) One might therefore be tempted to think of the recent garbage tax as the rats' revenge.

Well-intentioned laws have been backfiring for millennia. A Jewish statute recorded in the Bible required creditors to forgive all debts every sabbatical, or seventh year. For borrowers, the appeal of unilateral debt relief cannot be overstated, as the penalties for defaulting on a loan were severe: a creditor could even take a debtor's children into bondage.

If you were a creditor, however, you saw this debt-forgiveness program differently. Why loan money to some sandal maker if he could just tear up the note in Year Seven?

So creditors gamed the system by making loans in the years right after a sabbatical and pulling tight the purse strings in Years Five and Six. The result was a cyclical credit crunch that punished the very people the law was intended to help.

While some environmental laws indeed carry hidden costs, some contain unintended gains. Consider Australia's laws to cut the carbon monoxide (CO) emissions in car exhaust. Between 1997 and 2006, as CO emissions fell, so too did the Australian rate of suicide by exhaust asphyxiation.

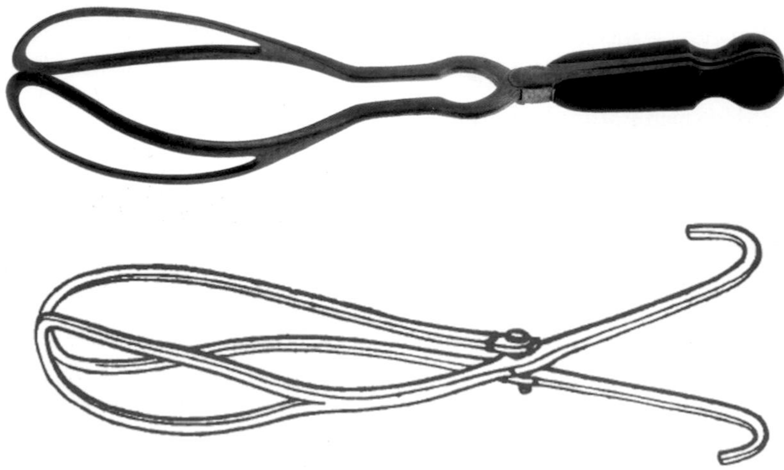

An obstetrical forceps from about 1851 and, beneath it, the earlier Chamberlen forceps, as illustrated in J. H. Aveling's book *The Chamberlens and the Midwifery Forceps.* While the Chamberlens hoarded their invention, Aveling points out, the forceps had actually been invented long before the Chamberlens came along: "It is beyond doubt a fact that Arabian surgeons [around the 10th and 11th centuries] used forceps to deliver the fetal head in difficult labours. [But] to whatever state of perfection they might have been brought, all knowledge of them had for centuries been lost, and re-invention had become a necessity."

Technology historians note that such "lost" inventions are quite common. For instance, archaeologists have discovered a 2,000-year-old mechanical computer used by the Greeks to calculate the position of the moon and the planets.

THE BRITISH COLUMBIA MEDICAL ASSOCIATION MEDICAL MUSEUM

But in the history of unintended consequences, few match the one uncovered by Ignatz Semmelweis: medical doctors, while in pursuit of lifesaving knowledge, conducted thousands upon thousands of autopsies, which, in turn, led to the loss of thousands upon thousands of lives.

It is heartening, of course, that Semmelweis's brilliant data deduction showed how to end this scourge. But our larger point, and the point of this chapter, is that Semmelweis's solution—sprinkling a bit of chloride of lime in the doctors' handwash—was remarkably simple and remarkably cheap. In a prosperous world, simple and cheap fixes sometimes get a bad rap; we are here to defend them.

There is another powerful, if bittersweet, example from the realm of childbirth: the forceps. It used to be that when a baby presented itself awkwardly, there was a good chance it would get stuck in the birth canal and endanger both mother and child. The forceps, a simple set of metal tongs, allowed a doctor or midwife to get a firm hold on the baby and adroitly pluck it out, headfirst, like a roast suckling pig from the oven.

As effective as it was, the forceps did not save as many lives as it should have. It is thought to have been invented in the early seventeenth century by a London obstetrician named Peter Chamberlen. The forceps worked so well that Chamberlen kept it a secret, sharing it only with sons and grandsons who continued in the family business. It wasn't until the mid-eighteenth century that the forceps passed into general use.

What was the cost of this technological hoarding? According to the surgeon and author Atul Gawande, "it had to have been millions of lives lost."

The most amazing thing about cheap and simple fixes is they often address problems that seem impervious to *any* solution. And yet almost invariably, a Semmelweis or a team of Semmelweises ride into view and save the day. History is studded with examples.

At the start of the Common Era, just over two thousand years ago, there were roughly 200 million people on earth. By the year 1000, that number

had risen only to 300 million. Even by 1750, there were just 800 million people. Famine was a constant worry, and the smart money said the planet couldn't possibly support much more growth. The population in England had been *decreasing*—"essentially because," as one historian wrote, "agriculture could not respond to the pressure of feeding extra people."

THOMAS MALTHUS

In 1798, the economist Thomas Malthus published *An Essay on the Principle of Population,* arguing that, barring disasters like war or plague, the future would bring mass starvation. As he saw it, population growth would be exponential while agricultural growth would be only linear, and thus would never keep pace. "I see no way by which man can escape from the weight of this law which pervades all animated nature," he wrote. "No fancied equality, no agrarian regulations in their utmost extent, could remove the pressure of it even for a single century."

Enter the Agricultural Revolution. A variety of innovations, none particularly complex—they included higher-yielding crops, better tools, and a more efficient use of capital—changed farming and, subsequently, the face of the earth. In late eighteenth-century America, "it took 19 out of 20 workers to feed the country's inhabitants and provide a surplus for export," wrote the economist Milton Friedman. Two hundred years later, only 1 of 20 American workers was needed to feed a far larger population while also making the United States "the largest single exporter of food in the world."

The Agricultural Revolution freed up millions of hands that went on to power the Industrial Revolution. By 1850, worldwide population had grown to 1.3 billion; by 1900, 1.7 billion; by 1950, 2.6 billion. And then things *really* took off. Over the next fifty years, the population more than doubled, reaching well beyond 6 billion. If you had to pick a single silver bullet that allowed this surge, it would be nitrate fertilizers, which are astonishingly cheap and effective. It wouldn't be much of an overstatement to say that nitrate fertilizer feeds the world. If it disappeared overnight, says the agricultural economist Will Masters, "most people's diets would revert to heaps of cereal grains and root crops, with animal products and fruits only for special occasions and for the rich."

Or consider the whale. Hunted since antiquity, by the nineteenth century it had become an economic engine that helped turn the United States into a powerhouse. Every square inch of it could be turned into *something*, so the whale afforded one-stop shopping for a fast-growing nation: material for the manufacture of paint and varnish; textiles and leather; candles and soap; clothing and of course food (the tongue was a particular delicacy). The whale was especially beloved by the finer sex, surrendering its body parts for corsets, collars, parasols, perfume, hairbrushes, and red fabric dye. (This last product was derived from, of all things, the whale's excrement.) Most valuable was whale oil, a lubricant for all sorts of machinery but most crucially used for lamp fuel. As the author Eric Jay Dolin declares in *Leviathan*, "American whale oil lit the world."

Out of a worldwide fleet of 900 whaling ships, 735 of them were American, hunting in all four oceans. Between 1835 and 1872, these ships reaped nearly 300,000 whales, an average of more than 7,700 a year. In a good year, the total take from oil and baleen (the whale's bonelike "teeth") exceeded $10 million, today's equivalent of roughly $200 million. Whaling was dangerous and difficult work, but it was the fifth-largest industry in the United States, employing 70,000 people.

And then what appeared to be an inexhaustible resource was—quite suddenly and, in retrospect, quite obviously—heading toward exhaustion. Too many ships were hunting for too few whales. A ship that once took a year at sea to fill its hold with whale oil now needed four years. Oil prices spiked accordingly, rocking the economy back home. Today, such an in-

THE WHALE FISHERY.
Whaling vessels at New Bedford wharves. (Sect. v, vol. ii, p. 232.)
From a photograph by T. W. Smillie.
PLATE 185.

A forest of whaling ships in New Bedford, Mass. The boom was ferocious—until whaling stocks were depleted.

NATIONAL OCEANIC AND ATMOSPHERIC ADMINISTRATION

dustry might be considered "too big to fail," but the whaling industry was failing indeed, with grim repercussions for all America.

That's when a retired railway man named Edwin L. Drake, using a steam engine to power a drill through seventy feet of shale and bedrock, struck oil in Titusville, Pennsylvania. The future bubbled to the surface. Why risk life and limb chasing underwater leviathans around the world, having to catch and carve them up, when so much energy was just waiting, in the nation's basement, to be pumped upstairs?

Oil was not only a cheap and simple fix but, like the whale, extraordinarily versatile. It could be used as lamp oil, a lubricant, and as a fuel for automobiles and home heating; it could be made into plastic and even nylon stockings. The new oil industry also provided lots of jobs for unemployed whalers and, as a bonus, functioned as the original Endangered Species Act, saving the whale from near-certain extinction.

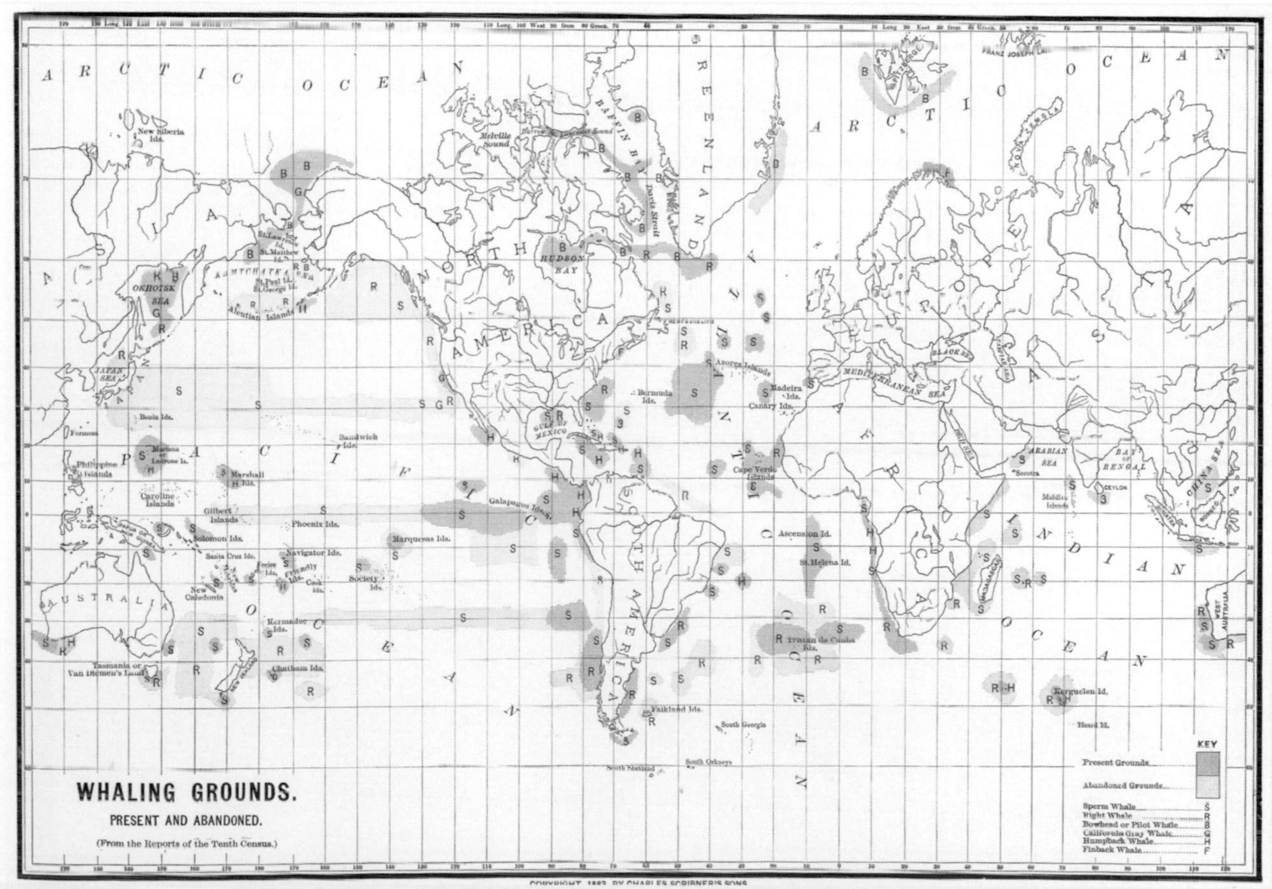

HENRY GANNETT AND FLETCHER W. HEWES, U.S. CENSUS OFFICE; PUBLISHED IN 1883 BY CHARLES SCRIBNER'S SONS, COURTESY DAVID RUMSEY ARCHIVE

In this 1880 map of whaling grounds, the light-blue fields represent areas that had already been exhausted.

Two men perched atop a Pennsylvania oil well in the 1860s, with another group assembled on its storage tank. Below, an 1872 map of the state, showing in green the oil fields pioneered by Edwin Drake in the state's northwest. Coal deposits are shown in blue, with iron in red.

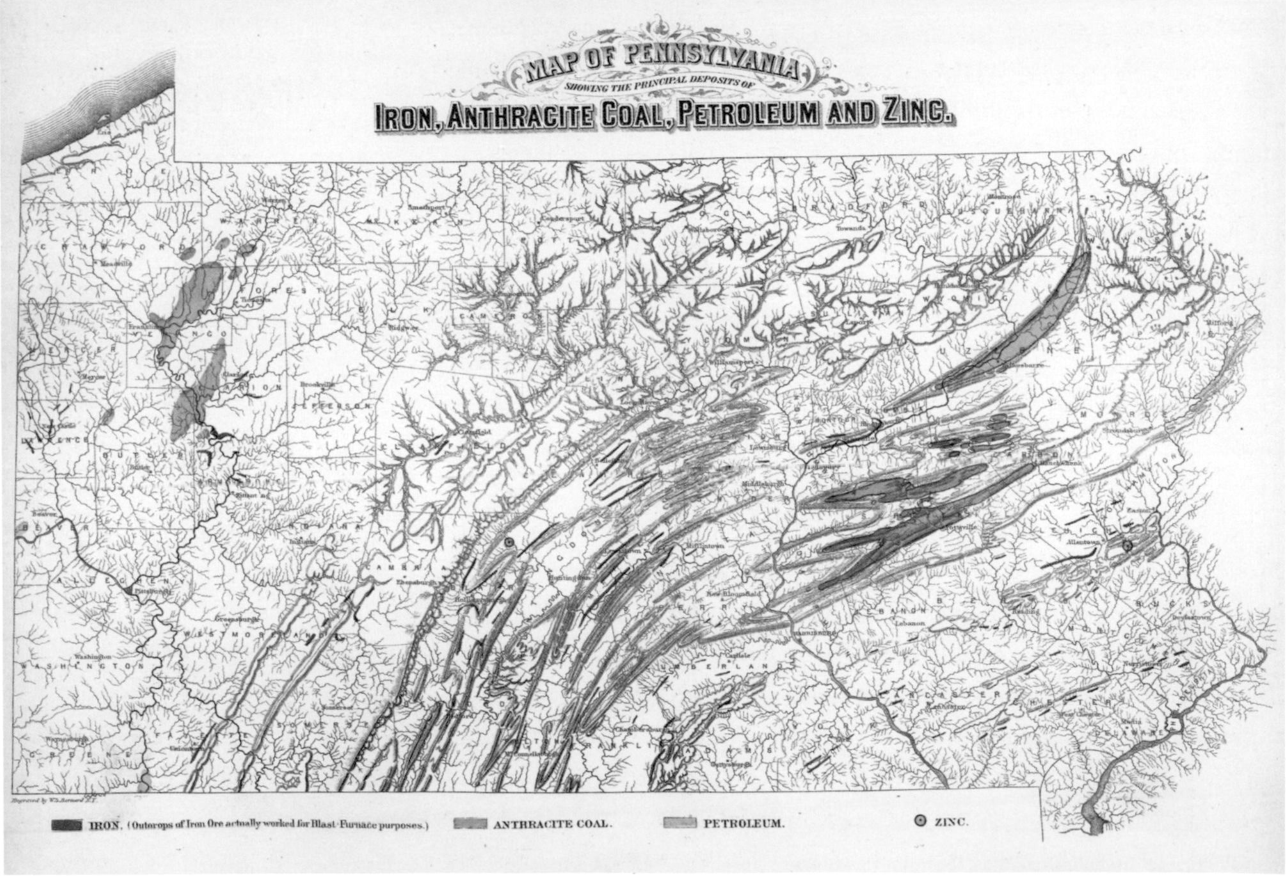

MAP OF PENNSYLVANIA
SHOWING THE PRINCIPAL DEPOSITS OF
IRON, ANTHRACITE COAL, PETROLEUM AND ZINC.

IRON. (Outcrops of Iron Ore actually worked for Blast-Furnace purposes.) ANTHRACITE COAL. PETROLEUM. ZINC.

TOP: WILLIAM J. PORTSER, LIBRARY OF CONGRESS; BOTTOM: ENGRAVED BY W. S. BARNARD, PUBLISHED BY STEDMAN, BROWN & LYON, PHILADELPHIA, 1872, COURTESY DAVID RUMSEY ARCHIVE

As petroleum replaced whale oil, what shall replace petroleum as the fuel of choice? Among the current contenders: algae, babassu, corn, *Jatropha,* halophytes, hemp, hydrogen, *Miscanthus,* poplar, restaurant grease, sorghum, soybeans, sugar, switchgrass, and willow.

By the early twentieth century, most infectious diseases—smallpox, tuberculosis, diphtheria, and the like—were on their way out. But polio refused to surrender.

It would be hard to invent a more frightening illness. "It was a children's disease; there was no prevention; there was no cure; every child everywhere was at risk," says David M. Oshinsky, author of the Pulitzer Prize–winning *Polio: An American Story.* "And what this really meant was that parents were absolutely frantic."

Polio was also a great mystery, spiking in summertime, its cause unknown. (In a classic case of mistaking correlation and causality, some researchers suspected that ice cream—consumed in far greater quantities in the summer—caused polio.) It was first thought to target immigrant slum children, especially boys, but it struck girls too, as well as kids in the leafiest suburbs. Even Franklin Delano Roosevelt, who was far removed from immigrant slums and, at thirty-nine, from childhood as well, contracted the disease.

Every outbreak prompted a new round of quarantines and panic. Parents kept their kids away from friends, from pools and parks and libraries. In 1916, the worst polio epidemic to date struck New York City. Out of 8,900 reported cases, 2,400 people died, most of them children under five. The disease roared on. Nineteen fifty-two was the worst year yet, with 57,000 reported cases nationwide, 3,000 of them fatal and 21,000 resulting in permanent paralysis.

Surviving a bad case of polio was only marginally better than dying. Some victims lost the use of their legs and lived in constant pain. Those with respiratory paralysis practically lived inside an "iron lung," a huge tank that did the work of their failed chest muscles. As the population of living polio victims grew, the cost of their medical care was staggering. "At a time when less than ten percent of the nation's families had any form of health insurance," Oshinsky writes, "the expense of boarding a polio patient (about $900 a year) actually exceeded the average annual wage ($875)."

America was by now the most powerful country on earth, the victor in

Franklin Delano Roosevelt was hardly the only well-known polio sufferer. Among the others:

FRIDA KAHLO (1907–1954): The painter's difficult life got off to a difficult start with polio at age six.

BROWNIE McGHEE (1915–1996): The legendary guitarist contracted polio when he was four, which kept him indoors practicing his instrument.

BEN BRADLEE (B. 1921): This newspaperman was hit with the disease as a teenager, and it left him paralyzed for months.

FRANCIS FORD COPPOLA (B. 1939): The future film director contracted polio at age ten and was bedridden for nine months.

JONI MITCHELL (B. 1943): Before she was diagnosed with polio at age nine, Mitchell wanted to be a dancer.

ITZHAK PERLMAN (B. 1945): Polio at the age of four left the violinist permanently disabled; he walks with crutches and performs seated.

FRANKLIN DELANO ROOSEVELT LIBRARY AND MUSEUM

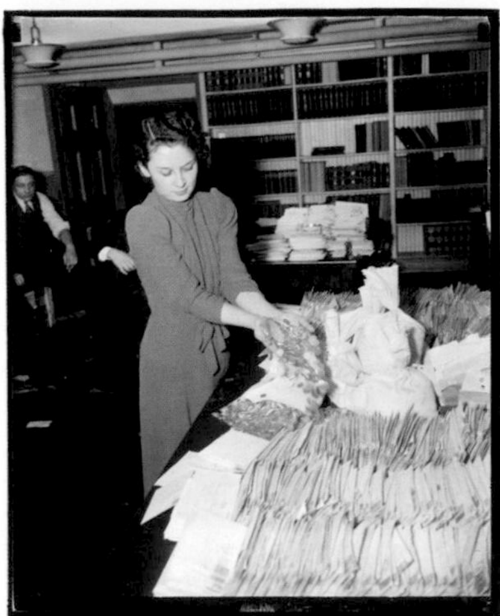

The March of Dimes was launched in 1938 with President Roosevelt asking Americans to mail their dimes to the White House to support the National Foundation for Infantile Paralysis. The response nearly overwhelmed the White House mail room, as seen in this 1939 photo.

By 1954, the foundation had become by far the highest-grossing medical charity in the country. The author David Oshinsky points out that financial support for polio was particularly outsized given the number of people suffering from the disease.

MONEY RAISED IN 1954 VS. NUMBER OF VICTIMS IN 1954

two world wars, possessor of a blindingly bright future. But there was legitimate concern that this single disease would consume such a large share of future health-care dollars that it would cripple the nation.

And then a vaccine was developed—a series of vaccines, really—and polio was effectively stamped out.

To call the vaccine a "simple" fix might seem to discount the tireless efforts of everyone who helped stop polio: the medical researchers (Jonas Salk and Albert Sabin chief among them); the fund-raising volunteers (the March of Dimes, Oshinsky writes, was "the largest charitable army the country had ever known"); even the non-human martyrs (thousands of monkeys were imported to be given experimental vaccines).

On the other hand, there is no simpler medical fix than a vaccine. Consider two of the major ways we try to thwart disease. The first is to invent a procedure or technology that helps fix a problem once it's arisen (open-heart surgery, for instance); these tend to be very costly. The second is to invent a medicine to prevent the problem before it happens; in the long run, these tend to be extraordinarily cheap. Health-care researchers have estimated that if a polio vaccine hadn't been invented, the United States would currently be caring for at least 250,000 long-term patients at an annual cost of at least $30 billion. And that doesn't even include "the intangible costs of suffering and death and of averted fear."

Polio is a stark example, but there are countless cheap and simple medical fixes. New ulcer drugs reduced the rate of surgery by roughly 60 percent; a later round of even cheaper drugs saved ulcer patients some $800 million a year. In the first twenty-five years after lithium was introduced to treat manic depression, it saved nearly $150 billion in hospitalization costs. Even the simple addition of fluoride to water systems has saved about $10 billion per year in dental bills.

As we noted earlier, deaths from heart disease have fallen substantially over the past few decades. Surely this can be attributed to expensive treatments like grafts, angioplasties, and stents, yes?

Actually, no: such procedures are responsible for a remarkably small share of the improvement. Roughly half of the decline has come from reductions in risk factors like high cholesterol and high blood pressure, both of which are treated by relatively cheap medicines. And much of the remaining decline is thanks to ridiculously inexpensive treatments like aspirin, heparin, ACE inhibitors, and beta-blockers.

It took a long time for effective ulcer drugs to arrive—mainly because doctors were mistaken about the cause of ulcers. The conventional wisdom held that stress or poor diets were to blame. In the 1940s, a young cardiologist named A. Stone Freedberg began to suspect that ulcers might be caused by bacteria. But he couldn't prove his theory, and most of his peers dismissed it, believing bacteria couldn't survive in the stomach's acidic environment. In the 1980s, a pair of Australian physicians isolated a bacterium, *Helicobacter pylori*, which they thought might be the villain. Their theory too was greeted with skepticism—until one of them, Barry Marshall, went so far as to prepare a batch of *H. pylori* in the lab and swallow it. Sure enough, he came down with an acute case of gastritis. Luckily, having just proven that a bacterium caused ulcers, Marshall knew he could cure himself with antibiotics. For their discovery, Marshall and Robin Warren won the Nobel Prize in Physiology or Medicine in 2005.

For years, doctors advocated drinking milk to treat ulcers. Indeed, milk alleviated gastric distress in the short term but, as it turned out, exacerbated the condition.

LIBRARY OF CONGRESS

By the early 1950s, automobile travel had become fantastically popular in the United States, with about 40 million cars on the road. But at the thirty-fifth annual convention of the National Automobile Dealers Association, held in January 1952, a vice president of the BFGoodrich tire company warned that the smooth ride might be over: "If the death rate continues upward it will seriously hurt the automobile business, as many people will quit driving."

Nearly 40,000 people died in U.S. traffic accidents in 1950. That's roughly the same number of deaths as today, but a straight-up comparison is very misleading, because far fewer miles were driven back then. The rate of death per mile driven was five times higher in 1950 than it is today.

Why so many fatalities then? Suspects were legion—faulty cars, poorly designed roads, careless drivers—but not much was known about the mechanics of car crashes. Nor was the auto industry exactly burning to find out.

Enter Robert Strange McNamara. Today he is best remembered as the much-maligned secretary of defense during the Vietnam War. One reason McNamara was so maligned was that he tended to make decisions based

While the annual number of U.S. traffic fatalities is higher today than it was in 1950, the rate of death has plummeted:

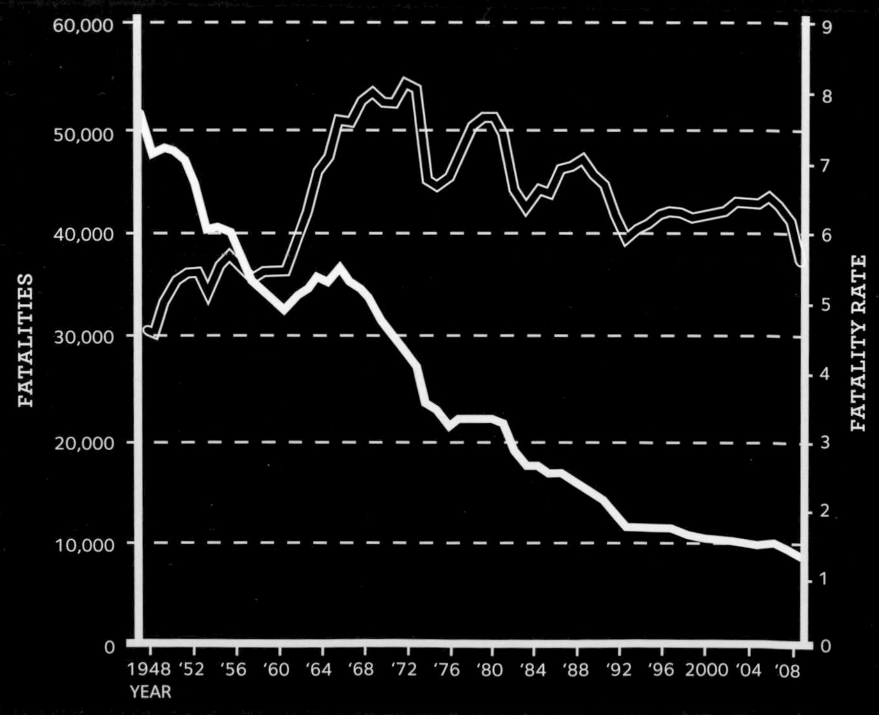

FATALITIES

FATALITIES PER 100 MILLION VEHICLE MILES TRAVELED

on statistical analysis rather than emotion or political considerations. In other words, he behaved like an economist.

This was no coincidence. He studied economics at Berkeley and went on to the Harvard Business School, where he stayed on as a young professor of accounting. McNamara volunteered when World War II broke out, and his analytical skills landed him in the Statistical Control Office of the Army Air Forces.

His team used data as a weapon to fight the war. For example, the abort rate among American bombers leaving England for daytime sorties over Germany was found to be unnaturally high, about 20 percent. The pilots gave a variety of explanations for failing to reach the target: a malfunctioning electrical system, a spotty radio, or illness. But a closer analysis of the data led McNamara to conclude that these reasons were "baloney." The real explanation, he said, was fear. "A helluva lot of them were going to be killed, they knew that, and they found reasons to not go over the target."

McNamara reported this to the commanding officer, the notoriously headstrong Curtis LeMay, who responded by flying the lead plane on bombing missions and vowing to court-martial any pilot who turned back. The abort rate, McNamara says, "dropped overnight."

After the war, the Ford Motor Company asked McNamara and others from his unit to bring their statistical wizardry to the auto industry. McNamara wanted to return to Harvard, but he and his wife had both racked up huge medical bills—from polio, of all things. So he took the job at Ford. He quickly rose through the ranks even though he wasn't a "car guy" in any traditional sense. "Instead," as one historian later wrote, "he was absorbed by such novel concepts as safety, fuel economy, and basic utility."

McNamara was particularly concerned with the deaths and injuries from automobile accidents. He asked the car guys what caused the problem. There were few statistics available, he was told.

Some aeronautical researchers at Cornell were trying to prevent airplane deaths, so McNamara commissioned them to look into auto crashes. They experimented by wrapping human skulls in different materials and dropping them down the stairwells in Cornell's dormitories. It turned out that human beings were no match for the hard materials used in car interiors. "In a crash, the driver was often impaled on the steering wheel," McNamara says. "The passenger was often injured because he'd hit the windshield or the header bar or the instrument panel." McNamara ordered new Ford models to have a safer steering wheel and a padded instrument panel.

In 1960, Robert S. McNamara became president of the Ford Motor Company. The first person to hold the post who wasn't a relative of Henry Ford himself, McNamara had always been a little out of step at Ford—a statistics man in the company of car guys, an academic in executive's clothing. Just a month after taking over Ford, McNamara left the company to join newly elected president John F. Kennedy as secretary of defense.

McNamara during a July 1965 news conference at the Department of Defense.

CORBIS

But the best fix, he realized, was also the simplest one. Rather than worrying about what a passenger's head would hit when he was flung about during an accident, wouldn't it be better to keep him from being flung at all? McNamara knew that airplanes had seat belts; why not cars?

"I calculated the number of deaths we'd prevent each year, which was very high," he says. "And this came at essentially no cost, with no great penalty for wearing them."

McNamara had all of Ford's company cars outfitted with seat belts. "I flew down to visit an assembly plant in Texas," he recalls. "The manager met me at the plane. I buckled my seat belt, and he said, 'What's the matter, you afraid of my driving?'"

That manager, it turned out, reflected a widespread sentiment about seat belts. McNamara's bosses saw them as "inconvenient, costly, and just a bunch of damn nonsense," he says. Even so, they followed his lead and put seat belts in the new Ford models.

McNamara was of course right: the seat belt would eventually save many lives. But the key word here is "eventually."

The brilliant ration-alist had encountered a central, frustrating tenet of human nature: *behavior change is hard*. The cleverest engineer or economist or politician or parent may come up with a cheap, simple solution to a problem, but if it requires people to change their behavior, it may not work. Every day, billions of people around the world engage in behaviors they know are bad for them—smoking cigarettes, gambling excessively, riding a motorcycle without a helmet.

Why? Because they want to! They derive pleasure from it, or a thrill, or just a break

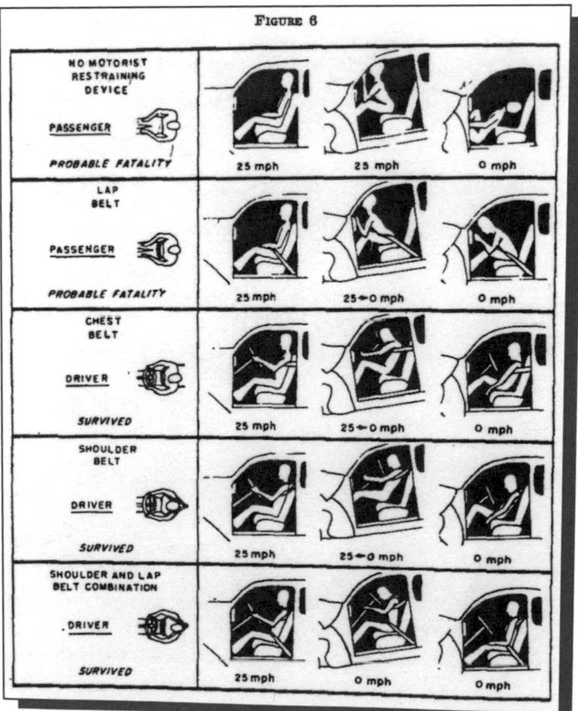

HEARINGS BEFORE A SUBCOMMITTEE OF THE HOUSE COMMITTEE ON INTERSTATE AND FOREIGN COMMERCE ON THE CRASHWORTHINESS OF AUTOMOBILE SEAT BELTS, APRIL 30, AUGUST 5–8, 1957

Among the early objections to seat belts was the suspicion that they were just a moneymaker for car companies. Consider the following exchange from a 1957 congressional hearing on the effectiveness of seat belts. The Ford executive Alex Haynes had just told Walter E. Rogers (D.-Tex.) that Ford spent $13 to install lap belts in the front seat of each car:

> **Rogers:** *There are a lot of people in this country that feel that a lot of gadgets are put on automobiles just to sell the gadget and that may be true. . . . Let me ask you this. What is the profit on a $13 item for a seat belt?*
>
> **Haynes:** *The profit?*
>
> **Rogers:** *Yes, insofar as the automobile company is concerned. Have you broken that down on a cost-profit basis?*
>
> **Haynes:** *I don't have the figures on profit but I will just hazard a guess. We haven't made very much at $13. We haven't made much profit if any.*

During that same hearing, a UCLA traffic engineer named Derwyn Severy presented evidence that a standard lap belt by itself wasn't even that effective; instead, he urged the use of a chest belt, shoulder belt, or the lap-and-shoulder belt that is commonplace today.

The subcommittee's verdict: automakers should install seat belts on a voluntary basis. It wasn't until 1966 that Congress required lap belts as a standard feature in new cars. American automakers argued that the lap-and-shoulder belt was too costly, and some safety advocates warned that the shoulder strap would cause more injuries than it prevented. (They would ultimately be proved very wrong.) The car-buying public was also unenthusiastic. "Many people ask us to take the seat belts out of their cars," one auto dealer told *The New York Times* in 1966. "They're afraid they'll mar the upholstery."

from the daily humdrum. And getting them to change their behavior, even with a fiercely rational argument, isn't easy.

And so it was with the seat belt. Congress began setting federal safety standards in the mid-1960s, but even fifteen years later, seat-belt use was laughably low: just 11 percent. Over time, the numbers crept upward, thanks to a variety of nudges: the threat of a traffic ticket; expansive public-awareness campaigns; annoying beeps and flashing dashboard lights if the belt wasn't buckled; and, eventually, a societal acceptance that wearing a seat belt wasn't an insult to anyone's driving ability. Seat-belt use rose to 21 percent by the mid-1980s, 49 percent by 1990, 61 percent by the mid-1990s, and today it is over 80 percent.

That's a big reason the per-mile auto fatality rate has fallen so much in the United States. Seat belts reduce the risk of death by as much as 70 percent; since 1975 they have saved roughly 250,000 lives. Traffic fatalities still claim more than 40,000 lives a year, but relatively speaking, driving isn't all that dangerous anymore. What makes the death toll so high is that so many Americans spend an enormous amount of time in their cars, racking up some 3 trillion miles per year. That translates into one death for every 75 million miles driven—or, put another way, if you drove 24 hours a day at 30 miles per hour, you could expect to die in a car accident only after driving for 285 straight years. Compared with the death rates in many countries in Africa, Asia, and the Middle East, where seat-belt use is far less prevalent, driving in the United States isn't much more dangerous than sitting on your couch.

And seat belts, at about $25 a pop, are one of the most cost-effective lifesaving devices ever invented. In a given year, it costs roughly $500 million to put them in every U.S. vehicle, which yields a rough estimate of $30,000 for every life saved. How does this compare with a far more complex safety feature like air bags? At an annual U.S. price of more than $4 billion, air bags cost about $1.8 *million* per life saved.

Robert McNamara, who recently passed away at the age of ninety-three, told us shortly before his death that he still wanted to get to 100 percent compliance on seat

In his 1871 essay "The Danger of Lying in Bed," Mark Twain sounds nearly like an economist as he considers the relative death rates of rail travel and staying in bed:

> *Between New York and Rochester the Erie [railroad] ran eight passenger-trains each way every day—16 altogether; and carried a daily average of 6,000 persons. That is about a million in six months—the population of New York City. Well, the Erie kills from 13 to 23 persons of its million in six months; and in the same time 13,000 of New York's million die in their beds! My flesh crept, my hair stood on end. "This is appalling!" I said. "The danger isn't in traveling by rail, but in trusting to those deadly beds. I will never sleep in a bed again."*

belts. "A lot of women often don't use the shoulder belt because they're uncomfortable, they're not designed to take account of the breasts," he said. "I think with very little thought, belts could be designed that are more comfortable and therefore increase the percentage of use."

He may or may not be right about women and seat belts. But without doubt there *is* one group of people for whom seat belts are poorly designed: children.

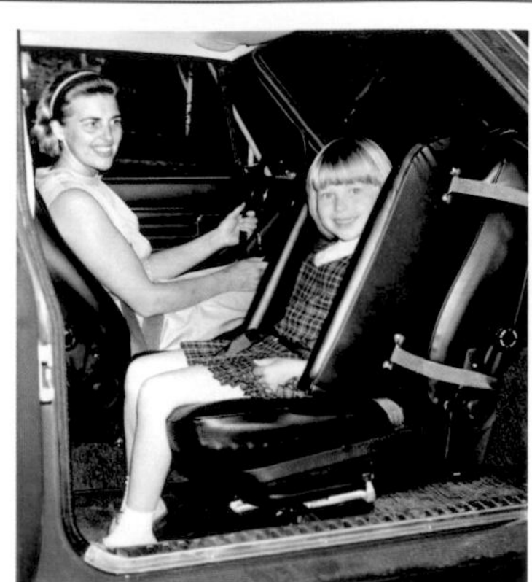

The earliest child safety seats came from the Swedish automaker Volvo in 1964. This 1967 version was designed by Bertil Aldman, who got the idea to mount rear-facing seats from the Gemini space missions, which had astronauts lying on their backs to protect against the g-forces of liftoff. It has by now come to be accepted that the backseat is much safer for children (and adults) than the front seat.

Sometimes it pays to be low status. When a family of four goes for a drive, the kids usually get shunted to the backseat while the mom or dad rides shotgun. The kids are luckier than they know: in the event of a crash, the backseat is far safer than the front. This is even truer for adults, who are larger and therefore more likely to smack into something hard when they sit up front. Unfortunately, while it's okay to consign the low-status kids to the rear seat, if the parents go out for a drive alone, it's a bit awkward for one of them to ride in the back while leaving the other up front in the martyr's seat.

Seat belts are now standard issue in the rear seat of all cars. But they were designed to fit grown-ups, not kids. If you try to strap in your three-year-old darling, the lap belt will be too loose and the shoulder belt will come across his neck or nose or eyebrows instead of his shoulder.

Here are the five leading causes of death among U.S. children ages 1 to 8, as a percentage of total, over the past quarter century:

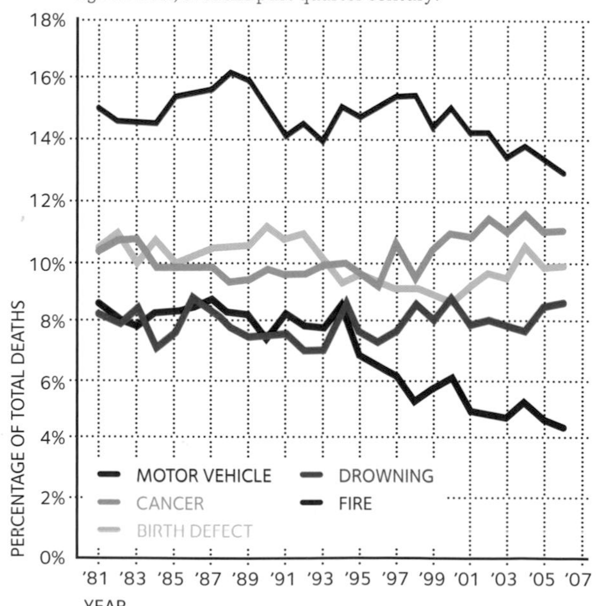

Fortunately, we live in a world that cherishes and protects children, and a solution was found: the child safety seat, commonly known as a car seat. Introduced in the 1960s, it was first embraced by only the most vigilant parents. Thanks to the advocacy of doctors, traffic-safety experts, and—surprise!—car-seat manufacturers, it came into wider use, and the government eventually joined the party. Between 1978 and 1985, every state in the United States made it illegal for children to ride in a car unless they were buckled into a safety seat that met federal crash-test standards.

Motor-vehicle accidents were the leading cause of death for U.S. children back then, and they still are today, but the rate of death has been falling. Most of the credit has gone to the car seat.

Safety isn't free, of course. Americans spend more than $300 million a year buying 4 million car seats. A single kid will typically inhabit three different seats over time: a rear-facing seat for infants; a larger, front-facing seat for toddlers; and a booster seat for older children. Moreover, if that kid has a sibling or two, his parents may have to buy an SUV or minivan to accommodate the width of the car seats.

Nor is the car-seat solution as simple as most people might like. Any given seat is a tangle of straps, tethers, and harnesses, built by one of dozens of manufacturers, and it must be anchored in place by a car's existing seat belt—whose configuration varies depending on *its* manufacturer, as does the shape and contour of the rear seat itself. Furthermore, those seat belts were designed to batten down a large human being, not a small, inanimate hunk of plastic. According to the National Highway Traffic Safety Administration (NHTSA), more than 80 percent of car seats are improperly installed. That's why so many parents trek to the local police station or firehouse for help with the seats. And that's why NHTSA runs a four-day National Standardized Child Passenger Safety Training Program for public-safety personnel, using a 345-page manual to teach proper installation.

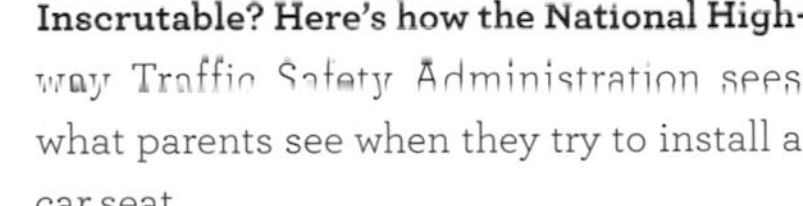
Inscrutable? Here's how the National Highway Traffic Safety Administration sees what parents see when they try to install a car seat.

TASKS FOR PROPER CHILD SEAT INSTALLATION (CARRIER WITH BASE)

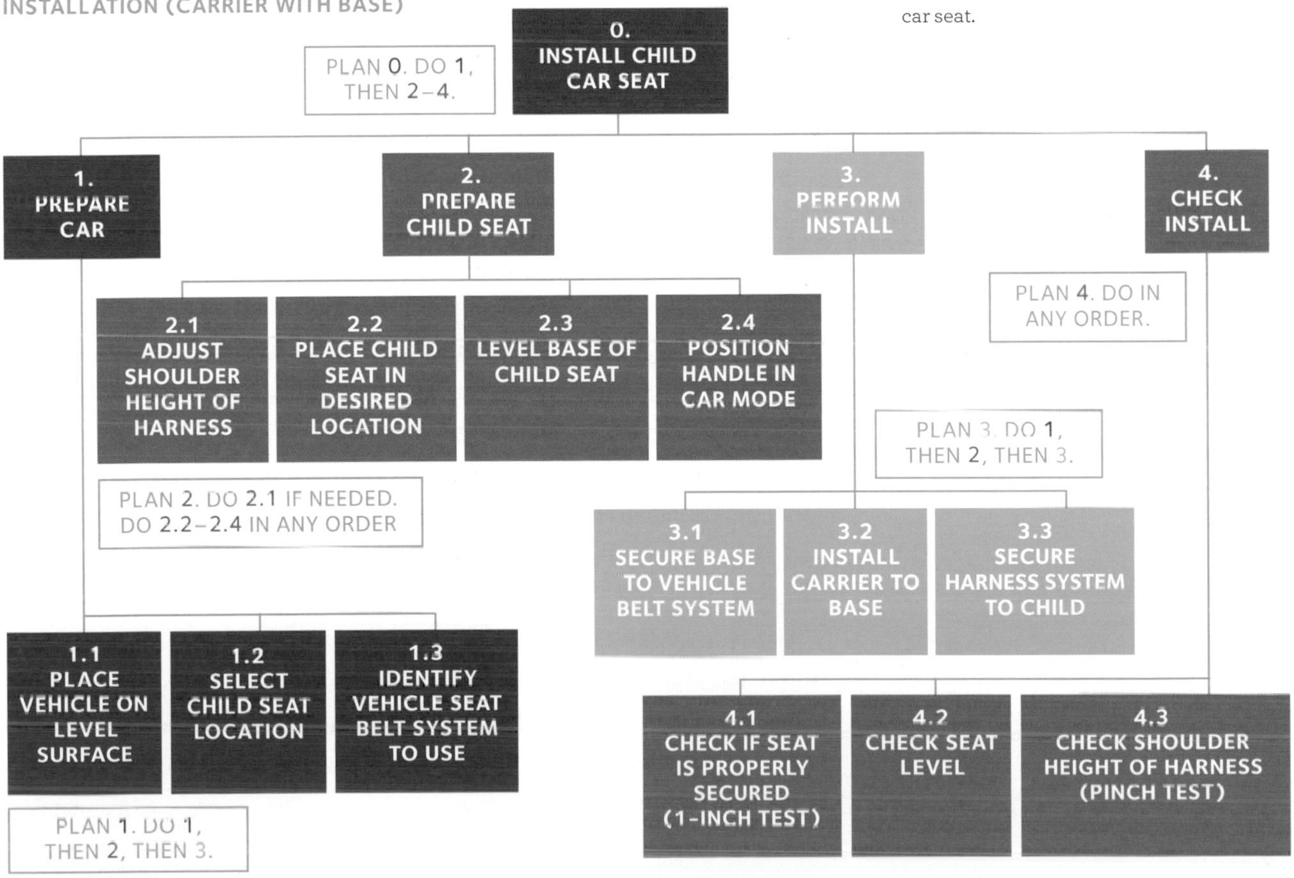

- 0. INSTALL CHILD CAR SEAT — PLAN 0. DO 1, THEN 2–4.
  - 1. PREPARE CAR — PLAN 1. DO 1, THEN 2, THEN 3.
    - 1.1 PLACE VEHICLE ON LEVEL SURFACE
    - 1.2 SELECT CHILD SEAT LOCATION
    - 1.3 IDENTIFY VEHICLE SEAT BELT SYSTEM TO USE
  - 2. PREPARE CHILD SEAT — PLAN 2. DO 2.1 IF NEEDED. DO 2.2–2.4 IN ANY ORDER
    - 2.1 ADJUST SHOULDER HEIGHT OF HARNESS
    - 2.2 PLACE CHILD SEAT IN DESIRED LOCATION
    - 2.3 LEVEL BASE OF CHILD SEAT
    - 2.4 POSITION HANDLE IN CAR MODE
  - 3. PERFORM INSTALL — PLAN 3. DO 1, THEN 2, THEN 3.
    - 3.1 SECURE BASE TO VEHICLE BELT SYSTEM
    - 3.2 INSTALL CARRIER TO BASE
    - 3.3 SECURE HARNESS SYSTEM TO CHILD
  - 4. CHECK INSTALL — PLAN 4. DO IN ANY ORDER.
    - 4.1 CHECK IF SEAT IS PROPERLY SECURED (1-INCH TEST)
    - 4.2 CHECK SEAT LEVEL
    - 4.3 CHECK SHOULDER HEIGHT OF HARNESS (PINCH TEST)

But who cares if car seats aren't so simple or cheap? Not every solution can be as elegant as we might like. Isn't it worth a police officer sacrificing four days of work to master such a valuable safety device? What matters is that car seats are *effective,* that they save children's lives. And according to NHTSA, they do, reducing the risk of fatality by a whopping 54 percent for children ages one to four.

Barry Myers, a biomedical engineer at Duke University, says it's not necessarily the surfaces of your car's interior that do the most damage in a car accident, but the weight of your body. "Our bodies are intensely fragile," he says. "They're not built to run around at 30 miles an hour and hit hard things." That's why even a good restraint system cannot always prevent death when a fast-moving human body comes to a sudden halt. Brain injuries can occur as the brain smashes against the inside of the skull. Ribs can crack and puncture the lungs. Internal organs bruise and rupture; under pressure, the stomach and intestines can burst like balloons and spill their contents into the body cavity. That said, all of these misfortunes are far likelier to befall an unrestrained passenger.

H. ARMSTRONG ROBERTS

Curious parents may have a question: a 54 percent reduction compared with *what*?

That answer can easily be found on NHTSA's own website. The agency maintains a trove of government data called the Fatality Analysis Reporting System (FARS), a compilation of police reports from all fatal crashes in the United States since 1975. It records every imaginable variable—the type and number of vehicles involved, their speed, time of day, where the passengers were sitting in the car—including what kind of safety restraints, if any, were being worn.

It turns out that a child in a car seat is 54 percent less likely to die than a child riding completely unrestrained—that is, with no car seat, no seat belt, no nothing. That makes sense. A car crash is a violent affair, and a lot of terrible things can happen to a mass of flesh and bone when it is traveling fast inside a heavy metal object that suddenly stops moving.

But how much better is the complicated and costly new solution (the car seat) than the cheap and simple old solution (the seat belt), even though the simple solution wasn't meant for kids?

Seat belts plainly won't do for children under two years old. They are simply too small, and a car seat is the best practical way to secure them. But what about older children? Laws vary by state, but in many cases car seats are mandatory until a child is six or seven years old. How much do those kids benefit from car seats?

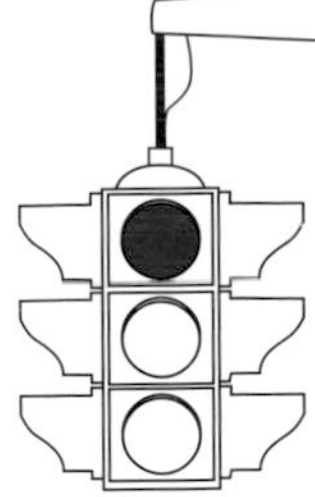

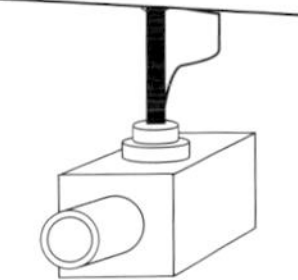

A quick look at the raw FARS data from nearly thirty years of crashes reveals a surprising result. For children two and older, the rate of death in crashes involving at least one fatality is almost identical for those riding in car seats and those wearing seat belts:

MODE OF RESTRAINT	INCIDENTS	DEATHS	CHILD'S DEATH RATE
CHILD SAFETY SEAT	6,835	1,241	18.2%
ADULT SEAT BELT	9,664	1,750	18.1%

It may be that these raw data are misleading. Perhaps kids who ride in car seats are in more violent crashes. Or maybe their parents drive more at night, or on more dangerous roads, or in less-safe vehicles?

But even the most rigorous econometric analysis of the FARS data yields the same results. In recent crashes and old ones, in vehicles large and small, in single-car crashes and pileups, there is no evidence that car seats are better than seat belts in saving the lives of children two and older. In certain kinds of crashes—rear-enders, for instance—car seats actually perform slightly worse.

So maybe the problem is, as NHTSA admits, that too many car seats are installed improperly. (You might argue that a forty-year-old safety device that only 20 percent of its users can install correctly may not be a great safety device to begin with; compared with car seats, the condoms worn by Indian men seem practically infallible.) Could it be that the car seat *is* a miracle device but that we just haven't learned to use it properly?

To answer this, we sought out crash-test data for a side-by-side comparison of seat belts and car seats. You wouldn't think this would be hard to find. After all, every car seat brought to the market must undergo crash testing to gain federal approval. But it appears that researchers have rarely, if ever, run parallel tests on child-sized crash-test dummies. So we decided to do it ourselves.

The idea was simple: we would commission two crash tests, one with a three-year-old-sized dummy in a car seat versus a three-year-old dummy in a lap-and-shoulder belt, the other with a six-year-old-sized dummy in

The proliferation of red-light cameras, placed at intersections to catch drivers who run traffic lights, would seem to present an obvious safety benefit. According to the Insurance Institute for Highway Safety, the cameras cut down the running of red lights by about 40 percent; a separate study found that this translates into a 32 percent reduction of side impact car crashes. But, as another study noted, the presence of cameras *increases* rear-impact crashes by more than 25 percent, apparently because drivers brake suddenly out of fear of being caught running the light. There's even some evidence that, on balance, there are more injuries with red-light cameras than without, although the data are inconclusive.

a booster seat versus a six-year-old dummy in a lap-and-shoulder belt. In each case, the test would simulate a thirty-mile-per-hour frontal collision.

We had a hard time finding a crash-test lab that would do our tests, even though we were willing to pay the $3,000 fee. (Hey, science doesn't come cheap.) After being turned down by what felt like every facility in America, we finally found one willing to take our money. Its director told us we couldn't name the lab, however, out of concern he might lose work from the car-seat manufacturers that were the core of his business. But, he said, he was "a fan of science," and he too wanted to know how things would turn out.

After flying in to this undisclosable location, we bought some new car seats at a Toys "R" Us and drove to the lab. But once the engineer on duty heard the particulars of our test, he refused to participate. It was an idiotic experiment, he said: *of course* the car seats would perform better—and besides, if we put one of his expensive dummies in a lap-and-shoulder belt, the impact would probably rip it to pieces.

It seemed odd to worry over the health of a crash-test dummy—aren't they made to be crashed?—but once we agreed to reimburse the lab if the seat-belted dummy was damaged, the engineer got to work, grumbling under his breath.

The lab conditions guaranteed that the car seats would perform optimally. They were strapped to old-fashioned bench-style rear seats, which

In the front seat, a crash-test dummy representing a three-year-old child is strapped into a brand-new, expertly installed car seat. The dummy in the rear seat, shown below in detail, was clearly too short for the adult-size lap-and-shoulder belt. And yet after the simulated crash in a hydraulic sled, the data showed that the seat-belted dummy did about as well as the dummy in the car seat, emerging with no injuries.

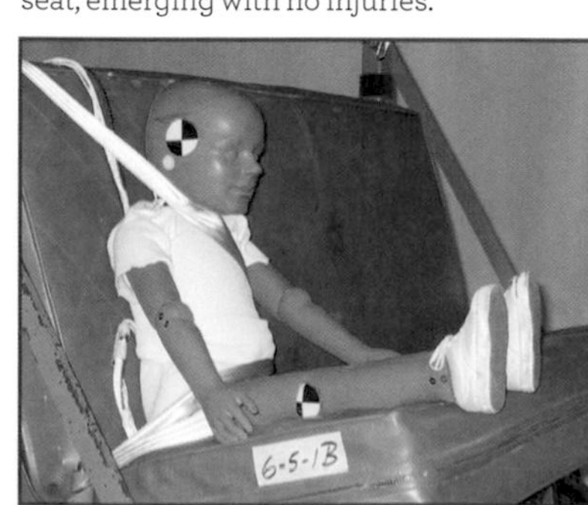

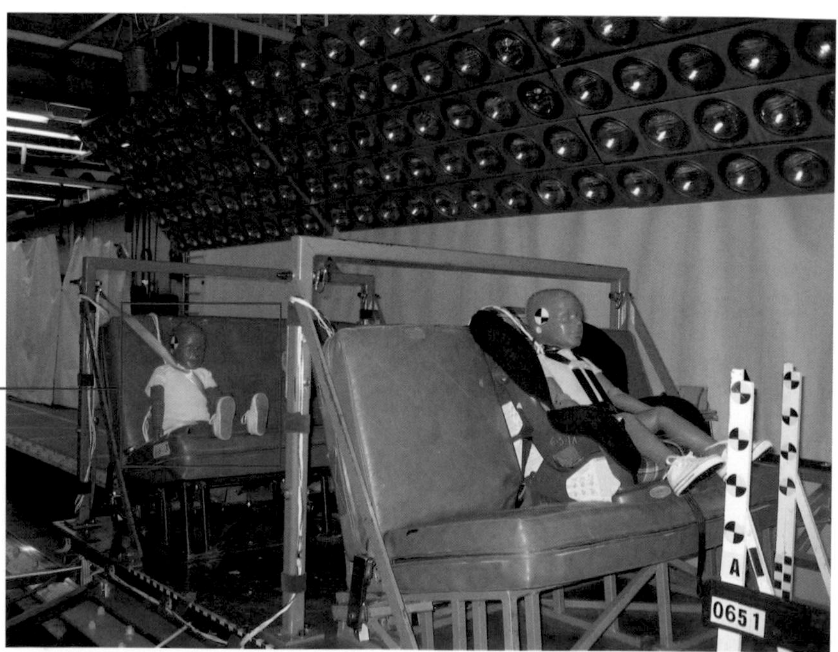

STEPHEN J. DUBNER

give a flush fit, by an experienced crash-test engineer who was presumably far better at securing a car seat than the average parent.

The chore was gruesome, from start to finish. Each child dummy, dressed in shorts, T-shirt, and sneakers, had a skein of wires snaking out of its body to measure head and chest damage.

First came the pair of three-year-olds, one in a car seat and the other in a lap-and-shoulder belt. The pneumatic sled was fired with a frightening bang. In real time, you couldn't see much (except that, to our relief, the seat-belted dummy remained in one piece). But watching the super-slow-motion video replay, you saw each dummy's head, legs, and arms jerk forward, fingers flailing in the air, before the head snapped back. The six-year-old dummies were next.

Within minutes, we had our results: the adult seat belts passed the crash test with flying colors. Based on the head- and chest-impact data, neither the children in the safety seats nor those in the seat belts would likely have been injured in this crash.

So how well did the old-fashioned seat belts work?

They exceeded every requirement for how a child safety seat should perform. Think of it this way: if we submitted our data from the seat-belted dummies to the federal government and said it came from the latest and greatest car seat, our "new" product—which is pretty much the same nylon

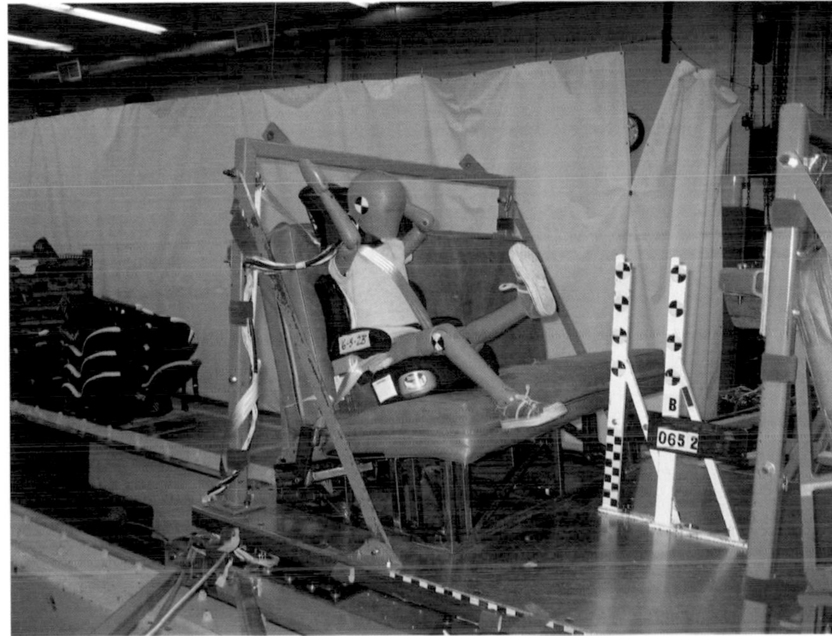

The six-year-old dummy on a booster seat, limbs askew after its crash test, which simulated a collision at 25 miles per hour. Even at this relatively low speed, the dummy was subjected to pressures up to 24 times the force of gravity.

strap Robert McNamara pushed for back in the 1950s—would easily win approval. Since a plain old seat belt can meet the government's safety standard for car seats, perhaps it's not very surprising that car-seat manufacturers turn out a product that can't beat the seat belt. Sad, perhaps, but not surprising.

As one can imagine, our lack of appreciation for car seats places us in a slim minority. (If we didn't have six young children between us, we might well be labeled child haters.) One compelling argument against our thesis is called "seat-belt syndrome." A group of prominent child-safety researchers, warning that crash-test dummies typically don't have sensors to measure neck and abdomen injuries, tell grisly emergency-room tales of the damage seat belts inflict upon children. These researchers gathered data by interviewing parents whose children were in car accidents, and concluded that booster seats reduce significant injury by roughly 60 percent relative to seat belts.

These researchers, many of whom actively care for injured children, are surely well-meaning. But are they right?

There are a variety of reasons why interviewing parents is not the ideal way to get reliable data. Parents may have been traumatized by the crash and will perhaps misremember details. There's also the question of whether the parents—whose names the researchers harvested from an insurance company's database—are being truthful. If your child was riding unrestrained in a car crash, you might feel strong social pressure (or, if you think the insurance company will raise your rates, financial pressure) to say your child was restrained. The police report will show whether or not the vehicle had a car seat, so you can't readily lie about that. But every backseat has a seat belt, so even if your child wasn't wearing one, you could say he was, and it would be difficult for anyone to prove otherwise.

Are there data sources other than parent interviews that could help us answer this important question about child injuries?

The FARS data set won't work because it covers only fatal accidents. We did, however, locate three other data sets that contain information on all crashes. One was a nationally representative database and two were from individual states, New Jersey and Wisconsin. Together, they cover more than 9 million crashes. The Wisconsin data set was particularly useful because it linked each crash to hospital-discharge data, allowing us to better measure the extent of the injuries.

What does an analysis of these data reveal?

For preventing *serious* injury, lap-and-shoulder belts once again performed as well as child safety seats for children aged two through six. But for more minor injuries, car seats did a better job, reducing the likelihood of injury by roughly 25 percent compared with seat belts.

So don't go throwing out your car seats just yet. (That would be illegal in all fifty states.) Children are such valuable cargo that even the relatively small benefit car seats seem to provide in preventing minor injuries may make them a worthwhile investment. There's another benefit that's hard to put a price tag on: a parent's peace of mind.

Or, looking at it another way, maybe that's the greatest *cost* of car seats. They give parents a misplaced sense of security, a belief they've done everything possible to protect their children. This complacency keeps us from striving for a better solution, one that may well be simpler and cheaper, and would save even more lives.

Imagine you were charged with starting from scratch to ensure the safety of all children who travel in cars. Do you really think the best solution

	New Jersey	Wisconsin
POPULATION (2009)	8,707,739	5,654,774
TOTAL AREA	7,417 SQ. MI.	54,310 SQ. MI.
PERCENTAGE URBAN	51%	3%
MEDIAN HOUSEHOLD INCOME (2008)	$70,347	$52,249
PERCENTAGE COMPLETING BACHELOR'S DEGREE (2004)	34.6%	25.6%
MILES OF PUBLIC ROADS	38,753	114,843
LICENSED DRIVERS PER 1,000 RESIDENTS OF ELIGIBLE AGE	841	911
ANNUAL VEHICLE-MILES TRAVELED PER CAPITA	8,480	10,210
SEAT-BELT USE (2008)	92%	74%
TOP FINE FOR FAILURE TO USE SEAT BELT, FIRST OFFENSE	$20	$10
MOTOR VEHICLE CRASH FATALITIES (2008)	590	605
TRAFFIC FATALITIES PER 100 MILLION MILES TRAVELED	.8	1.05
ADULTS WHO BINGE DRINK	14%	23%

A few vital statistics worth considering about New Jersey and Wisconsin.

is to begin with a device optimized for adults and use it to strap down some second, child-sized contraption? Would you really stipulate that this contraption be made by dozens of different manufacturers, and yet had to work in all vehicles even though each vehicle's seat has its own design?

So here's a radical thought: considering that half of all passengers who ride in the backseat of cars are children, what if seat belts were designed *to fit them in the first place*? Wouldn't it make more sense to take a proven solution—one that happens to be cheap and simple—and adapt it, whether through adjustable belts or fold-down seat inserts (which do exist, though not widely)—rather than relying on a costly, cumbersome solution that doesn't work very well?

The National Foundation for Infantile Paralysis, now known as the March of Dimes, also provided Jonas Salk with the initial financial support to start the Salk Institute, in 1962. With polio essentially a scourge of the past, the institute today carries out research on cancer, AIDS, Alzheimer's, and other diseases. Salk hired the architect Louis Kahn to design the Institute's campus in La Jolla, Calif.; it was one of Kahn's first major commissions and brought him worldwide acclaim. The campus, overlooking the Pacific Ocean, was designated a historic landmark in 1991.

GETTY IMAGES

But things seem to be moving in the opposite direction. Instead of pushing for a better solution to child auto safety, state governments across the United States have been raising the age when kids can graduate from car seats. The European Union has gone even further, requiring most children to stay in booster seats until they are twelve.

Alas, governments aren't exactly famous for cheap or simple solutions; they tend to prefer the costly-and-cumbersome route. Note that none of the earlier examples in this chapter were the brainchild of a government official. Even the polio vaccine was primarily developed by a private group, the National Foundation for Infantile Paralysis. President Roosevelt personally provided the seed money—it's interesting that even a sitting president chose the private sector for such a task—and the foundation then raised money and conducted the drug trials.

Nor was it the government that put seat belts in cars. Robert McNamara thought they would give Ford a competitive advantage. He was dead wrong. Ford had a hard time marketing the seat belt, since it seemed to remind customers that driving was inherently unsafe. This led Henry Ford II to complain to a reporter: "McNamara is selling safety but Chevrolet is selling cars."

Some problems, meanwhile, seem beyond the reach of any solution, simple or otherwise. Think of the devastation Mother Nature regularly dishes out. By comparison, traffic fatalities seem eminently manageable.

In 1926, a hurricane made landfall near what today is metropolitan Miami, Fla. It devastated a city of about 100,000 residents and caused, in 1926 dollars, an estimated $105 million in damages. Today, greater Miami has a population of more than 5 million. The environmental scientist Roger Pielke Jr. and the research meteorologist Christopher Landsea (yes, that's an aptonym) have calculated that if the same hurricane struck Miami today, it would cause $157 *billion* in damages, making it the most destructive hurricane in U.S. history. Using the same method—called "normalization"—Pielke and Landsea analyzed all major U.S. hurricanes since 1900. According to this normalized standard, here are the 10 most destructive U.S. hurricanes since 1900. Note that only 2 of them—Katrina and Andrew—have struck within the past 40 years.

RANK	NAME* (LOCATION)	CATEGORY	YEAR	DAMAGE
1	GREAT MIAMI (Fla., Ala.)	4–3	1926	$157 BILLION
2	KATRINA (La., Miss.)	3	2005	$ 81 BILLION
3	GALVESTON (Tex.)	4	1900	$ 78 BILLION
4	GALVESTON (Tex.)	4	1915	$ 62 BILLION
5	ANDREW (Fla., La.)	5–3	1992	$ 57 BILLION
6	NEW ENGLAND (Conn., Mass., N.Y., R.I.)	3	1938	$ 39 BILLION
7	11 (Fla.)	3	1944	$ 39 BILLION
8	LAKE OKEECHOBEE (Fla.)	4	1928	$ 34 BILLION
9	DONNA (Fla., N.C., N.Y.)	4–3	1960	$ 30 BILLION
10	CAMILLE (La., Miss.)	5	1969	$ 21 BILLION

*There was no standardized naming system for Atlantic hurricanes until 1953, when the U.S. Weather Bureau began attaching feminine names to severe storms. (Masculine names were added in 1979.) Before 1953, hurricanes were generally named for the areas they struck or were assigned a number (see "11," above) based on how many storms had preceded them that season. Some storms had multiple nicknames: the fast-moving New England Hurricane of 1938 is also sometimes called the Long Island Express.

Miami Beach after the 1926 hurricane.

Since 1900 more than 1.3 million people worldwide have been killed by hurricanes (or, as they are called in some places, typhoons or tropical cyclones). In the United States, the carnage has been lighter—roughly 20,000 deaths—but the financial losses have been steep, averaging more than $10 billion per year. In the space of just two recent years, 2004 and 2005, six hurricanes, including the killer Katrina, did a combined $153 billion in damages to the southeastern United States.

Why so much damage of late? More people have been moving to hurricane-prone areas (it's nice to live near the ocean, after all), and a lot of them built expensive vacation properties (which drive up the property-damage totals). **$** The irony is that many of these homeowners were lured to the ocean because of the *scarcity* of hurricanes in recent decades—and, perhaps, by the correspondingly low insurance rates.

From the mid-1960s until the mid-1990s, hurricane activity was depressed by the Atlantic Multidecadal Oscillation, a long-recurring climate cycle of sixty to eighty years during which the Atlantic Ocean gradually cools and then warms up again. The temperature change isn't drastic, just a couple of degrees. But it's enough to discourage hurricanes during the cool years and, as we've seen recently, empower them during the warm.

In some regards, hurricanes wouldn't seem to be such a hard problem to solve. Unlike other problems—cancer, for instance—their cause is well established, their location is predictable, and even their timing is known. Atlantic hurricanes generally strike between August 15 and November 15. They travel westward through "Hurricane Alley," a horizontal stretch of ocean running from the west coast of Africa through the Caribbean and into the southeastern United States. And they are essentially heat engines, massive storms created when the topmost layer of ocean water edges above a certain temperature (80 degrees Fahrenheit, or 26.7 degrees Celsius). That's why they start forming only toward summer's end, after the sun has had a few months to warm up the ocean.

At right, Hurricane Alley, as illustrated by the paths of the most destructive Atlantic storms from 1954 to 2008. And, below, the other swaths of ocean around the world where cyclonic storms form as the surface temperature rises.

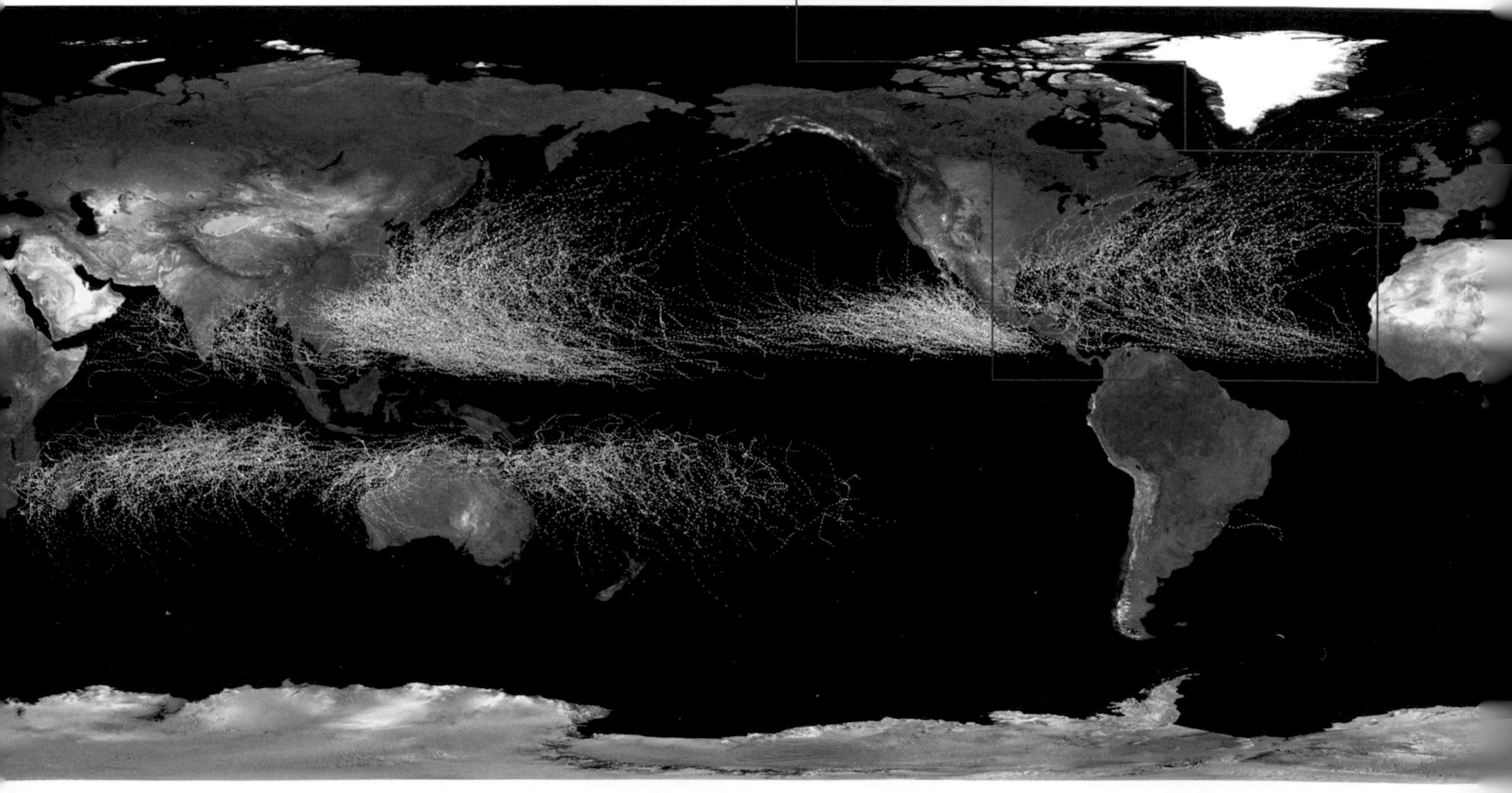

And yet for all their predictability, hurricanes represent a battle that humans seem to have lost. By the time a hurricane forms, there's really no way to fight it. All you can do is run away.

But outside of Seattle lives an intellectually venturesome fellow named Nathan who believes, along with some friends, that they've got a good hurricane solution. Nathan has a physics background, which is key, because that means he understands the thermal properties that define a hurricane. A hurricane isn't just a dynamo; it's a dynamo that comes without an "off" switch. Once it's begun amassing energy it cannot be shut down, and it's far too powerful to be blown back out to sea with a big fan.

That's why Nathan and his friends—most of whom are, like him, science geeks of some sort—want to dissipate the thermal energy *before* it has a chance to accumulate. In other words: prevent the water in Hurricane Alley from getting warm enough to form a destructive hurricane in the first place. Armies sometimes engage in a "scorched earth" policy, destroying anything that might be of value to the enemy. Nathan and his friends want to practice a "chilled ocean" policy to keep the enemy from destroying anything of value.

But, one might be tempted to ask, doesn't this constitute playing with Mother Nature?

"Of *course* it's playing with Mother Nature!" Nathan cackles. "You say that like it's a bad thing!"

Indeed, if we hadn't played with Mother Nature by using nitrate fertilizers to raise our crop yields, many readers of this book probably wouldn't exist today. (Or they would at least be too busy to read, spending all day scrounging for roots and berries.) Stopping polio was also a form of playing with Mother Nature. As are the levees we use to control hurricane flooding—even if, as in Hurricane Katrina, they sometimes fail.

A satellite image showing Hurricane Katrina—the white mass just left of center—on Aug. 27, 2005, along with a color-coded rendering of ocean temperatures. (Blue is cool; red is the warmest.) How much energy does a typical Atlantic hurricane contain? According to Kerry Emanuel, a climate scientist at MIT, in the neighborhood of three terawatts—or more than all the electricity consumed in China in 2007.

The anti-hurricane solution Nathan proposes is so simple that a Boy Scout might have dreamt it up (a very clever one, at least). It can be built with materials bought at a Home Depot, or maybe even filched from the dump.

"The trick is to modify the surface temperature of the water," Nathan says. "Now the interesting thing is that the surface layer of warm water

OPPOSITE AND INSERT: WIKIMEDIA USER NILFANION; NASA/GODDARD SPACE FLIGHT CENTER SCIENTIFIC VISUALIZATION STUDIO

is very thin, often less than 100 feet. And right beneath it is a bulk of very cold water. If you're skin-diving in many of these areas, you can feel the huge difference."

The warm surface layer is lighter than the cold water beneath, and therefore stays on the surface. "So what we need to do is fix that," he says.

It is a tantalizing puzzle—all that cold water, trillions upon trillions of gallons, lying just beneath the warm surface and yet impotent to defuse the potential disaster.

In this artist's rendering of a hurricane-busting device, the floating ring is supported by columns made from old tires. The water level inside the ring would be higher than the water level outside, thereby creating "hydraulic head," which forces the dangerously warm surface water down the tapering plastic tube at the ring's center.

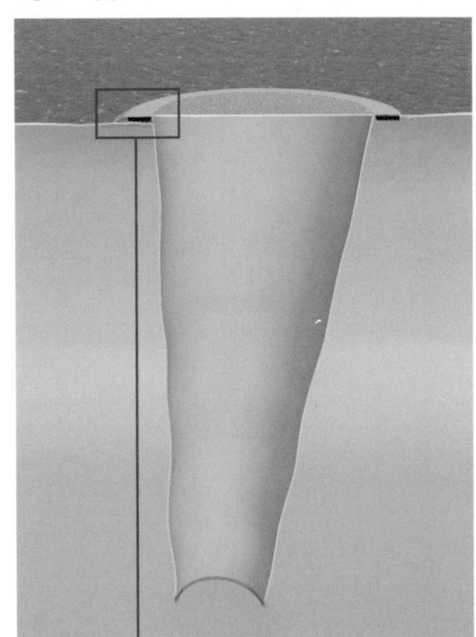

But Nathan has a solution. It is basically "an inner tube with a skirt," he says with a laugh. That is, a large floating ring, anywhere from thirty to three hundred feet across, with a long flexible cylinder affixed to the inside. The ring might be made from old truck tires, filled with foamed concrete and lashed together with steel cable. The cylinder, extending perhaps six hundred feet deep into the ocean, could be fashioned from polyethylene, aka the plastic used in shopping bags.

"That's it!" Nathan crows.

How does it work? Imagine one of these skirted inner tubes—a giant, funky, man-made jellyfish—floating in the ocean. As a warm wave splashes over the top, the water level inside the ring rises until it is higher than the surrounding ocean. "When you have water elevated above the surface in a tube like that," Nathan explains, "it's called 'hydraulic head.'"

Hydraulic head is a force, created by the energy put into the waves by wind. This force would push the warm surface water down into the long plastic cylinder, ultimately flushing it out at the bottom, far beneath the surface. As long as the waves keep coming—and they always do—the hydraulic head's force would keep pushing surface water into the cooler depths, which inevitably lowers the ocean's surface temperature. The process is low-impact, non-polluting, and slow: a molecule of warm surface water would take about three hours to be flushed out the bottom of the plastic cylinder.

Now imagine deploying these floats en masse in the patches of ocean where hurricanes grow. Nathan envisions "a picket fence" of them between Cuba and the Yucatán and another skein off the southeastern seaboard of the United States. They'd also be valuable in the South

© INTELLECTUAL VENTURES

China Sea and in the Coral Sea off the coast of Australia. How many would be needed? Depending on their size, a few thousand floats might be able to stop hurricanes in the Caribbean and the Gulf of Mexico.

A simple throwaway version of this contraption could be built for roughly $100 apiece, although the larger costs would come in towing and anchoring the floats. There's also the possibility of more durable and sophisticated versions, remote-controlled units that could be relocated to where they are most needed. A "smart" version could even adjust the rate at which it cools the surface water by varying the volume of warm water it takes in.

The most expensive float Nathan envisions would cost $100,000. Even at that price, allocating 10,000 of them around the world would cost just $1 billion—or one-tenth the amount of hurricane property damage incurred in a single year in the United States alone. As Ignatz Semmelweis learned about hand-washing and as millions of heart patients learned about cheap pills like aspirin and statins, an ounce of prevention can be worth a few tons of cure.

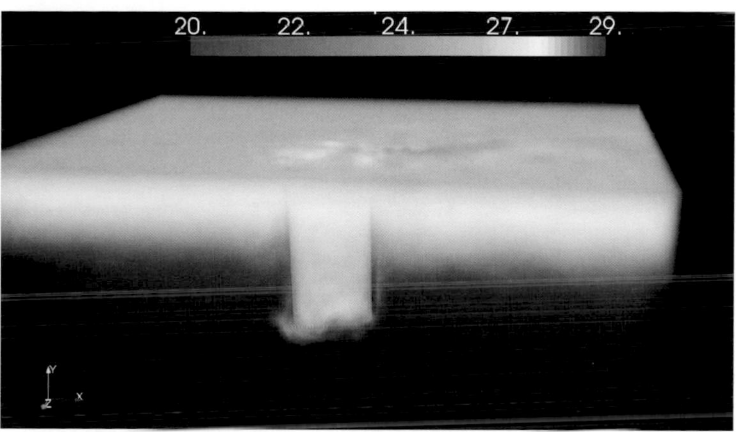

A computer model showing how the anti-hurricane device would work, flushing warmer water toward the cooler depths.

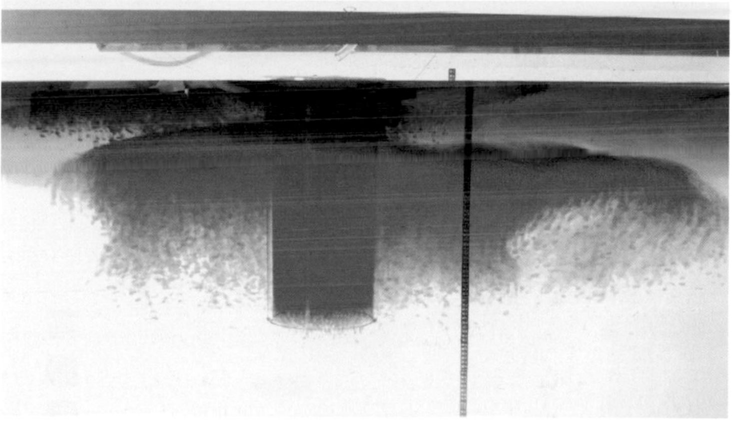

And a physical model, in miniature, housed in a large glass tank. The surface water, dyed red, is flushed out the bottom of the tube.

Nathan isn't yet sure the float will work. For months it has been undergoing intense computer modeling; soon it will be tried out in real water. But all indications are that he and his friends have invented a hurricane killer.

Even if it were capable of eliminating tropical storms entirely, that wouldn't be wise, since storms are part of the natural climate cycle and deliver much-needed rainfall to land. The real value comes from cooling down a Category 5 storm into a less destructive one. "You might be able to manipulate the monsoon rain cycle in tropical areas," Nathan enthuses, "and smooth out the boom-or-bust nature of rainfall in the Sahel in Africa, aiming to prevent starvation."

The float might also improve the ocean's ecology. As surface water heats up each summer, it becomes depleted of oxygen and nutrients, creating a

Here, based on data from the U.S. Geological Survey, is a map of the hurricanes expected to strike the U.S. every 100 years.

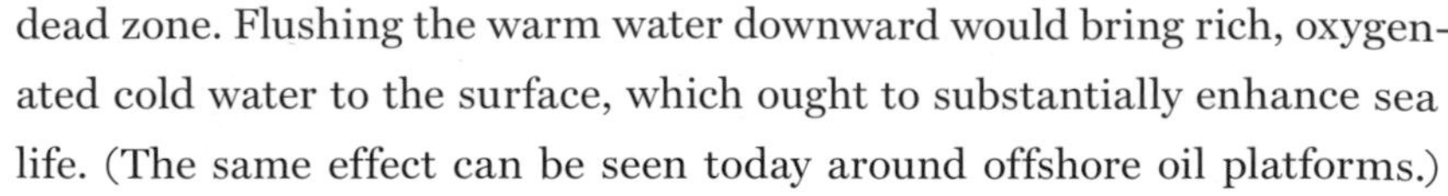

dead zone. Flushing the warm water downward would bring rich, oxygenated cold water to the surface, which ought to substantially enhance sea life. (The same effect can be seen today around offshore oil platforms.) The float might also help sink some of the excess carbon dioxide that has been absorbed by the ocean's surface in recent decades.

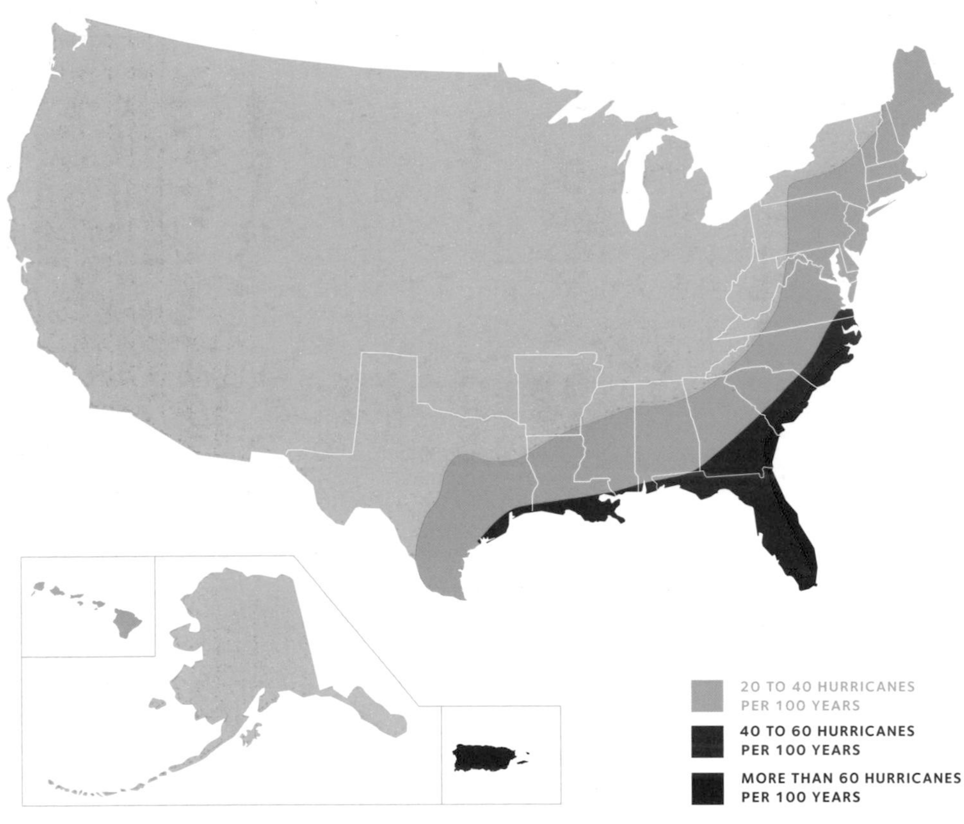

There remains, of course, the question of how, and by whom, these floats would be deployed. The Department of Homeland Security recently solicited hurricane-mitigation ideas from various scientists, including Nathan and his friends. Although such agencies rarely opt for cheap and simple solutions—it simply isn't in their DNA—perhaps an exception will be made in this case, for the potential upside is large and the harm in trying seems minimal.

As dangerous as hurricanes are, there looms within the realm of nature a far larger problem, one that threatens to end civilization as we know it: global warming. If only Nathan and his friends, such smart and creative thinkers who aren't afraid of simple solutions, could do something about *that* . . .

Could the next
Hurricane Katrina
be deleted?

CHAPTER 5

WHAT DO AL GORE AND MOUNT PINATUBO HAVE IN COMMON?

THE HEADLINES HAVE BEEN HARROWING, TO SAY THE LEAST. "Some experts believe that mankind is on the threshold of a new pattern of adverse global climate for which it is ill-prepared," one *New York Times* article declared. It quoted climate researchers who argued that "this climatic change poses a threat to the people of the world."

A *Newsweek* article, citing a National Academy of Sciences report, warned that climate change "would force economic and social adjustments on a worldwide scale." Worse yet, "climatologists are pessimistic that political leaders will take any positive action to compensate for the climatic change or even to allay its effects."

Who in his or her right mind wouldn't be scared of global warming?

But that's not what these scientists were talking about. These articles, published in the mid-1970s, were predicting the effects of global *cooling*.

Alarm bells had rung because the average ground temperature in the Northern Hemisphere had fallen by .5 degrees Fahrenheit (.28 degrees Celsius) from 1945 to 1968. Furthermore, there had been a large increase in snow cover and, between 1964 and 1972, a decrease of 1.3 percent in the amount of sunshine hitting the United States. *Newsweek* reported that the temperature decline, while relatively small in absolute terms, "has taken the planet about a sixth of the way toward the Ice Age average."

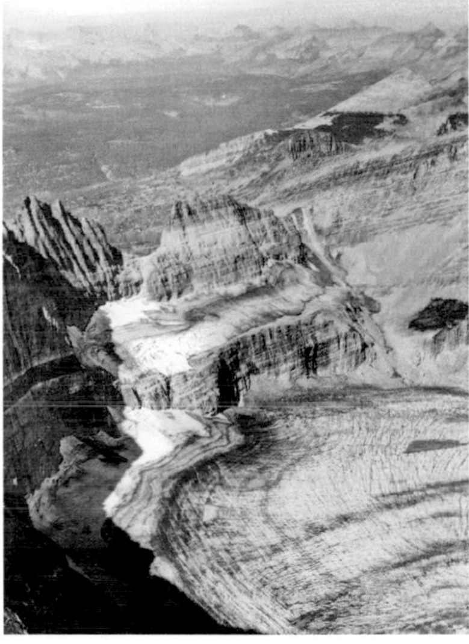

A 1938 photograph of the Grinnell Glacier in Glacier National Park in the northern Rocky Mountains. In the global-cooling predictions seized upon by the national media, glaciers like this one would have steadily advanced.

T. J. HILEMAN GLACIER NATIONAL PARK ARCHIVES

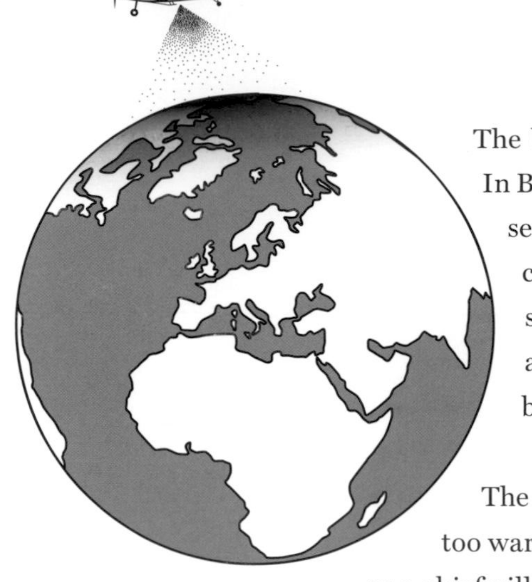

The big fear was a collapse of the agricultural system. In Britain, cooling had already shortened the growing season by two weeks. "[T]he resulting famines could be catastrophic," warned the *Newsweek* article. Some scientists proposed radical warming solutions such as "melting the arctic ice cap by covering it with black soot."

These days, of course, the threat is the opposite. The earth is no longer thought to be too cool but rather too warm. And black soot, rather than saving us, is seen as a chief villain. We have cast endless streams of carbon emissions skyward, the residue of all the fossil fuels we burn to heat and cool and feed and transport and entertain ourselves.

By so doing, we have apparently turned our tender planet into a greenhouse, fashioning in the sky a chemical scrim that traps too much of the sun's warmth and prevents it from escaping back into space. The "global cooling" phase notwithstanding, the average global ground temperature over the past hundred years has risen 1.3 degrees Fahrenheit (.7 degrees Celsius), and this warming has accelerated of late.

"[W]e are now so abusing the Earth," writes James Lovelock, the renowned environmental scientist, "that it may rise and move back to the hot state it was in fifty-five million years ago, and if it does most of us, and our descendants, will die."

There is essentially a consensus among climate scientists that the earth's temperature has been rising and, increasingly, agreement that human activity has played an important role. But the ways humans affect the climate aren't always as obvious as they seem.

It is generally believed that cars and trucks and airplanes contribute an ungodly share of greenhouse gases. This has recently led many right-minded people to buy a Prius or other hybrid car. But every time a Prius owner drives to the grocery store, she may be canceling out its emission-reducing benefit, at least if she shops in the meat section.

How so? Because cows—as well as sheep and other cud-chewing animals called ruminants—are wicked polluters. Their exhalation and flatulence and belching and manure emit methane, which by one common measure is about *twenty-five times more potent* as a greenhouse gas than the carbon dioxide released by cars (and, by the way, humans). The world's

As the earth has warmed, glaciers around the world have gone into retreat. Here is the Grinnell Glacier again, photographed in 2009 from the same vantage point as the picture on the previous page; it is now less than half the size. As of this writing, only 26 of the 150 glaciers in the park as of 1850 remain. Park officials predict that they will be gone entirely by 2020.

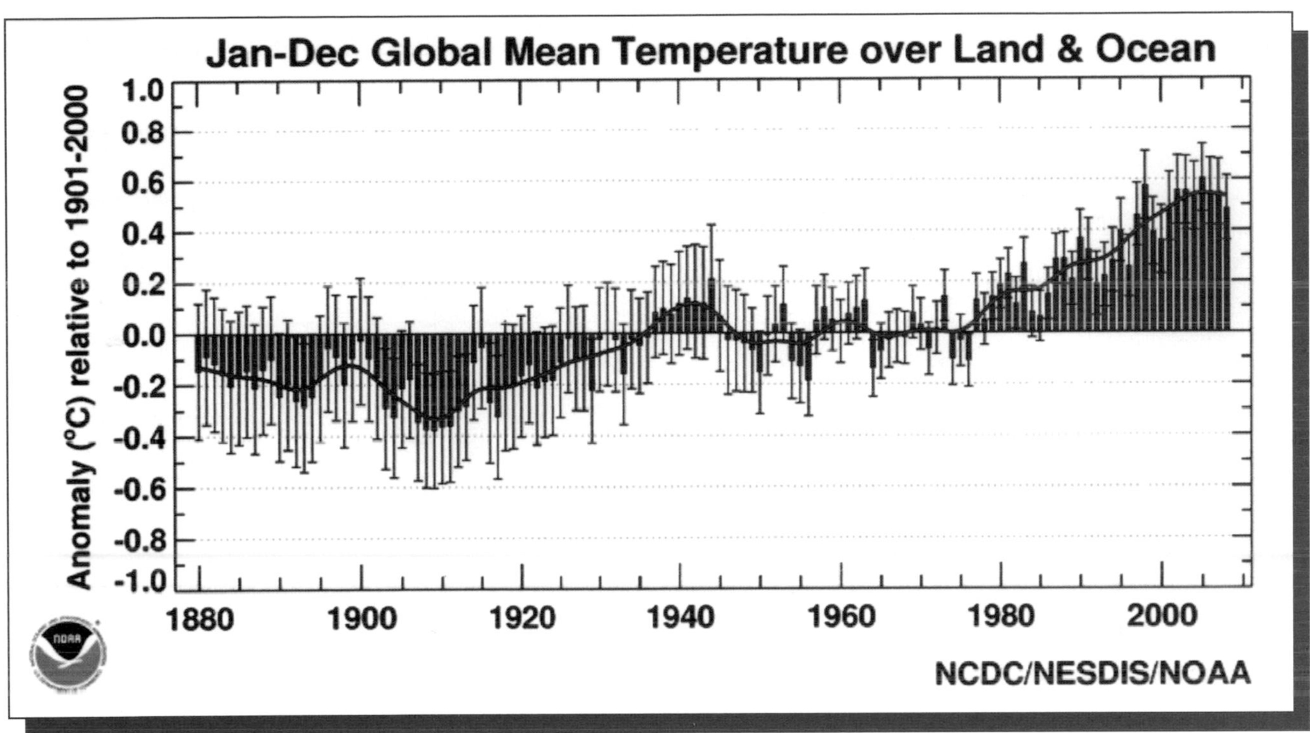

The National Oceanic and Atmospheric Administration's representation of global temperature anomalies—departures, that is, from the long-term average—combines a variety of temperature records from land, sea, and the atmosphere dating back to 1880.

ruminants are responsible for about 50 percent more greenhouse gas than the entire transportation sector.

Even the "locavore" movement, which encourages people to eat locally grown food, doesn't help in this regard. A recent study by two Carnegie Mellon researchers, Christopher Weber and H. Scott Matthews, found that buying locally produced food actually *increases* greenhouse-gas emissions. Why?

More than 80 percent of the emissions associated with food are in the production phase, and big farms are far more efficient than small farms. Transportation represents only 11 percent of food emissions, with delivery from producer to retailer representing only 4 percent. The best way to help, Weber and Matthews suggest, is to subtly change your diet. "Shifting less than one day per week's worth of calories from red meat and dairy products to chicken, fish, eggs, or a vegetable-based diet achieves more greenhouse-gas reduction than buying all locally sourced food," they write.

You could also switch from eating beef to eating kangaroo—because kangaroo farts, as fate would have it, don't contain methane. But just imagine the marketing campaign that would be needed to get Americans to take up 'roo-burgers. And think how

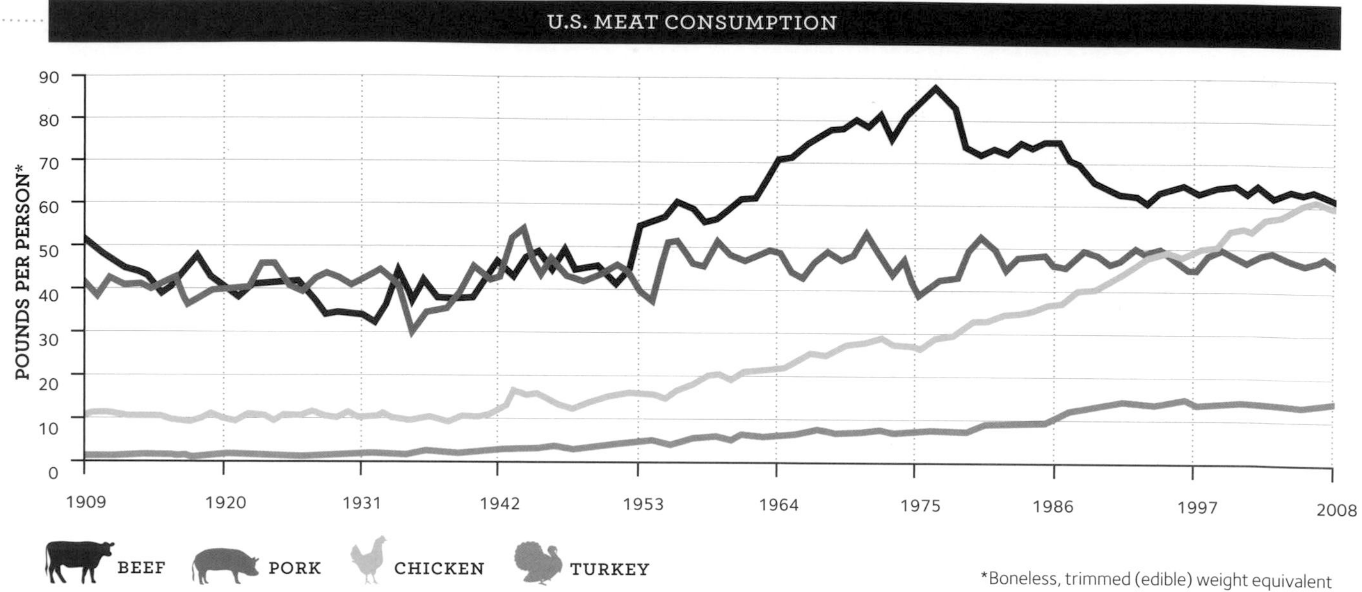

Over the past few decades, Americans *have* been eating less red meat and a lot more chicken. (Turkey consumption, meanwhile, has been on a slow and steady upward path, while **pork** has remained consistent.) The **beef** industry, troubled by this trend, funded research to find out why. It turns out that the public began to increasingly see **beef** as a health risk, thanks to recalls of tainted **beef** and a growing belief in the connection between red-meat consumption and heart disease. There's likely another reason: more women were entering the workforce. A study by the agricultural economists James Mintert, Glynn Tonsor, and Ted Schroeder found that for every 1 percent increase in female employment, **beef** consumption sank by .6 percent while chicken consumption rose by .6 percent. Why? Probably because **beef** takes longer than chicken to prepare, and because poultry producers did a good job marketing cheap and ready-to-cook chicken products. Furthermore, all those working women meant more household income, which meant more families eating in restaurants—where meals are less likely to contain **beef** than meals at home.

hard the cattle ranchers would lobby Washington to ban kangaroo meat. Fortunately, a team of Australian scientists is attacking this problem from the opposite direction, trying to replicate the digestive bacteria in kangaroos' stomachs so it can be transplanted to cows.

For a variety of reasons, global warming is a uniquely thorny problem.

First, climate scientists can't run experiments. In this regard, they are more like economists than physicists or biologists, their goal being to tease out relationships from existing data without the ability to, say, invoke a ten-year ban on cars (or cows).

Second, the science is extraordinarily complex. The impact of any single human activity—let's pretend we tripled the number of airplane flights, for instance—depends on many different factors: the gases emitted, yes, but also how the planes affect things like convection and cloud formation.

To predict global surface temperatures, one must take into account these and many other factors, including evaporation, rainfall, and, yes, animal emissions. But even the most sophisticated climate models don't do a very good job of representing such variables, and that obviously makes predicting the climatic future very difficult. By comparison, the risk models used by modern financial institutions seem quite reliable—but, as recent banking meltdowns have shown, that isn't always the case.

The imprecision inherent in climate science means we don't know with any certainty whether our current path will lead temperatures to rise two degrees or ten degrees. Nor do we really know if even a steep rise means an inconvenience or the end of civilization as we know it.

It is this specter of catastrophe, no matter how remote, that has propelled global warming to the forefront of public policy. If we were certain that warming would impose large and defined costs, the economics of the problem would come down to a simple cost-benefit analysis. Do the future benefits from cutting emissions outweigh the costs of doing so? Or are we better off waiting to cut emissions later—or even, perhaps, polluting at will and just learning to live in a hotter world?

The economist Martin Weitzman analyzed the best available climate models and concluded the future holds a 5 percent chance of a terrible-case scenario—a rise of more than 10 degrees Celsius.

There is of course great uncertainty even in this estimate of uncertainty. So how should we place a value on this relatively small chance of world-wide catastrophe?

MARTIN ACOSTA/REDUX

Scientists at Argentina's National Institute of Agricultural Technology are trying to figure out how to decrease cows' methane emissions. After inserting tubes into the rumen of a cow they named Metana (that's *methane* in Spanish), they siphoned off her digestive gases into a plastic tank strapped atop her back. The researchers found that the cow's methane production fell significantly when she ate a diet with fewer grains and more greens (alfalfa, for instance).

Uncertainty is often mistaken for risk, but there is a cardinal difference: risk, however great, can be measured; uncertainty cannot. How do people respond in the face of even a simple uncertainty? Consider a famous experiment that illustrates what is known as the Ellsberg paradox. (It was devised by Daniel Ellsberg, the same man who, much later in his career, leaked the Pentagon Papers to the *New York Times;* see page 131.) In one version of this experiment, there are two jars. The first jar, you are told, contains 50 red balls and 50 black balls. The second one also contains 100 red and black balls, but the number of each color is unknown. Your task is to pick one red ball out of either jar. Which jar do you choose? For all you know, there might be 99 red balls in the second jar. But most people pick from the first jar, suggesting that even a fifty-fifty risk is preferable to an immeasurable uncertainty. Economists have come to call this condition *ambiguity aversion.*

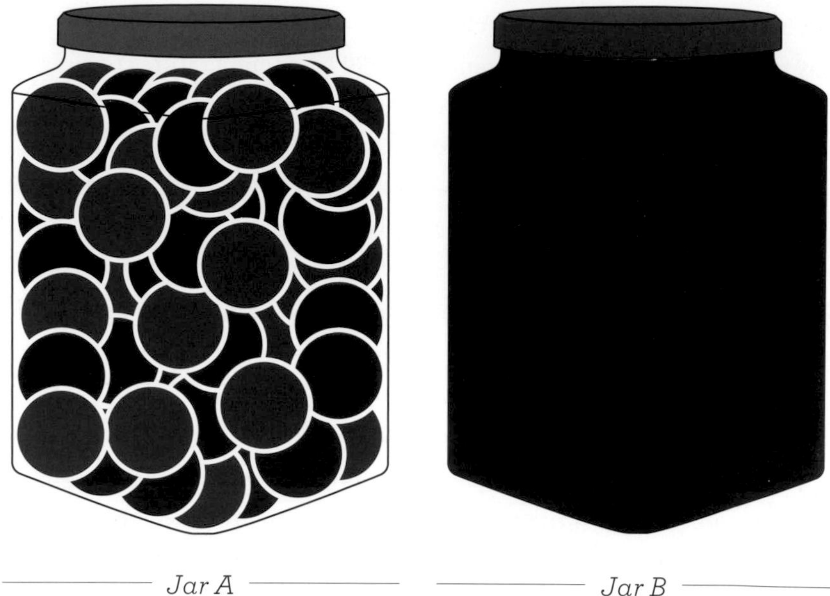

The economist Nicholas Stern, who prepared an encyclopedic report on global warming for the British government, suggested we spend 1.5 percent of global gross domestic product each year—that would be a $1.2 trillion bill as of today—to attack the problem.

But as most economists know, people are generally unwilling to spend a lot of money to avert a future problem, especially when its likelihood is so uncertain. One good reason for waiting is that we might have options in the future to avert the problem that cost far less than today's options.

Although economists are trained to be cold-blooded enough to sit around and calmly discuss the trade-offs involved in global catastrophe, the rest of us are a bit more excitable. And most people respond to uncertainty with more emotion—fear, blame, paralysis—than might be advisable. Uncertainty also has a nasty way of making us conjure up the very worst possibilities. (Think about the last time you heard a bump in the night outside your bedroom door.) With global warming, the worst possibilities are downright biblical: rising seas, hellish temperatures, plague upon plague, a planet in chaos.

It is understandable, therefore, that the movement to stop global warming has taken on the feel of a religion. The core belief is that humankind inherited a pristine Eden, has sinned greatly by polluting it, and must now suffer lest we all perish in a fiery apocalypse. James Lovelock, who might be considered a high priest of this religion, writes in a confessional language that would feel at home in any liturgy: "[W]e misused energy and overpopulated the Earth . . . [I]t is much too late for sustainable development; what we need is a sustainable retreat."

A "sustainable retreat" sounds a bit like wearing a sackcloth. To citizens of the developed world in particular, this would mean consuming less, using less, driving less—and, though it's uncouth to say it aloud, learning to live with a gradual depopulation of the earth.

If the modern conservation movement has a patron saint, it is surely Al Gore, the former vice president and recent Nobel laureate. His documentary film *An Inconvenient Truth* hammered home for millions the dangers of overconsumption. He has since founded the Alliance for Climate Protection, which describes itself as "an unprecedented mass persuasion exercise." Its centerpiece is a $300 million public-service campaign called "We," which urges Americans to change their profligate ways.

Gore's Oscar-winning film relied heavily on science but used spectacle as well; some critics have argued that he stretched credulity. One scene, for instance, showed endangered 700-foot-tall Arctic ice cliffs—"They are so majestic," Gore intoned. But those particular ice cliffs cannot be endangered because they apparently do not exist. The *Inconvenient Truth* scene was computer-generated footage lifted from the science-fiction film *The Day After Tomorrow*. "Yeah, that's our shot," Karen Goulekas, that film's visual effects supervisor, told ABC News. "That's a fully computer-generated shot. There's nothing real in there." Just because something isn't quite real, of course, doesn't mean it can't be scary.

Any religion, meanwhile, has its heretics, and global warming is no exception. Boris Johnson, a classically educated journalist who managed to become mayor of London, has read Lovelock—he calls him a "sacerdotal figure"—and concluded the following: "Like all the best religions, fear of climate change satisfies our need for guilt, and self-disgust, and that eternal human sense that technological progress must be punished by the gods. And the fear of climate change is like a religion in this vital sense, that it is veiled in mystery, and you can never tell whether your acts of propitiation or atonement have been in any way successful."

So while the true believers bemoan the desecration of our earthly Eden, the heretics point out that this Eden, long before humans arrived, once became so naturally thick with methane smog that it was rendered nearly lifeless. When Al Gore urges the citizenry to sacrifice their plastic shopping bags, their air-conditioning, their extraneous travel, the agnostics grumble that human activity accounts for just 2 percent of global carbon-dioxide emissions, with the remainder generated by natural processes like plant decay.

MICHAEL CAULFIELD/WIREIMAGE

The classic story of externalities is "the tragedy of the commons," first told by an English economist in an obscure pamphlet in 1833 and popularized by Garrett Hardin in 1968. The scenario goes like this: Imagine a pasture open to all the area's cattle ranchers, with no grazing restrictions whatsoever. Each rancher wants to add more animals to his herd, since it is in his own interest to do so; but the damage done to the public pasture from overgrazing is distributed among all ranchers. The pasture quickly becomes barren and useless, with everyone losing out. Such environmental externalities—deforestation, overfishing, and air pollution—are a constant danger. As Hardin writes: *"Each man is locked into a system that compels him to increase his herd without limit—in a world that is limited. Ruin is the destination toward which all men rush, each pursuing his own best interest in a society that believes in the freedom of the commons. Freedom in a commons brings ruin to all."*

TYRRELL PHOTOGRAPHIC COLLECTION, POWERHOUSE MUSEUM

Once you strip away the religious fervor and scientific complexity, an incredibly simple dilemma lies at the heart of global warming. Economists fondly call it an *externality.*

What's an externality? It's what happens when someone takes an action but someone else, without agreeing, pays some or all the costs of that action. An externality is an economic version of taxation without representation.

If you happen to live downwind from a fertilizer factory, the ammonium stench is an externality. When your neighbors throw a big party (and don't have the courtesy to invite you), their ruckus is an externality. Secondhand cigarette smoke is an externality, as is the stray gunshot one drug dealer meant for another that instead hit a child on the playground.

The greenhouse gases thought to be responsible for global warming are primarily externalities. When you have a bonfire in your backyard, you're not just toasting marshmallows. You're also emitting gases that, in a tiny way, help to heat the whole planet. Every time you get behind the wheel of a car, or eat a hamburger, or fly in an airplane, you are generating some by-products you're not paying for.

Imagine a fellow named Jack who lives in a lovely house—he built it himself—and comes home from work on the first warm day of summer. All he wants is to relax and cool off. So he cranks the air conditioner all the way

up. Maybe he thinks for a moment about the extra dollar or two he'll pay on his next electricity bill, but the cost isn't enough to deter him.

What he *doesn't* think about is the black smoke from the power plant that burns the coal that heats the water that turns to steam that fills the turbine that spins the generator that makes the power that cools the house that Jack built.

Nor will he think about the environmental costs associated with mining and trucking away that coal, or the associated dangers. In the United States alone, more than 100,000 coal miners died on the job over the past century, with another estimated 200,000 dying later from black lung disease. Thankfully, coal-mining deaths have plummeted in the United States, to a current average of about 36 per year. But if Jack happened to live in China, the local death externality would be much steeper: at least 3,000 Chinese coal miners die on the job each year.

It's hard to blame Jack for not thinking about all this. Modern technology is so proficient that it often masks the costs associated with our consumption. There's nothing visibly dirty about the electricity that feeds Jack's air conditioner. It just magically appears, as if out of a fairy tale.

If there were only a few Jacks in the world, or even a few million, no one would care. But as the global population hurtles toward 7 billion, all those externalities add up. So who should be paying for them?

In principle, this shouldn't be such a hard problem. If we knew how much it cost humankind every time someone used a tank of gas, we could simply levy a tax of that magnitude on the driver. The tax wouldn't necessarily convince him to cancel his trip, nor should it. The point of the tax is to make sure the driver faces the full costs of his actions (or, in economist-speak, to *internalize the externality*).

The revenues raised from these taxes could then be spread out across the folks who suffer the effects of a changing climate—people living in Bangladeshi lowlands, for instance, who will be flooded if the oceans rise

Black lung disease, caused by prolonged exposure to fine coal dust, can lead to scarred lung tissue, emphysema, and death. The rate of the disease among U.S. coal miners has fallen dramatically since 1969, when the federal government introduced regulations that include better mine ventilation, reduced airborne coal dust (by spraying down mine surfaces with water), and early preventive medical testing. In this 1974 photo, a miner at the Black Lung Laboratory of the Appalachian Regional Hospital in Beckley, West Virginia, takes a lung-capacity test.

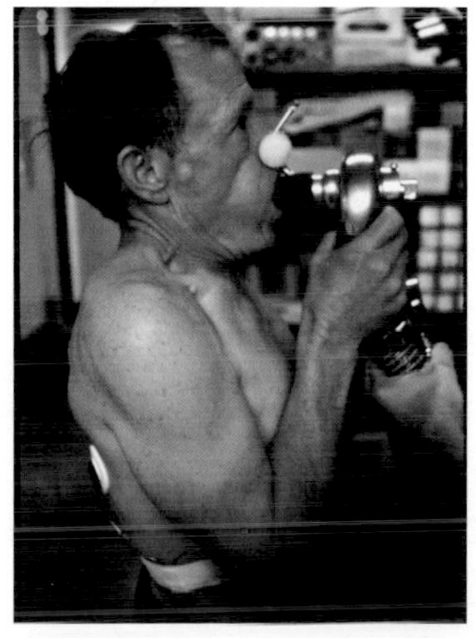

JACK CORN/ENVIRONMENTAL PROTECTION AGENCY

precipitously. If we chose exactly the right tax, the revenues could properly compensate the victims of climate change.

But when it comes to *actually* solving climate-change externalities through taxes, all we can say is good luck. Besides the obvious obstacles—like determining the right size of the tax and getting someone to collect it—there's the fact that greenhouse gases do not adhere to national boundaries. The earth's atmosphere is in constant, complex motion, which means that your emissions become mine and mine yours. Thus, *global* warming.

If, say, Australia decided overnight to eliminate its carbon emissions, that fine nation wouldn't enjoy the benefits of its costly and painful behavior unless everyone else joined in. Nor does one nation have the right to tell another what to do. The United States has in recent years sporadically attempted to lower its emissions. But when it leans on China or India to do the same, those countries can hardly be blamed for saying, *Hey, you got to free-ride your way to industrial superpowerdom, so why shouldn't we?*

When people aren't compelled to pay the full cost of their actions, they have little incentive to change their behavior. Back when the world's big cities were choked with horse manure, people didn't switch to the car because it was good for society; they switched because it was in their economic interest to do so. Today, people are being asked to change their behavior not out of self-interest but rather out of selflessness. This might make global warming seem like a hopeless problem unless—and this is what Al Gore is banking on—people are willing to put aside their self-interest and do the right thing even if it's personally costly. Gore is appealing to our altruistic selves, our externality-hating better angels.

Keep in mind that externalities aren't always as obvious as they seem.

To keep their cars from being stolen off the street, a lot of people lock the steering wheel with an anti-theft device like the Club. The Club is big and highly visible (it even comes in neon pink). By using a Club, you are explicitly telling a potential thief that your car will be hard to steal. The *implicit* signal, meanwhile, is that your neighbor's car—the one without a Club—is a much better target. So your Club produces a negative externality for your non-Club-using neighbor in the form of a higher risk that *his* car will be stolen. The Club is a perfect exercise in self-interest.

A device called LoJack, meanwhile, is in many ways the opposite of

COURTESY THE SEAWIFS PROJECT, NASA/GODDARD SPACE FLIGHT CENTER, AND ORBIMAGE; OCTOBER 22, 2004

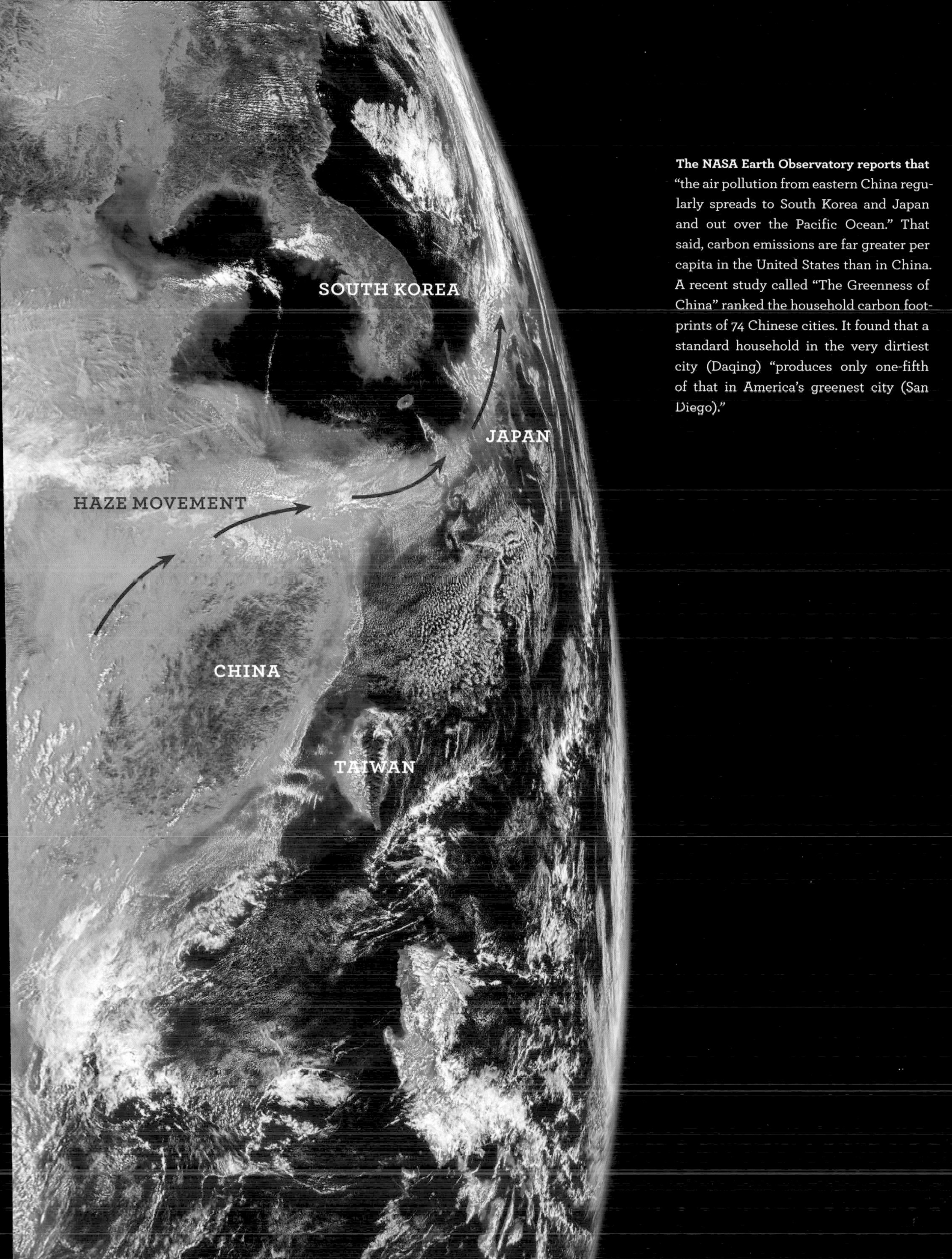

The NASA Earth Observatory reports that "the air pollution from eastern China regularly spreads to South Korea and Japan and out over the Pacific Ocean." That said, carbon emissions are far greater per capita in the United States than in China. A recent study called "The Greenness of China" ranked the household carbon footprints of 74 Chinese cities. It found that a standard household in the very dirtiest city (Daqing) "produces only one-fifth of that in America's greenest city (San Diego)."

Emboldened by its success in recovering cars, LoJack has made tracking devices for other valuables, like laptops and construction equipment. The company even offers a service called SafetyNet that helps you keep track of, say, a family member with Alzheimer's.

the Club. It is a small radio transmitter, not much larger than a deck of cards, hidden somewhere in or beneath the car where a thief can't see it. But if the car is stolen, the police can remotely activate the transmitter and follow its signal straight to the car.

Unlike the Club, LoJack doesn't stop a thief from stealing your car. So why bother installing it?

For one, it helps you recover the car, and fast. When it comes to auto theft, fast is important. Once your car has been missing more than a few days, you generally don't *want* it back, because it likely will have been stripped. Even if you don't want your car to be found, your insurance company does. So a second reason to install LoJack is that insurers will discount your premium. But perhaps the best reason is that LoJack actually makes it fun to have your car stolen.

There's a certain thrill to tracking a LoJack-equipped car, as if the hounds have just been released. The police spring into action, follow the radio signal, and nab the car thief before he knows what's happening. If you're lucky, he may even have filled up the gas tank for you.

Most stolen cars end up in chop shops, clandestine mini-factories that remove the car's most valuable parts and scrap the remains. The police have a hard time rooting out these operations—until, that is, LoJack comes around. Now the police simply follow the radio signal and, often, find the chop shop.

The people who run chop shops aren't stupid, of course. Once they real-

Putting aside the effectiveness of LoJack, auto theft is on a downward trend generally. This was part of an overall drop in crime, but auto theft fell more than any other major category. Why? Among the reasons: tougher enforcement and sentencing; better databases to track stolen cars and parts; and a variety of new anti-theft technologies. That said, auto theft is still a major drag on the U.S. economy. In 2008, $6.4 billion worth of motor vehicles were stolen. One of the most desirable parts: air bags, which are resold on the black market for $50 to $200.

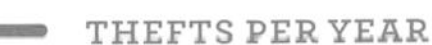

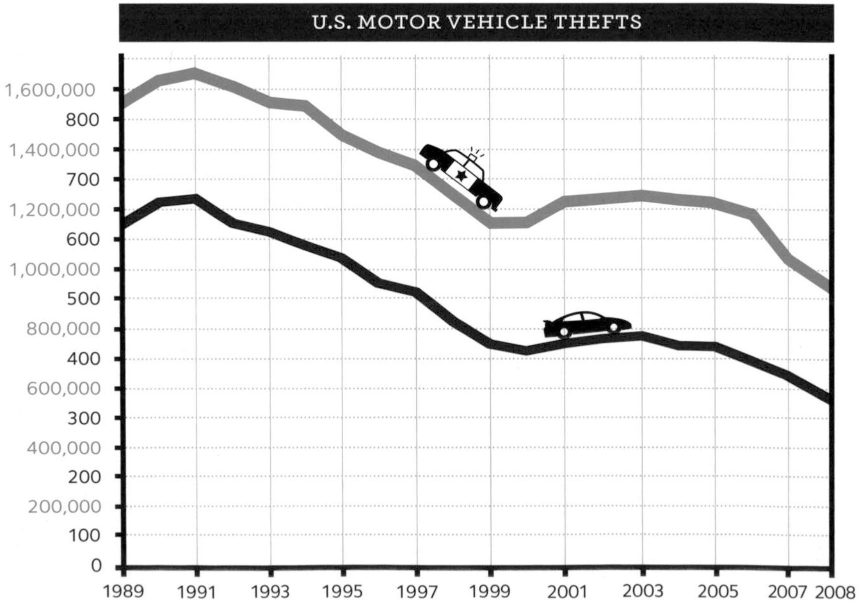

ize what's happening, they change their procedure. The thief, rather than driving the car straight to the shop, will leave it in a parking lot for a few days. If the car is gone when he returns, he knows it had LoJack. If not, he assumes it's safe to deliver it to the chop shop.

But the police aren't stupid either. When they find a stolen car in a parking lot, they may choose not to reclaim it right away. Instead, they watch the vehicle until the thief returns and let him lead them to the chop shop.

Just how difficult has LoJack made life for auto thieves?

For every additional percentage point of cars that have LoJack in a given city, overall thefts fall by as much as 20 percent. Since a thief can't tell which cars have LoJack, he's less willing to take a chance on any car. LoJack is relatively expensive, about $700, which means it isn't all that popular, installed in fewer than 2 percent of new cars. Even so, those cars create a rare and wonderful thing—a *positive* externality—for all the drivers who are too cheap to buy LoJack, because it protects their cars too.

That's right: not all externalities are negative. Good public schools create positive externalities because we all benefit from a society of well-educated people. (They also drive up property values.) Fruit farmers and beekeepers create positive externalities for each other: the trees provide free pollen for the bees and the bees pollinate the fruit trees, also at no charge. That's why beekeepers and fruit farmers often set up shop next to each other.

The externalities shared by farmers and beekeepers were discussed in a 1973 paper called "The Fable of the Bees: An Economic Investigation," by the economist Steven N. S. Cheung. In a footnote, Cheung makes the pithy assertion that "facts, like jade, are not only costly to obtain but also difficult to authenticate." Years later, Cheung was indicted by a U.S. federal grand jury for filing false tax returns and bank reports.

A jade market in Hong Kong.

The bad old days: a stolen car, minus the good parts, in New York City, circa 1986.

Most of the dramatic photos of Mount Pinatubo's 1991 eruption were, like this one, taken a few days before the main blasts:

On June 15, the day of the main blasts, the combina-tion of ashy sky and a passing typhoon made the volcano difficult to photograph. Here's one attempt:

Sixteen aircraft reported being damaged after flying through Pinatubo's ash. Smaller eruptions continued until at least 1994. Above, farmers back at work a few weeks after the main eruption.

One of the unlikeliest positive externalities on record came cloaked in a natural disaster.

In 1991, an eroded, wooded mountain on the Philippine island of Luzon began to rumble and spew sulfuric ash. It turned out that beloved old Mount Pinatubo was a dormant volcano. The nearby farmers and townspeople were reluctant to evacuate, but the geologists, seismologists, and volcanologists who rushed in ultimately persuaded most of them to leave.

Good thing, too: on June 15, Pinatubo erupted for nine furious hours. The explosions were so massive that the top of the mountain caved in on itself, forming what is known as a caldera, a huge bowl-shaped crater, its new peak 850 feet lower than the original mountaintop. Worse yet, the region was simultaneously being lashed by a typhoon. According to one account, the sky poured down "heavy rain and ash with pumice lumps the size of golf balls." Around 250 people died, mainly from collapsed roofs, and more died in the following days from mudslides. Still, thanks to the scientists' warnings, the death toll was relatively small.

Mount Pinatubo was the most powerful volcanic eruption in nearly one hundred years. Within two hours of the main blast, sulfuric ash had reached twenty-two miles into the sky. By the time it was done, Pinatubo had discharged more than 20 million tons of sulfur dioxide into the stratosphere. What effect did that have on the environment?

As it turned out, the stratospheric haze of sulfur dioxide acted like a layer of sunscreen, reducing the amount of solar radiation reaching the

VOLCANO	LOCATION	YEAR	VEI
TAMBORA	LESSER SUNDA ISLANDS (INDONESIA)	1815	7
BILLY MITCHELL	BOUGAINVILLE ISLAND (PAPUA NEW GUINEA)	1580 (± 20 YEARS)	6
HUAYNAPUTINA	SOUTHERN PERU	1600	6
LONG ISLAND	PAPUA NEW GUINEA	1660 (± 20 YEARS)	6
KRAKATOA	INDONESIA	1883	6
SANTA MARIA	WESTERN GUATEMALA	1902	6
NOVARUPTA	ALASKA PENINSULA	1912	6
PINATUBO	LUZON (PHILIPPINES)	1991	6

Meteorologists measure hurricanes with the Saffir-Simpson scale, which runs from categories 1 through 5. For earthquakes, geologists use the Richter magnitude scale, which has no upper limit, although no measured quake has ever hit magnitude 10. Volcanologists, meanwhile, use the Volcanic Explosivity Index (VEI), a 0–8 scale that takes into account the eruption's duration, the amount of material blown out of the volcano, and how high that material is sent into the sky. Some volcanoes cause disruptions far greater than their VEI would suggest—the recent eruptions of the Eyjafjallajökull volcano in Iceland, for instance. As of this writing, it was ranked only a 2 or 3 on the VEI, but because of its proximity to the jet stream, its ash cloud drifted over much of Europe and grounded thousands of airplanes.

OPPOSITE PAGE: TOP LEFT: DAVE HARLOW, U.S. GEOLOGICAL SURVEY; BOTTOM LEFT: RICHARD P. HOBLITT, U.S. GEOLOGICAL SURVEY; RIGHT: ASSOCIATED PRESS

earth. For the next two years, as the haze was settling out, the earth cooled off by an average of nearly 1 degree Fahrenheit, or .5 degrees Celsius. A single volcanic eruption practically reversed, albeit temporarily, the cumulative global warming of the previous hundred years.

Pinatubo created some other positive externalities too. Forests around the world grew more vigorously because trees prefer their sunlight a bit diffused. And all that sulfur dioxide in the stratosphere created some of the prettiest sunsets that people had ever seen.

Of course it was the global cooling that got scientists' attention. A paper in *Science* concluded that a Pinatubo-size eruption every few years would "offset much of the anthropogenic warming expected over the next century."

Even James Lovelock conceded the point: "[W]e might be saved," he wrote, "by an unexpected event such as a series of volcanic eruptions severe enough to block out sunlight and so cool the Earth. But only losers would bet their lives on such poor odds."

True, it probably would take a loser, or at least a fool, to believe a volcano could be persuaded to spew its protective effluvia into the sky at the proper intervals. But what if some foolish people thought Pinatubo could perhaps serve as a blueprint to stop global warming? The same sort of fools who, for instance, once believed that women *didn't* have to die in childbirth, that worldwide famine was *not* foreordained? While they're at it, could they also make their solution cheap and simple?

And if so, where might such fools be found?

In a nondescript section of Bellevue, Washington, a suburb of Seattle, lies a particularly nondescript series of buildings. There's a heating-and-air-conditioning company, a boat maker, a shop that fabricates marble tiles, and another building that used to be a Harley-Davidson repair shop. This last one is a windowless, charmless structure of about twenty thousand square feet whose occupant is identified only by a sheet of paper taped to the glass door. It reads "Intellectual Ventures."

Curb appeal—not. The entrance to the Intel-lectual Ventures laboratory.

STEPHEN J. DUBNER

Inside is one of the most unusual laboratories in the world. There are lathes and mold makers and 3D printers and many powerful computers, of course, but there is also an insectary where mosquitoes are bred so they can be placed in an empty fish tank and, from more than a hundred feet away, assassinated by a laser. This experiment is designed to thwart

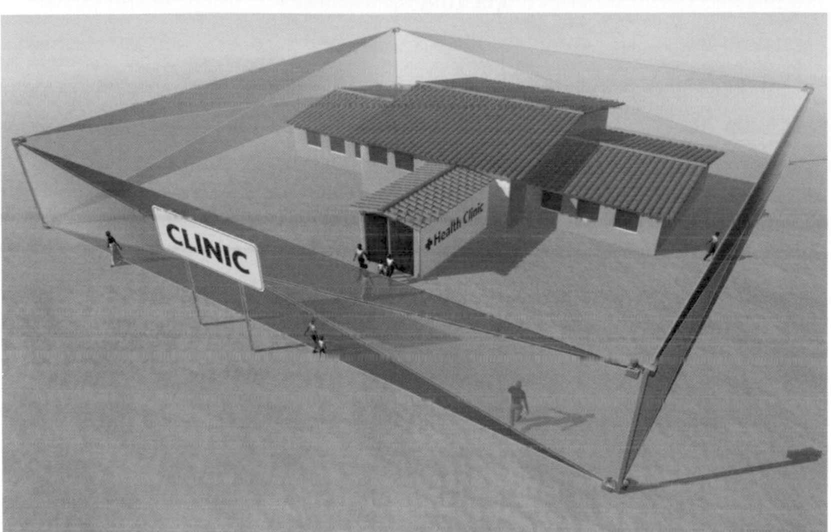

In a series of photos taken by a high-speed camera, a female mosquito is targeted and killed, demonstrating an anti-malaria laser system called a "photonic fence." The idea would be to create laser borders around areas like hospitals, schools, or fields of crops.

malaria. The disease is spread only by certain species of female mosquito, so the laser's tracking system identifies the females by wing-beat frequency—they flap more slowly than males because they are heavier—and zaps them.

Intellectual Ventures is an invention company. The lab, in addition to all the gear, is stocked with an elite assemblage of brainpower, scientists and puzzle-solvers of every variety. They dream up processes and products and then file patent applications, more than five hundred a year. The company also acquires patents from outside inventors, ranging from Fortune 500 companies to solo geniuses toiling in basements. IV operates much like a private-equity firm, raising investment capital and paying returns when its patents are licensed. The company currently controls more than twenty thousand patents, more than all but a few dozen companies in the world. This has led to some grumbling that IV is a "patent troll," accumulating patents so it can extort money from other companies, via lawsuit if necessary. But there is little hard evidence for such claims. A

more realistic assessment is that IV has created the first mass market for intellectual property.

Its ringleader is a gregarious man named Nathan, the same Nathan we met earlier, the one who hopes to enfeeble hurricanes by seeding the ocean with skirted truck tires. Yes, that apparatus is an IV invention. Internally it is known as the Salter Sink because it sinks warm surface water and was originally developed by Stephen Salter, a renowned British engineer who has been working for decades to harness the power of ocean waves.

By now it should be apparent that Nathan isn't just some weekend inventor. He is Nathan Myhrvold, the former chief technology officer at Microsoft. He co-founded IV in 2000 with Edward Jung, a biophysicist who was Microsoft's chief software architect. Myhrvold played a variety of roles at Microsoft: futurist, strategist, founder of its research lab, and whisperer-in-chief to Bill Gates. "I don't know anyone I would say is smarter than Nathan," Gates once observed.

Myhrvold, who is fifty years old, has been smart for a long time. Growing up in Seattle, he graduated from high school at fourteen and by the time he was twenty-three had earned, primarily at UCLA and Princeton, a bachelor's degree (mathematics), two master's degrees (geophysics/space physics and mathematical economics), and a Ph.D. (mathematical physics). He then went to Cambridge University to do quantum cosmology research with Stephen Hawking.

On a trip to the Falkland Islands in 2007, Myhrvold came upon a colony of gentoo penguins. They interested him as a naturalist, a photographer—and a physicist. When the gentoo is ready to relieve itself, it climbs onto the edge of its nest and fires a stream of excrement up to 40 centimeters away. "Penguins, it turns out, have amazing sphincter muscles," Myhrvold says. "And they are able to project like there's no tomorrow." To wit:

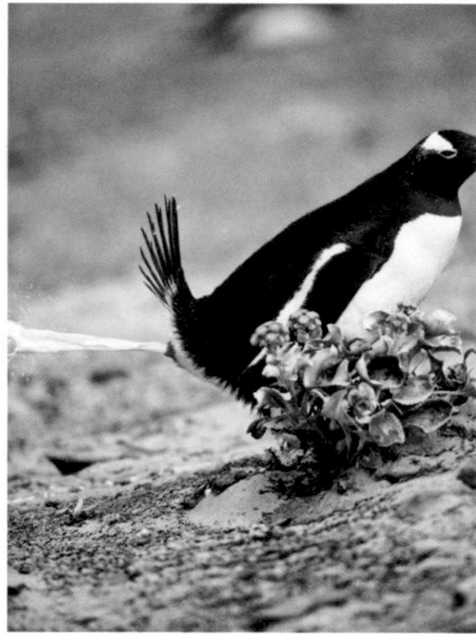

Myhrvold discovered that a pair of German engineers, Victor Benno Meyer-Rochow and Jozsef Gal, had already done some modeling on the subject for an academic paper:

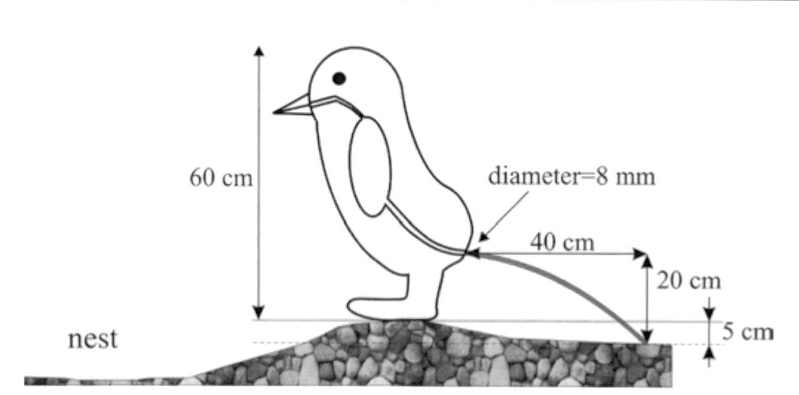

Fig. 1 Position of model penguin during defaecation and physical parameters used to calculate rectal pressure necessary to expel faecal material over a distance of 40 cm

"I can't tell you that particular bit of knowledge has changed my life," Myhrvold says, "but it is stored away with a million other weird things I have learned. Over time some of those do come back and help inform inventions in ways you could never expect. Arctic and Antarctic environments are the ones that will have the largest global-warming impact in the shortest amount of time, since global warming is mostly a high-latitude phenomenon. Penguins and polar bears suffer first—they are in some sense the miner's canary."

NATHAN MYHRVOLD

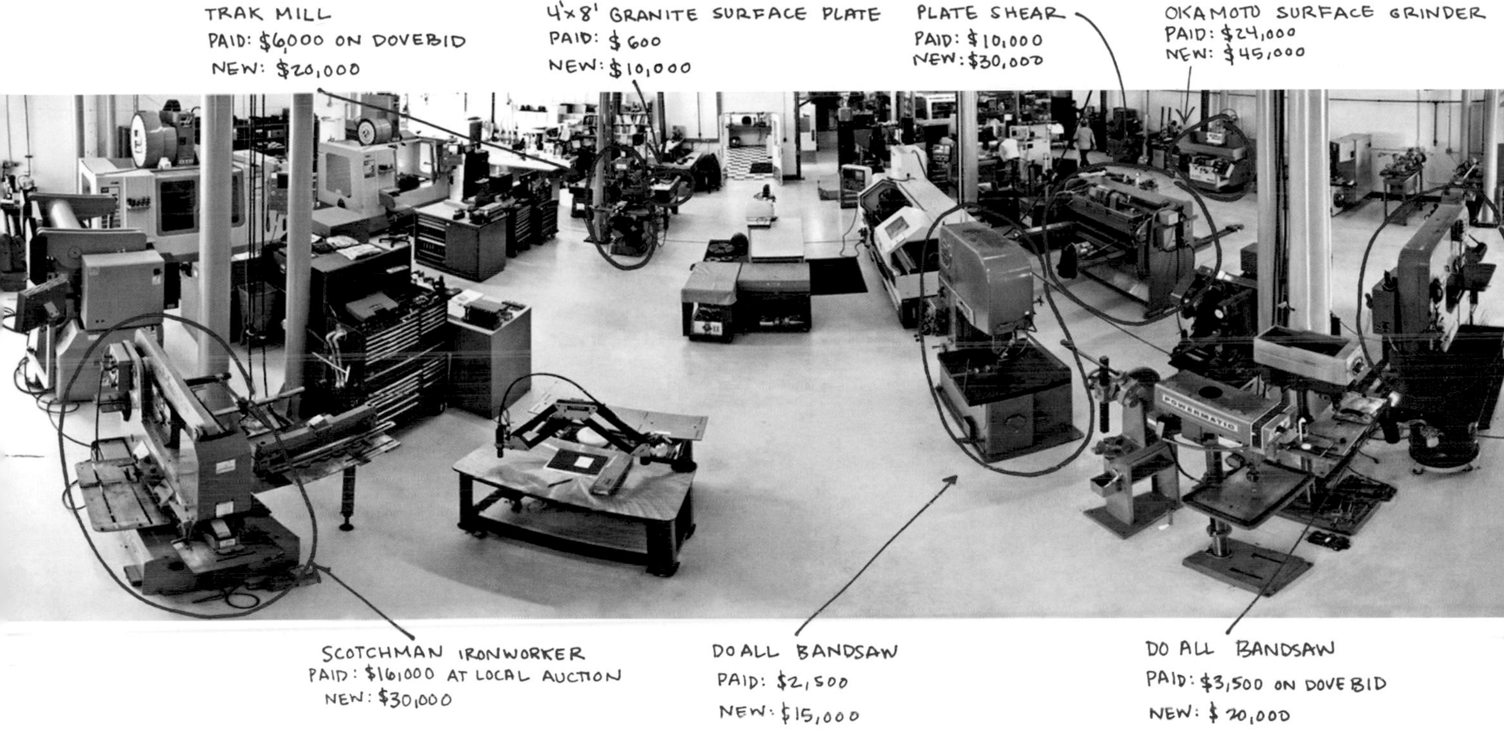

The machine shop at Intellectual Ventures includes nearly 6,000 square feet of precision tools and prototyping machines, many of them bought on the cheap. Here, as annotated by shop manager Mike Vinton, are a few of the bargains.

Myhrvold recalls watching the British science-fiction TV show *Dr. Who* when he was young: "The Doctor introduces himself to someone, who says, 'Doctor? Are you some kind of scientist?' And he says, 'Sir, I am *every* kind of scientist.' And I was, like, Yes! *Yes!* That is what I want to be: *every* kind of scientist!"

He is so polymathic as to make an everyday polymath tremble with shame. In addition to his scientific interests, he is an accomplished nature photographer, chef, mountain climber, and a collector of rare books, rocket engines, antique scientific instruments, and, especially, dinosaur bones: he is co-leader of a project that has dug up more *T. rex* skeletons than anyone else in the world. He is also—and this is hardly unrelated to his hobbies—very wealthy. In 1999, when he left Microsoft, he appeared on the Forbes list of the four hundred richest Americans.

At the same time—and this is how Myhrvold has managed to *stay* wealthy—he is famously cheap. As he walks through the IV lab pointing out his favorite tools and gadgets, his greatest pride is reserved for the items he bought on eBay or at bankruptcy sales. Though Myhrvold understands complexity as well as anyone, he is a firm believer that solutions should be cheap and simple whenever possible.

He and his compatriots are currently working on, among other projects:

Some of the Intellectual Ventures climate crew on the day of our visit. Nathan Myhrvold is at far left; John Latham (whom you'll meet on page 217) is the white-haired gentleman at the very rear; Lowell Wood is the man in tie-dye, with Ken Caldeira at far right, in a black shirt.

a better internal combustion engine; a way to reduce an airplane's "skin drag" and thus increase its fuel efficiency; and a new kind of nuclear power plant that would radically improve the future of worldwide electricity production. Although many of their ideas are just that—ideas—some have already started saving lives. The company has invented a process whereby a neurosurgeon who is attempting to repair an aneurysm can send IV the patient's brain-scan data, which are fed into a 3D printer that produces a life-size plastic model of the aneurysm. The model is shipped overnight to the surgeon, who can make a detailed plan to attack the aneurysm *before* cutting through the patient's skull.

It takes a healthy dose of collective arrogance for a small group of scientists and engineers to think they could simultaneously tackle many of the world's toughest problems. Fortunately, these folks have the requisite amount. They have already sent satellites to the moon, helped defend the United States against missile attack and, via computing advances, changed the way the world works. (Bill Gates is not only an investor in IV but an occasional inventor as well. The mosquito-zapping laser was a response to his philanthropic quest to eradicate malaria.) They have also conducted definitive scientific research in many fields, including climate science.

So it was only a matter of time before they began thinking about global warming. On the day we visited IV, Myhrvold convened roughly a dozen of his colleagues to talk about the problem and possible solutions. They sat around a long oval conference table, Myhrvold near one end.

They are a roomful of wizards, and yet without doubt Myhrvold is their Harry Potter. For the next ten or so hours, fueled by an astonishing amount of diet soda, he prodded and amplified, interjected and challenged.

Everyone in the room agrees that the earth has been getting warmer and they generally suspect that human activity has something to do with it. But they also agree that the standard global-warming rhetoric in the

STEVEN D. LEVITT

media and political circles is oversimplified and exaggerated. Too many accounts, Myhrvold says, suffer from "people who get on their high horse and say that our species will be exterminated."

Does he believe this?

"Probably not."

When *An Inconvenient Truth* is mentioned, the table erupts in a sea of groans. The film's purpose, Myhrvold believes, was "to scare the crap out of people." Although Al Gore "isn't technically lying," he says, some of the nightmare scenarios Gore describes—the state of Florida disappearing under rising seas, for instance—"don't have any basis in physical reality in any reasonable time frame. No climate model shows them happening."

But the scientific community is also at fault. The current generation of climate-prediction models are, as Lowell Wood puts it, "enormously crude." Wood is a heavyset and spectacularly talkative astrophysicist in his sixties who calls to mind a sane Ignatius J. Reilly. Long ago, Wood was Myhrvold's academic mentor. (Wood himself was a protégé of the physicist Edward Teller.) Myhrvold thinks Wood is one of the smartest men in the universe. Off the top of his head, Wood seems to know quite a bit about practically anything: the melt rate of the Greenland ice core (80 cubic kilometers per year); the percentage of unsanctioned Chinese power plants that went online in the previous year (about 20 percent); the number of times that metastatic cancer cells travel through the bloodstream before they land ("as many as a million").

Wood has achieved a great deal in science, on behalf of universities, private firms, and the U.S. government. It was Wood who dreamed up IV's mosquito laser assassination system—which, if it seems vaguely familiar, is because Wood also worked on the "Star Wars" missile-defense system at the Lawrence Livermore National Laboratory, from which he recently retired. (From fighting Soviet nukes to malarial mosquitoes: talk about a peace dividend!)

Today, at the IV think session, Wood is wearing a rainbow tie-dyed short-sleeve dress shirt with a matching necktie.

"The climate models are crude in space and they're crude in time," he continues. "So there's an enormous amount of natural phenomena they can't model. They can't do even giant storms like hurricanes."

What value is there in knowing the circulatory habits of cancer cells? One possibility: catching and killing them before they cause trouble. When Wood learned how widely cancer cells travel before they land, an obvious solution came to mind: a tiny filter, inserted into a person's bloodstream, to catch the offending cells. As it turned out, a professor of biomedical engineering at Cornell named Michael R. King was working on just such a filter. (It has already shown promise as both a cancer killer and a tool to harvest adult stem cells.) Below, an experimental version of the tubular blood filter and, beneath that, an illustration of how cancer cells would roll across the filter's surface (like a "lint brush," as King puts it), thereby binding to a protein that orders the cells to self-destruct.

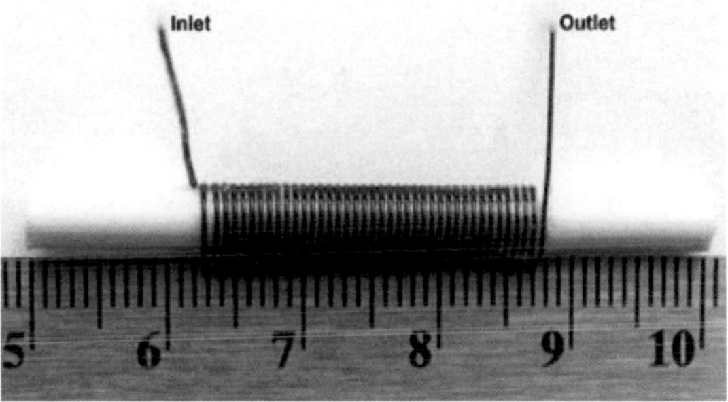

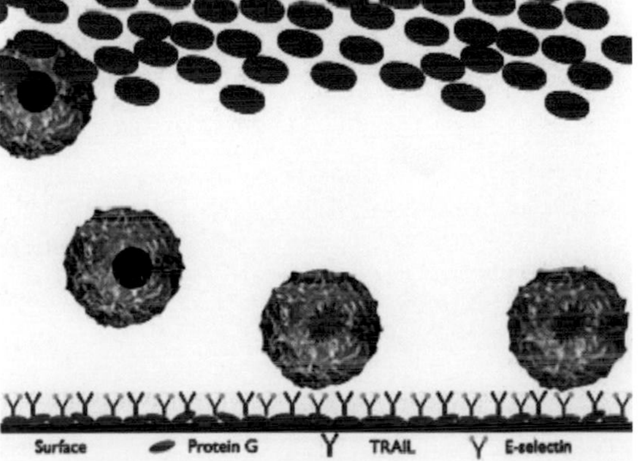

BOTH: KULDEEP RANA

In a provocative 2005 article called "Why Most Published Research Findings Are False," the epidemiologist John Ioannidis argued, "For many current scientific fields, claimed research findings may often be simply accurate measures of the prevailing bias." Even worse, Ioannidis wrote, the more popular the area of study, the more likely the research findings are to be false—in part because of increased pressure to chase funding or to publish the "most impressive" result.

The antidote to such biases? Ioannidis's answer: replication, replication, replication. That may work well in medical research. When it comes to climate predictions, however, replication is obviously a limited tool.

There are several reasons for this, Myhrvold explains. Today's models use a grid of cells to map the earth, and those grids are too large to allow for the modeling of actual weather. Smaller and more accurate grids would require better modeling software, which would require more computing power. "We're trying to predict climate change twenty to thirty years from now," he says, "but it will take us almost the same amount of time for the computer industry to give us fast enough computers to do the job."

That said, most current climate models tend to produce similar predictions. This might lead one to reasonably conclude that climate scientists have a pretty good handle on the future.

Not so, says Wood.

"Everybody turns their knobs"—that is, adjusts the control parameters and coefficients of their models—"so they aren't the outlier, because the outlying model is going to have difficulty getting funded." In other words, the economic reality of research funding, rather than a disinterested and uncoordinated scientific consensus, leads the models to approximately match one another. ■ It isn't that current climate models should be ignored, Wood says—but, when considering the fate of the planet, one should properly appreciate their limited nature.

As Wood, Myhrvold, and the other scientists discuss the various conventional wisdoms surrounding global warming, few, if any, survive unscathed.

The emphasis on carbon dioxide? "Misplaced," says Wood.

Why?

"Because carbon dioxide is not the major greenhouse gas. The major greenhouse gas is water vapor." But current climate models "do not know how to handle water vapor and various types of clouds. That is the elephant in the corner of this room. I hope we'll have good numbers on water vapor by 2020 or thereabouts."

Myhrvold cites a recent paper asserting that carbon dioxide may have had little to do with recent warming. Instead, all the heavy-particulate pollution we generated in earlier decades seems to have *cooled* the atmosphere by dimming the sun. That was the global cooling that caught scientists' attention in the 1970s. The trend began to reverse when we started cleaning up our air.

"So most of the warming seen over the past few decades," Myhrvold says, "might actually be due to *good environmental stewardship*!"

Not so many years ago, schoolchildren were taught that carbon dioxide is the naturally occurring lifeblood of plants, just as oxygen is ours. Today, children are more likely to think of carbon dioxide as a poison. That's because the amount of carbon dioxide in the atmosphere has increased substantially over the past one hundred years, from about 280 parts per million to 380.

But what people don't know, the IV scientists say, is that the carbon dioxide level some 80 million years ago—back when our mammalian ancestors were evolving—was at least 1,000 parts per million. In fact, that is the concentration of carbon dioxide you regularly breathe if you work in a new energy-efficient office building, for that is the level established by the engineering group that sets standards for heating and ventilation systems.

So not only is carbon dioxide plainly not poisonous, but changes in carbon-dioxide levels don't necessarily mirror human activity. Nor has atmospheric carbon dioxide been the trigger for global warming historically: ice-cap evidence shows that over the past several hundred thousand years, carbon dioxide levels have risen *after* a rise in temperature, not the other way around.

Beside Myhrvold sits Ken Caldeira, a soft-spoken man with a boyish face and a halo of curly hair. He runs an ecology lab at Stanford for the Carnegie Institution. Caldeira is among the most respected climate scientists in the world, his research cited approvingly by the most fervent environmentalists. He and a co-author coined the phrase "ocean acidification,"

The effort to curb air pollution has had large and obvious benefits. But a growing body of research argues that such measures had the unintended consequence of warming the earth. One study published by the American Geophysical Union concluded that as much as two-thirds of the warming in Europe since the 1980s was likely due to increased sunlight reaching the earth's surface thanks to less particulate pollution in the sky. (Another study put the figure more conservatively at no more than 50 percent.) A recent NASA study, meanwhile, found that 45 percent of Arctic warming over the last three decades was due to pollution—a strange double whammy of a finding that highlights the complex challenges posed by a global economy full of independent players: while reduced sulfate pollution from Europe and North America led to higher ground temperatures, black soot particles from increased industrial activity in Asia have absorbed sunlight in the atmosphere and caused warmer air temperatures.

the process by which the seas absorb so much carbon dioxide that corals and other shallow-water organisms are threatened. He also contributes research to the Intergovernmental Panel on Climate Change, which shared the 2007 Nobel Peace Prize with Al Gore for sounding the alarm on global warming. (Yes, Caldeira got a Nobel certificate.)

If you met Caldeira at a party, you would likely place him in the fervent-environmentalist camp himself. He was a philosophy major in college, for goodness' sake, and his very name—a variant of *caldera*, the craterlike rim of a volcano—aligns him with the natural world. In his youth (he is fifty-three now), he was a hard-charging environmental activist and all-around peacenik.

Caldeira is thoroughly convinced that human activity is responsible for some global warming and is more pessimistic than Myhrvold about how future climate will affect humankind. He believes "we are being incredibly foolish emitting carbon dioxide" as we currently do.

However, carbon dioxide may not be the right villain in this fight. For starters, as greenhouse gases go, it's not particularly efficient. "A doubling of carbon dioxide traps less than 2 percent of the outgoing radiation emitted by the earth," Caldeira says. Furthermore, atmospheric carbon dioxide is governed by the law of diminishing returns: each gigaton added to the air has less radiative impact than the previous one.

Since Ken Caldeira ushered the phrase "ocean acidification" into the scientific lexicon in a 2003 paper he co-authored with Michael E. Wickett, he has tried to draw public attention to the issue. In his testimony to Congress in 2008, he said that human carbon emissions would "affect ocean chemistry for tens of thousands of years and could harm marine life for millions of years."

In 2009, more than 150 marine scientists (Caldeira included) issued the Monaco Declaration, calling on governments to reduce carbon emissions. For his part, Caldeira would like to see a zero-carbon society: "If you're talking about mugging little old ladies, you don't say, 'What's our target rate of mugging little old ladies?' You say, 'Mugging little old ladies is bad, and we're going to try to eliminate it.'"

A dead coral reef, bleached white. Coral is vulnerable to both rising ocean temperatures and ocean acidification.

The massive eruption of Mount Pinatubo in 1991 left behind a 1.5-mile mountaintop caldera that quickly became a lake. Today it's a tourist destination.

LEFT: DAVID BURDICK, NATIONAL OCEANIC AND ATMOSPHERIC ADMINISTRATION / DEPARTMENT OF COMMERCE; RIGHT: JUAN PAULO, FLICKR

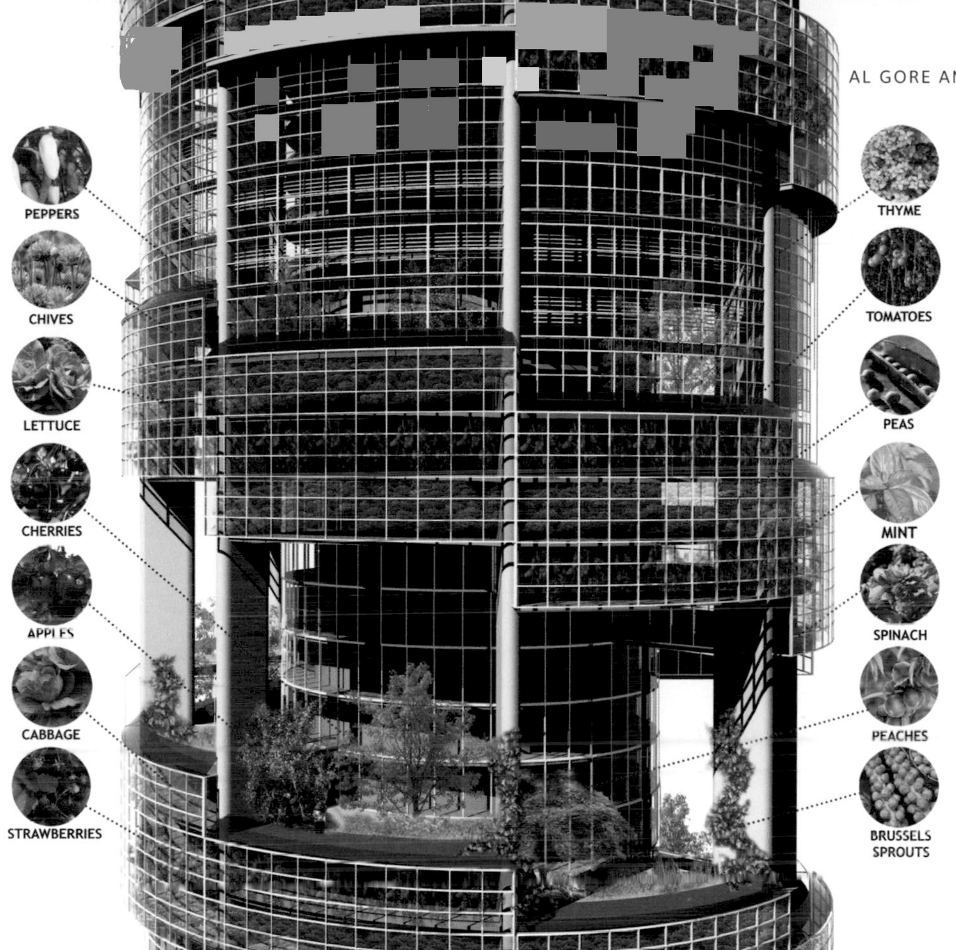

What will agriculture look like in the future? If it's up to Dickson Despommier, a professor of environmental health science at Columbia, much of it will be handled by "vertical farms," custom-built skyscrapers where crops would grow year-round in nutrient-rich liquids, immune to drought and sheltered from pests, with millions of consumers living nearby. This design, by the architect Blake Kurasek, would be 127 stories tall and yield 23 tons of produce per week.

BLAKE KURASEK

Caldeira mentions a study he undertook that considered the impact of higher carbon-dioxide levels on plant life. While plants get their water from the soil, they get their food—carbon dioxide, that is—from the air.

"Plants pay exceedingly dearly for carbon dioxide," Lowell Wood jumps in. "A plant has to raise about a hundred times as much water from the soil as it gets carbon dioxide from the air, on a molecule-lost-per-molecule-gained basis. Most plants, especially during the active part of the growing season, are water-stressed. They bleed very seriously to get their food."

So an increase in carbon dioxide means that plants require less water to grow. And what happens to productivity?

Caldeira's study showed that doubling the amount of carbon dioxide while holding steady all other inputs—water, nutrients, and so forth—yields a 70 percent increase in plant growth, an obvious boon to agricultural productivity.

"That's why most commercial hydroponic greenhouses have supplemental carbon dioxide," Myhrvold says. "And they typically run at 1,400 parts per million." ■

"Twenty thousand years ago," Caldeira says, "carbon-dioxide levels were

While most climate scientists label the 2000s the warmest decade on record, the warming trended downward toward the end of the decade, as seen in these data from the National Oceanic and Atmospheric Administration's National Climatic Data Center. A short-term decrease hardly negates a long-term trend, but the recent pause contributed to a growing public and political uncertainty about global warming's menace.

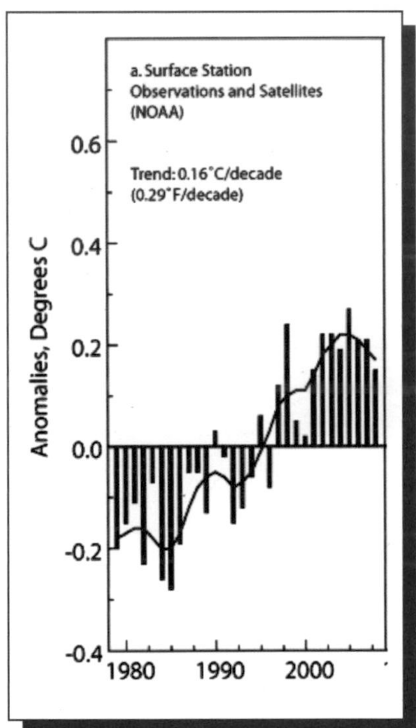

lower, sea level was lower—and trees were in a near state of asphyxiation for lack of carbon dioxide. There's nothing special about today's carbon-dioxide level, or today's sea level, or today's temperature. What damages us are *rapid* rates of change. Overall, more carbon dioxide is probably a *good* thing for the biosphere—it's just that it's increasing too fast."

The gentlemen of IV abound with further examples of global warming memes that are all wrong.

Rising sea levels, for instance, "aren't being driven primarily by glaciers melting," Wood says, no matter how useful that image may be for environmental activists. The truth is far less sexy. "It is driven mostly by water-warming—literally, the thermal expansion of ocean water as it warms up."

Sea levels *are* rising, Wood says—and have been for roughly twelve thousand years, since the end of the last ice age. The oceans are about 425 feet higher today, but the bulk of that rise occurred in the first thousand years. In the past century, the seas have risen less than eight inches.

As to the future: rather than the catastrophic thirty-foot rise some people have predicted over the next century—good-bye, Florida!—Wood notes that the most authoritative literature on the subject suggests a rise of about one and a half feet by 2100. That's much less than the twice-daily tidal variation in most coastal locations. "So it's a little bit difficult," he says, "to understand what the purported crisis is about."

Caldeira, with something of a pained look on his face, mentions a most surprising environmental scourge: trees. Yes, trees. As much as Caldeira personally lives the green life—his Stanford office is cooled by a misting water chamber rather than air-conditioning—his research has found that planting trees in certain locations actually exacerbates warming because comparatively dark leaves absorb more incoming sunlight than, say, grassy plains, sandy deserts, or snow-covered expanses.

Then there's this little-discussed fact about global warming: while the drumbeat of doom has grown louder over the past several years, the average global temperature during that time has in fact *decreased*.

In the darkened conference room, Myhrvold cues up an overhead slide that summarizes IV's views of the current slate of proposed global-warming solutions. The slide says:

- Too little
- Too late
- Too optimistic

Too little means that typical conservation efforts simply won't make much of a difference. "If you believe there's a problem worth solving," Myhrvold says, "then these solutions won't be enough to solve it. Wind power and most other alternative energy things are cute, but they don't scale to a sufficient degree. At this point, wind farms are a government subsidy scheme, fundamentally." What about the beloved Prius and other low-emission vehicles? "They're great," he says, "except that transportation is just not that big of a sector."

Also, coal is so cheap that trying to generate electricity without it would be economic suicide, especially for developing countries. Myhrvold argues that cap-and-trade agreements, whereby coal emissions are limited by quota and cost, can't help much, in part because it is already . . .

Too late. The half-life of atmospheric carbon dioxide is roughly one hundred years, and some of it remains in the atmosphere for thousands of years. So even if humankind immediately stopped burning all fossil fuel, the existing carbon dioxide would remain in the atmosphere for several generations. Pretend the United States (and perhaps Europe) miraculously converted overnight and became zero-carbon societies. Then pretend they persuaded China (and perhaps India) to demolish every coal-burning power plant and diesel truck. As far as atmospheric carbon dioxide is concerned, it might not matter all that much. And by the way, that zero-carbon society you were dreamily thinking about is way . . .

Too optimistic. "A lot of the things that people say would be a good thing probably aren't," Myhrvold says. As an example he points to solar power. "The problem with solar cells is that they're black, because they are designed to absorb light from the sun. But only about 12 percent gets turned into electricity, and the rest is reradiated as heat—which contributes to global warming." ■

Although a widespread conversion to solar power might seem appealing, the reality is tricky. The energy consumed by building the thousands of new solar plants necessary to replace coal-burning and other power plants would create a huge long-term "warming debt," as Myhrvold calls it. "Eventually, we'd have a great carbon-free energy infrastructure but only

Nathan Myhrvold expands on the challenges of solar power: "Efficiencies of 9 percent to 13 percent are typical for current widely deployed technology. In the future that will change, and some laboratory examples are better, but this is what people deploy now. So for every watt of electricity they generate, current solar cells throw about 10 watts into the climate as heat. Some of this heat would have occurred anyway when the light was absorbed by the ground, but the most effective solar cell installations are in deserts where the albedo is pretty high (.4 to .5) and there is little cloud cover, so the solar cells cause a bunch of heating that would not have otherwise occurred. A typical coal power plant gives off about 2 watts of thermal heat for each watt generated, so the direct thermal heating from solar plants is likely to be as large or larger than that from coal plants."

Solar panels in the Monegros Desert in Aragon, Spain.

RADIUS IMAGES/CORBIS

after making emissions and global warming worse every year until we're done building out the solar plants, which could take thirty to fifty years."

This hardly means the energy problem should be dismissed. That's why IV—along with inventors all over the world—are working toward the holy grail: cheaper and cleaner forms of energy.

But from an atmospheric perspective, energy represents what might be called the input dilemma. How about the *output* dilemma? What if the greenhouse gases we've already emitted *do* produce an ecological disaster?

Myhrvold is not blind to the possibility. He has probably thought about such scenarios in greater scientific detail than any climate doomsayer: a collapse of massive ice sheets in Greenland or Antarctica; a release of huge amounts of methane caused by the melting of Arctic permafrost; and, as he describes it, "a breakdown of the thermohaline circulation system in the North Atlantic, which would put an end to the Gulf Stream."

So what happens if the doomsayers turn out to be right? What if the earth *is* becoming dangerously warmer, whether because of our fossil-fuel profligacy or some natural climate cycle? We don't really want to sit back and stew in our own juices, do we?

The eruption of Mount St. Helens on May 18, 1980, blew debris 80,000 feet into the sky in less than fifteen minutes. Within three days, ash had reached the East Coast of the United States, and continued to spread around the world. The eruption sheared more than 1,300 feet off the mountain's summit, ejected 3.7 billion cubic yards of material, and killed fifty-seven people. Most of them died from asphyxiation as they were overtaken by the ash and superheated gases; the victims included a U.S. Geological Survey volcanologist who was observing the eruption from a ridge five miles away. As big an eruption as Mount St. Helens was, Mount Pinatubo was roughly ten times more powerful.

ROBERT KRIMMEL, U.S. GEOLOGICAL SURVEY

In 1980, when Myhrvold was a grad student at Princeton, Mount St. Helens erupted back home in Washington State. Even though he was nearly three thousand miles away, Myhrvold saw a thin layer of ash accumulating on his windowsill. "It's hard not to think about volcanic dust when it's raining down on your dorm room," he says, "although to be honest, my room was messy in many other ways."

Even as a kid, Myhrvold was fascinated by geophysical phenomena—volcanoes, sunspots, and the like—and their history of affecting the climate. The Little Ice Age intrigued him so much that he forced his family to visit the northern tip of Newfoundland, where Leif Eriksson and his Vikings reputedly made camp a thousand years earlier.

The connection between volcanoes and climate is hardly a new idea. Another polymath, Benjamin Franklin, wrote what seems to be the first scientific paper on the topic. In "Meteorological Imaginations and Conjectures," published in 1784, Franklin posited that recent volcanic eruptions in Iceland had caused a particularly harsh winter and a cool summer with "constant fog over all Europe, and [a] great part of North America." In 1815, the gargantuan eruption of Mount Tambora in Indonesia produced "The Year Without a Summer," a worldwide disaster that killed crops, prompted widespread starvation and food riots, and brought snow to New England as late as June.

As Myhrvold puts it: "All really big-ass volcanoes have some climate effects."

Volcanoes erupt all the time, all over the world, but truly "big-ass" ones are rare. If they weren't—well, we probably wouldn't be around to worry about global warming. The anthropologist Stanley Ambrose has argued that a supervolcanic explosion at Lake Toba on Sumatra, roughly seventy thousand years ago, blocked the sun so badly that it triggered an ice age that nearly wiped out *Homo sapiens*.

What distinguishes a big-ass volcano isn't just how much stuff it ejaculates, but where the ejaculate goes. The typical volcano sends sulfur dioxide into the troposphere, the atmospheric layer closest to the earth's surface. This is similar to what a coal-burning power plant does with its sulfur emissions. In both cases, the gas stays in the sky only a week or so before falling back to the ground as acid rain, generally within a few hundred miles of its origin.

But a big volcano shoots sulfur dioxide far higher, into the stratosphere. That's the layer that begins at about seven miles above the earth's surface, or six miles at the poles. Above that threshold altitude, there is a drastic change in a variety of atmospheric phenomena. The sulfur dioxide, rather than quickly returning to the earth's surface, absorbs stratospheric water vapor and forms an aerosol cloud that circulates rapidly, blanketing most of the globe. In the stratosphere, sulfur dioxide can linger for a year or more, and will thereby affect the global climate.

That's what happened in 1991 when Mount Pinatubo erupted in the Philippines. Pinatubo made Mount St. Helens look like a hiccup; it put more sulfur dioxide into the stratosphere than any volcano since Krakatoa, more than a century earlier. In the period between those two eruptions, the state of science had progressed considerably. A worldwide cadre of

Among the aftereffects of Krakatoa's eruption in 1883: garishly colorful sunsets around the world. Some modern art historians have concluded that the Norwegian painter Edvard Munch's *The Scream* records one such sunset. One evening that year, just as Krakatoa's ash cloud was affecting Scandinavia, Munch was walking down a road with two friends when, as he wrote in his journal:

> *The Sun set—all at once the sky became blood red—and I felt overcome with melancholy. I stood still and leaned against the railing, dead tired—clouds like blood and tongues of fire hung above the blue-black fjord and the city.... My friends went on, and I stood alone, trembling with anxiety. I felt a great, unending scream piercing through nature.*

Krakatoa apparently was not the only massive volcano to inspire a classic work of art. The 1815 eruption of Mount Tambora and the resultant "Year Without a Summer" is thought to have inspired the eighteen-year-old Mary Shelley to write *Frankenstein*.

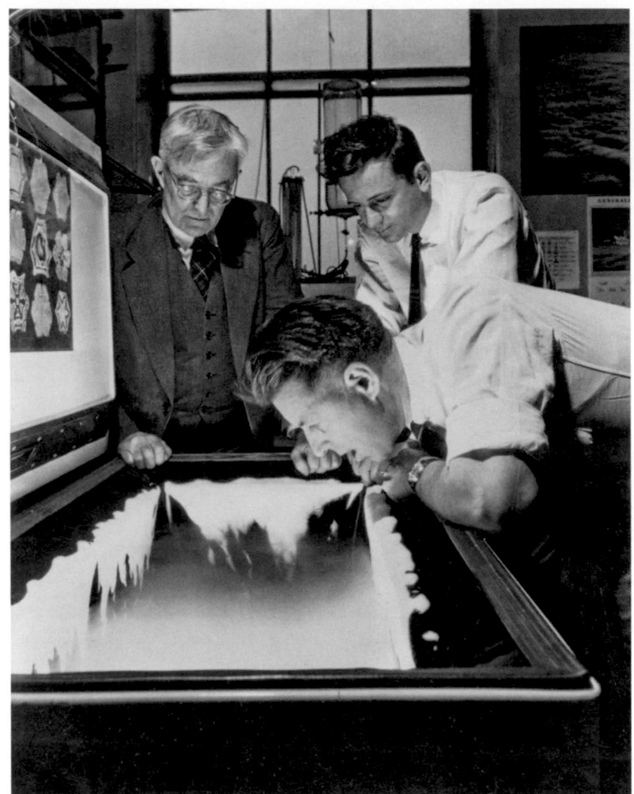

Project Cirrus, a joint venture between General Electric and the U.S. military, sought to research weather-modification technologies, including rain making. In this 1949 photo, Irving Langmuir (left) and Bernard Vonnegut look on as Vincent Schaefer tries to form ice crystals with his exhalations. Project Cirrus also tried to disrupt a hurricane by seeding it from an airplane with 180 pounds of crushed dry ice. The storm, which had been heading out into the Atlantic Ocean, veered westward and struck the Georgia coast, killing one person and injuring several more. As *Time* reported, a weatherman in Miami "hinted that last month's disastrous hurricane might have been not an act of God, but just a low Yankee trick." Ultimately, the U.S. Weather Bureau found that the hurricane had begun to head toward Georgia *before* the cloud seeding, and that Project Cirrus wasn't at fault.

SCHENECTADY MUSEUM; HALL OF ELECTRICAL HISTORY FOUNDATION/CORBIS

scientists was on watch at Pinatubo, equipped with modern technology to capture every measurable piece of data. The atmospheric aftereffects of Pinatubo were undeniable: a decrease in ozone, more diffuse sunlight, and, yes, a sustained drop in global temperature.

Nathan Myhrvold was working at Microsoft then, but he still followed the scientific literature on geophysical phenomena. He took note of the Pinatubo climate effects and, one year later, a 900-page report from the National Academy of Sciences called *Policy Implications of Greenhouse Warming*. It included a chapter on geoengineering, which the NAS defined as "large-scale engineering of our environment in order to combat or counteract the effects of changes in atmospheric chemistry."

In other words: if human activity is warming up the planet, could human ingenuity cool it down?

People have been trying to manipulate the weather forever. Just about every religion ever invented has a rain-making prayer. But secularists have stepped it up in recent decades. In the late 1940s, three General Electric scientists in Schenectady, New York, successfully seeded clouds with silver iodide. The trio included a chemist named Bernard Vonnegut; the project's public-relations man was his younger brother Kurt, who went on to become a world-class novelist—and in his writing, he used a good bit of the far-out science he picked up in Schenectady.

The 1992 NAS report gave a credibility boost to geoengineering, which until then had largely been seen as the province of crackpots and rogue governments. Still, some of the NAS proposals would have seemed outlandish even in a Vonnegut novel. A "multiple balloon screen," for instance, was meant to deflect sunlight by launching billions of aluminized balloons into the sky. A "space mirror" scheme called for fifty-five thousand reflective sails to orbit high above the earth.

The NAS report also raised the possibility of intentionally spreading sulfur dioxide in the stratosphere. The idea was attributed to a Belarusian climate scientist named Mikhail Budyko. After Pinatubo, there was no doubt that stratospheric sulfur dioxide cooled the earth. But wouldn't it be nice to not have to rely on volcanoes to do the job?

Unfortunately, the proposals for getting sulfur dioxide into the stratosphere were complex, costly, and impractical. Loading up artillery shells, for instance, and firing them into the sky. Or launching a fleet of fighter jets with high-sulfur fuel and letting their exhaust paint the stratosphere. "It was more science fiction than science," says Myhrvold. "None of the plans made any economic or practical sense."

The other problem was that many scientists, particularly nature-friendly ones like Ken Caldeira, found the very idea abhorrent. Dump chemicals in the atmosphere to reverse the damage caused by . . . dumping chemicals in the atmosphere? It was a crazy, hair-of-the-dog scheme that seemed to violate every tenet of environmentalism. Those who saw global warming as a religious issue could hardly imagine a more grievous sacrilege.

But the best reason to reject the idea, Caldeira thought, was that it simply wouldn't work.

That was his conclusion after hearing Lowell Wood give a lecture on stratospheric sulfur dioxide at a 1998 climate conference in Aspen. But being a scientist who prefers data to dogma—even if the environmental dogma in this case lay close to his heart—Caldeira ran a climate model to test Wood's claims. "The intent," he says, "was to put an end to all the geoengineering talk."

He failed. As much as Caldeira disliked the concept, his model backed up Wood's claims that geoengineering could stabilize the climate even in the face of a large spike in atmospheric carbon dioxide, and he wrote a paper saying so. Caldeira, the most reluctant geoengineer imaginable, became a convert—willing, at least, to explore the idea.

Which is how it comes to pass that, more than ten years later, Caldeira, Wood, and Myhrvold—the onetime peacenik, the onetime weapons architect, and the onetime Viking fanboy—are huddled together in a former Harley-Davidson repair shop showing off their scheme to stop global warming.

It wasn't just the cooling potential of stratospheric sulfur dioxide that surprised Caldeira. It was how little was needed to do the job: about thirty-four gallons per minute, not much more than the amount of water that comes out of a heavy-duty garden hose.

Warming is largely a polar phenomenon, which means that high-latitude

Pop quiz: Which Vonnegut brother published written works under which of the following titles?

1. *Nucleation Catalysis*
2. *Cat's Cradle*
3. *The Smell of Tornadoes*
4. *The Role of the Space Shuttle Videotapes in the Discovery of Sprites, Jets and Elves*
5. *Excelsior! We're Going to the Moon! Excelsior!*
6. *Chicken Plucking as Measure of Tornado Wind Speed*
7. *Luminous Phenomena in Nocturnal Tornadoes*
8. *Mother Night*
9. *A Vortex Whistle*
10. *2BR02B*
11. *Address to the American Physical Society*
12. *Thanasphere*
13. *Allegiance to Theory Changes With the Wind*
14. *Report on the Barnhouse Effect*
15. *Slaughterhouse-Five*
16. *Crude Altimeter*
17. *Little Drops of Water*
18. *Quaint Cumulus Convection Conviction*
19. *God Bless You, Mr. Rosewater*
20. *Presters*

Brothers Bernard (left) and Kurt Vonnegut.

ANSWERS:
Bernard: 1, 3, 4, 6, 7, 9, 13, 16, 18, 20
Kurt: 2, 5, 8, 10, 11, 12, 14, 15, 17, 19

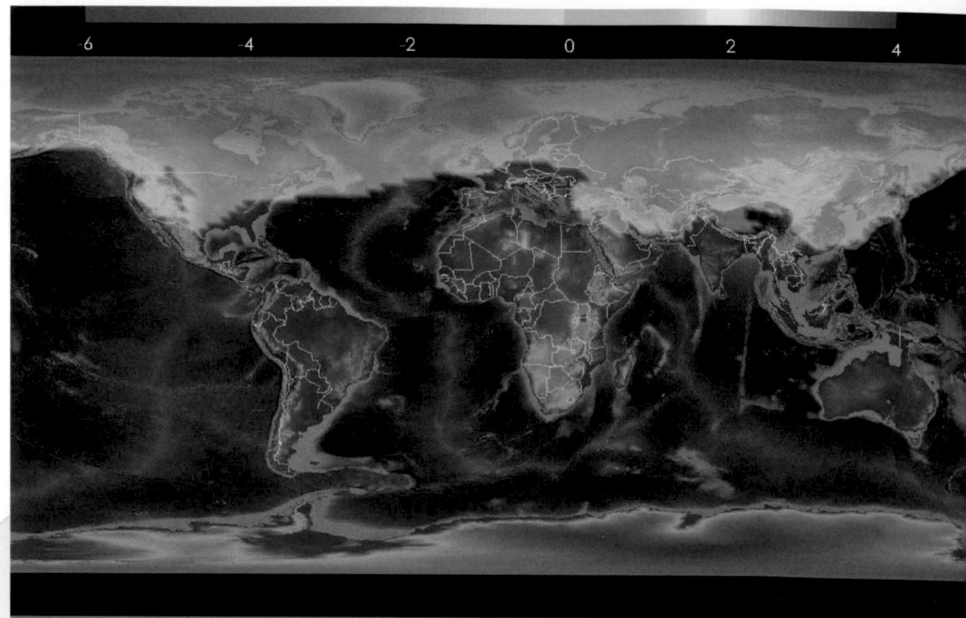

An Intellectual Ventures computer plot, by Ken Caldeira and Lowell Wood, showing the projected average temperature reduction (in degrees Celsius) over a fifty-year period if the "garden hose to the sky" were deployed at 60 degrees north latitude (just south of the Arctic Circle), assuming an atmospheric carbon-dioxide concentration of twice the preindustrial level, or roughly 50 percent higher than today's level.

areas are four times more sensitive to climate change than the equator. By IV's estimations, 100,000 tons of sulfur dioxide per year would effectively reverse warming in the high Arctic and reduce it in much of the Northern Hemisphere.

That may sound like a lot but, relatively speaking, it is a smidge. At least 200 *million* tons of sulfur dioxide already go into the atmosphere each year, roughly 25 percent from volcanoes, 25 percent from human sources like motor vehicles and coal-fired power plants, and the rest from other natural sources like sea spray.

So all that would be needed to produce a globe-changing effect is one-twentieth of 1 percent of current sulfur emissions, simply relocated to a higher point in the sky. How can this be? Myhrvold's answer: "Leverage!"

Leverage is the secret ingredient that distinguishes physics from, say, chemistry. Think back to the Salter Sink, IV's device for preventing hurricanes. Hurricanes are destructive because they gather up the thermal energy in the ocean's surface and convert it into physical force, a primordial act of leverage creation. The Salter Sink ruptures that process by using wave power to continually sink the warm water all through hurricane season.

"A kilogram of sulfur dioxide, emitted by a truck or a bus or a power plant into the troposphere, does much less good for you than in the stratosphere,"

THERMOSPHERE
372 MILES

MESOSPHERE
53 MILES

STRATOSPHERE
31 MILES

TROPOSPHERE
4–12 MILES

TOP: INTELLECTUAL VENTURES; BOTTOM: ATMOSPHERIC LAYER ALTITUDES: NASA; EARTH IMAGE: NASA/NSSDC

Myhrvold says. "So you get a huge leverage, and that's a pretty cool thing. That's why Archimedes said, 'If you give me a fulcrum, I can move the world.'"

So once you eliminate the moralism and the angst, the task of reversing global warming boils down to a straightforward engineering problem: how to get thirty-four gallons per minute of sulfur dioxide into the stratosphere?

The answer: a very long hose.

That's what IV calls this project—a "garden hose to the sky." Or, when they're feeling slightly more technical, a "stratospheric shield for climate stabilization." Considering its scientific forebear and the way it wraps the planet in a protective layer, perhaps it should be called Budyko's Blanket.

For anyone who loves cheap and simple solutions, things don't get much better. Here's how it works. At a base station, sulfur would be burned into sulfur dioxide and then liquefied. "The technology for doing this is well known," says Wood, "because early in the twentieth century, sulfur dioxide was the major refrigerant gas."

The hose, stretching from the base station into the stratosphere, would be about eighteen miles long but extremely light. "The diameter is just a couple inches, not some giant-ass pipe," says Myhrvold. "It's literally a specialized fire hose."

The hose would be suspended from a series of high-strength, helium-filled balloons fastened to the hose at 100- to 300-yard intervals (a "string of pearls," IV calls it), ranging in diameter from 25 feet near the ground to 100 feet near the top.

The liquefied sulfur dioxide would be sent skyward by a series of pumps, affixed to the hose at every 100 yards. These too would be relatively light, about forty-five pounds each—"smaller than the pumps in my swimming pool," Myhrvold says. There are several advantages to using many small pumps rather than one monster pump at the base station: a big ground pump would create more pressure, which, in turn, would require a far heavier hose; even if a few of the small pumps failed, the mission itself wouldn't; and using small, standardized units would keep costs down.

At the end of the hose, a cluster of nozzles

Lowell Wood challenged Myhrvold's quote of Archimedes: "Actually, he asked for a sufficiently long *lever*." To which Myhrvold huffed: "He needed a fulcrum too!"

It is not surprising that people like Wood and Myhrvold still admire the ancient Greek, one of history's greatest mathematicians and scientists. In addition to the theory of levers, Archimedes developed theories on measuring density and volume and came up with countless mechanical inventions, some of which are still used in one form or another.

When the Greek city of Syracuse was besieged by Rome in 214 B.C.E., Archimedes was enlisted to create war machines to defend it. Syracuse nevertheless fell; as history tells it, Archimedes was concentrating so hard on a mathematical problem that he hardly noticed a Roman soldier who burst into his home and killed him.

ARCHIMEDES erster erfinder scharpffsinniger vergleichung/
Wag vnd Gewicht/durch außfluß des Wassers.

A sixteenth-century German woodcut in which Archimedes explores the principle of displacement.

The key components of Intellectual Ventures' "garden hose to the sky" project to fight global warming include, from bottom to top: the base station, from which liquefied sulfur dioxide is pumped skyward; the very long hose, held aloft by V-shaped balloons; and weatherproof nozzles to spray sulfur dioxide into the stratosphere.

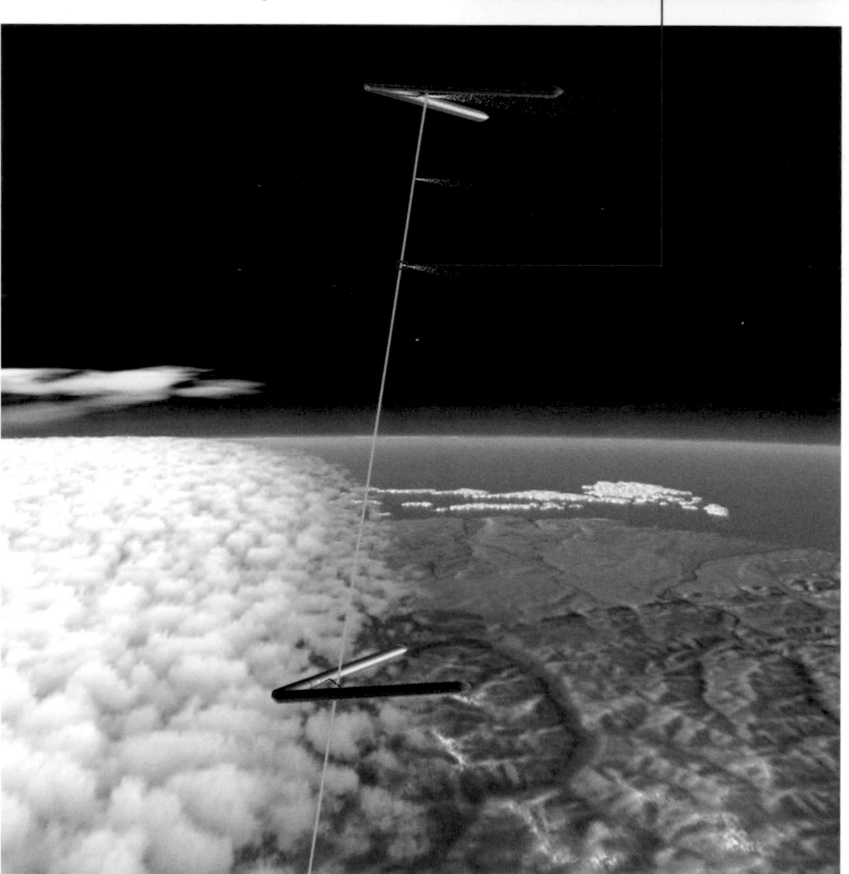

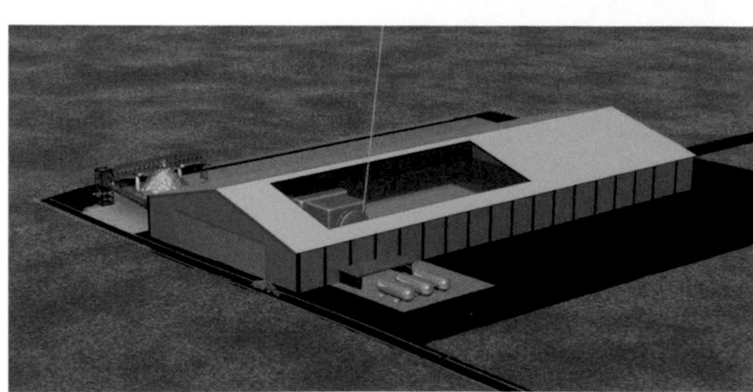

INTELLECTUAL VENTURES

would spritz the stratosphere with a fine mist of colorless liquid sulfur dioxide.

Thanks to stratospheric winds that typically reach one hundred miles per hour, the spritz would wrap around the earth in roughly ten days' time. That's how long it would take to create Budyko's Blanket. Because stratospheric air naturally spirals toward the poles, and because the Arctic regions are more vulnerable to global warming, it makes sense to spray the sulfur aerosol at high latitude—with perhaps one hose in the Southern Hemisphere and another in the Northern.

Myhrvold, in his recent travels, happened upon one potentially perfect site. Along with Bill Gates and Warren Buffett, he was taking a whirlwind educational tour of various energy producers—a nuclear plant, a wind farm, and so on. One of their destinations was the Athabasca Oil Sands in northern Alberta, Canada.

Billions of barrels of petroleum can be found there, but it is heavy, mucky crude. Rather than lying in a liquid pool beneath the earth's crust, it is mixed in, like molasses, with the surface dirt. In Athabasca you don't drill for oil; you mine it, scooping up gigantic shovels of earth and then separating the oil from its waste components.

One of the most plentiful waste components is sulfur, which commands such a low price that oil companies simply stockpile it. "There were big yellow mountains of it, like a hundred meters high by a thousand meters wide!"

Like industrial reincarnations of ancient step pyramids, the sulfur mountains built from Athabasca oil-sand waste dominate their landscape.

BOTH: NATHAN MYHRVOLD

says Myhrvold. "And they stair-step them, like a Mexican pyramid. So you could put one little pumping facility up there, and with one corner of one of those sulfur mountains, you could solve the whole global warming problem for the Northern Hemisphere."

It is interesting to think what might have happened if Myhrvold was around one hundred years ago, when New York and other cities were choking on horse manure. One wonders if, while everyone else looked at the mountains of dung and saw calamity, he might have seen opportunity.

On balance, Budyko's Blanket is a fiendishly simple plan. Considering the complexity of climate in general and how much we don't know, it probably makes sense to start small. With the fire-hose approach, you could begin with a trickle of sulfur and monitor the results. The amount could be easily dialed up or down—or, if need be, turned off. There is nothing permanent or irreversible about the process.

And it would be startlingly cheap. IV estimates the "Save the Arctic" plan could be set up in just two years at a cost of roughly $20 million, with an annual operating cost of about $10 million. If cooling the poles alone proved insufficient, IV has drawn up a "Save the Planet" version, with five worldwide base stations instead of two, and three hoses at each site. This would put about three to five times the amount of sulfur dioxide into the stratosphere. Even so, that would still represent less than 1 percent of current worldwide sulfur emissions. IV estimates this plan could be up and running in about three years, with a startup cost of $150 million and annual operating costs of $100 million.

For eleven years after Paul Crutzen re-ceived the Nobel Prize, the Antarctic ozone hole he helped identify grew larger. But after peaking in size in 2006, it began to heal, thanks to international agreements to phase out the use of ozone-depleting chlorofluorocarbons (CFCs). According to NASA estimates, it may take another fifty-plus years for the hole to fill itself in. The reversal of ozone depletion was a major environmental victory that often goes overlooked these days—and some advocates of carbon mitigation point to it as a template for their fight to stop global warming. A 2009 NASA paper suggested that if CFC emissions hadn't been curbed, nearly two-thirds of the planet's ozone layer would have been eaten away by 2065, allowing 650 percent more ultraviolet radiation to hit the surface.

But even this victory came with a potential cost: closing the ozone hole may accelerate global warming. That's because the hole's presence increased cloud cover over the Antarctic, cooling the polar region. As the hole vanishes, so, too, will those extra clouds.

Paul Crutzen in 1994, as director of the Max Planck Institute for Chemistry in Mainz, Germany. At right, a NASA rendering of the ozone hole at its maximum extent in 2006.

So Budyko's Blanket could effectively reverse global warming at a total cost of $250 million. Compared with the $1.2 trillion that Nicholas Stern proposes spending each year to attack the problem, IV's idea is, well, practically free. It would cost $50 million less to stop global warming than what Al Gore's foundation is paying just to increase public awareness about global warming.

And there lies the key to the question we asked at the beginning of this chapter: *What do Al Gore and Mount Pinatubo have in common?* The answer is that Gore and Pinatubo both suggest a way to cool the planet, albeit with methods whose cost-effectiveness are a universe apart.

This is not to dismiss the potential objections to Budyko's Blanket, which are legion. First of all, would it work?

The scientific evidence says yes. It is basically a controlled mimicry of Mount Pinatubo's eruption, whose cooling effects were exhaustively studied and remain unchallenged.

Perhaps the stoutest scientific argument in favor of the plan came from Paul Crutzen, a Dutch atmospheric scientist whose environmentalist bona fides run even deeper than Caldeira's. Crutzen won a Nobel Prize in 1995 for his research on atmospheric ozone depletion. And yet in 2006, he wrote an essay in the journal *Climatic Change* lamenting the "grossly unsuccessful" efforts to emit fewer greenhouse gases and acknowledging that an injection of sulfur in the stratosphere "is the only option available to rapidly reduce temperature rises and counteract other climatic effects."

Crutzen's embrace of geoengineering was considered such a heresy within the climate-science community that some peers tried to stop publication of his essay. How could the man reverently known as "Dr. Ozone" possibly endorse such a scheme? Wouldn't the environmental damage outweigh the benefits?

Actually, no. Crutzen concluded that damage to the ozone would be minimal. The sulfur dioxide would eventually settle out in the polar regions but in such relatively small amounts that there, too, significant harm was unlikely. If a problem did arise, Crutzen wrote, the sulfur injection "could be stopped on short notice . . . which would allow the atmosphere to return to its prior state within a few years."

Another fundamental objection to geoengineering is that it intentionally alters the earth's natural state. To that, Myhrvold has a simple answer: "We've *already* geoengineered the earth."

In just a few centuries, we will have burned up most of the fossil fuel that took 300 million years of biological accumulation to make. Compared with that, injecting a bit of sulfur into the sky seems pretty mild. As Lowell Wood points out, sulfur isn't even the optimal chemical for a stratospheric shield. Other, less noxious-sounding materials—aluminized plastic micro beads, for instance—could make an even more efficient sunscreen. But sulfur is the most palatable choice "simply because we've got the volcano proof of feasibility," Wood says, "and along with that, a proof of harmlessness."

Wood and Myhrvold do worry that Budyko's Blanket might create an "excuse to pollute." That is, rather than buying time for us to create new energy solutions, it would lure people into complacency. But blaming geoengineering for this, Myhrvold says, is like blaming a heart surgeon for saving the life of someone who fails to exercise and eats too many french fries.

Perhaps the single best objection to the garden hose idea is that it is *too* simple and *too* cheap. As of this writing, there is no regulatory frame-

COURTESY NASA GODDARD SPACE FLIGHT CENTER

work to prohibit anyone—a government, a private institution, even an individual—from putting sulfur dioxide in the atmosphere. (If there were, many of the world's nearly eight thousand coal-burning electricity units would be in a lot of trouble.) Still, Myhrvold admits that "it would freak people out" if someone unilaterally built the thing. But of course this depends on the individual. If it were Al Gore, he might snag a second Nobel Peace Prize. If it were Hugo Chávez, he'd probably get a prompt visit from some U.S. fighter jets.

In the months immediately after this book was first published in October 2009, several countries with whom the United States has historically had fraught relationships—including, yes, Hugo Chávez's Venezuela—did in fact carry out small-scale geoengineering projects.

The Chinese government, battling drought, seeded clouds with silver iodide—but, instead of rain, helped produce Beijing's earliest snowfall in twenty-two years.

In Moscow, Mayor Yuri Luzhkov announced a bid to keep the city snow-free all winter. Russian Air Force planes were enlisted to seed storm clouds, with the goal of making them dump their snow before reaching Moscow. Instead, the Russian capital was treated to a four-day blizzard that dropped a record-breaking two feet of snow.

Venezuela, like China, was experiencing a punishing drought. Chávez announced that he had obtained cloud-seeding equipment from Cuba and would personally oversee "bombing" campaigns to bring rain to his country. "I'm going in a plane," he told supporters. "Any cloud that crosses me, I'll zap it so that it rains." Rains did indeed fall on Venezuela, easing the drought. Whether this was a result of the cloud-seeding project, however, remains undecided, even among those in the Chávez government. "Where we have [sown] it has rained," said the president of the National Institute of Meteorology and Hydrology. "What I can't tell you, and it would be a lie, is how much water has fallen and if it has increased."

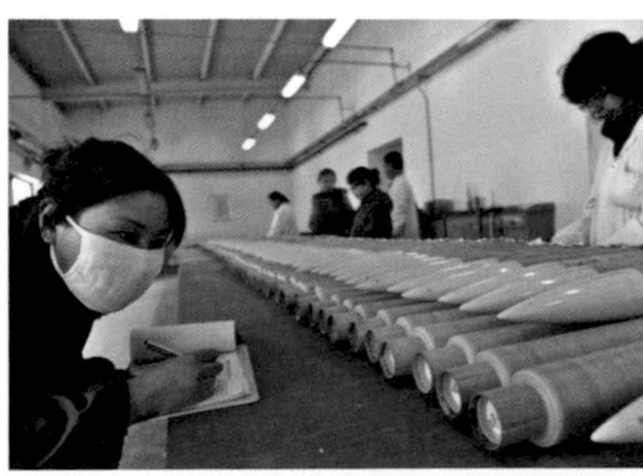

Factory workers in northwest China checking cloud-seeding rockets.

IMAGINECHINA VIA AP IMAGES

One can also imagine the wars that might break out over who controls the dials on Budyko's Blanket. A government that depends on high oil prices might like to crank up the sulfur to keep things extra cool; others, meanwhile, might be happier with longer growing seasons.

Lowell Wood recounts a lecture he once gave, during which he mentioned that a stratospheric shield could also filter out damaging ultraviolet rays. An audience member suggested that fewer ultraviolet rays would lead to more people getting rickets.

"My response," Wood says, "was that your pharmacist can take care of that with vitamin D, and it'll be better for your overall health as well."

All the rocket scientists, climate scientists, physicists, and engineers around the IV conference table chuckle at Wood's riposte. Then someone asks if IV, with Budyko's Blanket up its sleeve, should be working toward a rickets-prevention patent. Now they laugh louder.

But it's not entirely a joke. Unlike most of the patents IV owns, Budyko's Blanket has no clear route to profits. "If you were an investor of mine," Myhrvold says, "you might ask: 'Remind me again why you're working on this?'" Indeed, many of IV's most time-consuming projects, including a variety of AIDS and malaria solutions, are substantially pro bono work.

"This is the world's greatest philanthropist sitting on the other side of the table," Wood says with a chuckle and a nod toward Myhrvold. "Involuntarily so, but there he is."

As dismissive as Myhrvold can be toward the prevailing sentiments on global warming, he is quick to deny that he dismisses global warming itself. (If that were the case, he'd hardly spend so much of his company's resources working on solutions.) Nor is he arguing for an immediate deployment of Budyko's Blanket—but, rather, that technologies like it be researched and tested so they are ready to use if the worst climate predictions were to come true.

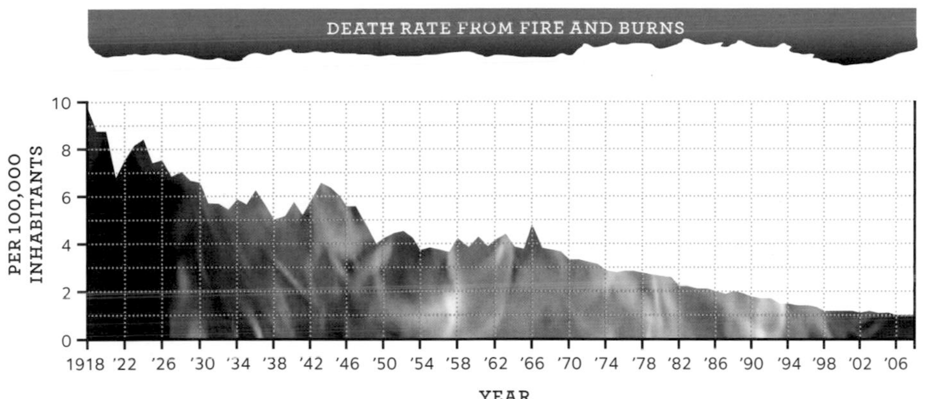

For a time, American history was regularly punctuated by catastrophic fires in which hotels and nightclubs, apartment blocks, and even entire cities burned to the ground. But the death rate due to fire has fallen an astonishing 90 percent over the past century, thanks to a variety of factors: the phasing-out of live-flame lights and fireplaces; the proliferation of fire extinguishers, smoke detectors, and sprinklers; the professionalization of firefighting; fireproof building materials and stricter building codes; and better medical treatment for fire victims.

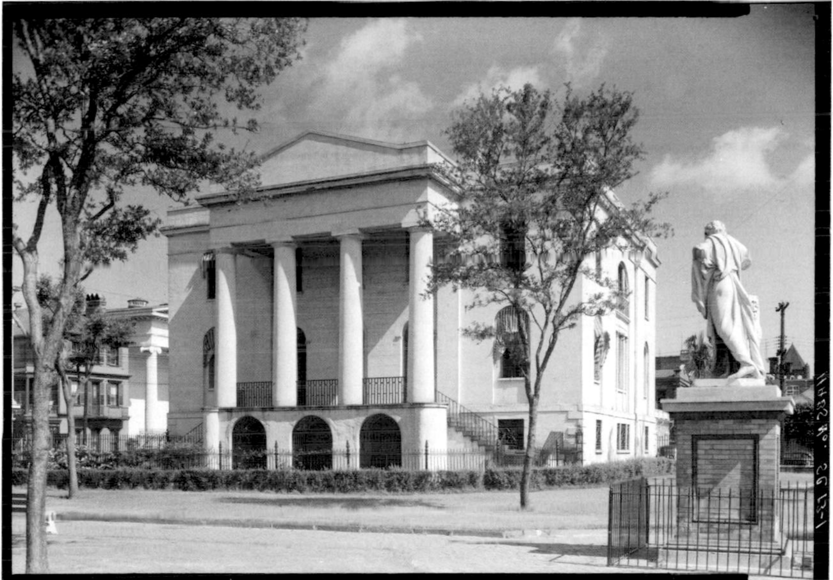

The nation's first fireproof building can be found in Charleston, South Carolina. Erected in the 1820s out of stone masonry, with brick floors, iron shutters, and a copper roof—which was stolen following the Civil War and replaced with tin—it once held the city's public records and is now home to the South Carolina Historical Society. The architect was Robert Mills, a Charleston native who would later design another fireproof structure: the Washington Monument.

"It's a bit like having fire sprinklers in a building," he says. "On the one hand, you should make every effort not to have a fire. But you also need something to fall back on in case the fire occurs anyway." Just as important, he says, "it gives you breathing room to move to carbon-free energy sources."

He is also eager to get geoengineering moving forward because of what he sees as "a real head of steam" that global-warming activists have gathered in recent years.

"They are seriously proposing doing a set of things that could have enormous impact—and we think probably negative impact—on human life," he says. "They want to divert a huge amount of economic value toward immediate and precipitous anti-carbon initiatives, without thinking things through. This will have a huge drag on the world economy. There are billions of poor people who will be greatly delayed, if not entirely precluded, from attaining a First World standard of living. In this country, we can pretty much afford the luxury of doing whatever we want on the energy-and-environment front, but other parts of the world would seriously suffer."

Certain new ideas, no matter how useful, are invariably seen as repugnant. As we mentioned earlier, a market for human organs—even though it might save tens of thousands of lives each year—is one such example.

Over time, some ideas do cross the repugnance barrier to become reality. Charging interest on loans. Selling human sperm and eggs. Profiting from a loved one's premature death. This last example of course describes how life insurance works. Today it is standard practice to wager on your own death in order to provide for your family. Until the mid-nineteenth century, life insurance was considered "a profanation," as the sociologist Viviana Zelizer writes, "which transformed the sacred event of death into a vulgar commodity."

Budyko's Blanket may simply be too repugnant a scheme to ever be given a chance. Intentional pollution? Futzing with the stratosphere? Putting the planet's weather in the hands of a few arrogant souls from Seattle? It is one thing for climate heavyweights like Paul Crutzen and Ken Caldeira to endorse such a solution. But they are mere scientists. The real heavyweights in this fight are people like Al Gore.

And what does he think of geoengineering?

"In a word," Gore has said, "I think it's nuts."

If the garden-hose-to-the-sky idea doesn't fly, IV has another proposal that relies on the same science but is perhaps slightly less repugnant. As it turns out, the amount of stratospheric sulfur necessary to cool the planet is equal to the amount that just a handful of coal-burning power plants already belch out. This second plan calls for simply extending the smokestacks at a few strategically located plants. So instead of spewing their sulfur-laden smoke several hundred feet into the air, these smokestacks would release it some eighteen miles high, into the stratosphere, where it would have the same net cooling effect as the garden-hose scheme.

This plan is appealing because it simply repurposes existing pollution without adding any more. Although an eighteen-mile-high smokestack

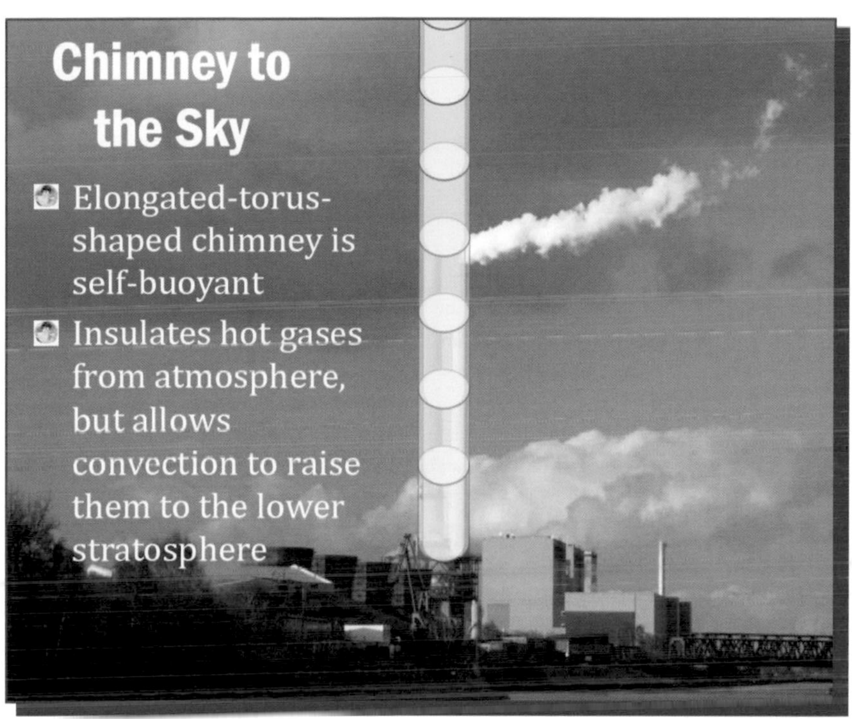

Chimney to the Sky
Elongated-torus-shaped chimney is self-buoyant
Insulates hot gases from atmosphere, but allows convection to raise them to the lower stratosphere

IV's "chimney to the sky," which would cool the earth by simply relocating existing smokestack pollution to the stratosphere.

might sound like a hard thing to build, IV has figured out how—essentially by attaching a long, skinny hot-air balloon to an existing power-plant smokestack, creating a channel that lets the hot sulfur gases rise by their own buoyancy into the stratosphere. This project is dubbed, naturally, "chimney to the sky."

And if even *that* plan is too repugnant, IV has something entirely different, a plan that is practically heavenly: a sky full of puffy white clouds.

This is the brainchild of John Latham, a British climate scientist who recently joined the IV stable of inventors. Latham is a gentle, soft-spoken man in his late sixties who is also a rather serious poet. So it caught his ear when, long ago, he stood on a mountaintop in North Wales with his eight-year-old son Mike, gazing down at a sunset, and the boy, pointing out how shiny the clouds were, called them "soggy mirrors."

See end pages of this chapter, pp. 228–229.

Precisely!

"On balance, the role of clouds is to produce a cooling," says Latham. "If clouds didn't exist in the atmosphere, the earth would be a lot hotter than it is now."

Even man-made clouds—the contrails from a jet plane, for instance—have a cooling effect. After the September 11 terrorist attacks, all commercial

1 In the early 1980s, John Latham came to know fellow atmospheric scientist Bernard Vonnegut (see page 206). Despite their friendship, the two men had a public disagreement in an academic journal about how lightning forms in thunderclouds. Shortly thereafter, Latham had a pleasant meeting with Bernard's younger brother Kurt, the novelist, who was visiting the U.K. on a book tour. A few weeks later, Latham received, as he recalls, a "violent letter" from Kurt. It was, he said, "totally unexpected":

Mar 21 83

Dear Professor Latham --

I have just read your sneering, impossibly conceited attack on my dear brother in the Quarterly Journal of the Royal Meteorological Society, and now understand that your smiles during our meeting in Manchester last month were as friendly as those of Count Dracula. Maybe you think you are funny, but you are as stupid as all the people who said Louis Pasteur was wrong about germs. They will have to find some real snotty English actor to play you when they make a movie about my brother's life. England may not be much good at science any more, but she sure has the actors still. We'll find one, by God, to nail you good.

Yours truly,

Kurt Vonnegut

2 Latham, shocked, phoned Bernard Vonnegut to make sense of the attack. Bernard "burst out laughing when he heard my voice," Latham said. Bernard then clued Latham in on Kurt's hobby of writing incendiary letters for a laugh. Latham promptly sat down at his own typewriter to reply:

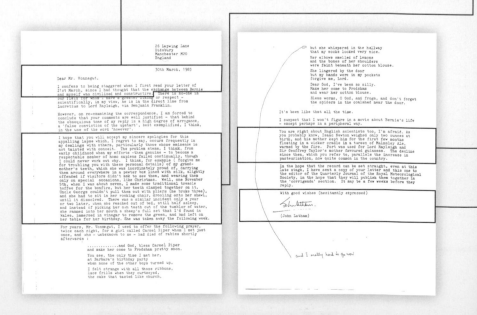

26 Lapwing Lane
Didsbury
Manchester M20
England

30th March, 1983

Dear Mr. Vonnegut,

I confess to being staggered when I first read your letter of 21st March, since I had thought that the exchange between Bernie and myself was civilized and constructive. There is no-one in our field for whom I have a greater liking or respect - scientifically, in my view, he is in the direct line from Lucretius to Lord Rayleigh, via Benjamin Franklin.

However, on re-examining the correspondence, I am forced to conclude that your comments are well justified - that behind the obsequious tone of my reply is a high degree of arrogance, a 'false conviction of the upstart', best exemplified, I think, in the use of the word 'however'.

I hope that you will accept my sincere apologies for this appalling lapse which, I regret to say, occurs frequently in my dealings with others, particularly those whose eminence is not tainted with conceit. The problem stems, I think, from early childhood when my efforts -then genuine - to become a respectable member of homo sapiens failed continually, though I could never work out why. I think, for example (forgive me for troubling you with these personal details) of my grandmother's teeth, which she was inordinately proud of, carrying them around everywhere in a pewter box lined with silk, slightly offended if visitors didn't ask to see them, and wearing them only on special occasions, like Christmas. Well, one November 5th, when I was about seven, I made some traditional treacle toffee for the bonfire, but her teeth clamped together on it, Uncle George couldn't pull them out with pliers (he broke three), and she had to sit in her rocking chair, drooling onto her shawl, until it dissolved. There was a similar incident only a year or two later, when she reached out of bed, still half asleep, and instead of picking her own teeth out of the tumbler of water, she rammed into her mouth a sheep's full set that I'd found in Wales, immersed in vinegar to remove the green, and had left on her table for her birthday. She was taken away the following week.

For years, Mr. Vonnegut, I used to offer the following prayer, twice each night, for a girl called Carmel Piper whom I met just once, and who - unbeknown to me - had died of rabies shortly afterwards :

.............and God, bless Carmel Piper
and make her come to Prodsham pretty soon.

You see, the only time I met her,
at Barbara's birthday party
when none of the other boys turned up,

I felt strange with all those ribbons,
lace frills when they curtseyed,
the cake that tasted like church,

but she whispered in the hallway
that my socks looked very nice.

Her elbows smelled of lemons
and the bones of her shoulders
were faint beneath her cotton blouse.

She lingered by the door
but my hands were in my pockets
forgive me, Lord.

Dear God, I've been so silly.
Make her come to Prodsham
and wear her cotton blouse.

Bless worms, O God, and frogs, and don't forget
the spiders in the coalshed near the door.

It's been like that all the time.

I suspect that I won't figure in a movie about Bernie's life - except perhaps in a peripheral way.

You are right about English scientists too, I'm afraid. As you probably know, Isaac Newton weighed only two ounces at birth, and his mother kept him for the first few months floating in a wicker cradle in a tureen of Malmsley Ale, warmed by the fire. Port was used for Lord Rayleigh and Sir Geoffrey Taylor's mother favoured guinness. The decline since then, which you refer to, parallels the increase in pasteurization, now quite common in the country.

In the hope that the record can be set straight, even at this late stage, I have sent a copy of your letter and this one to the editor of the Quarterly Journal of the Royal Meteorological Society, in the hope that they will publish them together in the 'corrigenda' section. It may be a few weeks before they reply.

With good wishes (hesitantly expressed)

(John Latham)

and I really had to go now

30th March, 1983

Dear Mr. Vonnegut,

I confess to being staggered when I first read your letter of 21st March, since I had thought that the exchange between Bernie and myself was civilized and constructive.

I hope that you will accept my sincere apologies for this appalling lapse which, I regret to say, occurs frequently in my dealings with others, particularly those whose eminence is not tainted with conceit. The problem stems, I think, from early childhood when my efforts -then genuine - to become a respectable member of homo sapiens failed continually, though I could never work out why. I think, for example (forgive me for troubling you with these personal details) of my grand-mother's teeth, which she was inordinately proud of, carrying them around everywhere in a pewter box lined with silk, slightly offended if visitors didn't ask to see them, and wearing them only on special occasions, like Christmas. Well, one November 5th, when I was about seven, I made some traditional treacle toffee for the bonfire, but her teeth clamped together on it, Uncle George couldn't pull them out with pliers (he broke three), and she had to sit in her rocking chair, drooling onto her shawl, until it dissolved. There was a similar incident only a year or two later, when she reached out of bed, still half asleep, and instead of picking her own teeth out of the tumbler of water, she rammed into her mouth a sheep's full set that I'd found in Wales, immersed in vinegar to remove the green, and had left on her table for her birthday. She was taken away the following week.

You are right about English scientists too, I'm afraid. As you probably know, Isaac Newton weighed only two ounces at birth, and his mother kept him for the first few months floating in a wicker cradle in a tureen of Malmsley Ale, warmed by the fire. Port was used for Lord Rayleigh and Sir Geoffrey Taylor's mother favoured guinness. The decline since then, which you refer to, parallels the increase in pasteurization, now quite common in the country.

With good wishes (hesitantly expressed)

(John Latham)

3 Then it was Kurt Vonnegut's turn to reply:

Apr 16 83

Dear Dr. Latham --

I feel as though I were waking up in a hospital, having taken a swing the night before at a stranger who happened to be the Heavyweight Boxing Champion of Europe. Nothing I have written (and I try hard to write well) matches the grace and cheerful music in your letter to me.

I am not surprised. I have spent a lot of time with scientists, and know how witty they can be.

Jewish persons in show business in this city have often given me this warning: "Never kid a kidder". Now I know what they mean.

Respectfully yours,

Kurt Vonnegut

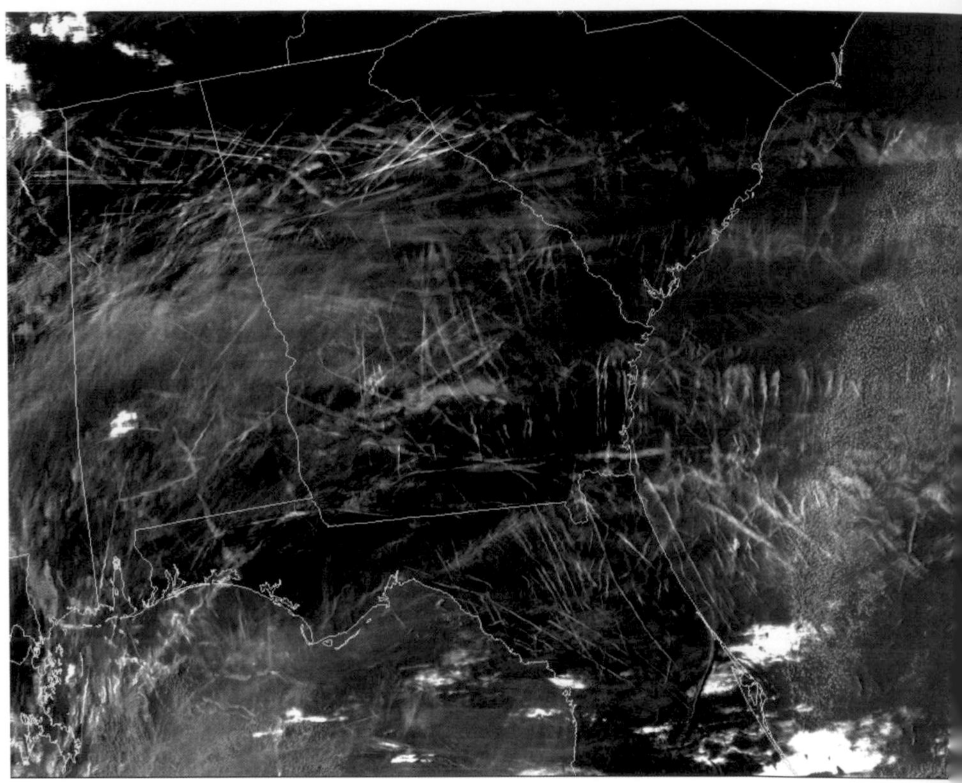

A 2004 photo of airplane contrails blanketing the southeastern United States. While some scientists detected a rise in daytime temperature after the 9/11 attacks due to the absence of sunlight-reflective contrails, further research by NASA's Patrick Minnis suggests that contrails may warm the earth rather than cool it. His argument: the cirrus clouds formed by contrails allow most sunlight through while trapping heat from below.

NASA LANGLEY RESEARCH CENTER

flights in the United States were grounded for three days. Using data from more than four thousand weather stations across the country, scientists found that the sudden absence of contrails accounted for a subsequent rise in ground temperature.

There are at least three essential ingredients for the formation of clouds: ascending air, water vapor, and solid particles known as cloud condensation nuclei. When planes fly, particles in the exhaust plume serve as the nuclei. Over landmasses, dust particles do the job. But there are far fewer cloud-friendly nuclei over the world's oceans, Latham explains, so the clouds contain fewer droplets and are therefore less reflective. As a result, more sunlight reaches the earth's surface. The ocean, because it is dark, is particularly good at absorbing the sun's heat.

By Latham's calculations, an increase of just 10 or 12 percent of the reflectivity of oceanic clouds would cool the earth enough to counteract even a doubling of current greenhouse gas levels. His solution: use the ocean itself to make more clouds.

As it happens, the salt-rich spray from seawater creates excellent nuclei for cloud formation. All you have to do is get the spray into the air several yards above the ocean's surface. From there, it naturally lofts upward to the altitude where clouds form.

IV has considered a variety of ways to make this happen. At the moment, the favorite idea is a fleet of wind-powered fiberglass boats, designed by Stephen Salter, with underwater turbines that produce enough thrust to kick up a steady stream of spray. Because there is no engine, there is no pollution. The only ingredients—seawater and air—are of course free. The volume of spray (and, therefore, of cloud reflectivity) would be easily adjustable. Nor would the clouds reach land, where sunshine is so important to agriculture. The estimated price tag: less than $50 million for the first prototypes and then a few billion dollars for a fleet of vessels large enough to offset projected warming at least until 2050. In the annals of cheap and simple solutions to vexing problems, it is hard to think of a more elegant example than John Latham's soggy mirrors—geoengineering that the greenest green could love.

That said, Myhrvold fears that even IV's gentlest proposals will find little favor within certain environmentalist circles. To him, this doesn't compute.

"If you believe that the scary stories could be true, or even possible, then you should also admit that relying only on reducing carbon-dioxide emissions is not a very good answer," he says. In other words: it's illogical to believe in a carbon-induced warming apocalypse *and* believe that such an apocalypse can be averted simply by curtailing new carbon emissions. "The scary scenarios could occur even if we make herculean efforts to reduce our emissions, in which case the only real answer is geoengineering."

Al Gore, meanwhile, counters with his own logic. "If we don't know enough to stop putting 70 million tons of global-warming pollution into the atmosphere every day," he says, "how in God's name can we know enough to precisely counteract that?"

But if you think like a cold-blooded economist instead of a warmhearted humanist, Gore's reasoning doesn't track. It's not that we don't *know how* to stop polluting the atmosphere. We don't *want* to stop, or aren't willing to pay the price.

Most pollution, remember, is a negative externality of our consumption. As hard as engineering or physics may be, getting human beings to change their behavior is probably harder. At present, the rewards for

A rendering of a seagoing vessel that would kick up salt spray and generate cloud-condensation nuclei, heightening the reflectivity—and therefore cooling ability—of oceanic clouds. The tall cylinders, known as Flettner rotors, use wind to create thrust for the ship. While the rotors may look futuristic, they actually represent another "lost" technology, first proven in the 1920s by the German inventor Anton Flettner. In 1925, a rotor-driven ship Flettner built (the *Buckau,* below) successfully crossed the North Sea. But his invention, coming at a time when wind propulsion had fallen out of fashion, didn't catch on. So Flettner went on to start an aircraft-engineering company and, in the 1930s, contributed greatly to the development of the helicopter.

TOP: ILLUSTRATION BY JOHN MACNEILL; BOTTOM: LIBRARY OF CONGRESS

An entire book could be written—an entire shelf of books, in fact—on the long-standing efforts by any number of parties around the world to encourage proper hand hygiene in medical settings. At right, the World Health Organization's step-by-step instructions.

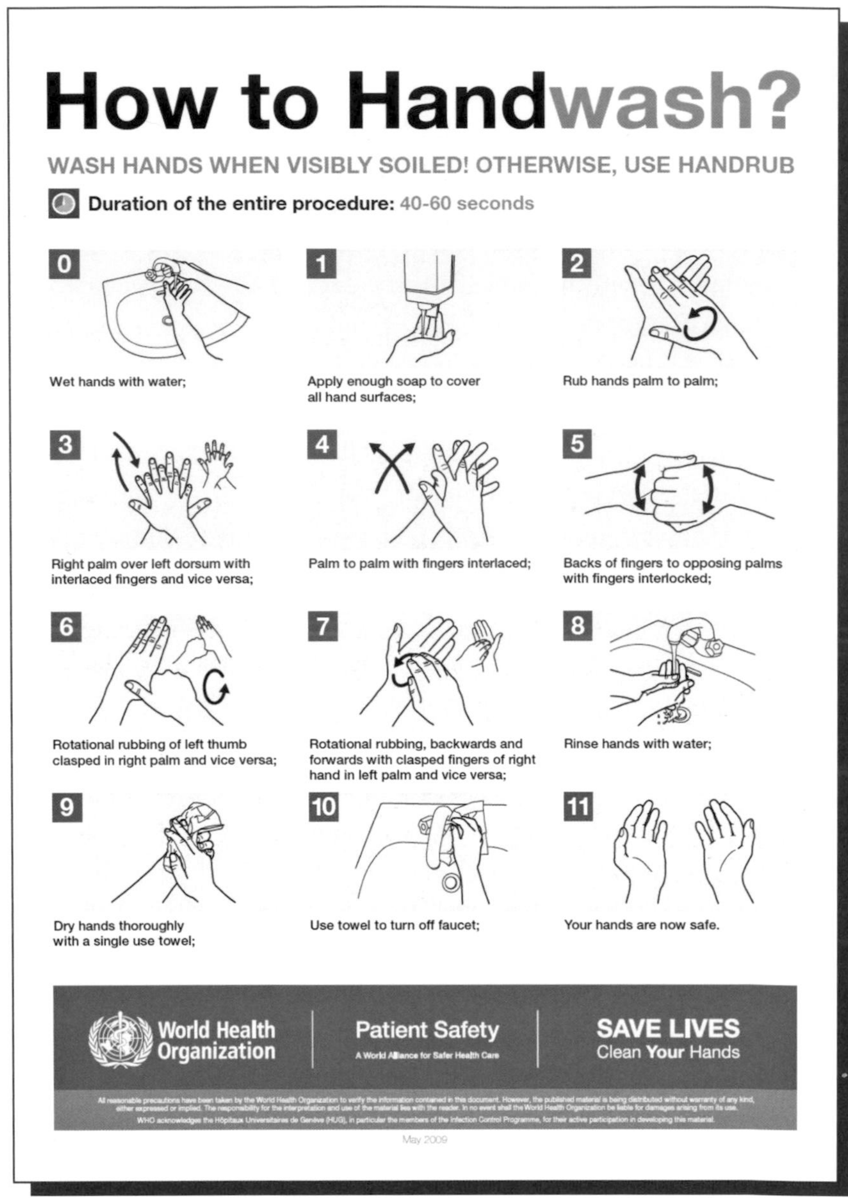

limiting consumption are weak, as are the penalties for overconsuming. Gore and other environmentalists are pleading for humankind to consume less and therefore pollute less, and that is a noble invitation. But as incentives go, it's not a very strong one.

And *collective* behavior change, as beguiling as that may sound, can be maddeningly elusive. Just ask Ignatz Semmelweis.

Back in 1847, when he solved the mystery of puerperal fever, Semmelweis was hailed as a hero—wasn't he?

Quite the opposite. Yes, the death rate in Vienna General's maternity ward plummeted when he ordered doctors to wash their hands after performing autopsies. Elsewhere, however, doctors ignored Semmelweis's findings. They even ridiculed him. Surely, they reasoned, such a ravaging illness could not be prevented simply by washing one's hands! Moreover, doctors of that era—not the humblest lot—couldn't accept the idea that they were the root of the trouble.

Semmelweis grew frustrated, and in time his frustration curdled into vitriol. He cast himself as a scorned messiah, labeling every critic of his theory a murderer of women and babies. His arguments were often nonsensical; his personal behavior became odd, marked by lewdness and sexual impropriety. In retrospect, it's safe to say that Ignatz Semmelweis was going mad. At the age of forty-seven, he was tricked into entering a sanitarium. He tried to escape, was forcibly restrained, and died within two weeks, his reputation shattered.

But that doesn't mean he wasn't right. Semmelweis was posthumously vindicated by Louis Pasteur's research in germ theory, after which it became standard practice for doctors to scrupulously clean their hands before treating patients.

So do contemporary doctors follow Semmelweis's orders?

A raft of recent studies have shown that hospital personnel wash or disinfect their hands in *fewer than half* the instances they should. And doctors are the worst offenders, more lax than either nurses or aides.

This failure seems puzzling. In the modern world, we tend to believe that dangerous behaviors are best solved by education. That is the thinking behind nearly every public-awareness campaign ever undertaken, from global warming to AIDS prevention to drunk driving. And doctors are the most educated people in the hospital.

In a 1999 report called "To Err Is Human," the Institute of Medicine estimated that between 44,000 and 98,000 Americans die each year because of preventable hospital errors—more than deaths from motor-vehicle crashes or breast cancer—and that one of the leading errors is wound infection. The best medicine for stopping infections? Getting doctors to wash their hands more frequently.

In the wake of this report, hospitals all over the country hustled to fix the

This book has discussed in several places the many different ways a person might die. In a given year, roughly 2.5 million people die in the U.S.—so many people that, if they were gathered up in one place, they would constitute our fourth-largest city, between Houston (2.2 million) and Chicago (2.9 million).

But considering that death is (as of this writing) inevitable, it may be that we fail to appreciate how good we have collectively become at forestalling it. For all the dramatic demises we worry about—accidents, terrorism, weather calamities—most of us will end up dying of natural causes, and at a remarkably advanced age; most people of past generations would have killed to live so long. Here's something to think about: roughly half of all the people who have ever lived to the age of sixty-five are living right now.

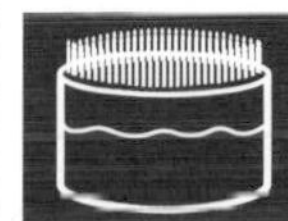

Back in the 1980s, the National Institutes of Health launched a campaign to promote hand-washing in hospitals and day-care centers. The promotional giveaway was a stuffed animal called T. Bear. Kids and doctors alike loved T. Bear—but they weren't the only ones. When a few dozen T. Bears were pulled from the wards after just one week to be examined, they were all found to have acquired at least one of a host of new friends: *Staphylococcus aureus, E. coli, Pseudomonas, Klebsiella pneumoniae,* and several others.

T. RÜGGEBERG/PLAINPICTURE/CORBIS

problem. Even a world-class hospital like Cedars-Sinai Medical Center in Los Angeles found it needed improvement, with a hand-hygiene rate of just 65 percent. Its senior administrators formed a committee to identify the reasons for this failure.

For one, they acknowledged, doctors are incredibly busy, and time spent washing hands is time not spent treating patients. Craig Feied, our emergency-room revolutionary from Washington, estimates that he often interacted with more than one hundred patients per shift. "If I ran to wash my hands every time I touched a patient, following the protocol, I'd spend nearly half my time just standing over a sink."

Sinks, furthermore, aren't always as accessible as they should be and, in patient rooms especially, they are sometimes barricaded by equipment or furniture. Cedars-Sinai, like a lot of other hospitals, had wall-mounted Purell dispensers for handy disinfection, but these too were often ignored.

Doctors' hand-washing failures also seem to have psychological components. The first might be (generously) called a perception deficit. During a five-month study in the intensive-care unit of an Australian children's hospital, doctors were asked to track their own hand-washing frequency. Their self-reported rate? Seventy-three percent. Not perfect, but not so terrible either.

Unbeknownst to these doctors, however, their nurses were spying on them, and recorded the docs' actual hand-hygiene rate: a paltry 9 percent.

Paul Silka, an emergency-room doctor at Cedars-Sinai who also served as the hospital's chief of staff, points to a second psychological factor: arrogance. "The ego can kick in after you've been in practice a while," he explains. "You say: 'Hey, *I* couldn't be carrying the bad bugs. It's the *other* hospital personnel.'"

Silka and the other administrators at Cedars-Sinai set out to change their colleagues' behavior. They tried all sorts of incentives: gentle cajoling via posters and e-mail messages; greeting doctors every morning with a bottle of Purell; establishing a Hand Hygiene Safety Posse that roamed the wards, giving a $10 Starbucks card to doctors who were seen properly washing their hands. You might think the highest earners in a hospital would be immune to a $10 incentive. "But none of them turned down the card," Silka says.

After several weeks, the hand-hygiene rate at Cedars-Sinai had increased but not nearly enough. This news was delivered by Rekha Murthy, the hospital's epidemiologist, during a lunch meeting of the Chief of Staff Advisory Committee. There were roughly twenty members, most of them top doctors in the hospital. They were openly discouraged by the report. When lunch was over, Murthy handed each of them an agar plate—a sterile petri dish loaded with a spongy layer of agar. "I would love to culture your hand," she told them.

They pressed their palms into the plates, which Murthy sent to the lab. The resulting images, Silka recalls, "were disgusting and striking, with gobs of colonies of bacteria."

Here were the most important people in the hospital, telling everyone else how to change their behavior, and yet even their own hands weren't clean! (And, most disturbingly, this took place at a lunch meeting.)

It may have been tempting to sweep this information under the rug. Instead, the administration decided to harness the disgusting power of the bacteria-laden handprints by installing one of them as the screen saver on computers throughout the hospital. For doctors—lifesavers by training, and by oath—this grisly warning proved more powerful than any other incentive. Hand-hygiene compliance at Cedars-Sinai promptly shot up to nearly 100 percent.

As word got around, other hospitals began copying the screen-saver solution. And why not? It was cheap, simple, and effective.

A happy ending, right?

Yes, but . . . think about it for a moment. Why did it take so much effort to persuade doctors to do what they have known to do since the age of Semmelweis? Why was it so hard to change their behavior when the price of compliance (a simple hand-wash) is so low and the potential cost of failure (the loss of a human life) so high?

Once again, as with pollution, the answer has to do with externalities.

When a doctor fails to wash his hands, his own life isn't the one that is primarily endangered. It is the next patient he treats, the one with the open wound or the compromised immune system. The dangerous bacteria that patient receives are a negative externality of

The life-saving screen saver used at Cedars-Sinai Medical Center. As word of its success got out, other hospitals around the country began asking Cedars for permission to use the same image.

Remember: Wash Your Hands

After Removing Gloves

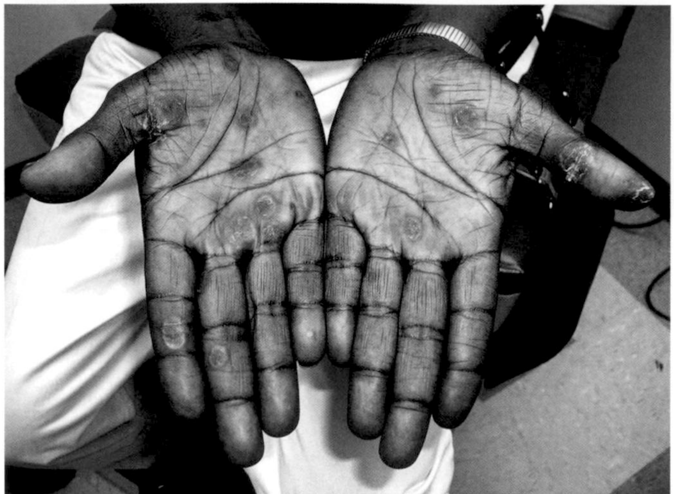

To be sure, even the most vigilant hand-washing won't keep certain bacteria from spreading. Syphilitic hand infections, for example, are highly contagious and will spread infectious bacteria no matter how often they are washed.

the doctor's actions—just as pollution is a negative externality of anyone who drives a car, jacks up the air conditioner, or sends coal exhaust up a smoke-stack. The polluter has insufficient incentive to not pollute, and the doctor has insufficient incentive to wash his hands.

This is what makes the science of behavior change so difficult.

So instead of collectively wringing our filthy hands about behavior that is so hard to change, what if we can come up with engineering or design or incentive solutions that supersede the need for such change?

That's what Intellectual Ventures has in mind for global warming, and that is what public-health officials have finally embraced to cut down on hospital-acquired infections. Among the best solutions: using disposable blood-pressure cuffs on incoming patients; infusing hospital equipment with silver ion particles to create an antimicrobial shield; and forbidding doctors to wear neckties because, as the U.K. Department of Health has noted, they "are rarely laundered," "perform no beneficial function in patient care," and "have been shown to be colonized by pathogens."

That's why Craig Feied has worn bow ties for years. He has also helped develop a virtual-reality interface that allows a gowned and gloved-up surgeon to scroll through X-rays on a computer without actually touching it—because computer keyboards and mice tend to collect pathogens at least as effectively as a doctor's necktie. And the next time you find yourself in a hospital room, don't pick up the TV remote control until you've disinfected the daylights out of it.

Perhaps it's not so surprising that it's hard to change people's behavior when someone else stands to reap most of the benefit. But surely we are capable of behavior change when our own welfare is at stake, yes?

Sadly, no. If we were, every diet would always work (and there would be no need for diets in the first place). If we were, most smokers would be ex-smokers. If we were, no one who ever took a sex-ed class would be party to an unwanted pregnancy. But knowing and doing are two different things, especially when pleasure is involved.

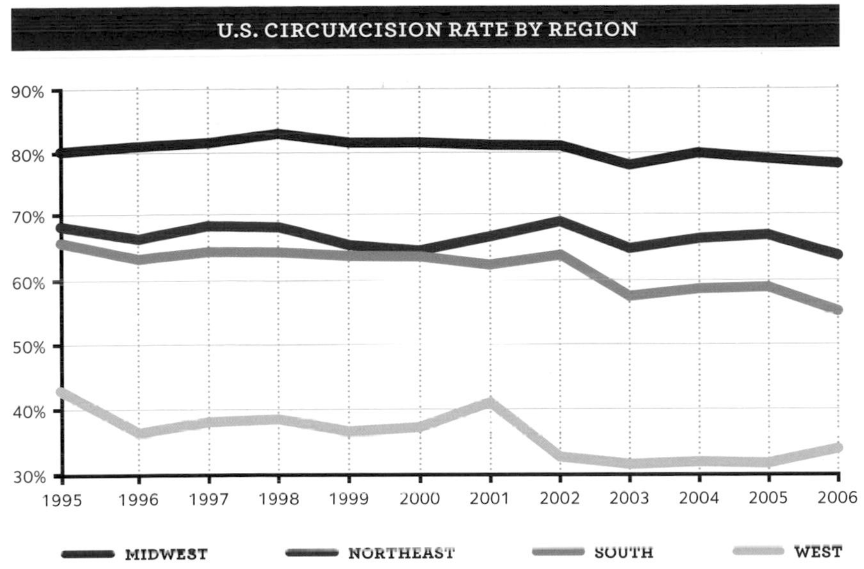

Around the world, about 3 of every 10 males are circumcised. Africa's rate is actually somewhat higher, although it varies dramatically from region to region. In Kenya, for example, 84 percent of adult men are circumcised; in Rwanda, only 10 percent are.

In the United States, meanwhile, the rate of circumcision peaked in 1965 at roughly 85 percent; today, about 56 percent of American boys are circumcised at birth. A variety of factors have driven this decline. In 1999, the American Academy of Pediatrics declared the procedure medically unnecessary. Subsequently, Medicaid programs in sixteen states withdrew coverage for circumcision. The circumcision rate today in those states' hospitals is 24 percent below the national average.

There's also a dramatic regional disparity in American circumcision, reflecting religious, ethnic, and social differences. It's nearly universal in the Midwest, whereas the West sees rates closer to the global mean.

Consider the high rate of HIV and AIDS in Africa. For years, public-health officials from around the world have been fighting this problem. They have preached all sorts of behavior change—using condoms, limiting the number of sexual partners, and so on. Recently, however, a French researcher named Bertran Auvert ran a medical trial in South Africa and came upon findings so encouraging that the trial was halted so the new preventive measure could be applied at once.

What was this magical treatment?

Circumcision. For reasons Auvert and other scientists do not fully understand, circumcision was found to reduce the risk of HIV transmission by as much as 60 percent in heterosexual men. Subsequent studies in Kenya and Uganda corroborated Auvert's results.

All over Africa, foreskins began to fall. "People are used to policies that target behaviors," said one South African health official, "but circumcision is a surgical intervention—it's cold, hard steel."

The decision to undergo an adult circumcision is obviously a deeply personal one. We would hardly presume to counsel anyone in either direction. But for those who *do* choose circumcision, a simple word of advice: before the doctor gets anywhere near you, please make sure he washes his hands.

FOLLOWING PAGES: GUY EDWARDES/GETTY IMAGES

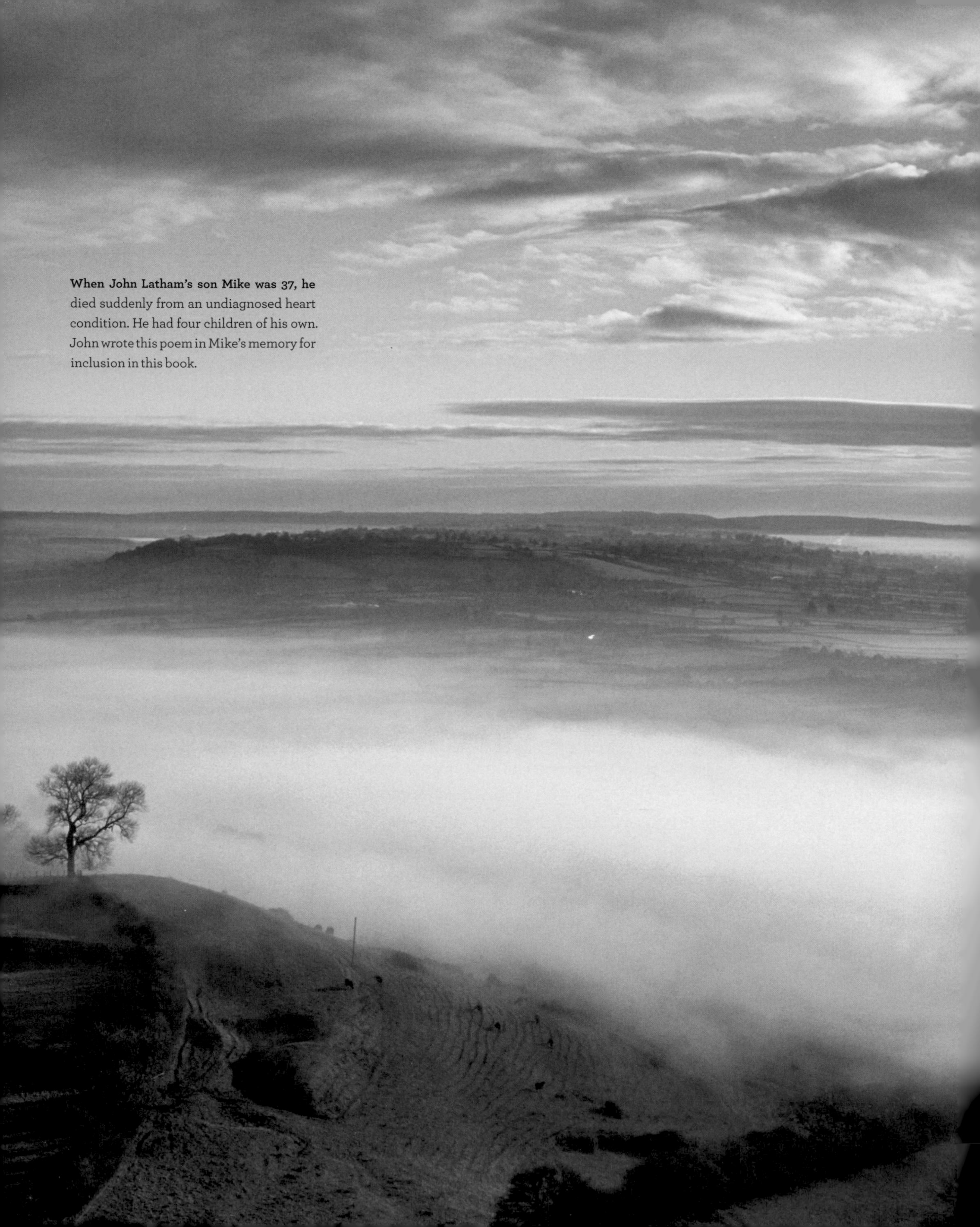

When John Latham's son Mike was 37, he died suddenly from an undiagnosed heart condition. He had four children of his own. John wrote this poem in Mike's memory for inclusion in this book.

Soggy Mirrors

(for Mike)

He's ten years old, we've climbed Moel Eilio today,
we look out over Caernarfon, the Irish Sea, to a sky
on fire, thin stratus flaunting colour. He nudges me
and points: *Dad! Those clouds. Why do they shine?*
I tell him they're made of tiny water drops, millions,
even billions, bouncing sunlight off towards the sky.
Again I'm on the summit, four decades on, scarlets
just as vivid, clouds as shallow, shiny as before. But
he's not here, the silence is oppressive. He's sailed
away into an early sunset, unknowing, no farewell.
I can almost conjure his asthmatic voice as he turned
to me and laughed: *Those clouds are soggy mirrors!*

EPILOGUE

MONKEYS ARE PEOPLE TOO

THE BRANCH OF ECONOMICS CONCERNED WITH ISSUES LIKE inflation, recessions, and financial shocks is known as macroeconomics. When the economy is going well, macroeconomists are lauded as heroes; when it turns sour, as it did recently, they catch a lot of the blame. In either case, the headlines go to the macroeconomists.

We hope that after reading this book, you'll realize there is a whole different breed of economist out there—*micro*economists—lurking in the shadows. They seek to understand the choices that individuals make, not just in terms of what they buy but also how often they wash their hands and whether they become terrorists.

Some of these microeconomists do not even limit their research to the human race.

Keith Chen, the son of Chinese immigrants, is a hyper-verbal, sharp-dressing thirty-three-year-old with spiky hair. After an itinerant upbringing in the rural Midwest, Chen attended Stanford, where after a brief infatuation with Marxism, he made an about-face and took up economics. Now he is an associate professor of economics at Yale.

His research agenda was inspired by something written long ago by Adam Smith, the founder of classical economics: "Nobody ever saw a dog make a fair and deliberate exchange of one bone for another with another

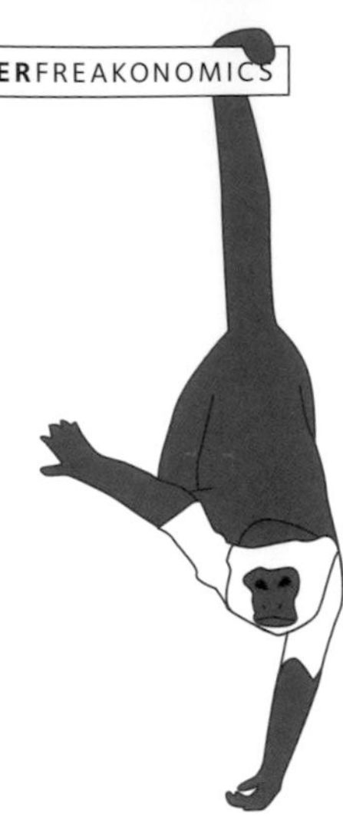

dog. Nobody ever saw one animal by its gestures and natural cries signify to another, *this is mine, that yours; I am willing to give this for that.*"

In other words, Smith was certain that humankind alone had a knack for monetary exchange.

But was he right?

In economics, as in life, you'll never find the answer to a question unless you're willing to ask it, as silly as it may seem. Chen's question was simply this: *What would happen if I could teach a bunch of monkeys to use money?*

Chen's monkey of choice was the capuchin, a cute, brown New World monkey about the size of a one-year-old child, or at least a scrawny one-year-old who has a very long tail. "The capuchin has a small brain," Chen says, "and it's pretty much focused on food and sex." (This, we would argue, doesn't make the capuchin so different from many people we know, but that's another story.) "You should really think of a capuchin as a bottomless stomach of want. You can feed them marshmallows all day, they'll throw up, and then come back for more."

To an economist, this makes the capuchin an excellent research subject.

Chen, along with Venkat Lakshminarayanan, went to work with seven capuchins at a lab set up by the psychologist Laurie Santos at Yale–New Haven Hospital. In the tradition of monkey labs everywhere, the capuchins were given names—in this case, derived from characters in James Bond films. There were four females and three males. The alpha male was named Felix, after the CIA agent Felix Leiter. He was Chen's favorite.

The monkeys lived together in a large, open cage. Down at one end was a much smaller cage, the testing chamber, where one monkey at a time could enter to take part in experiments. For currency, Chen settled on a one-inch silver disc with a hole in the middle—"kind of like Chinese money," he says.

The first step was to teach the monkeys that the coins had value. This took some effort. If you give a capuchin a coin, he will sniff it and, after determining he can't eat it (or have sex with it), he'll toss it aside. If you repeat this several times, he may start tossing the coins *at you,* and hard.

So Chen and his colleagues gave the monkey a coin and then showed a treat. Whenever the monkey gave the coin back to the researcher, it got the treat. It took many months, but the monkeys eventually learned that the coins could buy the treats.

It turned out that individual monkeys had strong preferences for different treats. A capuchin would be presented with twelve coins on a tray—his budget constraint—and then be offered, say, Jell-O cubes by one researcher and apple slices by another. The monkey would hand his coins to whichever researcher held the food he preferred, and the researcher would fork over the goodies.

Chen now introduced price shocks and income shocks to the monkeys' economy. Let's say Felix's favorite food was Jell-O, and he was accustomed to getting three cubes of it for one coin. How would he respond if one coin suddenly bought just two cubes?

To Chen's surprise, Felix and the others responded rationally. When the price of a given food rose, the monkeys bought less of it, and when the price fell, they bought more. The most basic law of economics—that the demand curve slopes downward—held for monkeys as well as humans.

Now that he had witnessed their rational behavior, Chen wanted to test the capuchins for *ir*rational behavior. He set up two gambling games. In the first, a capuchin was shown one grape and, dependent on a coin flip, either got only that grape or won a bonus grape as well. In the second game, the capuchin started out seeing two grapes, but if the coin flip went against him, the researchers took away one grape and the monkey got only one.

In both cases, the monkey got the same number of grapes on average. But the first gamble was framed as a potential gain while the second was framed as a potential loss.

How did the capuchins react?

Given that the monkeys aren't very smart in the first place, you might assume that any gambling strategy was well beyond their capabilities. In that case, you'd expect them to prefer it when a researcher initially offered them two grapes instead of one. But precisely the opposite happened! Once the monkeys figured out that the two-grape researcher sometimes withheld the second grape and that the one-grape researcher sometimes added a bonus grape, the monkeys strongly preferred the one-grape researcher. A rational monkey wouldn't have cared, but these irrational monkeys suffered from what psychologists call "loss aversion." They behaved as if the pain from losing a grape was greater than the pleasure from gaining one.

Up to now, the monkeys appeared to be as rational as humans in their

use of money. But surely this last experiment showed the vast gulf that lay between monkey and man.

Or did it?

The fact is that similar experiments with human beings—day traders, for instance—had found that people make the same kind of irrational decisions at a nearly identical rate. The data generated by the capuchin monkeys, Chen says, "make them statistically indistinguishable from most stock-market investors."

So the parallels between human beings and these tiny-brained, food-and-sex monkeys remained intact. And then, as if Chen needed any further evidence of these parallels, the strangest thing happened in the lab.

Felix scurried into the testing chamber, just as he'd done countless times before, but on this day, for reasons Chen could never understand, Felix did not gather up the twelve coins on the tray and use them to buy food. Instead, he flung the entire tray's worth of coins back into the communal cage and, fleeing the testing chamber, dashed in after them—a bank heist followed by a jailbreak.

There was chaos in the big cage, with twelve coins on the floor and seven monkeys going after them. When Chen and the other researchers went inside to get the coins, the monkeys wouldn't give them up. After all, they had learned that the coins had value. So the humans resorted to bribing the capuchins with treats. This taught the monkeys another valuable lesson: crime pays.

Then, out of the corner of his eye, Chen saw something remarkable. One monkey, rather than handing his coin over to the humans for a grape or a slice of apple, instead approached a second monkey and gave it to her. Chen had done earlier research in which monkeys were found to be altruistic. Had he just witnessed an unprompted act of monkey altruism?

After a few seconds of grooming—*bam!*—the two capuchins were having sex.

What Chen had seen wasn't altruism at all, but rather the first instance of monkey prostitution in the recorded history of science.

And then, just to prove how thoroughly the monkeys had assimilated the concept of money, as soon as the sex was over—it lasted about eight seconds; they're monkeys, after all—the capuchin who'd received the coin promptly brought it over to Chen to purchase some grapes.

This episode sent Chen's mind spinning. Until now, the researchers had run narrowly defined money experiments with one monkey at a time.

What if Chen could introduce money directly into the monkeys' lives? The research possibilities were endless.

Alas, Chen's dream of capuchin capitalism never came to pass. The authorities who oversaw the monkey lab feared that introducing money to the capuchins would irreparably damage their social structure.

They were probably right.

If the capuchins were so quick to turn to prostitution as soon as they got hold of some money, just imagine how quickly the world would be overrun with monkey murderers and monkey terrorists, with monkey polluters who contribute to global warming and monkey doctors who fail to wash their hands. Future generations of monkeys, of course, would come along and solve these problems. But there would always be something to fix—like the monkeys' pigheaded insistence that all their children ride in car seats . . .

ACKNOWLEDGMENTS

★ JOINTLY, WE'D FIRST LIKE TO THANK ALL THE PEOPLE WHO let us tell their stories in this book. For every person named in the text, there were usually five or ten more who contributed in various ways. Thanks to all of you. We are also greatly indebted to the many scholars and researchers whose work is cited in the book.

Suzanne Gluck of William Morris Endeavor is an agent like no other, and we are lucky to have her. She has many extraordinary colleagues, including Tracy Fisher, Raffaella De Angelis, Cathryn Summerhayes, Erin Malone, Sarah Ceglarski, Caroline Donofrio, and Eric Zohn, all of whom have been a big help, as have others at WME, past and present.

At William Morrow/HarperCollins, we've had a great time working with our wonderful editor Henry Ferris, and Dee Dee DeBartlo is unfailingly hardworking and cheerful. There are many others to thank—Brian Murray, Michael Morrison, Liate Stehlik, Lynn Grady, Peter Hubbard, Danny Goldstein, and Frank Albanese among them—as well as those who've moved on, especially Jane Friedman and Lisa Gallagher. For tea, sympathy, and more, thanks to Will Goodlad, Stefan McGrath, and Thi Dinh at Penguin UK (who also provide excellent British children's books for our offspring).

The New York Times has allowed us, in its pages and on our blog, to run some of this book's ideas up the flagpole. Thanks especially to Gerry

Marzorati, Paul Tough, Aaron Retica, Andy Rosenthal, David Shipley, Sasha Koren, Jason Kleinman, Brian Ernst, and Jeremy Zilar.

The Harry Walker Agency has given us more opportunities to meet more incredible people than we ever thought possible, and they are a joy to work with. Thanks to Don Walker, Beth Gargano, Cynthia Rice, Kim Nisbet, Mirjana Novkovic, and everyone else there.

Linda Jines continues to prove that she has no peer when it comes to naming things.

And thanks especially to all the readers who take the time to send along their clever, fascinating, devious, and maddening ideas for us to pursue.

PERSONAL ACKNOWLEDGMENTS

I owe an enormous debt to my many co-authors and colleagues, whose great ideas fill this book, and to all the kind people who have taken the time to teach me what I know about economics and life. My wife, Jeannette, and our children, Amanda, Olivia, Nicholas, and Sophie, make every day a joy, even though we miss Andrew so much. I thank my parents, who showed me it was okay to be different. Most of all, I want to thank my good friend and co-author Stephen Dubner, who is a brilliant writer and a creative genius.

S.D.L.

People like Sudhir Venkatesh, Allie, Craig Feied, Ian Horsley, Joe De May Jr., John List, Nathan Myhrvold, and Lowell Wood make me grateful every day that I became a writer. They are full of insights and surprises that are a joy to learn. Steve Levitt is not only a great collaborator but a wonderful economics teacher as well. For outstanding research assistance, thanks to Rhena Tantisunthorn, Rachel Fershleiser, Nicole Tourtelot, Danielle Holtz, Nell Boeschenstein, Dwyer Gunn, and especially Ryan Hagen, who did great work on this book and will write great books of his own one day. To Ellen, my extraordinary wife, and to the fantastic creatures known as Solomon and Anya: you are all pretty damn swell.

S.J.D.

NOTES

AN EXPLANATORY NOTE

xvi–xvii HOW SOME OTHER PARTNERS HAVE SPLIT THEIR LOOT: For **Orville and Wilbur Wright,** see Mark Eppler, *The Wright Way* (AMACOM, 2004); for **Steve Jobs and Steve Wozniak,** see Owen W. Linzmayer, *Apple Confidential 2.0* (No Starch Press, 2004); for **George Washington and Martha Dandridge Custis,** see Joseph J. Ellis, *His Excellency: George Washington* (Random House, 2005); for **Lou Costello and Bud Abbott,** see Joey Green, *How They Met: Fateful Encounters of Famous Lovebirds, Rivals, Partners in Crime, and Other Strange Bedfellows* (Black Dog Publishing, 2003); for **Coco Chanel and Pierre Wertheimer,** see Dana Thomas, "The Power Behind the Cologne," *The New York Times,* February 24, 2002.

xvii DR. FART SPEAKS: Michael Levitt was christened "one of the world's leading authorities on the science of flatulence" in Jeffrey Kluger, "What a Gas," *Discover,* April 1, 1995.

INTRODUCTION: PUTTING THE FREAK IN ECONOMICS

1–3 THE PERILS OF WALKING DRUNK: The brilliant economist Kevin Murphy called our attention to the relative risk of walking drunk. For background on **the dangers of drunk driving,** see Steven D. Levitt and Jack Porter, "How Dangerous Are Drinking Drivers?" *Journal of Political Economy* 109, no. 6 (2001). / 1–2 One of the benefits of a cumbersome federal bureaucracy is that it hires tens of thousands of employees to staff hundreds of agencies that collect and organize endless reams of statistical data. The National Highway Traffic Safety Administration (NHTSA) is one such agency, and it supplies definitive and valuable data on traffic safety. Regarding the **proportion of miles driven drunk,** see "Impaired Driving in the United States," NHTSA, 2006. / 2 For **drunk pedestrian deaths,** see "Pedestrian Roadway Fatalities," NHTSA, DOT HS 809 456, April 2003. / 2 For **drunk driving deaths,** see "Traffic Safety Facts 2006," NHTSA, DOT HS 810 801, March 2008. / 2 **"They lie down to rest on country roads":** see William E. Schmidt, "A Rural Phenomenon: Lying-in-the-Road Deaths," *The New York Times,* June 30, 1986. / 2 The **number of Americans of driving age:** here and elsewhere in this book, population statistics and characteristics are generally drawn from U.S. Census Bureau data. / 3 **"Friends Don't Let Friends . . .":** By total happenstance, we recently met one of the creators of the original slogan "Friends Don't Let Friends Drive Drunk." Her name is Susan Wershba Zerin. In the early 1980s, she worked at the Leber Katz Partners ad agency in New York and was the account manager on a pro bono anti-drunk-driving campaign for the U.S. Department of Transportation. "Elizabeth Dole, the secretary of transportation, was our key contact," she recalls. The phrase "Friends Don't Let Friends Drive Drunk" was written as the campaign's internal strategic statement, but it proved so memorable in-house that it was adopted as the campaign's tagline.

3–7 THE UNLIKELY SAVIOR OF INDIAN WOMEN: This section draws substantially from Robert Jensen and Emily Oster, "The Power of TV: Cable Television and Women's Status in India," *Quarterly Journal of Economics* 124, no. 3 (2009). For more on **living standards in India,** see the United Nations Human Development Report for India; "National Family Health Survey (NFHS-3), 2005–06, India," the International Institute for Population Sciences and Macro Intl.; and "India Corruption Study 2005," Center for Media Studies, Transparency International, India. / 3 The **Smile Train** story comes from author interviews with Brian Mullaney of Smile Train; see also Stephen J. Dubner and Steven D. Levitt, "Bottom-Line Philanthropy," *The New York Times Magazine,* March 9, 2008. / 3 For more on the persistence of **dowry in India,** see Siwan Anderson, "Why Dowry Payments Declined with Modernization in Europe but Are Rising in India," *Journal of Political Economy* 111, no. 2 (April 2003); Sharda Srinivasan and Arjun S. Bedi, "Domestic Violence and Dowry: Evidence from a South Indian Village," *World Development* 35, no. 5 (2007); and Amelia Gentleman, "Indian Brides Pay a High Price," *The International Herald Tribune,* October 22, 2006. / 4 On the **unwantedness of girls in India** and the use of ultrasounds to identify them for abortion, see NFHS-3 report; and Peter Wonacott, "India's Skewed Sex Ratio Puts GE Sales in Spotlight," *The Wall Street Journal,* April 19, 2007; and Neil Samson Katz and Marisa Sherry, "India: The Missing Girls," *Frontline,* April 26, 2007. / 4 For more on **the "missing women" of India,** see Amartya Sen, "More Than 100 Million Women Are Missing," *The New York Review of Books,* December 20, 1990; Stephan Klasen and Claudia Wink, published in K. Basu and R. Kanbur (eds.), *Social Welfare, Moral Philosophy and Development: Essays in Honour of Amartya Sen's Seventy-Fifth Birthday* (Oxford University Press, 2008); and Swami Agnivesh, Rama Mani, and Angelika Koster-Lossack, "Missing: 50 Million Indian Girls," *The New York Times,* November 25, 2005. See also Stephen J. Dubner and Steven D.

Levitt, "The Search for 100 Million Missing Women," *Slate,* May 24, 2005, which reported on Emily Oster's finding of a connection between missing women and hepatitis B; but see also Steven D. Levitt, "An Academic Does the Right Thing," Freakonomics blog, *The New York Times,* May 22, 2008, in which the hepatitis conclusion was found to be faulty. / 4 **Son worship in China:** see Therese Hesketh and Zhu Wei Xing, "Abnormal Sex Ratios in Human Populations: Causes and Consequences," *Proceedings of the National Academy of Sciences* 103, no. 6 (September 5, 2006); and Sharon LaFraniere, "Chinese Bias for Baby Boys Creates a Gap of 32 Million," *The New York Times,* April 10, 2009. / 4 Information about **bride burning, wife beating, and other domestic atrocities** can be found in Virendra Kumar, Sarita Kanth, "Bride Burning," *The Lancet* 364, supp. 1 (December 18, 2004); B. R. Sharma, "Social Etiology of Violence Against Women in India," *Social Science Journal* 42, no. 3 (2005); "India HIV and AIDS Statistics," AVERT, available at www.avert.org/indiaaids.htm; and Kounteya Sinha, "Many Women Justify Wife Beating," *The Times of India,* October 12, 2007. / 5 **"The condom is not optimized for India":** see Rohit Sharma, "Project Launched in India to Measure Size of Men's Penises," *British Medical Journal,* October 13, 2001; Damian Grammaticus, "Condoms 'Too Big' for Indian Men," *BBC News,* December 8, 2006; and Madhavi Rajadhyaksha, "Indian Men Don't Measure Up," *The Times of India,* December 8, 2006. For **average penis sizes** in select countries, see Eduardo A. Gómez de Diego, "Average Penis Size Worldwide," Andromedical metastudy available at: http://www.andromedical.com/world-penis-sizes. / 5 **Ultrasound in India:** see Alka Gupta, "Female Foeticide in India" available at: www.unicef .org/india/media_3285.htm. / 5 **Apni Beti, Apna Dhan** is described in Fahmida Jabeen and Ravi Karkara, *Government Support to Parenting in Bangladesh and India* (Save the Children Sweden, Kathmandu, December 2005). / 7 **Indian TV ratings** provided by TAM Media Research.

8 FIREFIGHTING, AN AWE-INSPIRING BUSINESS: For more on mythical firefighter **Big Mose** and the perils and promise of life in New York City, see Pete Hamill, *Downtown* (Little, Brown and Company, 2004); see also Richard Plunz, *A History of Housing in New York City* (Columbia University Press, 1990).

8–11 DROWNING IN HORSE MANURE: See Joel Tarr and Clay McShane, "The Centrality of the Horse to the Nineteenth-Century American City," in *The Making of Urban America,* ed. Raymond Mohl (Rowman & Littlefield, 1997); Eric Morris, "From Horse Power to Horsepower," *Access,* no. 30, Spring 2007; Ann Norton Greene, *Horses at Work: Harnessing Power in Industrial America* (Harvard University Press, 2008). Also based on author interviews with Morris, McShane, and David Rosner, Ronald H. Lauterstein Professor of Sociomedical Sciences at Columbia University. / 8 **ASPCA history:** author interviews with Clay McShane of Northeastern University. / 10 **Climate change will "destroy planet Earth as we know it":** see Martin Weitzman, "On Modeling and Interpreting the Economics of Catastrophic Climate Change," *The Review of Economics and Statistics* 91, no. 1 (February 2009). / 11 **The case of the stolen horse manure** is recounted in two *Boston Globe* articles by Kay Lazar: "It's Not a Dung Deal," June 26, 2005; and "Economics Professor Set to Pay for Manure," August 2, 2005.

11–13 WHAT IS "FREAKONOMICS," ANYWAY? **Gary Becker, the original freakonomist,** has written many books, papers, and articles that should be widely read, including *The Economic Approach to Human Behavior, A Treatise on the Human Family,* and *Human Capital.* See also his Nobel Prize acceptance speech, "The Economic Way of Looking at Life," Nobel Lecture, University of Chicago, December 9, 1992; and *The Nobel Prizes/Les Prix Nobel 1992: Nobel Prizes, Presentations, Biographies, and Lectures,* ed. Tore Frängsmyr (The Nobel Foundation, 1993). / 12 **"Our job in this book is to come up with such questions":** as the renowned statistician John Tukey once reportedly said, "An approximate answer to the right question is worth a great deal more than a precise answer to the wrong question." / 12 **One breast, one testicle:** for this thought, a hat tip to the futurist Watts Wacker.

13–16 SHARK-ATTACK HYSTERIA: The *Time* magazine cover package appeared on July 30, 2001, and included Timothy Roche, "Saving Jessie Arbogast." / 13 The definitive source for **shark-attack statistics** is the International Shark Attack File, compiled by the Florida Museum of Natural History at the University of Florida. / 16 **Elephant deaths:** see *People and Wildlife: Conflict or Co-existence?* ed. Rosie Woodroffe, Simon Thirgood, and Alan Rabinowitz (Cambridge University Press, 2005). For more on elephants attacking humans, see Charles Siebert, "An Elephant Crackup?" *The New York Times Magazine,* October 8, 2006.

14–15 GARY BECKER DECISION TREE: Material drawn from Gary Becker's autobiography in *The Nobel Prizes/Les Prix Nobel 1992;* Richard Thompson, "Profile: Economist of the Mind," *The Independent,* October 18, 1992; podcast of interview with Gary Becker, hosted by Russ Roberts, Library of Economics and Liberty, July 10, 2006; and Steven D. Levitt, "Guity Becker Roasts Gary Becker," Freakonomics blog, *The New York Times,* April 16, 2006.

CHAPTER 1: HOW IS A STREET PROSTITUTE LIKE A DEPARTMENT-STORE SANTA?

21 MEET LASHEENA: She is one of the many street prostitutes who participated in Sudhir Venkatesh's fieldwork, summarized in much further detail later in the chapter and contained in Steven D. Levitt and Sudhir Alladi Venkatesh, "An Empirical Analysis of Street-Level Prostitution," working paper, September 2007. / 21 **Off-the-books revenue:** see Sudhir Venkatesh, *American Project* (Harvard University Press, 2000).

22 HARD TO BE A WOMAN: For historic life expectancy, see Vern Bullough and Cameron Campbell, "Female Longevity and Diet in the Middle Ages," *Speculum* 55, no. 2 (April 1980). / 22 **Executed as witches:** see Emily Oster, "Witchcraft, Weather and Economic Growth in Renaissance Europe," *Journal of Economic Perspectives* 18, no. 1 (Winter 2004); the 1533 account of an execution at Schiltach, Germany, is attributed to Stefan Hamer, with illustration by Erhard Schön. It was translated for this edition by Martin Bäumel and Joshua Clemente Bonilla. / 22 **Breast ironing:** see Randy Joe

Sa'ah, "Cameroon Girls Battle 'Breast Ironing,' " *BBC News*, June 23, 2006; as many as 26 percent of Cameroonian girls undergo the procedure, often by their mothers, upon reaching puberty. / 22 **The plight of Chinese women:** see the U.S. State Department's "2007 Country Reports on Human Rights Practices"; for long-term consequences of foot binding, see Steven Cummings, Xu Ling, and Katie Stone, "Consequences of Foot Binding Among Older Women in Beijing, China," *American Journal of Public Health* 87, no. 10 (1997).

22–24 DRAMATIC IMPROVEMENT IN WOMEN'S LIVES: The **advancement of women in higher education** is derived from two reports by the U.S. Department of Education's National Center for Education Statistics: *120 Years of American Education: A Statistical Portrait* (1993); and *Postsecondary Institutions in the United States: Fall 2007, Degrees and Other Awards Conferred: 2006–07, and 12-Month Enrollment: 2006–07* (2008). / 23 **Even Ivy League women** trail men in salaries: see Claudia Goldin and Lawrence F. Katz, "Transitions: Career and Family Lifecycles of the Educational Elite," *AEA Papers and Proceedings*, May 2008. / 23 **Wage penalty for overweight women:** see Dalton Conley and Rebecca Glauber, "Gender, Body Mass and Economic Status," National Bureau of Economics Research working paper, May 2005. / 23 **Women with bad teeth:** see Sherry Glied and Matthew Neidell, "The Economic Value of Teeth," NBER working paper, March 2008; for "beauty premium," see Jeff Biddle and Daniel Hamermesh, "Beauty, Productivity and Discrimination: Lawyers' Looks and Lucre," *Journal of Labor Economics* 16, no. 1 (1998). / 23–24 **The price of menstruation:** see Andrea Ichino and Enrico Moretti, "Biological Gender Differences, Absenteeism and the Earnings Gap," *American Economic Journal: Applied Economics* 1, no. 1 (2009). / 24 **Title IX creates jobs for women; men take them:** see Betsey Stevenson, "Beyond the Classroom: Using Title IX to Measure the Return to High School Sports," the Wharton School, University of Pennsylvania, June 2008; Linda Jean Carpenter and R. Vivian Acosta, "Women in Intercollegiate Sport: A Longitudinal, National Study Twenty-Seven-Year Update, 1977–2004"; and Christina A. Cruz, *Gender Games: Why Women Coaches Are Losing the Field* (VDM Verlag, 2009). For the WNBA disparity, see Mike Terry, "Men Dominate WNBA Coaching Ranks," *The Los Angeles Times*, August 2, 2006.

24–29 PREWAR PROSTITUTION: The section was drawn from a variety of archival sources and books, including: *The Social Evil in Chicago* (aka the Chicago Vice Commission report), American Vigilance Association, 1911; George Jackson Kneeland and Katharine Bement Davis, *Commercialized Prostitution in New York City* (The Century Co., 1913); Howard Brown Woolston, *Prostitution in the United States*, vol. 1, *Prior to the Entrance of the United States into the World War* (The Century Co., 1921); and *The Lost Sisterhood: Prostitution in America, 1900–1918* (The Johns Hopkins University Press, 1983). For more information on the Everleigh Club, see Karen Abbott's fascinating book *Sin in the Second City* (Random House, 2007).

28–29 DRUG DEALERS, NOT BUYERS, DO THE TIME: See Ilyana Kuziemko and Steven D. Levitt, "An Empirical Analysis of Imprisoning Drug Offenders," *Journal of Public Economics* 88 (2004); also, the U.S. Sentencing Commission's *2008 Sourcebook of Federal Sentencing Statistics*.

29–46 THE STREET PROSTITUTES OF CHICAGO: This section is largely drawn from Steven D. Levitt and Sudhir Alladi Venkatesh, "An Empirical Analysis of Street-Level Prostitution," working paper. Venkatesh's Grateful Dead obsession was recounted in author interviews.

30–31 LYING TO THE OPORTUNIDADES CLERK: See César Martinelli and Susan Parker, "Deception and Misreporting in a Social Program," *Journal of the European Economic Association* 7, no. 4 (2009). This paper was brought to our attention by the journalist Tina Rosenberg.

33–34 LOSING VIRGINITY TO A PROSTITUTE, THEN AND NOW: See Charles Winick and Paul M. Kinsie, *The Lively Commerce: Prostitution in the United States* (Quadrangle Books, 1971), citing a paper by P. H. Gebhard presented to the December 1967 meeting of the American Association for the Advancement of Science; and Edward O. Laumann, John H. Gagnon, Robert T. Michael, and Stuart Michaels, *The Social Organization of Sexuality: Sexual Practices in the United States* (The University of Chicago Press, 1994). / 33 **Anti-Flirt Club:** see "10 Girls Start Wars on Auto Invitation," *The Washington Post*, February 28, 1923. / 34 **U.S. tariffs:** drawn from the United States International Trade Commission's Trade DataWeb.

36 A 1-IN-1,200 CHANCE: see the Book of Odds at www.bookofodds.com.

36–38 WHY DID ORAL SEX GET SO CHEAP? See Bonnie L. Halpern-Felsher, Jodi L. Cornell, Rhonda Y. Kropp, and Jeanne M. Tschann, "Oral Versus Vaginal Sex Among Adolescents: Perceptions, Attitudes, and Behavior," *Pediatrics* 115 (2005); Stephen J. Dubner and Steven D. Levitt, "The Economy of Desire," *The New York Times Magazine*, December 11, 2005; Tim Harford, "A Cock-and-Bull Story: Explaining the Huge Rise in Teen Oral Sex," *Slate*, September 2, 2006. / 37 **"Ease of exit"** is a phrase used by Dr. Michael Rekart of the University of British Columbia in an author interview; see also Michael Rekart, "Sex-Work Harm Reduction," *The Lancet* 366 (2005).

39 PRICE DISCRIMINATION: For more information on Dr. Leonard's hair and pet trimmers, see Daniel Hamermesh, "To Discriminate You Need to Separate," Freakonomics blog, *The New York Times*, May 8, 2008. Gender gap in **"keeping up appearances":** see "Average Annual Spending for Men/Women Who Live Alone, by Age Group," Bureau of Labor Statistics, 2003.

40–41 HIGH AIDS RATE AMONG MALE PROSTITUTES' CUSTOMERS: See K. W. Elifson, J. Boles, W. W. Darrow, and C. E. Sterk, "HIV Seroprevalence and Risk Factors Among Clients of Female and Male Prostitutes," *Journal of Acquired Immune Deficiency Syndromes and Human Retrovirology* 20, no. 2 (1999). For the **high rate among female prisoners,** see "HIV in Prisons, 2006," Bureau of Justice Statistics, April 22, 2008.

41–44 PIMPACT > RIMPACT: See Igal Hendel, Aviv Nevo, and François Ortalo-Magné, "The Relative Performance of Real Estate Marketing Platforms: MLS versus FSBOMadison.com," *American Economic Review* 99, no. 5 (2009); and Steven D. Levitt and Chad Syverson, "Antitrust Implications of Outcomes

When Home Sellers Use Flat-Fee Real Estate Agents," *Brookings-Wharton Papers on Urban Affairs*, 2008.

45 THE ECONOMICS OF PIRACY: see Peter Leeson, *The Invisible Hook* (Princeton University Press, 2009).

46–48 FEMINISM AND TEACHING: The **occupations of women in 1910** are taken from the 1910 U.S. Census. / 46 **Percentage of women as teachers:** see Claudia Goldin, Lawrence F. Katz, and Ilyana Kuziemko, "The Homecoming of American College Women: The Reversal of the College Gender Gap," *Journal of Economic Perspectives* 20, no. 4 (Fall 2006). Thanks to Kuziemko for additional calculations. / 46 **Work opportunities multiplying:** see Raymond F. Gregory, *Women and Workplace Discrimination: Overcoming Barriers to Gender Equality* (Rutgers University Press, 2003). / 46-47 **Baby formula as "unsung hero":** see Stefania Albanesi and Claudia Olivetti, "Gender Roles and Technological Progress," National Bureau of Economic Research working paper, June 2007. / 47-48 The **erosion of teacher quality:** see Marigee P. Bacolod, "Do Alternative Opportunities Matter? The Role of Female Labor Markets in the Decline of Teacher Supply and Teacher Quality, 1940–1990," *Review of Economics and Statistics* 89, no. 4 (November 2007); Harold O. Levy, "Why the Best Don't Teach," *The New York Times*, September 9, 2000; and John H. Bishop, "Is the Test Score Decline Responsible for the Productivity Growth Decline," *American Economic Review* 79, no. 1 (March 1989). / 48 **"One pushback against the teacher brain drain":** see Associated Press, "Teach for America: The 2009 Class," May 28, 2009; other statistics provided by TFA.

47 AMALGAMATED ORDER OF REAL BEARDED SANTAS: see Jim Carlton, "These Santas Are Keeping a List, and Not All Have Been Nice," *The Wall Street Journal*, July 10, 2008.

48–49 EVEN TOP WOMEN EARN LESS: See Justin Wolfers, "Diagnosing Discrimination: Stock Returns and CEO Gender," *Journal of the European Economic Association* 4, nos. 2–3 (April–May 2006); and Marianne Bertrand, Claudia Goldin, and Lawrence F. Katz, "Dynamics of the Gender Gap for Young Professionals in the Financial and Corporate Sectors," National Bureau of Economic Research working paper, January 2009.

50 DO MEN LOVE MONEY THE WAY WOMEN LOVE KIDS? The **cash-incentive gender-gap experiment** was reported in Roland G. Fryer, Steven D. Levitt, and John A. List, "Exploring the Impact of Financial Incentives on Stereotype Threat: Evidence from a Pilot Study," *AEA Papers and Proceedings* 98, no. 2 (2008). / 50 The **boy-girl experiment:** see Uri Gneezy, Muriel Niederle, and Aldo Rustichini, "Performance in Competitive Environments: Gender Differences," *Quarterly Journal of Economics* 118, no. 3 (2003).

50–52 CAN A SEX CHANGE BOOST YOUR SALARY? See Kristen Schilt and Matthew Wiswall, "Before and After: Gender Transitions, Human Capital, and Workplace Experiences," *B.E. Journal of Economic Analysis & Policy* 8, no. 1 (2008). Further information for this section was drawn from author interviews with Ben Barres and Deirdre McCloskey; see also Robin Wilson, "Leading Economist Stuns Field by Deciding to Become a Woman," *Chronicle of Higher Education,* February 16, 1996; and Shankar Vedantam, "He, Once a She, Offers Own View on Science Spat," *The Wall Street Journal,* July 13, 2006. **"How is a transgendered person like a ginkgo tree?":** see Steven D. Garber, *The Encyclopedia of New York City* (Yale University Press, 1995); the tree's fruit has been causing trouble since at least the late nineteenth century, when William R. Smith, superintendent of New York City's Botanic Gardens, complained, "The only objection [to the ginkgo tree] is the bad odor the fruit has when matured. My first handling of it cost me three hours' time and a bar of soap to be rid of it" (see *The New York Times,* "Growth of Trees for Shade or Beauty," November 29, 1895).

52–58 WHY AREN'T THERE MORE WOMEN LIKE ALLIE? As detailed in this book's explanatory note, we met Allie thanks to a mutual acquaintance. Allie is not her real name, but all other facts about her are true. Over the past few years, we have both spent a considerable amount of time with her (all fully clothed), as this section was based on extensive interviews, a review of her ledgers, and the occasional guest lectures she delivered at the University of Chicago for Levitt's class "The Economics of Crime." Several students said this was the single-best lecture they had in all their years at the university, which is both a firm testament to Allie's insights and a brutal indictment of Levitt and the other professors. See also Stephen J. Dubner, "A Call Girl's View of the Spitzer Affair," Freakonomics blog, *The New York Times,* March 12, 2008.

57 REALTORS FLOCK TO A REAL-ESTATE BOOM: See Stephen J. Dubner and Steven D. Levitt, "Endangered Species," *The New York Times Magazine,* March 5, 2006.

CHAPTER 2: WHY SHOULD SUICIDE BOMBERS BUY LIFE INSURANCE?

61–63 RAMADAN AND OTHER BIRTH EFFECTS: The section on **prenatal daytime fasting** was drawn from Douglas Almond and Bhashkar Mazumder, "The Effects of Maternal Fasting During Ramadan on Birth and Adult Outcomes," National Bureau of Economic Research working paper, October 2008. / 62 **The natal roulette affects horses too:** see Bill Mooney, "Horse Racing; A Study on the Loss of Foals," *The New York Times,* May 2, 2002; and Frank Fitzpatrick, "Fate Stepped in for Smarty," *The Philadelphia Inquirer,* May 26, 2004. / 62 **Econ horses:** Thoroughbred names must adhere to Jockey Club rules, which stipulate that names cannot be "considered in poor taste" and furthermore cannot be longer than eighteen letters; consist entirely of initials (NASDAQ, for example, or CDO); or consist entirely of numbers (although numbers above 30 may be used if they are spelled out). The Thoroughbred names, vital statistics, and lifetime earnings data in this section were drawn from equibase.com. / 63 **The "Spanish Flu" effect:** see Douglas Almond, "Is the 1918 Influenza Pandemic Over? Long-Term Effects of *In Utero* Influenza Exposure in the Post-1940 U.S. Population," *Journal of Political Economy* 114, no. 4 (2006); and Douglas Almond and Bhashkar Mazumder, "The 1918 Influenza Pandemic and Subsequent Health Outcomes: An Analysis of SIPP Data," *Recent Developments in Health Economics* 95, no. 2 (May 2005). / 63 **Albert Aab versus Albert Zyzmor:** see Liran Einav and Leeat Yariv, "What's in a Surname? The Effects of Surname Initials on Academic Success," *Journal of*

Economic Perspectives 20, no. 1 (2006); and C. Mirjam van Praag and Bernard M. S. van Praag, "The Benefits of Being Economics Professor A (and not Z)," Institute for the Study of Labor discussion paper, March 2007.

63–66 THE BIRTHDATE BULGE AND THE RELATIVE-AGE EFFECT: See Stephen J. Dubner and Steven D. Levitt, "A Star Is Made," *The New York Times Magazine*, May 7, 2006; K. Anders Ericsson, Neil Charness, Paul J. Feltovich, and Robert R. Hoffman, *The Cambridge Handbook of Expertise and Expert Performance* (Cambridge University Press, 2006); K. Anders Ericsson, Ralf Th. Krampe, and Clemens Tesch-Romer, "The Role of Deliberate Practice in the Acquisition of Expert Performance," *Psychological Review* 100, no. 3 (1993); Werner Helsen, Jan Van Winckel, and A. Mark Williams, "The Relative Age Effect in Youth Soccer Across Europe," *Journal of Sports Sciences* 23, no. 6 (June 2005); and Greg Spira, "The Boys of Late Summer," *Slate*, April 16, 2008. As explained in a side note in this section, we originally planned to write an entire chapter in *SuperFreakonomics* about the acquisition of talent—that is, when a person is very good at a given thing, what is it that makes him or her so good? But our plans changed when several books were recently published on this theme. That said, many people gave generously of their time and insights during our research on this abandoned chapter, and we remain indebted to them. Anders Ericsson was extremely helpful, as were Werner Helsen, Paula Barnsley, Gus Thompson, and several others. We are especially grateful to Takeru Kobayashi, the competitive-eating champion from Japan, for his time, insights, and willingness during a New York visit to try out a Papaya King hot dog as well as a Hebrew National, even though he's not particularly fond of hot dogs except when he's eating eight or ten of them per minute. It was the ultimate busman's holiday, and Kobayashi could not have been more gracious. / 65 **Chess, memory, and expertise:** see K. Anders Ericsson and Walter Kintsch, "Long-Term Working Memory," ICS Technical Report 94-01 (1994); as well as pioneering work in this area by W. G. Chase and H. A. Simon, "The Mind's Eye in Chess," in *Visual Information Processing* ed. W. G. Chase (Academic Press, 1976); and A. de Groot, *Thought and Choice and Chess* (Mouton, 1978).

66–68 WHO BECOMES A TERRORIST? See Alan B. Krueger, *What Makes a Terrorist* (Princeton University Press, 2007); Claude Berrebi, "Evidence About the Link Between Education, Poverty and Terrorism Among Palestinians," Princeton University Industrial Relations Section working paper, 2003; and Krueger and Jita Maleckova, "Education, Poverty and Terrorism: Is There a Causal Connection?" *Journal of Economic Perspectives* 17, no. 4 (Fall 2003). See also Robert A. Pape, *Dying to Win: The Strategic Logic of Suicide Terrorism* (Random House, 2005). / 67 **Terrorists and engineers:** see Diego Gambetta and Steffen Hertog, "Engineers of Jihad," University of Oxford working paper, 2007. / 67 **The University of Wisconsin bombing:** see Mike Davis, *Buda's Wagon: A Brief History of the Car Bomb* (Verso, 2007). / 68 For more on **terrorists' goals,** see Mark Juergensmeyer, *Terror in the Mind of God* (University of California Press, 2001). / 68 **Terrorism hard to define:** see Associated Press, "Muslim Nations Fail to Define Terrorism," April 3, 2002.

68–71 WHY TERRORISM IS SO CHEAP AND EASY: **The murder count in the Washington, D.C., metro area** was provided by the Federal Bureau of Investigation, which collects crime statistics from local police departments. The Washington,

D.C., Metropolitan Statistical Area includes the district itself and surrounding counties in Maryland, Virginia, and West Virginia. For more on the **impact of the Washington sniper attacks,** see Jeffrey Schulden et al., "Psychological Responses to the Sniper Attacks: Washington DC, Area, October 2002," *American Journal of Preventive Medicine* 31, no. 4 (October 2006). / 69 Figures for **airport security screenings** come from the Federal Bureau of Transportation Statistics. / 69 **Financial impact of 9/11:** see Dick K. Nanto, "9/11 Terrorism: Global Economic Costs," *Congressional Research Service,* 2004. / 69 **Extra driving deaths after 9/11:** see Garrick Blalock, Vrinda Kadiyali, and Daniel Simon, "Driving Fatalities after 9/11: A Hidden Cost of Terrorism," Cornell University Department of Applied Economics and Management working paper, 2005; Gerd Gigerenzer, "Dread Risk, September 11, and Fatal Traffic Accidents," *Psychological Science* 15, no. 4 (2004); Michael Sivak and Michael J. Flannagan, "Consequences for Road Traffic Fatalities of the Reduction in Flying Following September 11, 2001," *Transportation Research* 7, nos. 4–5 (July–September 2004); and Jenny C. Su et al., "Driving Under the Influence (of Stress): Evidence of a Regional Increase in Impaired Driving and Traffic Fatalities After the September 11 Terrorist Attacks," *Psychological Science* 20, no. 1 (December 2008). / 70 **Our inflated fear of terrorism:** see Krueger, *What Makes a Terrorist?*; and Nate Silver, "The Odds of Airborne Terror," FiveThirtyEight.com, December 27, 2009. / 71 **Back-dated stock options:** see Mark Maremont, Charles Forelle, and James Bandler, "Companies Say Backdating Used in Days After 9/11," *The Wall Street Journal,* March 7, 2007. / 71 **Police resources shifted to terrorism:** see Selwyn Raab, *Five Families: The Rise, Decline, and Resurgence of America's Most Powerful Mafia Empires* (Macmillan, 2005); Janelle Nanos, "Stiffed," *New York,* November 6, 2006; Suzy Jagger, "F.B.I. Diverts Anti-Terror Agents to Bernard Madoff $50 Billion Swindle," *The Times* (London), December 22, 2008; and Eric Lichtblau, "Federal Cases of Stock Fraud Drop Sharply," *The New York Times,* December 24, 2008. / 71 **Influenza and airline travel:** see John Brownstein, Cecily Wolfe, and Kenneth Mandl, "Empirical Evidence for the Effect of Airline Travel on Interregional Influenza Spread in the United States," *PloS Medicine,* October 2006. / 71 **Crime drop in D.C.:** see Jonathan Klick and Alexander Tabarrok, "Using Terror Alert Levels to Estimate the Effect of Police on Crime," *Journal of Law and Economics* 48, no. 1 (April 2005). / 71 **A California pot bonanza:** see "Home-Grown," *The Economist,* October 18, 2007; and Jeffrey Miron, "The Budgetary Implications of Drug Prohibition," Harvard University, December 2008.

71–78 THE MAN WHO FIXES HOSPITALS: This section is based primarily on author interviews with Craig Feied as well as other members of his team, including Mark Smith. We also benefited substantially from Rosabeth Moss Kanter and Michelle Heskett, "Washington Hospital Center," a four-part series in *Harvard Business School,* July 21, 2002, N9-303-010 through N9-303-022. / 72 **Emergency medicine as a specialty:** see Derek R. Smart, *Physician Characteristics and Distribution in the U.S.* (American Medical Association Press, 2007). / 72 **E.R. statistics:** see Eric W. Nawar, Richard W. Niska, and Jiamin Xu, "National Hospital Ambulatory Medical Care Survey: 2005 Emergency Department Summary," *Advance Data from Vital and Health Statistics,* Centers for Disease Control, June 29, 2007; and information gleaned from the Federal Agency for Healthcare Research and Quality (AHRQ), as well as these AHRQ reports: Pamela Owens and Anne Elixhauser, "Hospital Admissions That Began in the Emergency Department, 2003"; and Healthcare Cost and Utilization Project (H-CUP) Statistical Brief no. 1., February 2006. / 73 **"Isordil" and "Plendil":** see Rob Waters, "Precarious Prescriptions," *Salon,* May 5, 1999. / 75 **"It's about what you do in the first sixty minutes":** drawn from Fred D. Baldwin, "It's All About Speed," *Healthcare Informatics,* November 2000. / 75 **"Cognitive drift":** see R. Miller, "Response Time in Man-Computer Conversational Transactions," *Proceedings of the AFIPS Fall Joint Computer Conference,* 1968; and B. Shneiderman, "Response Time and Display Rate in Human Performance with Computers," *Computing Surveys,* 1984.

78–85 WHO ARE THE BEST AND WORST DOCTORS IN THE ER?: This section is based primarily on Mark Duggan and Steven D. Levitt, "Assessing Differences in Skill Across Emergency Room Physicians," working paper. / 78 The **negative effect of doctor report cards:** see David Dranove, Daniel Kessler, Mark McClellan, and Mark Satterthwaite, "Is More Information Better?" *Journal of Political Economy* 111, no. 3 (2003). / 78 **Doctors and "a variety of job-related tests":** N. K. Choudhry, R. H. Fletcher, and S. B. Soumerai, "Systematic Review: The Relationship between Clinical Experience and Quality of Health Care," *Annals of Internal Medicine* 142, no. 4 (2005); Anders Ericsson, "Deliberate Practice and the Acquisition and Maintenance of Expert Performance in Medicine and Related Domains," *Academic Medicine* 79 (2004); and Geoff Norman, Kevin Eva, Lee Brooks, and Stan Hamstra, "Expertise in Medicine and Surgery," in *The Cambridge Handbook of Expertise and Expert Performance,* ed. Anders Ericsson, Neil Charness, Paul J. Feltovich, and Robert R. Hoffman (Cambridge University Press, 2006). / 79 **Animal bites:** see Gregory Erickson, A. Kristopher Lappin, and Kent A. Vilet, "The Ontogeny of Bite-Force Performance in American Alligator *(Alligator mississippiensis),*" *Journal of Zoology* 260 (2003); for the incident involving the Thai zoo crocodile and the veterinarian, see David Byers, "Vet's Arm Is Reattached After Croc Attack," *The Times* (London), April 12, 2007. / 80 **Death in TV hospitals:** see Amir Hetsroni, "If You Must Be Hospitalized, Television Is Not the Place," *Communication Research Reports* 26 (October 2009). / 82 ***E. coli:*** see "*Escherichia coli* O157:H7: General Information," National Center for Zoonotic, Vector-Borne, and Enteric Diseases, Centers for Disease Control and Prevention. / 83 **Personal health-care spending:** see Charles Roehrig, George Miller, Craig Lake, and Jenny Bryant, "National Health Spending by Medical Condition, 1996–2005," *Health Affairs* 28, no. 2 (February 2009). / 85 **Do doctors' strikes save lives?:** see Robert S. Mendelsohn, *Confessions of a Medical Heretic* (Contemporary Books, 1979); and Solveig Argeseanu Cunningham, Kristina Mitchell, K. M. Venkat Narayan, and Salim Yusuf, "Doctors' Strikes and Mortality: A Review," *Social Science and Medicine* 67, no. 11 (December 2008).

86–87 WAYS TO POSTPONE DEATH: **Win a Nobel Prize:** see Matthew D. Rablen and Andrew J. Oswald, "Mortality and Immortality," University of Warwick, January 2007; and Donald MacLeod, "Nobel Winners Live Longer, Say Researchers," *The Guardian,* January 17, 2007. **Make the Hall of Fame:** see David J. Becker, Kenneth Y. Chay, and Shailender Swaminathan, "Mortality and the Baseball Hall of Fame: An Investigation into the Role of Status in Life Expectancy," iHEA 2007 6th World Congress: Explorations in Health Economics paper. **Buy annuities:** see Thomas J. Phillipson and Gary S. Becker, "Old-Age

Longevity and Mortality-Contingent Claims," *Journal of Political Economy* 106, no. 3 (1998). **Be religious:** see Ellen L. Idler and Stanislav V. Kasl, "Religion, Disability, Depression, and the Timing of Death," *American Journal of Sociology* 97, no. 4 (January 1992). **Be patriotic:** see David McCullough, *John Adams* (Simon & Schuster, 2001). **Beat the estate tax:** Joshua Gans and Andrew Leigh, "Did the Death of Australian Inheritance Taxes Affect Deaths?" *Topics in Economic Analysis and Policy* (Berkeley Electronic Press, 2006).

87–90 THE TRUTHS ABOUT CHEMOTHERAPY: This section was drawn in part from interviews with practicing oncologists and oncology researchers including Thomas J. Smith, Max Wicha, Peter D. Eisenberg, and Jerome Groopman, as well as several participants at "Requirements for the Cure for Cancer," an off-the-record 2007 conference organized by Arny Glazier and the Van Andel Research Institute. (Thanks to Rafe Furst for the invitation.) See also Thomas G. Roberts Jr., Thomas J. Lynch Jr., Bruce A. Chabner, "Choosing Chemotherapy for Lung Cancer Based on Cost: Not Yet," *Oncologist,* June 1, 2002; Scott Ramsey et al., "Economic Analysis of Vinorelbine Plus Cisplatin Versus Paclitaxel Plus Carboplatin for Advanced Non-Small-Cell Lung Cancer," *Journal of the National Cancer Institute* 94, no. 4 (February 20, 2002); Graeme Morgan, Robyn Wardy, and Michael Bartonz, "The Contribution of Cytotoxic Chemotherapy to 5-Year Survival in Adult Malignancies," *Clinical Oncology* 16 (2004); Guy Faguet, *The War on Cancer: An Anatomy of Failure, a Blueprint for the Future* (Springer Netherlands, 2005); Neal J. Meropol and Kevin A. Schulman, "Cost of Cancer Care: Issues and Implications," *Clinical Oncology* 25, no. 2 (January 2007); and Bruce Hillner and Thomas J. Smith, "Efficacy Does Not Necessarily Translate to Cost Effectiveness: A Case Study in the Challenges Associated With 21st-Century Cancer Drug Pricing," *Journal of Clinical Oncology* 27, no. 13 (May 2009). / 87 **"The first chemotherapy drug":** see "Doctors Have Faith in Ehrlich's '606,'" *The New York Times,* February 9, 1912. / 88 **The price of cigarettes:** for U.S. tax and smoking rates, see Bill Orzechowski and Rob Walker, *The Tax Burden on Tobacco,* vol. 42 (February 2008); for prevalence of smoking by country, see World Health Organization Report on the Global Tobacco Epidemic, 2009; for average price of cigarettes around the world, see "The Price of a Puff," *The Economist,* December 10, 2009. / 89 **"The deep and abiding desire not to be dead":** This quote was misremembered by Tom Smith from Thomas Finucane, "How Gravely Ill Becomes Dying: A Key to End-of-Life Care," *Journal of the American Medical Association* 282 (1999).

90 LIVING LONG ENOUGH TO DIE FROM CANCER: See Bo E. Honore and Adriana Lleras-Muney, "Bounds in Competing Risks Models and the War on Cancer," *Econometrica* 76, no. 6 (November 2006).

91 WAR: NOT AS DANGEROUS AS YOU THINK?: Derived from "U.S. Active Duty Military Deaths 1980 through 2008 (as of April 22, 2009)," prepared by the Defense Manpower Data Center for Department of Defense; thanks to a reader named Adam Smith (seriously) for alerting us to these data.

91–98 HOW TO CATCH A TERRORIST: This section is drawn from "Identifying Terrorists Using Banking Data," Steven D. Levitt and A. Danger Powers, working paper; and from author interviews with Ian Horsley (a pseudonym), primarily in London. / 92 **Anthrax:** see Scott Shane, "FBI, Laying Out Evidence, Closes Anthrax Case," *The New York Times,* February 19, 2010; and "Ameranthrax Investigative Summary," U.S. Federal Bureau of Investigation, February 2010. / 93 **Bank fraud in the U.K:** gleaned from the Association for Payment Clearing Services (APACS); for fraud by category, see the APACS report *Fraud: The Facts 2009.* / 93 **Card skimming:** see Brian Krebs, "Would You Have Spotted the Fraud?" at KrebsOnSecurity.com, January 15, 2010. / 95 **False positives in cancer screening:** see Jennifer Miller Croswell et al., "Cumulative Incidence of False-Positive Results in Repeated, Multimodal Cancer Screening," *Annals of Family Medicine* 7 (2009). / 95 **Mike Lowell:** see Jimmy Golen, "Lowell: Baseball Held to Higher Standard," The Associated Press, January 18, 2008. / 96–97 **Release of terror suspects:** see Alan Travis, "Two-Thirds of U.K. Terror Suspects Released Without Charge," *The Guardian,* May 12, 2009. / 98 **Fly on a wall:** author interview with Michael Dickinson.

CHAPTER 3: UNBELIEVABLE STORIES ABOUT APATHY AND ALTRUISM

101–104 KITTY GENOVESE AND THE "38 WITNESSES": This section, as well as the section at the end of the chapter about Kitty Genovese, benefited greatly from the time and input of Joseph De May Jr., who created a now-defunct online repository of documentary evidence about the murder at www.kewgardenshistory.com. We are also indebted to many others who contributed their knowledge of the case in interviews or correspondence, including Andrew Blauner, Mike Hoffman, Jim Rasenberger, Charles Skoller, Jim Solomon, and Harold Takooshian. And we drew extensively from some of the many books and articles written about the murder, including: Martin Gansberg, "37 Who Saw Murder Didn't Call the Police: Apathy at Stabbing of Queens Woman Shocks Inspector," *The New York Times,* March 27, 1964; A.M. Rosenthal, *Thirty-Eight Witnesses: The Kitty Genovese Case* (Melville House, 2008; originally published 1964 by McGraw-Hill); Elliot Aronson, *The Social Animal,* 5th ed. (W.H. Freeman and Co., 1988); Joe Sexton, "Reviving Kitty Genovese Case, and Its Passions," *The New York Times,* July 25, 1995; Malcolm Gladwell, *The Tipping Point* (Little, Brown, 2000); Jim Rasenberger, "Nightmare on Austin Street," *American Heritage,* October 2006; Charles Skoller, *Twisted Confessions* (Bridgeway Books, 2008); Rachel Manning, Mark Levine, and Alan Collins, "The Kitty Genovese Murder and the Social Psychology of Helping: The Parable of the 38 Witnesses," *American Psychologist* 62, no. 6 (2007). / 101 **Weather conditions in Queens** were provided by the National Weather Service. / 103 **Genovese and the Holocaust:** see Maureen Dowd, "20 Years After the Murder of Kitty Genovese, the Question Remains: Why?" *The New York Times,* March 12, 1984. Dowd cites R. Lance Shotland, a professor of psychology at Pennsylvania State University, who noted that "probably no single incident has caused social psychologists to pay as much attention to an aspect of social behavior as Kitty Genovese's murder." / 103 **Bill Clinton's statement** about the Genovese murder comes from his remarks at the AmeriCorps Public Safety Forum in New York City, March 10, 1994.

104–110 CRIME AND TELEVISION IN AMERICA: This section is primarily drawn from Steven D. Levitt and Matthew Gentzkow, "Measuring the Impact of TV's Introduction on Crime," working paper. See also Matthew Gentzkow, "Television and Voter Turnout," *Quarterly Journal of Economics* 121, no. 3 (August 2006); and Matthew Gentzkow and Jesse M. Shapiro, "Preschool Television Viewing and Adolescent Test Scores: Historical Evidence from the Coleman Study," *Quarterly Journal of Economics* 123, no. 1 (February 2008). / 105-106 **Prison overcrowding and the ACLU "experiment":** see Steven D. Levitt, "The Effect of Prison Population Size on Crime Rates: Evidence from Prison Overcrowding Litigation," *The Quarterly Journal of Economics* 11, no. 2 (May 1996). / 106 **Provisions for newly released inmates:** provided by the Commonwealth of Virginia's Department of Corrections. / 107 **The rise and fall of murder in America:** see Steven D. Levitt, "Understanding Why Crime Fell in the 1990s," *Journal of Economic Perspectives* 18, no. 1 (Winter 2004); supplemented by *Crime in the United States,* published annually by the Federal Bureau of Investigation. See also Steven D. Levitt and Stephen J. Dubner, *Freakonomics* (William Morrow, 2005). / 109 **"Electronic babysitter":** see "Television Not an Electronic Babysitter, Program Executive Tells Parent Congress," *The New York Times,* May 24, 1950.

110–111 FAMILY ALTRUISM?: See Gary Becker, "Altruism in the Family and Selfishness in the Marketplace," *Economica* 48, no. 189, New Series (February 1981); and B. Douglas Bernheim, Andrei Shleifer, and Lawrence H. Summers, "The Strategic Bequest Motive," *Journal of Political Economy* 93, no. 6 (December 1985). / 111 **The Maintenance of Parents Act:** for the full text of Singapore's law, see statutes.agc.gov.sg.

111–112 AMERICANS ARE FAMOUSLY ALTRUISTIC: These figures are drawn from an Indiana University Center on Philanthropy study. From 1996 to 2006, overall American giving increased from $139 billion to $295 billion (inflation-adjusted), which represents an increase from 1.7% of GDP to 2.6% of GDP. See also David Leonhardt, "What Makes People Give," *The New York Times,* March 9, 2008. / 112 For more on **disaster donations and TV coverage,** see Philip H. Brown and Jessica H. Minty, "Media Coverage and Charitable Giving After the 2004 Tsunami," *Southern Economic Journal* 75, no. 1 (2008); and Alexei Barrionuevo, "Fears of Lawlessness Prompt Show of Force in Chile," *The New York Times,* March 3, 2010.

113 THE VALUE OF LAB EXPERIMENTS: **Galileo's acceleration experiment** is related in Galileo Galilei, *Dialogue Concerning Two New Sciences,* trans. Henry Crew and Alfonso de Salvio, 1914. **Richard Feynman's point** about the primacy of experimentation comes from his *Lectures on Physics,* ed. Matthew Linzee Sands (Addison-Wesley, 1963); for Feynman's conclusions about the *Challenger* explosion, see "Personal Observations on Reliability of Shuttle," Appendix F to *Report of the Presidential Commission on the Space Shuttle Challenger Accident* (June 6, 1986).

113–116 ULTIMATUM AND DICTATOR: The first paper on **Ultimatum** as it is commonly known is Werner Guth, Rolf Schmittberger, and Bernd Schwarze, "An Experimental Analysis of Ultimatum Bargaining," *Journal of Economic Behavior and Organization* 3, no. 4 (1982). For a good background on the evolution of such games, see Steven D. Levitt and John A. List, "What Do Laboratory Experiments Measuring Social Preferences Tell Us About the Real World," *Journal of Economic Perspectives* 21, no. 2 (2007). See also Daniel Kahneman, Jack

L. Knetsch, and Richard Thaler, "Fairness as a Constraint on Profit Seeking: Entitlements in the Market," *American Economic Review* 76, no. 4 (September 1986); Robert Forsythe, Joel L. Horowitz, N. E. Savin, and Martin Sefton, "Fairness in Simple Bargaining Experiments," *Games and Economic Behavior* 6, no. 3 (May 1994); Colin F. Camerer, *Behavioral Game Theory* (Princeton University Press, 2003); and John A. List, "Dictator Game Giving Is an Experimental Artifact," working paper, 2005. / 114 **Smile Train:** drawn from author interviews. / 115 **Monkey altruism:** see Stephen J. Dubner and Steven D. Levitt, "Monkey Business," *The New York Times Magazine,* June 5, 2005.

116–118 ORGAN TRANSPLANTS: The **first successful long-term kidney transplant** was performed at the Peter Bent Brigham Hospital in Boston by Joseph Murray in December 1954, as related in Nicholas Tilney, *Transplant: From Myth to Reality* (Yale University Press, 2003). / 116–117 **"Donorcyclists":** see Stacy Dickert-Conlin, Todd Elder, and Brian Moore, "Donorcycles: Do Motorcycle Helmet Laws Reduce Organ Donations?" Michigan State University working paper, 2009. / 117 **"Presumed consent"** laws in Europe: see Alberto Abadie and Sebastien Gay, "The Impact of Presumed Consent Legislation on Cadaveric Organ Donation: A Cross-Country Study," *Journal of Health Economics* 25, no. 4 (July 2006). / 117 **The Iranian kidney program** is described in Ahad J. Ghods and Shekoufeh Savaj, "Iranian Model of Paid and Regulated Living-Unrelated Kidney Donation," *Clinical Journal of the American Society of Nephrology* 1 (October 2006); and Benjamin E. Hippen, "Organ Sales and Moral Travails: Lessons from the Living Kidney Vendor Program in Iran," Cato Institute, *Policy Analysis,* no. 614, March 20, 2008. / 117 The **exchange between Dr. Barry Jacobs and Rep. Al Gore** took place in the hearings before the Subcommittee on Health and the Environment to consider H.R. 4080, October 17, 1983. / 117 **What if you want your kidney back?:** see Larry McShane, "Long Island Doctor Richard Batista to Estranged Wife: Give Me My Kidney Back or $1.5M," *New York Daily News,* January 8, 2009; and Bill Hutchinson, "Judge Rejects Long Island Doctor Richard Batista's Bid to Charge Estranged Wife for Kidney," *New York Daily News,* February 26, 2009.

118–128 JOHN LIST, GAME-CHANGER: This section is drawn primarily from author interviews with John A. List, as well as a number of his many, many papers, several written in collaboration with Steven D. Levitt. These papers include: List, "Does Market Experience Eliminate Market Anomalies?" *Quarterly Journal of Economics* 118, no. 1 (2003); Glenn Harrison and List, "Field Experiments," *Journal of Economic Literature* 42 (December 2004); List, "Dictator Game Giving Is an Experimental Artifact," working paper, 2005; List, "The Behavioralist Meets the Market: Measuring Social Preferences and Reputation Effects in Actual Transactions," *Journal of Political Economy* 14, no. 1 (2006); Levitt and List, "Viewpoint: On the Generalizability of Lab Behaviour to the Field," *Canadian Journal of Economics* 40, no. 2 (May 2007); Levitt and List, "What Do Laboratory Experiments Measuring Social Preferences Tell Us About the Real World," *Journal of Economic Perspectives* 21, no. 2 (2007); List, "On the Interpretation of Giving in Dictator Games," *Journal of Political Economy* 115, no. 3 (2007); List and Todd L. Cherry, "Examining the Role of Fairness in High Stakes Allocation Decisions," *Journal of Economic Behavior & Organization* 65, no. 1 (2008); Levitt and List, "Homo Economicus Evolves," *Science,* February 15, 2008; Levitt, List, and David Reiley, "What Happens in the Field Stays in the Field: Professionals Do Not Play Minimax in Laboratory Experiments," National Bureau of Economic Research Working Paper, 2009. Levitt and List, "Field Experiments in Economics: The Past, the Present, and the Future," *European Economic Review* 53, no. 1 (January 2009). Note that other researchers have begun questioning whether altruism seen in the lab is an artifact of the experiment itself; notably, see Nicholas Bardsley, "Experimental Economics and the Artificiality of Alteration," *Journal of Economic Methodology* 12, no. 2 (2005). / 118 **The other John List:** see Robert D. McFadden, "Suspect in 5 Killings in 1971 Caught with Aid of TV Show," *The New York Times*, June 2, 1989. / 119 **"Another notable economist-golfer":** see Donald Edward Moggridge, *Maynard Keynes: An Economist's Biography* (Routledge, 1992). / 120 **Vernon Smith:** see *The Nobel Prizes/Les Prix Nobel 2002: Nobel Prizes, Presentations, Biographies, and Lectures*, ed. Tore Frängsmyr (The Nobel Foundation, 2003). / 121 **The Honus Wagner T206** card: see Michael O'Keeffe and Teri Thompson, *The Card: Collectors, Con Men, and the True Story of History's Most Desired Baseball Card* (William Morrow, 2007); and O'Keeffe, "The Infamous 1909 T206 Honus Wagner, Once Owned by Wayne Gretzky, Displayed in Cooperstown," *New York Daily News*, April 17, 2010. / 123 **"Visualize whirled peas":** see William J. Szlemko et al., "Territorial Markings as a Predictor of Driver Aggression and Road Rage," *Journal of Applied Social Psychology* 38, no. 6 (May 21, 2008). / 126 **Nicholas Bardsley:** see his paper "Dictator Game Giving: Altruism or Artefact?" *Experimental Economics* 11, no. 2 (June 2008). / 126 **"Just those sophomores"** and "scientific do-gooders": see R. L. Rosenthal, *Artifact in Behavioral Research* (Academic Press, 1969); / 126 **"A higher need for approval"** and menstruating females: see Richard L. Doty and Colin Silverthorne, "Influence of Menstrual Cycle on Volunteering Behavior," *Nature* 254 (1975). / 127 **The boss washing her hands:** see Kristen Munger and Shelby J. Harris, "Effects of an Observer on Hand Washing in a Public Restroom," *Perceptual and Motor Skills* 69 (1989). / 127 **The "honesty box" experiment:** see Melissa Bateson, Daniel Nettle, and Gilbert Roberts, "Cues of Being Watched Enhance Cooperation in a Real-World Setting," *Biology Letters* 2, no. 3 (September 2006). Along these same lines, consider another clever field experiment, this one conducted in thirty Dutch churches by a young economist named Adriaan R. Soetevent. In these churches, the collection was taken up in a closed bag that was passed along from person to person, row to row. Soetevent got the churches to let him switch things up, randomly substituting an open collection basket for the closed bags over a period of several months. He wanted to know if the added scrutiny changed the donation patterns. (An open basket lets you see how much money has already been collected as well as how much your neighbor puts in.) Indeed it did: with open baskets, the churchgoers gave more money, including fewer small-denomination coins, than with closed bags—although, interestingly, the effect petered out once the open baskets had been around for a while. See Soetevent, "Anonymity in Giving in a Natural Context—a Field Experiment in 30 Churches," *Journal of Public Economics* 89 (2005). / 128 A **"stupid automaton":** see A. H. Pierce, "The Subconscious Again," *Journal of Philosophy, Psychology, & Scientific Methods* 5 (1908). / 128 **"Forced cooperation":** see Martin T. Orne, "On the Social Psychological Experiment: With Particular Reference to Demand Characteristics and Their Implications," *American Psychologist* 17, no. 10 (1962); for more on **Orne, Anne Sexton, and Patricia Hearst,** see Eric Nagourney, "Martin Orne, 72, Psychiatrist and Expert on Hypnosis, Dies," *The New York Times*, February 17, 2000. / 128 **"Why Nazi officers obeyed":** see Stanley Milgram, "Behavioral Study of Obedience," *Journal of Abnormal and Social Psychology* 67, no. 4 (1963). / 128 The **Stanford prison experiments:** see Craig Haney, Curtis Banks, and Philip Zimbardo, "Interpersonal Dynamics in a Simulated Prison," *International Journal of Criminology and Penology* 1 (1973).

129–130 "IMPURE ALTRUISM": **Americans as top givers:** see "International Comparisons of Charitable Giving," Charities Aid Foundation briefing paper, November 2006. And for the correspondingly strong tax incentives, see David Roodman and Scott Standley, "Tax Policies to Promote Private Charitable Giving in DAC Countries," Center for Global Development, working paper 82, February 2006. / 129 **"Impure" and "warm-glow" altruism:** see James Andreoni, "Giving with Impure Altruism: Applications to Charity and Ricardian Equivalence," *Journal of Political Economy* 97 (December 1989); and Andreoni, "Impure Altruism and Donations to Public Goods: A Theory of Warm-Glow Giving," *Economic Journal* 100 (June 1990). / 129 **The economics of panhandling:** see Gary S. Becker, "Spouses and Beggars: Love and Sympathy," in *Accounting for Tastes* (Harvard University Press, 1998). / 129 **Organ transplant waiting lists:** this information was gleaned from the U.S. Department of Health and Human Services' Organ Procurement and Transplant Network website, at www.optn.org. Further material was generated by the economist Julio Jorge Elias of the State University of New York, Buffalo. See also Becker and Elias, "Introducing Incentives in the Market for Live and Cadaveric Organ Donations," *Journal of Economic Perspectives* 21, no. 3 (Summer 2007); and Stephen J. Dubner and Steven D. Levitt, "Flesh Trade," *The New York Times Magazine*, July 9, 2006. / 130 **"Once repugnant, now accepted":** see Alvin E. Roth, "Repugnance as a Constraint on Markets," *Journal of Economic Perspectives* 21, no. 3 (Summer 2007). / 130 **No waiting list in Iran:** see Benjamin E. Hippen, "Organ Sales and Moral Travails: Lessons from the Living Kidney Vendor Program in Iran," Cato Institute, *Policy Analysis*, no. 614, March 20, 2008; and Stephen J. Dubner, "Human Organs for Sale, Legally, in . . . *Which* Country?" Freakonomics blog, *The New York Times*, April 29, 2008.

130–137 KITTY GENOVESE REVISITED: See the notes at the top of this chapter section for a list of the sources we relied upon for the reappraisal of the case. This second section drew substantially on interviews with Joseph De May Jr. and Mike Hoffman, as well as A.M. Rosenthal's book *Thirty-Eight Witnesses*. / 131 **A.M. Rosenthal's Kevin Bacon score** was calculated using the Oracle of Bacon, at oracleofbacon.org. / 131 **"The number 38 is also":** for surviving **Shakespeare plays,** see William Shakespeare, *The Oxford Shakespeare: The Complete Works,* 2nd ed., ed. Stanley Wells, Gary Taylor, John Jowett, and William Montgomery (Oxford University Press, 2005); for **John Lennon ranking,** see "The Immortals," *Rolling Stone,* April 21, 2005; for **Smith & Wesson chairman tenure,** see "Harper's Index," *Harper's,* May 2004, as well as Associated Press, "Ex-Armed Robber Resigns as Head of Smith & Wesson," February 26, 2004; for the brief **war with Zanzibar,** see Ian Hernon, *Britain's Forgotten Wars: Colonial Campaigns of the 19th Century* (The History Press, 2003); for **people not entitled to an opinion:** see *The Onion,* "Study: 38 Percent of People Not Actually Entitled to Their Opinion," May 23, 2007. / 137 **Winston Moseley's dangerous car:** see Ralph Nader, *Unsafe at Any Speed: The Designed-in Dangers of the American Automobile* (Grossman, 1965).

138–139 PANHANDLERS' SIGNS: Author interviews with James McWilliams, to whom we are indebted for loaning us some of his signs, which were photographed by Jessica Zadnik.

CHAPTER 4: THE FIX IS IN—AND IT'S CHEAP AND SIMPLE

141 MATERNAL DEATH RATES: For recent figures, see "Maternal Mortality in 2005: Estimates Developed by WHO, UNICEF, UNFPA, and the World Bank," World Health Organization, 2007; and "Achievements in Public Health, 1900–1999: Healthier Mothers and Babies," *The Centers for Disease Control and Prevention Morbidity and Mortality Weekly Report,* October 1, 1999. For historical rates, see Irvine Loudon, "Maternal Mortality in the Past and Its Relevance to Developing Countries Today," *American Journal of Clinical Nutrition* 72, no. 1 (July 2000).

142–146 IGNATZ SEMMELWEIS COMES TO THE RESCUE: The story of Ignatz Semmelweis has been told variously over the years, but perhaps the most impressive telling is Sherwin B. Nuland, *The Doctor's Plague: Germs, Childbed Fever, and the Strange Story of Ignatz Semmelweis* (Atlas Books, 2003). This may be because Nuland is a physician himself. We have drawn substantially from his book, and we are greatly indebted. See also Ignatz Semmelweis, "The Etiology, Concept, and Prophylaxis of Childbed Fever," trans. K. Codell Carter (University of Wisconsin Press, 1983; originally published 1861). Note: *Puerpera* is Latin for a woman who has given birth. / 143 **"The very male faculty":** see Martha Clevenger, "From Lay Practitioner to Doctor of Medicine: Woman Physicians in St. Louis, 1860–1920," in *Gateway Heritage* (The Missouri Historical Society, 1987). / 144 **New York's missing suicides:** see Hugh P. Whitt, "Where Did the Bodies Go? The Social Construction of Suicide Data, New York City, 1976–1992," *Sociological Inquiry* 76, no. 2 (2006); James Barron, "Koch Dismisses Gross, Faulting His Leadership," *The New York Times,* October 30, 1987; and Philip Shenon, "Broad Deterioration in Coroner's Office Charged," *The New York Times,* January 30, 1985.

146–147 UNINTENDED CONSEQUENCES: For an overview, see Stephen J. Dubner and Steven D. Levitt, "Unintended Consequences," *The New York Times Magazine,* January 20, 2008. / 146 For the **Americans with Disabilities Act,** see Daron Acemoglu and Joshua D. Angrist, "Consequences of Employment Protection? The Case of the Americans with Disabilities Act," *Journal of Political Economy* 109, no. 5 (2001). / 147 For the **Endangered Species Act,** see Dean Lueck and Jeffrey A. Michael, "Preemptive Habitat Destruction Under the Endangered Species Act," *Journal of Law and Economics* 46 (April 2003); and John A. List, Michael Margolis, and Daniel E. Osgood, "Is the Endangered Species Act Endangering Species?" National Bureau of Economic Research working paper, December 2006. / 147 **Avoiding the trash tax:** for the **"Seattle Stomp,"** the **Charlottesville woods-dumping,** and other tactics, see Don Fullerton and Thomas C. Kinnaman, "Household Responses to Pricing Garbage by the Bag," *American Economic Review* 86, no. 4 (September 1996); for **German food-flushing,** see Roger Boyes, "Children Beware: The Rats Are Back and Hamelin Needs a New Piper," *The Times* (London), December 17, 2008; for **backyard burning in Dublin,** see S. M. Murphy, C. Davidson, A. M. Kennedy, P. A. Eadie, and C. Lawlor, "Backyard Burning," *Journal of Plastic, Reconstructive & Aesthetic Surgery* 61, no. 1 (February 2008). / 147 **Australian emissions and suicides:** see David M. Studdert, Lyle C. Gurrin, Uma Jatkar, and Jane Pirkis, "Relationship between Vehicle Emissions Laws and Incidence of Suicide by Motor Vehicle Exhaust Gas in Australia, 2001–06: An Ecological Analysis," *PLoS Medicine* (January 2010). / 147 **The sabbatical backlash:** see Solomon Zeitlin, "Prosbol: A Study in Tannaitic Jurisprudence," *The Jewish Quarterly Review* 37, no. 4 (April 1947). (Thanks to Leon Morris for the tip.)

148 FORCEPS HOARDING: See James Hobson Aveling, *The Chamberlens and the Midwifery Forceps* (J. & A. Churchill, 1882); Atul Gawande, "The Score: How Childbirth Went Industrial," *The New Yorker,* October 2, 2006; and Stephen J. Dubner, "Medical Failures, and Successes Too: A Q&A with Atul Gawande," Freakonomics blog, *The New York Times,* June 25, 2007. / 148 For more on an **ancient astrological computer,** see John Noble Wilford, "Discovering How Greeks Computed in 100 B.C.," *The New York Times,* July 31, 2008.

148–149 MORE FOOD, MORE PEOPLE: See "The World at Six Billion," *United Nations,* 1999; Mark Overton, *Agricultural Revolution in England: The Transformation of the Agrarian Economy, 1500–1850* (Cambridge University Press, 1996); and Milton Friedman and Rose Friedman, *Free to Choose* (Harvest, 1990; originally published 1979). Information from Will Masters, a professor of agricultural economics at Purdue, came from an author interview. For a stunning exhibition of Masters's mastery at setting theories of agricultural economics to verse, see Stephen J. Dubner, "Why Are Kiwis So Cheap?" Freakonomics blog, *The New York Times,* June 4, 2009.

149–153 CONSIDER THE WHALE: The rise and fall of whale hunting is beautifully told in Eric Jay Dolin, *Leviathan: The History of Whaling in America* (W.W. Norton & Company, 2007). See also Charles Melville Scammon, *The Marine Mammals of the Northwestern Coast of North America: Together with an Account of the American Whale-Fishery,* 1874; Alexander Starbuck, *History of the American Whale Fishery From Its Earliest Inception to the Year 1876,* published by the author in 1878; and Paul Gilmour, "Saving the Whales, Circa 1852," letter to the editor, *The Wall Street Journal,* December 6, 2008.

153–155 THE MYSTERIES OF POLIO: See David M. Oshinsky, *Polio: An American Story* (Oxford University Press, 2005), a truly excellent book on the topic; and "The Battle Against Polio," *NewsHour with Jim Lehrer,* PBS, April 24, 2006. / 153 The **fallacious polio/ice-cream link** was raised by David Alan Grier, a statistician at George Washington University, in Steve Lohr, "For Today's Graduate, Just One Word: Statistics," *The New York Times,* August 5, 2009. / 153 **Other well-known polio sufferers:** for **Frida Kahlo,** see Valmantas Budrys, "Neurological Deficits in the Life and Works of Frida Kahlo," *European Neurology* 55, no. 1 (2006); for **Brownie McGhee** and **Joni Mitchell,** see Holly George-Warren, Patricia Romanowski, and Jon Pareles, eds., *The Rolling Stone Encyclopedia of Rock & Roll* (Fireside, 2001); for **Ben Bradlee,** see Benjamin C. Bradlee, *A Good Life* (Simon & Schuster, 1996); for **Francis Ford Coppola,** see Gene D. Phillips, *Godfather: The Intimate Francis Ford Coppola* (University Press of Kentucky, 2004); for **Itzhak Perlman,** see Boris Schwarz, *Great Masters of the Violin: From Corelli and Vivaldi to Stern, Zukerman, and Perlman* (Simon

& Schuster, 1983). / 155 For estimated **cost savings of the polio vaccines,** see Kimberly M. Thompson and Radboud J. Duintjer Tebbens, "Retrospective Cost-Effectiveness Analysis for Polio Vaccination in the United States," *Risk Analysis* 26, no. 6 (2006); and Tebbens et al., "A Dynamic Model of Poliomyelitis Outbreaks: Learning from the Past to Help Inform the Future," *American Journal of Epidemiology* 162, no. 4 (July 2005). / 155 For more on **the development of ulcer drugs,** see Lawrence K. Altman, "Two Win Nobel Prize for Discovering Bacterium Tied to Stomach Ailments," *The New York Times,* October 4, 2005; and Altman, "A. Stone Freedberg, Pioneer in Study of Ulcers, Dies at 101," *The New York Times,* August 23, 2009. / 155 For **other cheap and simple medical fixes,** see Marc W. Kirschner, Elizabeth Marincola, and Elizabeth Olmsted Teisberg, "The Role of Biomedical Research in Health Care Reform," *Science* 266 (October 7, 1994); and Earl S. Ford et al., "Explaining the Decrease in U.S. Deaths from Coronary Disease, 1980–2000," *New England Journal of Medicine* 356, no. 23 (June 7, 2007).

156 THE KILLER CAR: For **number of cars in the 1950s,** see "Topics and Sidelights of the Day in Wall Street: Fuel Consumption," *The New York Times,* May 25, 1951. For **industry fears** over safety concerns, see "Fear Seen Cutting Car Traffic, Sales," *The New York Times,* January 29, 1952. The **number and rate of U.S. traffic deaths** were drawn from "Motor Vehicle Traffic Fatalities, 1900–2007," Table FI-200, Federal Highway Administration, January 2009; and NHTSA's Fatality Analysis Reporting System.

156–160 THE STRANGE STORY OF ROBERT MCNAMARA'S SEAT BELT: This section is based on a number of sources, including author interviews with McNamara shortly before his death. See also "A Life in Public Service: Conversation with Robert McNamara," April 16, 1996, by Harry Kreisler, part of the Conversations with History series, Institute of International Studies, University of California, Berkeley; *The Fog of War: Eleven Lessons from the Life of Robert S. McNamara,* directed by Errol Morris, 2003, Sony Pictures Classics; Richard Alan Johnson, *Six Men Who Built the Modern Auto Industry* (MotorBooks/MBI Publishing Company, 2005); and Johnson, "The Outsider: How Robert McNamara Changed the Automobile Industry," *American Heritage,* Summer 2007. / 158 For **objections to seat belts,** see U.S. Congress, House, *Automobile Seat Belts: Hearings before a subcommittee of the Committee on Interstate Foreign Commerce, on the crashworthiness of automobile seat belts,* 85th Cong., 1st sess., April 30, August 5, 6, 7, and 8, 1957" also Walter Rugaber, "Car Safety Found Low Sales Point: Few Dealers Say Public Is Showing More Interest in It," *The New York Times,* January 18, 1966; and John D. Morris, "Shoulder Strap Rule for Cars Stands," *The New York Times,* October 9, 1967. / 159 **Seat belt usage over time:** see Steven D. Levitt and Jack Porter, "Sample Selection in the Estimation of Air Bag and Seat Belt Effectiveness," *The Review of Economics and Statistics* 83, no. 4 (November 2001). / 159 For **lives saved by seat belts,** see Donna Glassbrenner, "Estimating the Lives Saved by Safety Belts and Air Bags," National Highway Traffic Safety Administration, paper no. 500; and "Lives Saved in 2008 by Restraint Use and Minimum Drinking Age Laws," NHTSA, June 2009. / 159 **3 trillion miles driven per year:** gleaned from U.S. Bureau of Transportation Statistics. / 159 **Dangerous roads on other continents:** see "Road Safety: A Public Health Issue," World Health Organization, March 29, 2004. / 159 The **cost of a life saved by a seat**

belt versus an air bag: see Levitt and Porter, "Sample Selection in the Estimation of Air Bag and Seat Belt Effectiveness." / 159 Samuel Langhorne Clemens (as Mark Twain) first published **"The Danger of Lying in Bed"** in *Galaxy*, February 1871.

160–168 HOW MUCH GOOD DO CAR SEATS DO? This section is primarily based on Steven D. Levitt, "Evidence That Seat Belts Are as Effective as Child Safety Seats in Preventing Death for Children," *The Review of Economics and Statistics* 90, no. 1 (February 2008); Levitt and Joseph J. Doyle, "Evaluating the Effectiveness of Child Safety Seats and Seat Belts in Protecting Children from Injury," *Economic Inquiry* (August 2008); and Levitt and Stephen J. Dubner, "The Seat-Belt Solution," *The New York Times Magazine*, July 10, 2005. For a brief **history of child safety seats,** see Charles J. Kahane, "An Evaluation of Child Passenger Safety: The Effectiveness and Benefits of Safety Seats," National Highway Traffic Safety Administration, February 1986. / 160 For more on **Bertil Aldman,** see Francis Capistrano, "Volvo Tackles Child Safety in Forum," *BusinessWorld*, August 17, 2004; and "Volvo Improves Safety for Children," *Motor Trend*, February 2009. / 160 **Leading causes of death among children:** drawn from the National Center for Injury Prevention and Control, Centers for Disease Control and Prevention. / 161 **Inscrutable?:** See *Drivers' Mistakes When Installing Child Seats*, National Highway Traffic Safety Administration, DOT HS 811 234, December 2009. / 162 **Barry Myers:** drawn from author interviews. / 163 **Red-light cameras:** see R. A. Retting et al., "Evaluation of Red Light Camera Enforcement in Fairfax, Va., USA," *ITE Journal* 69 (1999); R. A. Retting et al., "Evaluation of Red Light Camera Enforcement in Oxnard, California," *Accident Analysis and Prevention* 31 (1999); R. A. Retting, S. A. Ferguson, and A. S. Hakkert, "Effects of Red Light Cameras on Violations and Crashes: A Review of the International Literature," *Traffic Injury Prevention* 4 (2003); and Nicholas J. Garber et al., *The Impact of Red Light Cameras (Photo-Red Enforcement) on Crashes in Virginia*, Virginia Department of Transportation, Virginia Transportation Research Council, research report, June 2007. / 166 **"A group of prominent child-safety researchers":** see Flaura K. Winston, Dennis R. Durbin, Michael J. Kallan, and Elisa K. Moll, "The Danger of Premature Graduation to Seat Belts for Young Children," *Pediatrics* 105 (2000); and Dennis R. Durbin, Michael R. Elliott, and Flaura K. Winston, "Belt-Positioning Booster Seats and Reduction in Risk of Injury Among Children in Vehicle Crashes," *Journal of the American Medical Association* 289, no. 21 (June 4, 2003). / 167 **Wisconsin vs. New Jersey:** statistics drawn from the U.S. Census Bureau; Federal Highway Administration; the National Institute on Alcohol Abuse and Alcoholism, and "Traffic Safety Facts, Crash Stats," NHTSA, 2009. The Centers for Disease Control and Prevention defines binge drinking for men as the consumption of five or more drinks in a single sitting, and for women as the consumption of four drinks or more in a single sitting.

168 SALK INSTITUTE/LOUIS KAHN: See Louis I. Kahn and John Lobell, *Between Silence and Light: Spirit in the Architecture of Louis I. Kahn* (Shambhala, 1979).

168–170 HURRICANE STATISTICS: Data on **worldwide hurricane deaths** were provided by the Emergency Events Database, hosted by the Université catholique de Louvain; the U.S. death count was obtained from the National Hurricane Research Division of the National Oceanic and Atmospheric Association. The **economic cost in the United States alone:** see Roger Pielke Jr. et al., "Normalized Hurricane Damage in the United States: 1900–2005," *Natural Hazards Review,* February 2008. For more on **the Atlantic Multidecadal Oscillation,** see Stephen Gray, Lisa Graumlich, Julio Betancourt, and Gregory Pederson, "A Tree-Ring Based Reconstruction of the Atlantic Multidecadal Oscillation since 1567 A.D.," *Geophysical Research Letters* 31 (June 17, 2004); Mihai Dima, "A Hemispheric Mechanism for the Atlantic Multidecadal Oscillation," *Journal of Climate* 20 (October 2006); David Enfield, Alberto Mestas-Nuñez, and Paul Trimble, "The Atlantic Multidecadal Oscillation and Its Relation to Rainfall and River Flows in the Continental U.S.," *Geophysical Research Letters* 28 (May 15, 2001); and Clive Thompson, "The Five-Year Forecast," *New York,* November 27, 2006.

171–175 "AN INTELLECTUALLY VENTURESOME FELLOW NAMED NATHAN": This section is drawn from author interviews with Nathan and his colleagues, whom the reader will meet in fuller detail in chapter 5. Neal Stephenson—yes, the same one who writes phantasmagorical novels—was particularly helpful in walking us through some of the details and showing computer simulations. The hurricane killer described is also known as Jeffrey A. Bowers et al., "Water Alteration Structure Applications and Methods," U.S. Patent Application 20090173386, July 9, 2009. Among the "et al." authors is one William H. Gates III. The abstract from the patent application reads like this: "A method is generally described which includes environmental alteration. The method includes determining a placement of at least one vessel capable of moving water to lower depths in the water via wave induced downwelling. The method also includes placing at least one vessel in the determined placement. Further, the method includes generating movement of the water adjacent the surface of the water in response to the placing." / 171 **"How much energy does a major hurricane contain?":** See "The Power of a Hurricane," Kerry A. Emanuel, Massachusetts Institute of Technology, available at http://citeseerx.ist.psu.edu/viewdoc/download?doi=10.1.1.23.3121&rep=rep1&type=pdf.

CHAPTER 5: WHAT DO AL GORE AND MOUNT PINATUBO HAVE IN COMMON?

177–178 LET'S MELT THE ICE CAP!: For the section on **global cooling,** see Harold M. Schmeck Jr., "Climate Changes Endanger World's Food Output," *The New York Times,* August 8, 1974; Peter Gwynne, "The Cooling World," *Newsweek,* April 28, 1975; Walter Sullivan, "Scientists Ask Why World Climate Is Changing; Major Cooling May Be Ahead," *The New York Times,* May 21, 1975. Ground temperatures over the past 100 years can be found in "Climate Change 2007: Synthesis Report," U.N. Intergovernmental Panel on Climate Change (IPCC). / 178 **Grinnell Glacier:** see Robert M. Krimmel, "Glaciers of North America," U.S. Geological Survey Professional Paper 1386-J-2; and Michael Jamison, "Warming Climate Shrinking Glacier Park's Glaciers," *USA Today,* October 15, 2007.

178 JAMES LOVELOCK: All Lovelock quotes in this chapter can be found in *The Revenge of Gaia: Earth's Climate Crisis and the Fate of Humanity* (Basic Books,

2006). Lovelock is a scientist perhaps best known as the originator of the Gaia hypothesis, which argues that the earth is essentially a living organism much like (but in many ways superior to) a human being. He has written several books on the subject, including the foundational *Gaia: The Practical Science of Planetary Medicine* (Gaia Books, 1991).

178–180 COWS ARE WICKED POLLUTERS: **The potency of methane** as a greenhouse gas as compared with carbon dioxide was calculated by the climate scientist Ken Caldeira, of the Carnegie Institution for Science, based on the IPCC's Third Assessment Report. **Ruminants produce more greenhouse gas than transportation sector:** see "Livestockff's Long Shadow: Environmental Issues and Options," Food and Agriculture Organization of the United Nations, Rome, 2006; and Shigeki Kobayashi, "Transport and Its Infrastructure," chapter 5 from IPCC Third Assessment Report, September 25, 2007.

179 WELL-MEANING LOCAVORES: See Christopher L. Weber and H. Scott Matthews, "Food-Miles and the Relative Climate Impacts of Food Choices in the United States," *Environmental Science and Technology* 42, no. 10 (April 2008); see also James McWilliams, "On Locavorism," Freakonomics blog, *The New York Times,* August 26, 2008; and McWilliams's book *Just Food* (Little, Brown, 2009).

179–180 EAT MORE KANGAROO: See "Eco-friendly Kangaroo Farts Could Help Global Warming: Scientists," Agence France-Presse, December 5, 2007. / 180 For **trends in American meat consumption,** see Rosanna Mentzer Morrison, Jean C. Buzby, and Hodan Farah Wells, "Guess Who's Turning 100? Tracking a Century of American Eating," *Amber Waves* (USDA, Economic Research Service, March 2010); and James Mintert, Glynn Tonsor, and Ted Schroeder, *U.S. Beef Demand Drivers and Enhancement Opportunities: A Research Summary* (Kansas State University, 2009).

180–183 GLOBAL WARMING AS A "UNIQUELY THORNY PROBLEM": For the **"terrible-case scenario,"** see Martin L. Weitzman, "On Modeling and Interpreting the Economics of Catastrophic Climate Change," *The Review of Economics and Statistics* 91, no. 1 (February 2009). / 181 **Metana, the research cow:** see Associated Press, "Device Measures Cows' Methane Impact," February 8, 2010. / 182 **A Stern warning:** see Nicholas Herbert Stern, *The Economics of Climate Change: The Stern Review* (Cambridge University Press, 2007). / 182 There is much to be read about **the influence of uncertainty,** especially as it compares with its cousin risk. The Israeli psychologists Amos Tversky and Daniel Kahneman, whose work is generally credited with giving ultimate birth to behavioral economics, conducted pioneering research on how people make decisions under pressure and found that uncertainty leads to "severe and systematic errors" in judgment. (See "Judgment Under Uncertainty: Heuristics and Biases," from *Judgment Under Uncertainty: Heuristics and Biases,* ed. Daniel Kahneman, Paul Slovic, and Amos Tversky [Cambridge University Press, 1982].) The **Ellsberg paradox** was first proposed by Daniel Ellsberg in "Risk, Ambiguity, and the Savage Axioms," *The Quarterly Journal of Economics* 75, no. 4 (1961). We wrote about the difference between risk and uncertainty in a *New York Times Magazine* column ("The Jane Fonda Effect," September 16, 2007), in which we wondered whether nuclear energy, risks and all, is now seen as preferable to the uncertainties of global warming. / 183 **Al Gore's "We" campaign:** see www.climateprotect.org and Andrew C. Revkin, "Gore Group Plans Ad Blitz on Global Warming," *The New York Times,* April 1, 2008. / 183 ***An Inconvenient Truth* special effects:** see Sam Champion, "Realistic Good and Bad Science; Legitimate Science in TV and Film," *20/20,* ABC News, April 18, 2008. / 183 **The heretic Boris Johnson:** see Boris Johnson, "We've Lost Our Fear of Hellfire, but Put Climate Change in Its Place," *The Daily Telegraph,* February 2, 2006. / 183 **"Rendered nearly lifeless":** see Peter Ward, *The Medea Hypothesis: Is Life on Earth Ultimately Self-Destructive?* (Princeton University Press, 2009); and Drake Bennett, "Dark Green: A Scientist Argues That the Natural World Isn't Benevolent and Sustaining: It's Bent on Self-Destruction," *The Boston Globe,* January 11, 2009. / 183 **Human activity and carbon emissions:** see Kenneth Chang, "Satellite Will Track Carbon Dioxide," *The New York Times,* February 22, 2009; read more about NASA's view of carbon dioxide at http://oco.jpl.nasa.gov/science/.

184–185 NEGATIVE EXTERNALITIES AND COAL MINING: see Garrett Hardin, "The Tragedy of the Commons: The population problem has no technical solution; it requires a fundamental extension in morality," *Science,* December 13, 1968. / 185 For **American coal worker deaths,** see the U.S. Department of Labor, Mine Safety and Health Administration, "Coal Fatalities for 1900 Through 2008"; and Jeff Goodell, *Big Coal: The Dirty Secret Behind America's Energy Future* (Houghton Mifflin, 2007). Deaths from **black lung** were gleaned from National Institute for Occupational Safety and Health reports; for more, see Kris Maher, "Black Lung on Rise in Mines, Reversing Trend," *The Wall Street Journal,* December 15, 2009. **Chinese coal worker deaths** were reported by the Chinese government to be 4,746 in 2006, 3,786 in 2007, and 3,215 in 2008; these numbers are likely underestimates. See "China Sees Coal Mine Deaths Fall, but Outlook Grim," Reuters, January 11, 2007; and "Correction: 3,215 Coal Mining Deaths in 2008," *China.org.cn,* February 9, 2009.

186–189 LOJACK: See Ian Ayres and Steven D. Levitt, "Measuring Positive Externalities from Unobservable Victim Precaution: An Empirical Analysis of LoJack," *Quarterly Journal of Economics* 113, no. 8 (February 1998).

187 POLLUTION WITHOUT BORDERS: See "Pollution Over China Blows Out to Sea," NASA Earth Observatory *Image of the Day* blog, October 29, 2004; see also Siqi Zheng, Rui Wang, Edward L. Glaeser, and Matthew E. Kahn, "The Greenness of China: Household Carbon Dioxide Emissions and Urban Development," NBER Working Paper no. 15621, December 2009.

189 APPLE TREES AND HONEY BEES: See J. E. Meade, "External Economies and Diseconomies in a Competitive Situation," *Economic Journal* 62, no. 245 (March 1952); and Steven N. S. Cheung, "The Fable of the Bees: An Economic Investigation," *Journal of Law and Economics* 16, no. 1 (April 1973). For more on Cheung's legal issues, see Stephen J. Dubner, "Not as Authentic as It Seems," Freakonomics blog, *The New York Times,* March 23, 2009; also Duff Wilson, "The Art of Deception: Eminent Economist Tied to Fake Antiques," *The Seattle Times,* January 27, 2003; and Emily Heffter, "Art Gallery Settles Fraud Case," *The Seattle Times,* October 29, 2005.

190–192 MOUNT PINATUBO: For one dramatic telling of the eruption, see Barbara Decker, *Volcanoes* (Macmillan, 2005); for a more by-the-numbers approach, see "The Cataclysmic 1991 Eruption of Mount Pinatubo, Philippines," U.S. Geological Survey Fact Sheet 113-97. For its effect on global climate, see: Richard Kerr, "Pinatubo Global Cooling on Target," *Science*, January 1993; P. Minnis et al., "Radiative Climate Forcing by the Mount Pinatubo Eruption," *Science*, March 1993; Gregg J. S. Bluth et al., "Stratospheric Loading of Sulfur from Explosive Volcanic Eruptions," *Journal of Geology*, 1997; Brian J. Soden et al., "Global Cooling After the Eruption of Mount Pinatubo: A Test of Climate Feedback by Water Vapor," *Science*, April 2002; and T.M.L. Wigley, "A Combined Mitigation/Geoengineering Approach to Climate Stabilization," *Science*, October 2006. For the effect of the eruption on aviation, see Thomas J. Casadevall, Perla J. Delos Reyes, and David J. Schneider, "The 1991 Pinatubo Eruptions and Their Effects on Aircraft Operations," U.S. Geological Survey (1999). / 191 For **other recent major eruptions,** see Smithsonian Institution, Global Volcanism Program, "Large Holocene Eruptions"; and Kate Ravilious, "Volcanoes: Be Afraid, Be Very Afraid—The Supervolcano Is Coming," *Sydney Morning Herald*, April 16, 2010. For Eyjafjallajökull, see Alan Cowell, Nicola Clark, and Liz Robbins, "Air Travel Chaos Deepens into Weekend," *The New York Times*, April 15, 2010.

192–222 INTELLECTUAL VENTURES AND GEOENGINEERING: This section is primarily drawn from a visit we made to the Intellectual Ventures lab in Bellevue, Washington, in early 2008, and from subsequent interviews and correspondence with Nathan Myhrvold, Ken Caldeira, Lowell Wood, John Latham, Bill Gates, Rod Hyde, Neal Stephenson, Pablos Holman, and others. During our visit to IV, several other people contributed to the conversation, including Shelby Barnes, Wayt Gibbs, John Gilleand, Jordin Kare, Casey Tegreene, and Chuck Witmer. . . . **Conor and Cameron Myhrvold,** Nathan's college-age sons, also participated. They have already stepped into the invention racket themselves with a "wearable/portable protection system for a body," or a human air bag. From the patent application: "In an embodiment, system 100 may be worn by a locomotion-challenged person to cushion against prospective falls or collisions with environmental objects. In another embodiment, system 100 may be worn by athletes in lieu of traditional body-padding, helmets, and/or guards. In another embodiment, system 100 may be worn by people riding bicycles, skate-boarding, skating, skiing, snow-boarding, sledding and/or while engaged in various other sports or activities." . . . **For some interesting further reading on their father,** see: Ken Auletta, "The Microsoft Provocateur," *The New Yorker*, May 12, 1997; "Patent Quality and Improvement," Myhrvold's testimony before the Subcommittee on the Courts, the Internet and Intellectual Property, Committee on the Judiciary, House of Representatives, Congress of the United States, April 28, 2005; Jonathan Reynolds, "Kitchen Voyeur," *The New York Times Magazine*, October 16, 2005; Nicholas Varchaver, "Who's Afraid of Nathan Myhrvold," *Fortune*, July 10, 2006; Malcolm Gladwell, "In the Air; Annals of Innovation," *The New Yorker*, May 12, 2008; Amol Sharma and Don Clark, "Tech Guru Riles the Industry by Seeking Huge Patent Fees," *The Wall Street Journal*, September 18, 2008; Mike Ullman, "The Problem Solver," *Washington CEO*, December 2008. . . . **Myhrvold is himself famous** for writing—in particular, many long, provocative, extravagantly detailed memos that are intended primarily for internal use. See Auletta, above, for a good discussion of some of Myhrvold's Microsoft memos. Perhaps his greatest memo to date is one he wrote for his current company, back in 2003. It is called "What Makes a Great Invention?" We hope it will someday be made available for public consumption. / 192–193 **Mosquito laser assassination:** for more fascinating detail, see Robert A. Guth, "Rocket Scientists Shoot Down Mosquitoes with Lasers," *The Wall Street Journal,* March 14–15, 2009. / 194 **"I don't know anyone [who] is smarter than Nathan":** see Auletta, above. / 194 **Penguin poop:** see Victor Benno Meyer-Rochow and Jozsef Gal, "Pressures Produced When Penguins Pooh—Calculations on Avian Defaecation," *Polar Biology* 27, no. 1 (2003). / 195 **More T. rex skeletons:** see Gladwell, above; based also on correspondence with the paleontologist Jack Horner, with whom Myhrvold collaborates in hunting for dinosaur bones. / 196 **Definitive research . . . including climate science:** see, e.g., Edward Teller, Lowell Wood, and Roderick Hyde, "Global Warming and Ice Ages: I. Prospects for Physics-Based Modulation of Global Change," 22nd International Seminar on Planetary Emergencies, Erice (Sicily), Italy, August 20–23, 1997; Ken Caldeira and Lowell Wood, "Global and Arctic Climate Engineering: Numerical Model Studies," *Philosophical Transactions of the Royal Society,* November 13, 2008. / 196 **For the next ten hours or so:** During a break, if you were to casually ask Myhrvold a question of interest—his take on, say, whether an asteroid strike was indeed responsible for the extinction of dinosaurs—he is apt to regale you with a long narrative history of the various competing theories, the logic (and caveats) behind the ultimate winning theory, and the fallacies (and lesser truths) behind the losers. On this particular question, Myhrvold's short answer is: yes. / 197 **Wood himself was a protégé:** for an excellent exploration of geoengineering that is also a dual profile of Lowell Wood and Ken Caldeira, see Chris Mooney, "Can a Million Tons of Sulfur Dioxide Combat Climate Change?" *Wired,* June 23, 2008. / 197 **"As many as a million":** see Gladwell, above. / 197 For the **"value of knowing"** the travel habits of cancer cells, see "Engineers Use Blood's Hydrodynamics to Manipulate Stem, Cancer Cells," *ScienceDaily,* January 28, 2008; Lauren Gold, "Researcher Invents Lethal 'Lint Brush' to Capture and Kill Cancer Cells in the Bloodstream," *Cornell Chronicle,* December 10, 2008; and Michael King et al., "Biomolecular Surfaces for the Capture and Reprogramming of Circulating Tumor Cells," *Journal of Bionic Engineering* 6, no. 4 (December 2009). / 198 **Myhrvold cites a recent paper:** see Robert Vautard, Pascal Yiou, and Geert Jan van Oldenborgh, "Decline of Fog, Mist and Haze in Europe Over the Past 30 Years," *Nature Geoscience* 2, no. 115 (2009); and Rolf Philipona, Klaus Behrens, and Christian Ruckstuhl, "How Declining Aerosols and Rising Greenhouse Gases Forced Rapid Warming in Europe Since the 1980s," *Geophysical Research Letters* 36 (2009). / 198 **"A provocative 2005 article":** see John P. A. Ioannidis, "Why Most Published Research Findings Are False," *PLoS Medicine,* August 2005. / 199 **The carbon dioxide you breathe in a new office building:** derived from guidelines of the American Society of Heating, Refrigerating, and Air-Conditioning Engineers. / 199 **Carbon dioxide is not poison:** for a trenchant overview of the current state of thinking about atmospheric carbon dioxide, see William Happer, "Climate Change," Statement before the U.S. Senate Environment and Public Works Committee, February 25, 2009; data also gleaned from the Department of Energy's Carbon Dioxide Information Analysis Center. / 199 **Carbon dioxide levels rise *after* a rise in temperature:** see Jeff Severinghaus, "What Does the Lag of CO_2 Behind Temperature in Ice Cores Tell Us About

Global Warming," *RealClimate*, December 3, 2004. / 199 For **the complicated consequences of air pollution,** see Vautard et al. and Philipona et al., cited above, as well as Drew Shindell and Greg Faluvegi, "Climate Response to Regional Radiative Forcing During the Twentieth Century," *Nature Geoscience* 2 (2009). / 199–200 **"Ocean acidification":** see Ken Caldeira and Michael E. Wickett, "Oceanography: Anthropogenic Carbon and Ocean pH," *Nature* 425 (September 2003); and Elizabeth Kolbert, "The Darkening Sea," *The New Yorker*, November 20, 2006. / 200 **Hard-charging environmental activist:** see Mooney, above, for interesting reading on Caldeira's background. / 201 **Caldeira mentions a study:** see Caldeira et al., "Impact of Geoengineering Schemes on the Terrestrial Biosphere," *Geophysical Research Letters* 29, no. 22 (2002). / 201 **Vertical farming:** see Dickson Despommier, *The Vertical Farm: The World Grows Up* (Thomas Dunne Books, 2010); see also Blake Kurasek, "The Living Skyscraper: Farming the Urban Skyline, Chicago, Illinois" (master's thesis, University of Illinois at Urbana-Champaign, 2008). / 202 **Trees as environmental scourge:** see Caldeira et al., "Climate Effects of Global Land Cover Change," *Geophysical Research Letters* 32 (2005); and Caldeira et al., "Combined Climate and Carbon-Cycle Effects of Large-Scale Deforestation," *Proceedings of the National Academy of Sciences* 104, no. 16 (April 17, 2007). / 203 **The half-life of atmospheric carbon:** see Archer et al., "Atmospheric Lifetime of Fossil Fuel Carbon Dioxide," *Annual Review of Earth and Planetary Sciences* 37 (2009). / 203 **Myhrvold on solar:** see Nathan Myhrvold, "Are Solar Panels Really Black? And What Does That Have to Do With the Climate Debate?" Freakonomics blog, *The New York Times*, October 20, 2010. / 204 **"Would put an end to the Gulf Stream":** see Thomas F. Stocker and Andreas Schmittner, "Influence of Carbon Dioxide Emission Rates on the Stability of the Thermohaline Circulation," *Nature* 388 (1997); and Brad Lemley, "The Next Ice Age," *Discover*, September 2002. / 204 **Mount St. Helens:** see "Mount St. Helens, Washington, May 18, 1980 Eruption Summary," U.S. Geological Survey (1997). / 204 **The northern tip of Newfoundland:** this former Norse settlement is known as L'Anse aux Meadows. / 205 **Benjamin Franklin's volcanic suspicion:** see Benjamin Franklin, "Meteorological Imaginations and Conjectures," *Memoirs of the Literary and Philosophical Society of Manchester*, December 22, 1784; and Karen Harpp, "How Do Volcanoes Affect World Climate?" *Scientific American*, October 4, 2005. / 205 **"Year Without a Summer":** see Robert Evans, "Blast from the Past," *Smithsonian*, July 2002. / 205 **Lake Toba super volcano:** see Stanley H. Ambrose, "Late Pleistocene Human Population Bottlenecks, Volcanic Winter, and Differentiation of Modern Humans," *Journal of Human Evolution* 34, no. 6 (1998). / 205 **Volcanoes in art and literature:** see Richard Panek, "'The Scream,' East of Krakatoa," *The New York Times*, February 8, 2004; Donald W. Olson, Russell L. Doescher, and Marilynn S. Olson, "When the Sky Ran Red: The Story Behind *The Scream*," *Sky & Telescope*, February 2004; and Bill Philips, "Frankenstein and Mary Shelley's 'Wet Ungenial Summer,'" *Atlantis*, December 2006. / 206 **The Vonnegut brothers make rain:** see William Langewiesche, "Stealing Weather," *Vanity Fair*, May 2008. For more on **Project Cirrus** and its hurricane-killing experiment, see "Science: Yankee Meddling?" *Time*, November 10, 1947; Jay Barnes and Steve Lyons, *Florida's Hurricane History* (UNC Press, 2007); and Bob Sheets and Jack Williams, *Hurricane Watch: Forecasting the Deadliest Storms on Earth* (Vintage, 2001). / 206 **The idea was attributed to . . . Mikhail Budyko:** see M. I. Budyko, "Climatic Changes," American Geophysical Society,

Washington, D.C., 1977. Improbably, Ken Caldeira did postdoctoral work at Budyko's institute in Leningrad and met his future wife there. / 207 **Which Vonnegut wrote what?** By **Bernard Vonnegut:** With D. Turnbull, "Nucleation Catalysis," *Industrial and Engineering Chemistry* (1952); "A Vortex Whistle," *Journal of the Acoustical Society of America* (1954); "Luminous Phenomena in Nocturnal Tornadoes," *Science* (1966); with J. R. Weyer, "Crude Altimeter," *Science* (1970); "Chicken Plucking as Measure of Tornado Wind Speed," *Weatherwise* (1975); "Presters," *Weather* (1991); "Allegiance to Theory Changes With the Wind," *EOS Forum* (1994); "Quaint Cumulus Convection Conviction," *American Geophysical Union* (1997); with Howard G. Altschule, "The Smell of Tornadoes," *Weatherwise* (1997); and with William L. Boeck, Otha H. Vaughan Jr., R. J. Blakeslee, and Marx Brook, "The Role of the Space Shuttle Videotapes in the Discovery of Sprites, Jets and Elves," *Journal of Atmospheric and Solar-Terrestrial Physics* (1998). By **Kurt Vonnegut:** "Report on the Barnhouse Effect," published in *Collier's Weekly*, February 11, 1950; *Mother Night* (Fawcett, 1961); *Cat's Cradle* (Holt, 1963); *God Bless You, Mr. Rosewater* (Dell, 1965); *Slaughterhouse-Five* (Dell, 1969); "Excelsior! We're Going to the Moon! Excelsior!" as well as "Address to the American Physical Society," published in *Wampeters, Foma and Granfalloons* (Dell, 1989); "2BR02B," as well as "Thanasphere," published in *Bagombo Snuff Box* (G. P. Putnam's Sons, 1999); and "Little Drops of Water," published in *Look at the Birdie* (Delacorte Press, 2009). / 208 Current data on **global atmospheric carbon-dioxide concentration** is available from NOAA's Earth System Research Laboratory, www.esrl.noaa.gov/gmd/ccgg/trends. / 209 An account of the death of **Archimedes** is relayed by Plutarch in his *Life of Marcellus,* written in 75 C.E. Marcellus was the commanding Roman general of the siege of Syracuse; as Plutarch writes, he was dismayed to learn that Archimedes had been slain by of one of his soldiers. / 212–213 **Perhaps the stoutest scientific argument:** see Paul J. Crutzen, "Albedo Enhancement by Stratospheric Sulfur Injections: A Contribution to Resolve a Policy Dilemma?" *Climatic Change,* 2006. / 212 **Ozone depletion:** see Michael Carlowicz, "New Simulation Shows Consequences of a World Without Earth's Natural Sunscreen," NASA Goddard Space Flight Center, March 2009; and Paul A. Newman et al., "What Would Have Happened to the Ozone Layer if Chlorofluorocarbons (CFCs) Had Not Been Regulated?" *Atmospheric and Chemistry Physics* (2009). / 213–214 **There is no regulatory framework:** for further reading, see "The Sun Blotted Out from the Sky," Elizabeth Svoboda, *Salon.com,* April 2, 2008. / 214 For **recent small-scale geoengineering projects,** see: Simon Shuster, "Moscow Mayor Promises a Winter Without Snow," *Time,* October 16, 2009; Tania Branigan, "Nature Gets a Helping Hand as Snow Blankets Beijing," *The Guardian,* November 2, 2009; "Chavez Asking Cubans to 'Bomb Clouds' Amid Drought," Reuters, November 15, 2009; Christopher Toothaker, "Chavez Says Drought Threatens Hydroelectric Dams," Associated Press, December 7, 2009; "China Blames Freak Storm on Global Warming," *Sydney Morning Herald*, January 5, 2010; Charlie Devereux, "Venezuela Tries to Make it Rain," Reuters, February 11, 2010; United Press International, "Moscow Sees Record Amount of Snow," February 23, 2010; and Daniel Cancel, "Chavez Says Cuban 'Cloud Bombing' Eases Power Crisis," *BusinessWeek,* April 16, 2010. / 215 For **U.S. fire deaths:** see *Injury Facts,* National Safety Council, 2010; and Alan F. Hoskin, "Trends in Unintentional-Injury Deaths During the 20th Century," *Statistical Bulletin,* Metropolitan Life Insurance Company, April–June 2000; for **"the nation's first**

fireproof building," see Gene Waddell, "Robert Mills's Fireproof Building," *The South Carolina Historical Magazine,* April 1979. / 216 **Certain new ideas . . . are invariably seen as repugnant:** the dean of repugnance studies is the Harvard economist Alvin E. Roth, whose work can be seen at the Market Design blog. See also: Stephen J. Dubner and Steven D. Levitt, "Flesh Trade," *The New York Times Magazine,* July 9, 2006; and Viviana A. Zelizer, "Human Values and the Market: The Case of Life Insurance and Death in 19th-Century America," *American Journal of Sociology* 84, no. 3 (November 1978). / 216 **Al Gore is quoted** here and elsewhere in Leonard David, "Al Gore: Earth Is in 'Full-Scale Planetary Emergency,'" *Space.com,* October 26, 2006. / 217 **The "soggy mirrors" plan:** see John Latham, "Amelioration of Global Warming by Controlled Enhancement of the Albedo and Longevity of Low-Level Maritime Clouds," *Atmospheric Science Letters* 3, no. 2 (2002). / 220 **Contrail clouds:** see David J. Travis, Andrew M. Carleton, and Ryan G. Lauritsen, "Climatology: Contrails Reduce Daily Temperature Range," *Nature,* August 8, 2002; Travis, "Regional Variations in U.S. Diurnal Temperature Range for the 11–14 September 2001 Aircraft Groundings: Evidence of Jet Contrail Influence on Climate," *Journal of Climate* 17 (March 1, 2004); Andrew M. Carleton et al., "Composite Atmospheric Environments of Jet Contrail Outbreaks for the United States," *Journal of Applied Meteorology and Climatology* 47 (February 2008); and Patrick Minnis, "Contrails, Cirrus Trends, and Climate," *American Meteorological Society* 17 (April 15, 2004). / 221 **Flettner rotors:** see Ernst-Heinrich Hirschel, Horst Prem, and Gero Madelung, *Aeronautical Research in Germany: From Lilienthal until Today* (Springer, 2004); and G. B. Seybold, "A Sailing Ship Without Sails; New Wonder of the Seas," *Popular Science,* February 1925. / 222 **Fighting global warming with individual behavior change:** the difficulty of this endeavor was illustrated, if indirectly, by Barack Obama as he ran for president in 2008. While preparing for a debate, Obama was caught on tape complaining about how shallow the debates could be: "So when Brian Williams [of NBC News] is asking me about what's a personal thing that you've done [that's green], and I say, you know, 'Well, I planted a bunch of trees.' And he says, 'I'm talking about personal.' What I'm thinking in my head is, 'Well, the truth is, Brian, we can't solve global warming because *I* f—ing changed light bulbs in my house. It's because of something collective.' " As reported in "Hackers and Spending Sprees," *Newsweek* web exclusive, November 5, 2008.

222–226 DIRTY HANDS AND DEADLY DOCTORS: For **Semmelweis's sad ending,** see Sherwin B. Nuland, *The Doctor's Plague: Germs, Childbed Fever, and the Strange Story of Ignatz Semmelweis* (Atlas Books, 2003). / 223 **"A raft of recent studies":** see Didier Pittet, "Improving Adherence to Hand Hygiene Practice: A Multidisciplinary Approach," *Emerging Infectious Diseases,* March–April 2001. / 223 **"To Err Is Human":** Linda T. Kohn, Janet Corrigan, and Molla S. Donaldson, *To Err Is Human: Building a Safer Health System* (National Academies Press, 2000). / 223 For the **total number of U.S. deaths,** see: Jiaquan Xu et al., "Deaths: Preliminary Data for 2007," *National Vital Statistics Reports* 58, no. 1 (August 19, 2009). / 224 **T. Bear:** see Walter T. Hughes et al., "The Nosocomial Colonization of T. Bear," *Infection Control* 10 (1986). / 224–225 **Cedars-Sinai Medical Center:** see Stephen J. Dubner and Steven D. Levitt, "Selling Soap," *The New York Times Magazine,* September 24, 2006. It was Dr. Leon Bender, a urologist at Cedars-Sinai, who led us to this story. / 224

The Australian study: see J. Tibbals, "Teaching Hospital Medical Staff to Handwash," *Medical Journal of Australia* 164 (1996). / 226 **"Among the best solutions":** for disposable blood pressure cuffs, see Kevin Sack, "Swabs in Hand, Hospital Cuts Deadly Infections," *The New York Times,* July 27, 2007; for the silver-ion antimicrobial shield, see Craig Feied, "Novel Antimicrobial Surface Coatings and the Potential for Reduced Fomite Transmission of SARS and Other Pathogens," unpublished manuscript, 2004; for neckties, see Associated Press, "British Hospitals Ban Long Sleeves and Neckties to Fight Infection," September 17, 2007.

227 FORESKINS ARE FALLING: See Ingrid T. Katz and Alexi A. Wright, "Circumcision—A Surgical Strategy for HIV Prevention in Africa," *New England Journal of Medicine* 359, no. 23 (December 4, 2008); also drawn from author interview with Katz. **Circumcision rates in the U.S. and elsewhere,** see Brian G. Williams et al., "The Potential Impact of Male Circumcision on HIV in Sub-Saharan Africa," *PLoS Medicine,* July 2006; Arleen A. Leibowitz et al., "Determinants and Policy Implications of Male Circumcision in the United States," *American Journal of Public Health* 99, no. 1 (2009); and "United States Circumcision Incidence," the Circumcision Reference Library.

EPILOGUE: MONKEYS ARE PEOPLE TOO

231–235 See Stephen J. Dubner and Steven D. Levitt, "Monkey Business," *The New York Times Magazine,* June 5, 2005; Venkat Lakshminarayanan, M. Keith Chen, and Laurie R. Santos, "Endowment Effect in Capuchin Monkeys," *Philosophical Transactions of the Royal Society* 363 (October 2008); and M. Keith Chen and Laurie Santos, "The Evolution of Rational and Irrational Economic Behavior: Evidence and Insight from a Non-Human Primate Species," chapter from *Neuroeconomics: Decision Making and the Brain,* ed. Paul Glimcher, Colin Camerer, Ernst Fehr, and Russell Poldrack (Academic Press, Elsevier, 2009). / 231 **"Nobody ever saw a dog":** see Adam Smith, *An Inquiry into the Nature and Causes of the Wealth of Nations,* ed. Edwin Cannon (University of Chicago Press, 1976; originally published in 1776). / 234 **Day traders are also loss-averse:** see Terrance Odean, "Are Investors Reluctant to Realize Their Losses?" *Journal of Finance* 53, no. 5 (October 1998).

INDEX

Note: Italicized page numbers refer to picture captions and sidebars.